"The book is a self-composite in terms of explaining the concept, definition and computation of statistical methods with numerical examples and with MS Excel. . . . In addition to beginning students, researchers, and teachers in social sciences, business, and management, the book is useful to all in other subjects if they wish to pursue a quantitative approach."

Professor M R Narayana, *Fiscal Policy Institute, Bengaluru*

"*Basic Computational Techniques for Data Analysis: An Exploration in MS Excel (second edition)* is quite handy for mastering computational techniques in Excel and could be a lifelong companion, much beyond a student's educational career. The authors D Narayana, Sharad Ranjan, and Nupur Tyagi, have filled a gap that was lying vacant for more than three decades."

Sudip Mohapatra, *Senior Economist, IMF*

"This book by Professors Narayana, Ranjan, and Tyagi skillfully and uniquely combines Excel-based tools for statistical and financial analysis with the revised version, even including ways for growth rate calculation and use of Census data gainfully for research. It is a very useful text for economics students and communicators to help them make meaningful inferences from data."

Professor Sukhpal Singh, *Indian Institute of Management, Ahmedabad*

"This is an important and comprehensive work on various data analysis techniques. It provides an in-depth and clear understanding on the use of multiple data with a systematic and stepwise explanation of statistical and financial concepts – a must-read for everyone in the domain."

Dr K S James, *Director and Senior Professor,*
International Institute for Population Sciences, Mumbai

BASIC COMPUTATIONAL TECHNIQUES FOR DATA ANALYSIS

This book is designed to equip students to navigate through MS Excel and basic data computation methods, which are essential tools in research or professional settings and in classrooms.

It illustrates the concepts used in research and data analysis and economic and financial decision-making in business and in daily life. The book will help students acquire knowledge and develop skills in statistical techniques and financial analysis using MS Excel. With illustrations and examples, it will help the readers to:

- Visualize, present, and analyze data through MS Excel spreadsheets and tables and create personal or business spreadsheets
- Learn how to work with spreadsheets, use formulae, and perform calculations and analysis
- Create tables including Pivot Tables
- Become familiar with basic statistical and financial measures
- Design creative spread sheets and communicate effectively in business using spreadsheets and data analysis

This revised and updated second edition will be an essential resource for students of economics, commerce, management, and other social science subjects, and will be useful to those studying econometrics, financial technology, basic computational techniques, data analysis, and applied economics.

Content

The book is developed through three phases, with each phase standing on its own as well as providing a foundation for the next. In the first phase, Excel is introduced for the students to learn entry of data, manipulation of data, carrying out operations and develop presentations. The second phase introduces basic statistical measures of data summarisation and analysis, following which these are illustrated in Excel spreadsheets with the techniques introduced in the first phase. In addition, a few advanced tools of statistical analysis are introduced and illustrated in Excel. The third phase introduces financial measures of common use, their general computation and working them out in Excel.

The book intends to illustrate the concepts used in economic and financial decision-making in business and in daily life; it helps demonstrate a deeper understanding from both theoretical and practical perspectives. An effort has been made to make the book student-friendly by using simple language and giving a number of illustrations in each chapter, solved in such a simple manner that they can be easily understood by the students. Practical questions have been included at the end of each chapter so that the students can independently solve them and test their understanding of the concepts and computations introduced in the chapter.

Outcome

At the end, students will be able to describe what a spreadsheet is and what Excel's capabilities are and can work with elements that make up the structure of a worksheet. They will be able to work with spreadsheets and enter data in Excel, use formulae and calculations, and create tables, charts and pivot tables. They will be familiar with basic statistical and financial measures of general use. They will be able to do basic computations in statistics and finance in Excel. Students will acquire the capacity to create personal and/or business spreadsheets following current professional and/or industry standards. Their potential for critical thinking to design and create spreadsheets and communicate in a business setting using spreadsheet vocabulary will be enhanced.

In the digital age, students necessarily need to know data, data sources and how to 'dirty' their hands with data. There can be no substitute to 'talking through numbers'. The book introduces students to a variety of Indian and International data sources and teaches them how to import data-be it social, economic, financial and so on-to the Excel sheet. Once they master it, the data world is there for them to conquer!

The educational background required for the student to understand the text is some basic English and Mathematics of school-leaving level. Some flair for numbers will be an asset and for them it will be a breeze; others will have to make an effort but ample illustrations and practice questions make life simple, whether it is basic statistics or slightly intricate finance!

D Narayana is Former Director of the Gulati Institute of Finance and Taxation, Thiruvananthapuram, and Chairman of Kerala Public Expenditure Review Committee. He is a renowned economist, researcher, and statistician. He holds a PhD from Indian Statistical Institute (ISI), Kolkata. He held the Reserve Bank of India (RBI) Chair at Centre for Development Studies (CDS), Thiruvananthapuram from 2001 to 2012. He has published numerous articles in reputed national and international journals on health, state finance, decentralization, issues of SC/ST Communities, agriculture, irrigation, and migrant labour and has authored and co-edited many books. He also served as a member of many important committees, including the Expert Committee on Goods and Services Tax (GST), committee for revising the rates for the medical procedures under the centrally sponsored Rashtriya Swasthya Bima Yojana (RSBY), and the Contributory Pension Review Committee, constituted by the Government of Kerala.

Sharad Ranjan is a professor in economics at Zakir Husain Delhi College (Evening) (University of Delhi) with a teaching experience of nearly three decades. He is a PhD from the Centre for Economic Studies and Planning, Jawaharlal Nehru University, New Delhi. He has published many research papers in various journals and has also authored five books. He has conducted workshops on financial literacy for the Securities and Exchange Board of India (SEBI) as a resource person and has also co-supervised and evaluated PhD theses.

Nupur Tyagi is assistant professor at Gargi College, University of Delhi. She completed her post-graduation and MPhil from Delhi School of Economics, University of Delhi. Her areas of interest are finance and accounting.

BASIC COMPUTATIONAL TECHNIQUES FOR DATA ANALYSIS

An Exploration in MS Excel

Second Edition

D Narayana, Sharad Ranjan, and Nupur Tyagi

Routledge
Taylor & Francis Group

LONDON AND NEW YORK

Cover image credit: © Getty Images

Second edition published 2023
by Routledge
4 Park Square, Milton Park, Abingdon, Oxon, OX14 4RN

and by Routledge
605 Third Avenue, New York, NY 10158

Routledge is an imprint of the Taylor & Francis Group, an informa business

© 2023 D Narayana, Sharad Ranjan, and Nupur Tyagi

The right of D Narayana, Sharad Ranjan, and Nupur Tyagi to be identified as authors of this work has been asserted in accordance with sections 77 and 78 of the Copyright, Designs and Patents Act 1988.

First edition published by Sage 2020

British Library Cataloguing-in-Publication Data
A catalogue record for this book is available from the British Library

ISBN: 978-1-032-45935-6 (hbk)
ISBN: 978-1-032-50354-7 (pbk)
ISBN: 978-1-003-39812-7 (ebk)

DOI: 10.4324/9781003398127

Typeset in Bembo
by Apex CoVantage, LLC

CONTENTS

List of figures   ix
List of tables   xiv
Preface to the second edition   xv
Acknowledgements   xvi
List of abbreviations   xvii

 1 Getting Started With Microsoft Excel   1

 2 Basic Arithmetic Operations in Excel   15

 3 Data: Input Into Excel and Sources   33

 4 Visualization of Data Using Charts in Excel   60

 5 Measures of Central Tendency   75

 6 Measures of Dispersion   101

 7 Correlation Coefficient   130

 8 Regression Analysis   154

 9 Hypothesis Testing in Regression Analysis   177

10 Understanding Growth Rates   191

11 Growth Rate Using Regression Analysis   204

12 Compounding: Future Value of Money   218

13 Investment Decision Criteria: NPV and IRR   230

14 Loan Amortization   247

Web References   262
Answer key   263
Appendix 1: Present Value and Future Value Tables   272
Appendix 2: t-Distribution: Critical Values of t   277
Index   279

FIGURES

1.1	Layout of Excel Worksheet	2
1.2	Finding the Number of Rows and Columns in Data	4
1.3	Profile of Rural Workers	4
1.4	Formatting Decimal Points	5
1.5	Formatting Decimal Points Using Home Tab	6
1.6	Formatting Up to Two Decimal Points	6
1.7	Step 1 in Sorting Data	7
1.8	Step 2 in Sorting Data	7
1.9	Step 3 in Sorting Data	8
1.10	Hidden Column	9
1.11	Filtering Data Through Key Commands	10
1.12	Filtering Data Through Tabs	10
1.13	Filtering Data Using Text Filters	11
1.14	Custom Filter	11
1.15	Number Filters	12
1.16	Copy and Paste of Filtered Data	13
1.17	Freezing/Unfreezing of Panes	13
2.1	Data of Workers Employed in Non-Farm Activities	16
2.2	Step 1 in Adding Up Cells	17
2.3	Step 2 in Adding Up Cells	17
2.4	Subtracting of Cells	18
2.5	Method 1 of Multiplication of Cells	19
2.6	Method 2 of Multiplication of Cells	19
2.7	Division Function in Excel	20
2.8	Absolute Cell Reference	21
2.9	Usage of the AutoSum Function	22
2.10	Usage of SUMIF Function	23
2.11	The MAX Function	23
2.12	The MIN Function	24

2.13 The COUNT Function   24
2.14 The COUNTIF Function   25
2.15 The Power Function   26
2.16 Sales Data of a Company   27
2.17 Inserting of a Pivot Table   27
2.18 Illustration of a Pivot Table Template   28
2.19 Summary of Results   28
2.20 Step 1 in Data Filtering in Pivot Table   29
2.21 Step 2 in Data Filtering in Pivot Table   29
2.22 Summarizing of Values   30
2.23 Forms of Summarized Values   31
3.1   Adding Form to Quick Access Toolbar   35
3.2   Adding Form to Quick Access Toolbar   36
3.3   DBIE Website: Statistics   38
3.4   Data on Real Sector in DBIE Website   38
3.5   Exporting Data (Sector-wise)   40
3.6   Census of India Website: Home Page   41
3.7   Downloading Census Data   42
3.8   Downloading Census Data   43
3.9   Downloading Census Data   43
3.10 Downloading Census Data   44
3.11 Downloading Census Data   44
3.12 The MoSPI Website   45
3.13 The Downloading of Reports at MoSPI   46
3.14 Statistical Publications Provided by MoSPI   46
3.15 Press Release   47
3.16 Downloading of Tables Data on MoSPI Website   47
3.17 Step 1 in Microdata Catalogue   48
3.18 Step 2 in Microdata Catalogue (NADA)   48
3.19 Step 3 in Microdata Catalogue (National Data Archive)   49
3.20 National Data Bank   49
3.21 The New NSE Website   50
3.22 Step 1 in Downloading Historical Reports – NSE   50
3.23 Step 2 in Downloading Historical Reports – NSE   51
3.24 Step 3 in Downloading Historical Reports – NSE   51
3.25 Step 1 in Historical Data of a Company – NSE   51
3.26 Step 2 in Historical Data of a Company – NSE   52
3.27 Step 3 in Historical Data of a Company – NSE   52
3.28 Step 1 in Downloading Historical Data – BSE   53
3.29 Step 2 in Downloading Historical Data – BSE   53
3.30 Step 3 in Downloading Historical Data – BSE   53
3.31 Step 4 in Downloading Historical Data – BSE   54
3.32 Step 5 in Downloading Historical Data – BSE   54
3.33 World Bank Open Data   54
3.34 Downloading Data: Indicator-wise   55
3.35 Downloading Data: Country-wise   55

3.36 Downloading Data: Combination of an Indicator and Country   56
3.37 Downloading Data: Combination of an Indicator and Multiple Countries 56
3.38 UNdata Website   57
3.39 Step 1 in Downloading of Data Series   58
3.40 Step 2 in Downloading of Data Series   58
3.41 Step 3 in Downloading of Data Series   58
3.42 Step 4 in Downloading of Data Series   59
4.1   Per Capita Gross Domestic Product (2011 PPP $)   61
4.2   Line Graph in Excel   62
4.3   Labelling of Chart   62
4.4   Per Capita GDP of SAARC Countries, 2010–2018   64
4.5   Steps of Depicting Per Capita GDP of SAARC Countries, 2010–2018 in
      Column Chart   65
4.6   Column Chart Depicting Per Capita GDP   65
4.7   The Histogram: Direct Method   67
4.8   The Histogram: Another Method   69
4.9   Steps in Labelling Pie Chart, Motor Vehicle Production 2008–2009   70
4.10 Pie Chart of Motor Vehicle Production 2009–2010   71
4.11 The Scatter Plot of Company ABC   72
5.1   Step 1 in Calculating the Mean   78
5.2   Step 2 in Calculating the Mean   78
5.3   Step 3 in Calculating the Mean   79
5.4   Step 1 in Calculating the Median   83
5.5   Step 2 in Calculating the Median   83
5.6   Step 3 in Calculating the Median   84
5.7   Step 1 in Calculating the Mode   85
5.8   Step 2 in Calculating the Mode   86
5.9   Step 3 in Calculating the Mode   86
5.10 Calculating the Mode Using Graph   87
5.11 Step 1 in Calculating the Mode Using MAX   88
5.12 Step 2 in Calculating the Mode Using MAX   89
5.13 Step 1 in Calculating the Weighted Arithmetic Mean   91
5.14 Step 2 in Calculating the Weighted Arithmetic Mean   92
5.15 Step 1 in Calculating the Geometric Mean   93
5.16 Step 2 in Calculating the Geometric Mean   94
5.17 Step 1 in Calculating the Harmonic Mean   97
5.18 Step 2 in Calculating the Harmonic Mean   97
6.1   Scatter Plot for Scores of Class A   102
6.2   Scatter Plot for Scores of Class B   102
6.3   Step 1 in Calculation of Range   104
6.4   Step 2 in Calculation of Range   105
6.5   Step 1 in Calculation of Standard Deviation   108
6.6   Step 2 in Calculation of Standard Deviation   108
6.7   Step 1 in Calculation of Variance   112
6.8   Step 2 in Calculation of Variance   112
6.9   Step 1 in Calculation of Skewness   117

6.10 Step 2 in Calculation of Skewness   118
6.11 Histogram   118
6.12 Step 1 in Calculation of Kurtosis   121
6.13 Step 2 in Calculation of Kurtosis   122
6.14 Step 1 in Data Analysis (Descriptive Statistics)   124
6.15 Step 2 in Data Analysis (Descriptive Statistics)   124
6.16 Step 3 in Data Analysis (Descriptive Statistics)   125
7.1   Step 1 in Calculation of Covariance   133
7.2   Step 2 in Calculation of Covariance   134
7.3   Positive Correlation   135
7.4   Negative Correlation   135
7.5   No Correlation   136
7.6   Step 1 in Calculation of Correlation   139
7.7   Step 2 in Calculation of Correlation   139
7.8   Step 1 in Calculation of the Pearson Correlation Coefficient   140
7.9   Step 2 in Calculation of Pearson Correlation Coefficient   140
7.10 Step 1 in Calculation of Correlation   141
7.11 Step 2 in Calculation of Correlation Using Data Analysis   141
7.12 Step 3 in Calculation of Correlation Using Data Analysis   142
7.13 Scatter Plot Showing Linear Relationship Between the Monthly Rate of
      Returns on Sensex (X) and Nifty 50 (Y)   143
7.14 Step 1 in Calculation of the Spearman Correlation Coefficient   148
7.15 Step 2 in Calculation of the Spearman Correlation Coefficient   148
7.16 Step 3 in Calculation of the Spearman Correlation Coefficient   149
7.17 Step 4 in Calculation of the Spearman Correlation Coefficient   149
7.18 Relationship Between Hours of Work and Average Cost   151
8.1   Graphical Representation of Regression Line   156
8.2   Regression Line With Positive Slope ($\beta_1 > 0$)   156
8.3   Regression Line With Negative Slope ($\beta_1 < 0$)   157
8.4   Regression Line With Constant Slope ($\beta_1 = 0$)   157
8.5   Step 1 in Calculating Regression Parameters   161
8.6   Step 2 in Calculating Regression Parameters   162
8.7   Step 3 in Calculating Regression Parameters   162
8.8   Step 4 in Calculating Regression Parameters   163
8.9   Step 1 Regression Analysis (Predicting the Dependent Variable)   164
8.10 Step 2 in Regression Analysis (Predicting the Dependent Variable)   165
8.11 Population (PRF) and Sample Regression Functions (SRF)   166
8.12 Graphical Representation of Three Types of Variations   168
8.13 Regression Analysis Dialogue Box   171
8.14 Regression Analysis (Summary Output)   172
8.15 Regression Analysis (Residual Output)   172
8.16 Regression Analysis: Promotional Expense Line Fit Plots   173
9.1   Rejection Areas for a Two-Tailed Test   179
9.2   Rejection Areas for a One-Tailed Test   180
9.3   Regression Analysis Output: Residual Degrees of Freedom   182
9.4 t-Distribution p-Value > alpha (α)   184

9.5	*t*-Distribution *p*-Value < alpha (α)	184
9.6	*t*-Distribution Computed *p*-Value < alpha (α)	185
9.7	Regression Analysis Output (95% Confidence Intervals)	186
9.8	Test Results of the Regression Equation Displayed in the Excel Sheet	186
10.1	Step 1 in the Calculation of Average Annual Growth Rate	195
10.2	Step 2 in the Calculation of Average Annual Growth Rate	195
10.3	Step 3 in the Calculation of Average Annual Growth Rate	196
10.4	Calculation of Compound Annual Growth Rate	199
10.5	Calculation of Compound Annual Growth Rate	200
10.6	Calculation of Compound Annual Growth Rate Using RRI Function	201
10.7	Calculation of Compound Annual Growth Rate Using RRI Function	201
10.8	Calculation of Compound Annual Growth Rate Using RRI Function	202
10.9	Calculation of Compound Annual Growth Rate Using RRI Function	202
11.1	Step 1 in Calculation of Compound Annual Growth Rate	207
11.2	Step 2 in Calculation of Compound Annual Growth Rate	208
11.3	Steps 3, 4, and 5 in Calculation of Compound Annual Growth Rate	208
11.4	Step 6 in Calculation of Compound Annual Growth Rate Using OLS Method (Summary Output)	209
11.5	Steps 1 and 2 in the Calculation of Regression Coefficients Using the LINEST Function	212
11.6	Steps 3 and 4 in the Calculation of Regression Coefficients Using the LINEST Function	212
11.7	Step 5 in the Calculation of Regression Coefficients Using the LINEST Function	213
11.8	Step 1 in Calculation of Regression Coefficients Using LOGEST Function	215
11.9	Steps 2 and 3 in Calculation of Regression Coefficients Using the LOGEST Function	216
11.10	Steps 4 and 5 in Calculation of Regression Coefficients Using the LOGEST Function	216
12.1	Impact of Compounding in Investment	221
12.2	Calculating Future Value Using Excel	224
12.3	Calculating Future Value of Annuity Using Excel	228
13.1	Calculating NPV Using Excel	234
13.2	Calculating IRR Using Excel	239
13.3	Calculating IRR of Endowment Plans	240
13.4	Calculating IRR in a Money-Back Policy	241
13.5	Calculating XIRR	242
14.1	Calculating EMI Using the Fixed Rate Method	248
14.2	Calculating Outstanding Loan Amount Using PV Method	253
14.3	Calculating EMI Amount Using Excel	254
14.4	CUMPRINC Function in Excel	255
14.5	CUMIPMT Function in Excel	256
14.6	PPMT Function in Excel	257
14.7	IPMT Function in Excel	258
14.8	Effective Annual Rate Function	260

TABLES AND ILLUSTRATIONS

Tables

9.1	Type 1 and Type 2 Errors	179
9.2	t-Distribution Table	183
12.1	Future Value Interest Factor Table	223
12.2	Timeline of a Cash Flow	225
12.3	Future Annuity Value Table	227
A-1	Future Value Interest Factors for One Rupee Compounded at r Percent for n Periods: $FVIF_{r,n} = (1 + r)^n$	273
A-2	Future Value Interest Factors for a One-Rupee Annuity Compounded at r Percent for n Periods: $FVIFA_{r,n} = (1 + r)^n - 1/r$	274
A-3	Present Value Interest Factors for One Rupee Discounted at r Percent for n Periods: $PVIF_{r,n} = 1/(1 + r)^n$	275
A-4	Present Value Interest Factors for a One-Rupee Annuity Discounted at r Percent for n Periods: $PVIFA = [1 - 1/(1 + r)^n] / r$	276

PREFACE TO THE SECOND EDITION

First and foremost, we wish to thank the readers for the overwhelming response to the first edition of the book. Continuing with our endeavour to provide a holistic approach to the financial concepts and statistical techniques illustrated in the first edition, the second edition of the book seeks to add on to that knowledge base. We have made two major additions to the second edition – first, this edition includes a section called *Census of India* in Chapter 3. The section provides a look into data available on the Census of India websites and discusses in detail the tools and methods to access and use this database. This is an important source of demographic data widely available in the public domain and extensively used by the researchers. Moreover, the importance of Census data for research, analysis, and evaluation of different aspects of the Indian economy is known to one and all. It is the largest and the diverse data source for a complete understanding of the social, economic, and demographic dimensions of the country. To fill this gap, we have incorporated this essential topic to familiarize them with the Census data and to facilitate its utilization for research purposes.

Secondly, the second edition includes additional chapters on *growth rates*. In the field of social sciences, *the study of changes* in different variables over time is of key importance – be it GDP growth rates, growth in investment levels, profits, etc. Beyond the introduction of the basic concepts, it is imperative to learn the computational techniques for arriving at the growth figures for the analysis purpose. Keeping this in mind, the new chapter has been added to give readers a glimpse into these techniques of analysis. We strongly feel that the book would be incomplete with the exclusion of the preceding.

We believe that the revised edition will be truly beneficial to the readers.

ACKNOWLEDGEMENTS

The authors wish to acknowledge Shagishna K for the research assistance rendered throughout the preparation of the book. She read the entire text; made suggestions; reworked sections, figures, and tables; and formatted the chapters. The book in its present form became a reality at such quick time by her unstinted commitment.

Sharad Ranjan wishes to acknowledge:

Prof C P Chandrasekhar for his guidance and for suggesting various sources to understand concepts related to finance.

Mr Amit Rohilla, assistant professor, Gargi College for giving the liberty to bother him for discussing various concepts.

His daughter, Hariti Tyagi, and niece, Vadanya, spent a lot of time making suggestions on various aspects related to the book.

His wife, Nidhi, for all the moral support and relieving him from many responsibilities throughout.

His friend Raushan Kumar, associate professor, Zakir Husain Delhi College (Evening) for his continuous guidance and encouragement.

Lastly, his father, Late Dr R C Tyagi, who made every effort to provide him the best of education to reach this stage.

Nupur Tyagi wishes to acknowledge her grandparents Mr J.K. Tyagi and Mrs. Satya, Mr R.D. Sharma, and Mrs. Prem Sharma for their blessings. She is grateful to her parents, Mr Rajeev Tyagi and Mrs. Madhu Tyagi, for being her inspiration, guide, and support and always encouraging her to give best and work hard. She is thankful to her husband, Ashwarj Bhargava, and her sister, Shipra Tyagi, for constant motivation, support, and valuable suggestions.

ABBREVIATIONS

APR	Annual percentage rate
BSE	Bombay Stock Exchange
CAGR	Compound annual growth rate
CSV	Comma-separated values
DBIE	Database on Indian Economy
EAR	Effective annual rate
EMI	Equated monthly instalment
FVIF	Future value interest factor
GDP	Gross domestic product
IIP	Index of industrial production
IRR	Internal rate of return
JNU	Jawaharlal Nehru University
MIRR	Modified internal rate of return
MNC	Multinational corporation
MoSPI	Ministry of Statistics and Programme Implementation
NAV	Net Asset Value
NPV	Net present value
NSE	National Stock Exchange
OLS	Ordinary least squares
PRF	Population regression functions
PV	Present value
PVAF	Present value annuity factor
PVF	Present value factor
PVIFA	Present value interest factor of annuity
RBI	Reserve Bank of India
SI	Simple interest
SRF	Sample regression functions
XIRR	Extended internal rate of return

1

GETTING STARTED WITH MICROSOFT EXCEL

Learning Objectives

After reading this chapter, the readers will be able to understand

- Basics of the Excel program
- How to find the number of rows and columns
- Formatting the decimal places
- Sorting of data
- Unhiding or hiding some of the rows and columns
- Filtering the data using various methods
- Freezing worksheet panes

Excel is a spreadsheet/worksheet program that most people use, be it businessmen, college students, researchers, financial analysts, and many more. Released in 1985, it is now widely used. Its popularity arises out of its ability to do mass arithmetic calculations like addition, subtraction, multiplication, and division of thousands of numbers simultaneously. It automates calculations and even supports complex functions when used with other functions included in the software. Further, it is a perfect tool for creating graphs and tables for visual data analysis. In fact, it does much more. Not only does it aggregate and simplify numbers for data management, but it also processes raw data for deeper data analysis. Hence, working knowledge of Excel is considered vitally important in today's world, irrespective of professionals in any field. The following section is an introduction to the Excel program. At this point, no prior knowledge of software is assumed.

DOI: 10.4324/9781003398127-1

1.1 Glimpse of Excel

The display of a newly opened Excel spreadsheet is presented in Figure 1.1. A quick display of a few outlines that help handle data analysis is described to assist in a beginner's comprehension. It contains certain comment boxes with explanations. Before elucidation, click the **Ribbon Display Option** on the top-right corner of the document and select **Show Tabs**. Selecting the **Auto-hide Option** will hide **tabs** from the display sheet, making it difficult to go ahead with our data analysis.

- **Quick Access Toolbar**: The Quick Access Toolbar consists of favourite commands. By default, it displays commands such as Save, Undo, and Redo. As we proceed with the data analysis, we may frequently use more commands such as **Sort**, **Copy**, and **Format**, etc., which can be added to the **Quick Access Toolbar** using the drop-down arrow. From the drop-down list, we can choose several functions arranged alphabetically by selecting **More Commands**
- **Tabs:** The tabs on the ribbon area are **File**, **Home**, **Insert**, **Page Layout**, **View**, and **Help**. Each tab contains groups. The groups are further separated by a vertical line. Various functions are listed in these groups, which can be used as per requirement. The **Home** tab contains the most frequently used commands in Excel

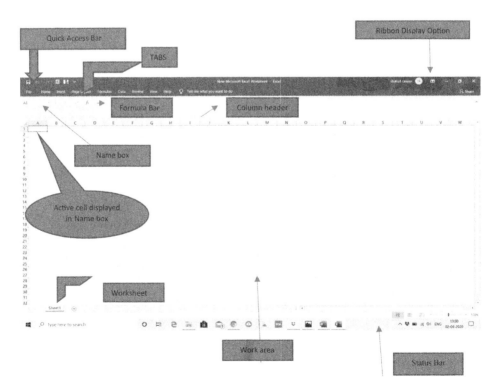

FIGURE 1.1   Layout of Excel Worksheet

- **Name box:** It displays the selected cell in the spreadsheet. Alternatively, one can type cell box number and press **Enter** to reach the desired cell
- **Formula Bar:** The **Formula Bar** displays the data or formula entered in the active cell. This **Formula Bar** may also be used to edit entered data or formulas. The active cell displays the results of the formula entered while we see the formula itself in the **Formula Bar**
- **Work Area:** The entire cell area where data can be placed is called the **work area**. These cells are conspicuous in the format of rows and columns. The entire **work area** consists of 1,048,576 rows and 16,384 columns. The easiest way to find the number of rows can be observed by selecting any cell and then pressing **Ctrl+Down** arrow on the keyboard. Similarly, **Ctrl+Right** arrow is pressed for the number of columns
- **Worksheet:** In Excel, a sheet is generally called a **Worksheet**. It is listed at the bottom of the document. A worksheet can be considered a single sheet of paper where calculations are performed. Any workbook contains at least one worksheet by default, subject to a maximum of 255 worksheets. Each sheet can have its name. It can be renamed by right-clicking on the worksheet tab. A new sheet can be created by clicking on the **Insert Sheet** icon if the data is large enough as well as heterogeneous. The sheets can be **deleted**, **renamed**, **moved**, or **copied** by right-clicking that worksheet tab
- **Zoom In and Zoom Out:** In most cases, one can quickly use the minus and plus symbols in the **Status Bar** to zoom the document
- **Adjustment of Column Width in the Work Area:** It may sometimes happen that the data/text entered in a cell exceeds the width of a cell. To adjust this overlapping to another cell, place the cursor at the end of the respective **column header** until this appears. Now double click this sign, and the size of the column will adjust automatically to the cell having the lengthiest data.

1.2 Basic Data Manipulation

With this level of familiarity, this section illustrates the techniques necessary to handle data. Specifically, we will see how to move across cells in a spreadsheet, for example, how to move from the top of a column to the bottom of the column, how to format cells, how to **Sort** various columns in the spreadsheet and how to **hide/unhide** some of the columns. To explain it, in Figure 1.2, we have taken hypothetical data of rural workers engaged in non-farm activities in a village. This data pertains to 25 workers only; in real life, the data may run into thousands of rows and hundreds of columns.

1.3 Finding the Number of Rows and Columns in Data

In a given data, one wants to determine how many workers are engaged in non-farm activities. In other words, how many rows of data are in this file. An easy way to find this is by pressing the cursor on A1 and pressing the **Ctrl+Down** arrow. Notice that the file has 25 workers. Remember, the very first row is **header** row. To find out the number of columns, press **Ctrl+Right** arrow, and it takes to the last column of the data. The data in the sheet can further be selected by pressing **Shift+Ctrl+Down** and **Shift+Ctrl+Right** keys (Figure 1.2).

1.4 Formatting Decimal Places

It may be noted in Figure 1.3 that the cells in land-owned data have values up to different decimal places. For example, the worker with ID number 1 owns 0.7534 acres of land or value up to four decimal places, whereas the worker with ID number 3 owns 2.258 acres of land up to three decimal places. If we wish to organize all the land data consistently so that all cells display values up to two decimal places, then select the entire **column** of data cells. Right-click any cell in this column,

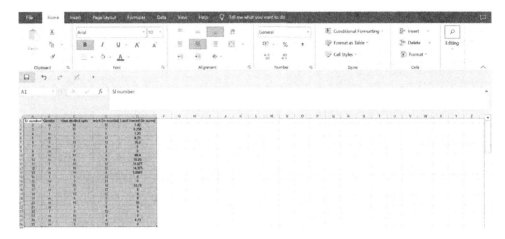

FIGURE 1.2 Finding the Number of Rows and Columns in Data

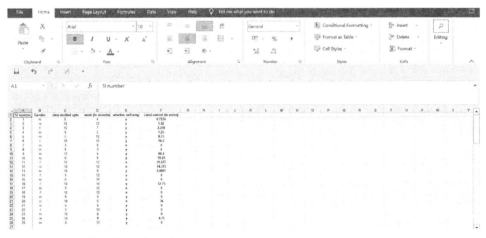

FIGURE 1.3 Profile of Rural Workers

- Press **Format cells**
- Select **Number**, and choose the number of decimal places (Figure 1.4). If two decimal places are selected, data in all the cells will be transformed into two decimal places
- Press **OK**.

Alternatively, as displayed in Figure 1.5, the data in the chosen cells may be converted directly into desired decimal places by choosing **Numbers** in the **Home** tab and selecting desired decimal points. Notice that all the decimal places are shortened or rounded off to two decimal places using either method (Figure 1.6).

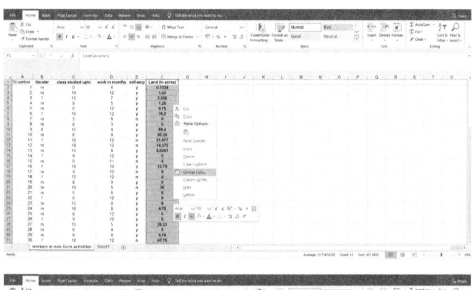

FIGURE 1.4 Formatting Decimal Points

FIGURE 1.5 Formatting Decimal Points Using Home Tab

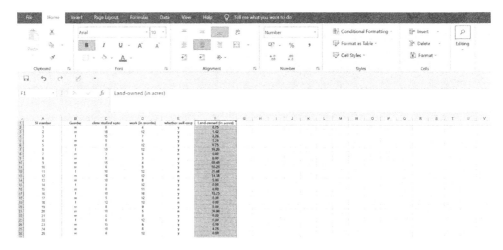

FIGURE 1.6 Formatting Up to Two Decimal Points

1.5 Sorting Data

Let us **Sort** our data according to the number of months workers have worked in ascending order. That is, we wish to list the workers who have not worked at all at the beginning of the list and those during the whole year at the end of the list. We wish to further **Sort** the workers as per their identity in column 1 in ascending order. We start by selecting the entire data file. An easy way to select is to first place the cursor in the very first cell, which is the A1 cell, press **Ctrl+Shift+Right** arrow and then **Ctrl+Shift+Down** arrow. The entire data is selected now.

- Click **Data**
- **Select Sort** opens up the following dialogue box (Figure 1.7).

Alternatively, the same dialogue box also opens up under *Custom Sort* in Sort and Filter in the Home tab (Figure 1.8).

- **Sort** by work in months by order, **Smallest to Largest**
  Now we wish to **Sort** it further by worker ID
- Click **Add Level**

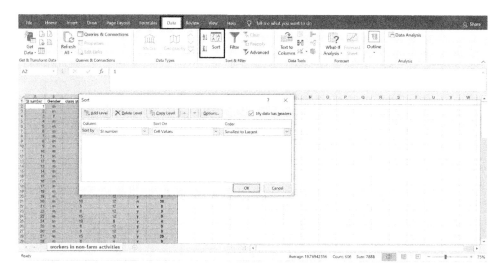

FIGURE 1.7 Step 1 in Sorting Data

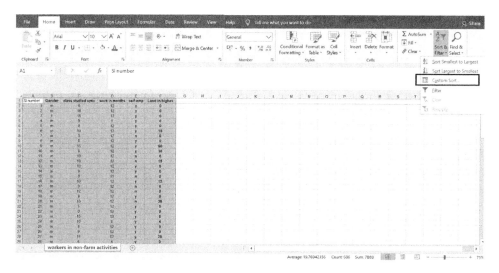

FIGURE 1.8 Step 2 in Sorting Data

- A new level (*Then by*) is added. Select the ID number from the drop-down box, and choose **Smallest to Largest** order because we want the serial IDs in ascending order. Since our data has headers, we need to make sure that the box with **My data has headers** is checked (Figure 1.9).
- Click **OK**
- The data has been sorted according to the ascending order of work in months and *within* work in months, with their serial IDs again in ascending order.

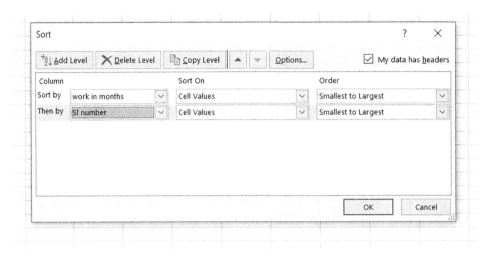

FIGURE 1.9 Step 3 in Sorting Data

1.6 Unhide and Hide Rows and Columns

When dealing with a heavy spreadsheet with many numbers of **rows** and **columns**, it is sometimes helpful to **unhide** or **hide** some of the **rows** and **columns** to see better the information one needs to analyze. If we do not wish to see some of the **column/s** (for example, self-employed in Figure 1.10),

- Select the **column** you do not wish to see
- **Right-click** the column
- Select **Hide**.

It can be noted from the table that **Column** E is not displayed. It does not delete the **column** but **hides** it. To **unhide** it again,

- Select both the adjacent **columns** of the hidden column
- **Right-click** the column
- Select **Unhide**. The hidden data is now visible again. The same method can be followed in the case of **rows** also.

1.7 Filtering Data

A **Filter** is an important tool in data analysis. It helps us display data selectively, according to the criteria set by a researcher. It may be noted again that the data we have in our example is selective, but the real-life data may be massive. In our ongoing example, a **Filter** needs to be applied if we wish to see gender-related data of female workers only. Similarly, other headers can accordingly be **Filtered**. A straightforward action to apply Filter is to hold **Shift+Ctrl** and press L. The columns should now have drop-down arrows next to each header, as shown in Figure 1.11.

A	B	C	D	F	G	H	I	J	K
Sl number	Gender	class studied upto	work (in months)	Land-owned (in acres)					
1	m	0	4	0.7534					
2	m	18	12	1.42					
3	f	15	7	2.258					
4	m	9	5	1.25					
5	m	0	12	0.75					
6	f	10	12	16.2					
7	m	3	6	0					
8	m	8	3	0					
9	m	15	4	60.4					
10	m	8	9	55.25					
11	f	10	12	31.677					
12	m	18	12	14.375					
13	m	10	8	5.0001					
14	f	9	12	0					
15	m	0	11	0					
16	f	10	10	12.75					
17	m	9	12	0					
18	f	12	12	0					
19	m	8	9	0					
20	m	10	5	36					
21	m	5	8	0					
22	f	0	12	0					
23	m	15	6	0					
24	m	10	8	4.75					
25	m	8	12	0					

FIGURE 1.10   Hidden Column

Another way to do it is by placing the cursor on any cell within the data range and selecting **Filter** in the **Data** tab. The outcome will be the same. One can also press the **Home** tab and select **Sort & Filter** (Figure 1.12). From the drop-down box, choose **Filter**. The box has **Text Filters** and **Number Filters** if the data is in text or numbers, respectively.

Suppose we are interested in looking at gender-based data, that is, of female workers who are employed in non-farm activities. To view it, click the drop-down arrow for the column of Gender to be filtered to display. **Uncheck** the box **Select All**, and **Check** the 'female' box again. Click **OK**. The data now shown is of female workers only.

Additional **Filters** can further be applied to other columns to narrow down the results. For instance, we wish to identify those female workers who have worked in all the months of the year. To do it, place the cursor on the work in months **Filter**, **Uncheck** the box **Select All** and **Check** the 12-month box again and click **OK**. The **Filters** can be cleared by pressing **Filter** again or **Clear** in the **Data** tab.

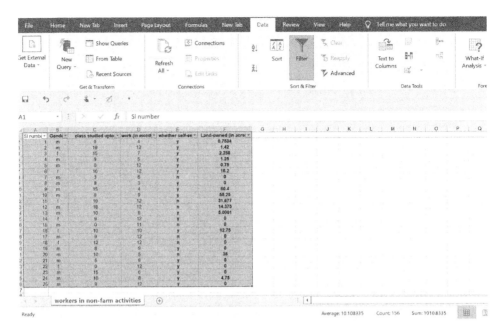

FIGURE 1.11 Filtering Data Through Key Commands

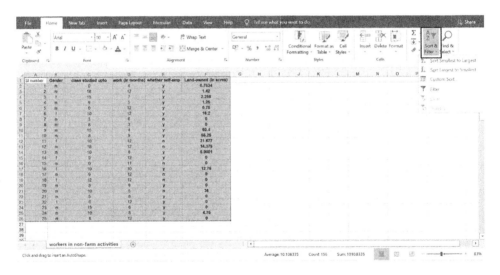

FIGURE 1.12 Filtering Data Through Tabs

Advanced **Filter** tools can be used for further insight into the data, both textual and numeral, according to the format of data given. For text data, click on the drop-down arrow of the column to be filtered (in our example, it is gender), click **Text Filters**, and the desired option like **Equals**, **Does not Equal**, **Begins With**, **Ends With** and **Contains** may be chosen (Figure 1.13). A **Custom filter** dialogue box appears immediately after selecting the desired criteria from the option **Text filter** (Figure 1.14).

FIGURE 1.13   Filtering Data Using Text Filters

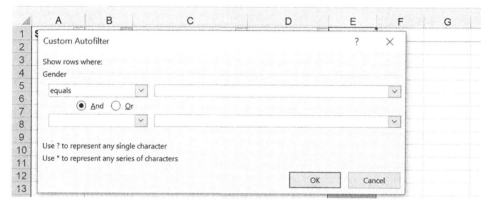

FIGURE 1.14   Custom Filter

Similarly, the relevant options in Number Filters like Equals, Does not Equal, Greater Than, Greater Than or Equal To, Less Than or Equal To and Between and Custom Filter can be analyzed (Figure 1.15).

Once the data is filtered, we can **copy** and **paste** the data into another sheet for deeper investigation. To do it, keep the cursor in any of the data cell, press **Ctrl+A** and again **Ctrl+C**. The data is now selected and copied. To paste it into the new sheet, open it, place the cursor on the cell we want copied data to be pasted, and press **Ctrl+V** (Figure 1.16). The data is now ready for scrutiny by the researcher.

1.8   Freezing Worksheet Panes

The **Freezing Panes** utility is used when the size of data is large so that the complete data is not displayed at one point in time. Resultantly, the researcher tends to lose track of what each of these columns/rows belongs to while scrolling down or right. In such a situation,

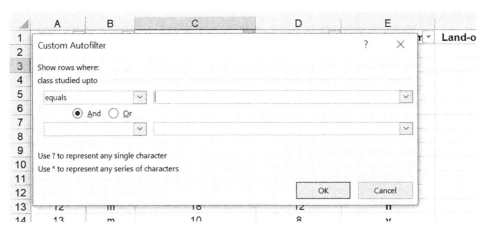

FIGURE 1.15   Number Filters

Freezing Panes is the technique to freeze the panes so that the **headers** of the first **rows** and **columns** can be viewed even after scrolling across the worksheet. As shown in Figure 1.17, the steps to freeze the first **column** are given as follows.

- Click **View** tab
- Select **Freeze Panes**, then from the drop-down box
- Then from the drop-down box select **Freeze First Column**.

    The first **column** is **frozen** (or locked) now. Scrolling to the right, we will no longer lose sight of the first column. Likewise, to **freeze** the top **row**,

- First **Unfreeze Panes** from **Freeze Panes** drop-down box
- Select Freeze Top Row.

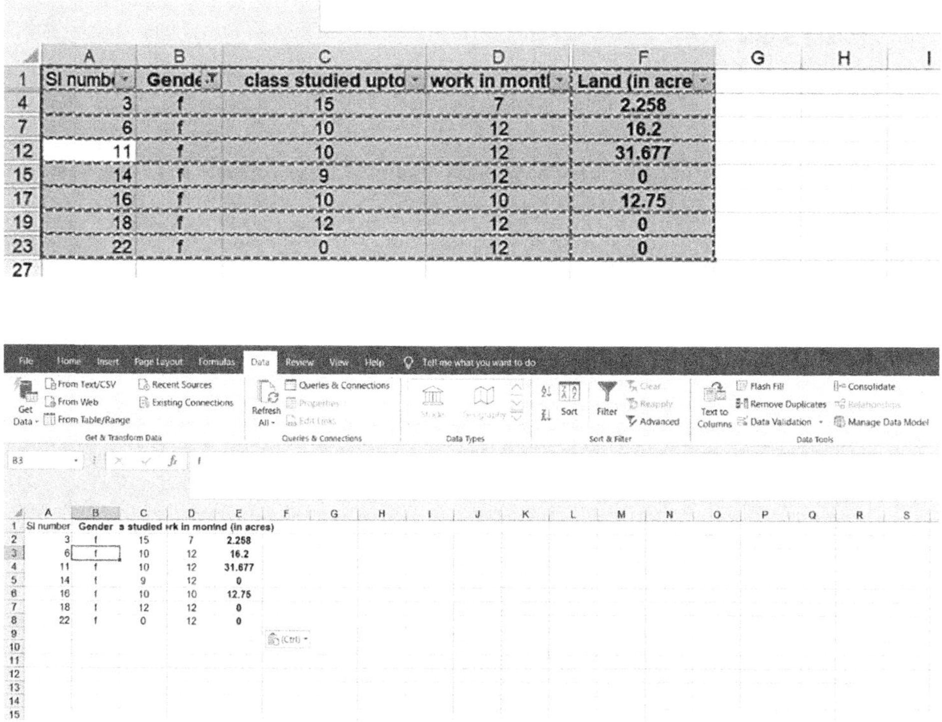

	A	B	C	D	F	G	H	I
1	Sl numb	Gende	class studied upto	work in montl	Land (in acre			
4	3	f	15	7	2.258			
7	6	f	10	12	16.2			
12	11	f	10	12	31.677			
15	14	f	9	12	0			
17	16	f	10	10	12.75			
19	18	f	12	12	0			
23	22	f	0	12	0			
27								

FIGURE 1.16   Copy and Paste of Filtered Data

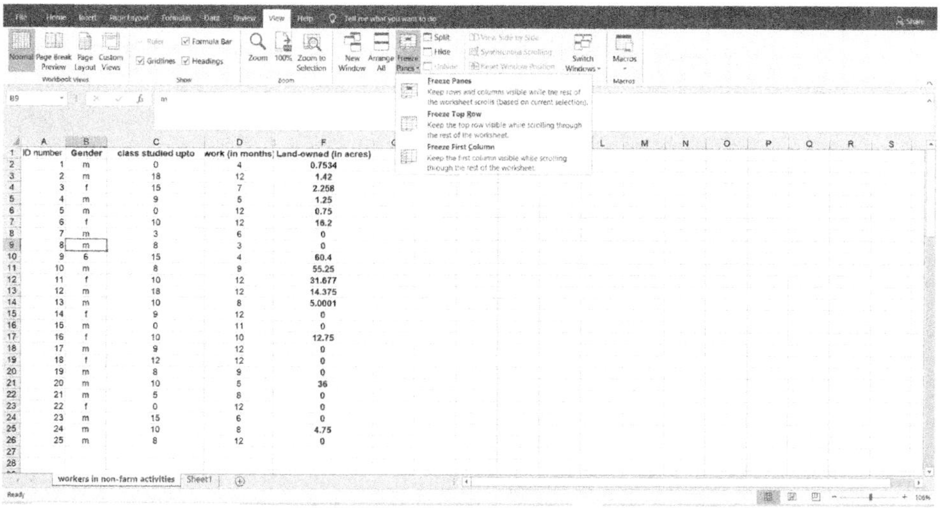

FIGURE 1.17   Freezing/Unfreezing of Panes

Further, in a situation when we need to **freeze** both the Top **row** and first **column,**

- Click on **Freeze Panes** in **View** tab
- Select **Unfreeze Panes** from the drop-down box
- Place the cursor on the intersection point of the first data point (cell B2)
- Select **Freeze Panes** in **View** tab
- Select the first option of **Freeze Panes**. The first **row** and **column** will remain visible while scrolling data to the right or down.

With these introductory techniques, we will learn how to perform arithmetic manipulation in Excel in the next chapter.

2
BASIC ARITHMETIC OPERATIONS IN EXCEL

Learning Objectives

After reading this chapter, the readers will be able to understand

- Basic arithmetic operations in Excel such as addition, subtraction, multiplication, and division
- Performing calculations using functions such as SUMIF, COUNT and COUNTIF, MAX and MIN
- Use of relative and absolute cell references
- Creating Pivot Tables in Excel

This chapter imparts an understanding of basic arithmetic operations in Excel. Such operations are necessary for undertaking any study. In particular, entering a formula in the spreadsheet to perform basic operations like addition, subtraction, multiplication, and division are introduced. Some other commands, namely **SUMIF**, **COUNT** and **COUNTIF**, **MAX** and **MIN** are also introduced. How to **copy** and **paste** the formula across the spreadsheet is presented. To learn these functions, we use the dataset of workers engaged in non-farm activities considered in Chapter 1. This time, however, additional information on their income and expenses is also presented, as shown in Figure 2.1.

2.1 Addition

We wish to determine the total monthly income a worker earns with ID number 1. To figure it out, we need to aggregate his monthly wages and income earned from other sources given in cells G2 and H2, respectively. Let us find the calculation in column J and name it *total*

DOI: 10.4324/9781003398127-2

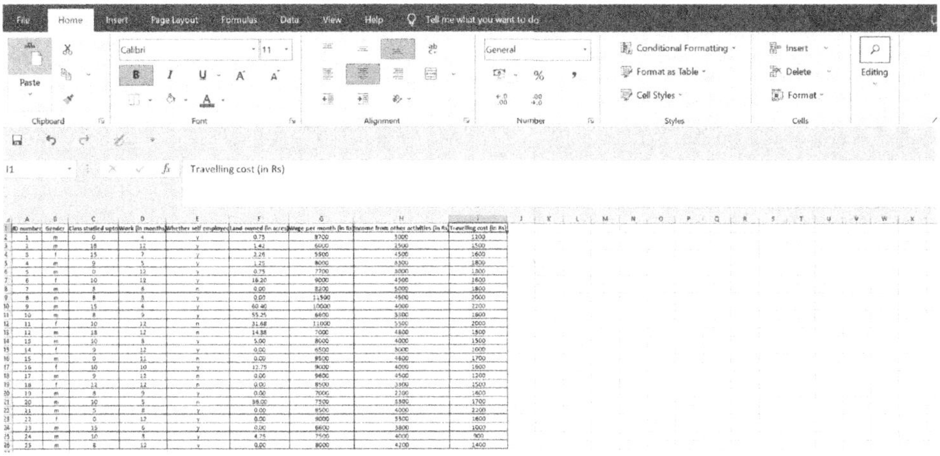

FIGURE 2.1 Data of Workers Employed in Non-Farm Activities

income earned. Corresponding to G2 and H2 cells, place the cursor in cell J2, where we want the calculation result to appear.

- Press the '=' key to start writing the formula
- Click on the first cell which is to be added (or write the name of the cell), press + (that is, the plus sign), and click on the second cell that needs to be added (or simply write the name of the cell)
- Press **Enter** for the result.

Another practical approach is the following:

- Press the **Insert function** (f_x) key. It automatically brings in = in **Formula Bar,** and a **dialogue box** pops up
- Search for a function **SUM** or select a function straightaway from the given options (Figure 2.2)
- Select the cells intended to be **summed.** The cells may be added up by either giving a **Range** (G2: H2 as in our example) or maybe entered separately in Number 2, Number 3 and so on (Figure 2.3)
- Press **OK** for the answer.

We can **copy** the formula by selecting the cell and taking the cursor to the bottom right of the cell until we see a thin plus (+) sign and double click. Notice that the entire column gets populated by the formula displaying the total income of all the workers.

2.2 Subtraction

We now may want to look at the net income of the workers. In our example, net income is obtained by subtracting the travelling cost from total income. In our Excel sheet example, the total income earned is given in column J. So, to find out, first, the net income of worker with ID number 1, we place the cursor in cell K2, where we want the calculation

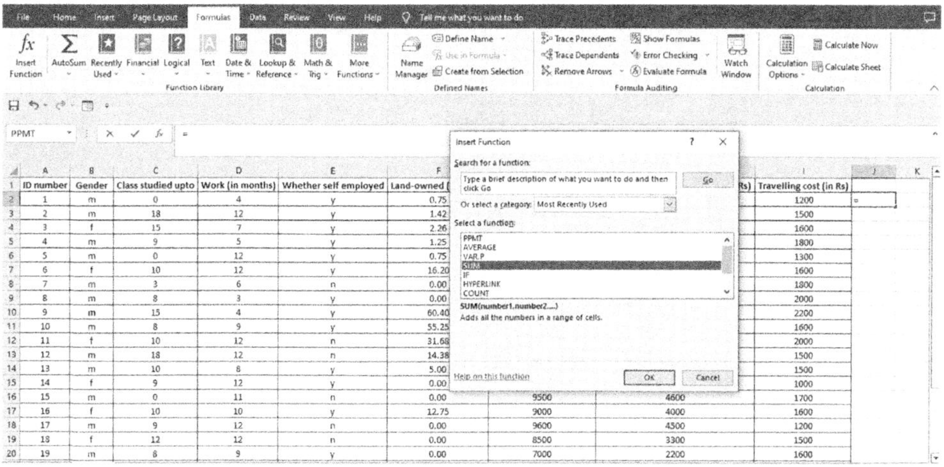

FIGURE 2.2   Step 1 in Adding Up Cells

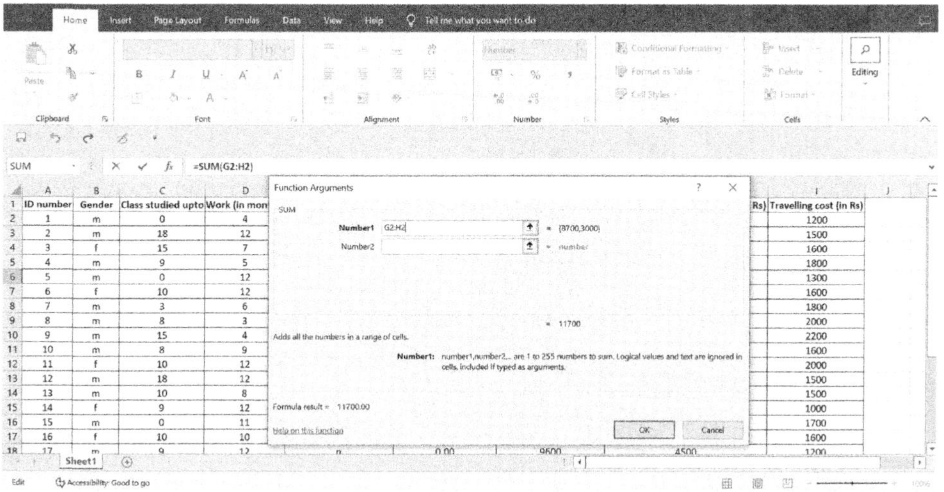

FIGURE 2.3   Step 2 in Adding Up Cells

result to appear and we then type '=' to begin the formula. We may next write either J2 (where total income earned of the worker with ID number 1 is given) straightway or select the cell J2 and then put a minus (−) sign. Write I2 (which represents the travelling cost) or select cell I2. Press **Enter**. This will lead to the answer we are looking for. Thus, the formula comes out as **=J2−I2** (Figure 2.4). It may be noted that there is no **SUBTRACT** function in Excel.

To know the net income earned by the rest of the workers, that is, to copy the formula in the rest of the cells, we follow the step mentioned earlier, that is, taking the cursor to the bottom right of the cell till we see a thin plus (+) sign and then double-clicking on it. Thus, we get the result for the remaining cells as well.

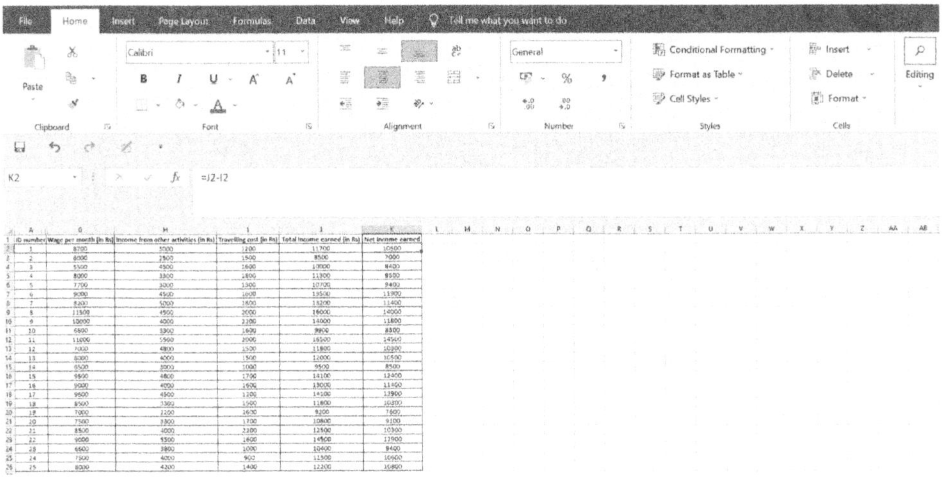

FIGURE 2.4 Subtracting of Cells

2.3 Multiplication

In addition to the aforementioned information, one may be curious to know the total income earned by these workers in a year. To arrive at final income earnings in a year, we need to multiply the monthly income by the number of months they worked. It can be seen that the data of the number of months worked by a worker is given in column D. The worker with ID number 1 worked for four months a year, the worker with ID 2 worked round the year, the worker with ID 3 for seven months a year, and so on. The total annual income earned is specified in column J, as shown. Multiplication of cells of columns D and J will give us the annum income levels. All workers' annual income results are to be presented in cells of L.

For the first worker (ID number 1) whose work in months and total income earned are placed in cells D2 and J2, we place the cursor on the corresponding cell K2.

- In this K2 cell, type '=', then click on the cell that contains the first number we want to multiply
- Type '*' and click on the second cell we want to multiply
- Press **Enter** for the results (Figure 2.5).

The second method to approach it is as follows:

- Press the **Insert function** (f_x) key. It automatically brings in '=' in the **Formula Bar** and a **dialogue box** shows up
- Select category **Math & Trig**
- Select the function **Product** and
- Press **OK**. It leads to another pop-up, as shown in Figure 2.6.

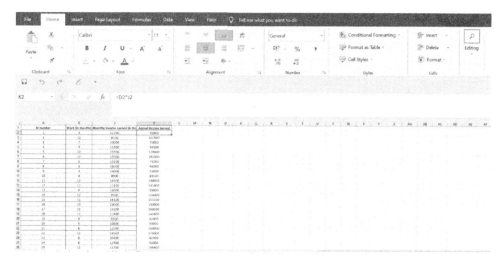

FIGURE 2.5   Method 1 of Multiplication of Cells

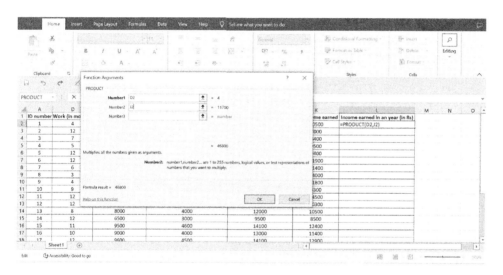

FIGURE 2.6   Method 2 of Multiplication of Cells

- In the **Number 1** and **Number 2** boxes, enter the numbers to be multiplied respectively. We can now see that the worker with ID number 1 collected ₹46,800 a year.
- It may be noted that if multiplication figures are more than two, the **Number** boxes can be extended accordingly
- Press **OK** for the report
- We can **copy** and **paste** the formula in the same manner, followed earlier.

2.4 Division

To find out the average monthly wages of the entire workforce in our data, the annual income earned by the worker needs to be divided by the total number of months in a year, that is, 12. To carry out this calculation, in our dataset, cells of column L2 are to be divided by respective cells in column D2.

For this, we first select the column in which such calculations are to be pursued (column M in our example). Place the cursor in cell M2, corresponding to the data figure of the worker with ID number 1. In our earlier illustrations, an arithmetic operation was carried out by first pressing '=' sign. We follow the same method here. Select the cell L2 representing the total income earned in a year and press the forward-slash (/) sign which does the division job. We divide it by cell D2 representing the number of months worked in a year by the worker and press **Enter**.

We can now see that the average income earned by the worker with ID number 1 is ₹11,700. The formula for the remaining cells can be copied accordingly. It may be noted that there is no **divide** function in Excel. However, if we are interested only in the integer portion of a division and discard the remainder, then we can use the **QUOTIENT** function in **Insert function**.

QUOTIENT (numerator, denominator), where

the numerator (required) is the dividend, that is, the number to be divided and,
the denominator (required) is the divisor, the number to divide by.

When two numbers divide evenly with no remainder, the division symbol and a **QUOTIENT** formula return the same result. For example, both **= 46800/4 and = QUOTIENT (46800, 4)** return 11700 (Figure 2.7).

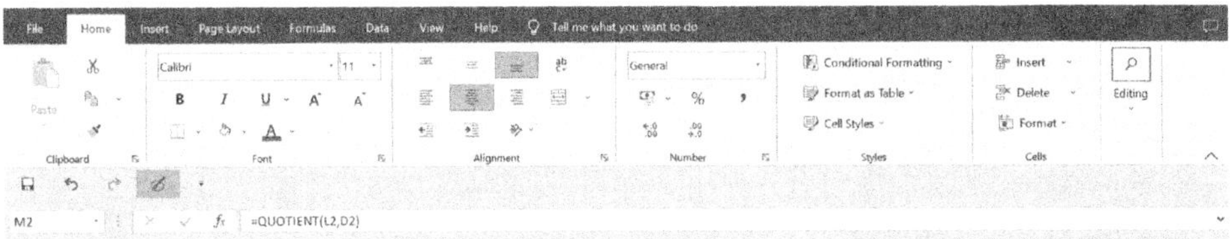

M2 =QUOTIENT(L2,D2)

	D	G	H	J	K	L	M
1	Work (in months)	Wage per month (in Rs)	Income from other activities (in Rs)	Total Income earned (in Rs)	Net Income earned	Income earned in an year (in Rs)	Average Income per month (In Rs)
2	4	8700	3000	11700	10500	46800	11700
3	12	6000	2500	8500	7000	102000	8500
4	7	5500	4500	10000	8400	70000	10000
5	5	8000	3300	11300	9500	56500	11300
6	12	7700	3000	10700	9400	128400	10700
7	12	9000	4500	13500	11900	162000	13500
8	6	8200	5000	13200	11400	79200	13200
9	3	11500	4500	16000	14000	48000	16000
10	4	10000	4000	14000	11800	56000	14000
11	9	6600	3300	9900	8300	89100	9900
12	12	11000	5500	16500	14500	198000	16500
13	12	7000	4800	11800	10300	141600	11800
14	8	8000	4000	12000	10500	96000	12000
15	12	6500	3000	9500	8500	114000	9500
16	11	9500	4600	14100	12400	155100	14100
17	10	9000	4000	13000	11400	130000	13000
18	12	9600	4500	14100	12900	169200	14100

FIGURE 2.7 Division Function in Excel

2.5 Relative and Absolute References

A formula containing a cell address is called a cell reference. For example, (=B1) refers to the value of the current cell, that is, the value of B1. So far, the calculations performed in our examples by **copy** and **paste** were *relative*. They were relative in the sense that after copying the function, the latter cell takes the *relative* reference of the preceding cell. For example, the Division function used for calculating average income per month for the worker with ID number 1, takes the formula M2 '=L2/D2'. Similarly, the same formula applies to the worker with ID number 2 in cell M3 (=L3/D3) with an incremental row number.

However, when we talk about *absolute* cell reference, we fix a particular cell by inserting a $ sign and then performing calculations. In Figure 2.8, we examine per worker income share (in Column M) relative to aggregate income (in Cell J28). To determine it, we first calculate the aggregate income of all workers. The next step is dividing an individual's annual income while keeping aggregate income constant ($J$28), as seen in Figure 2.8. Without the $ sign, the formula in cell M3 will become '=J3/J29*100', which will be meaningless. By carefully going through column M, we can figure out the denominator being fixed with the help of $ sign.

2.6 AutoSum Function

One of the basic functions used in Excel is the **SUM** function. Calculating the sum of many values can often be a complex task. We can use the **SUM** function to ease up the task. There are many ways to perform this function. In our ongoing discussion on Excel data of workers employed in non-farm activities, we want to find the sum of the incomes of workers given in columns A and B by using the **SUM** function. Place the cursor in cell C2, corresponding to the data of worker 1. Now type =**SUM** and select the cells to be summed up. Press **Enter**.

An alternative easy way is also depicted in Figure 2.9. To operate this, place the cursor in the cell where we desire the answer to appear (e.g., C2). Select **AutoSum** in the **Home** tab

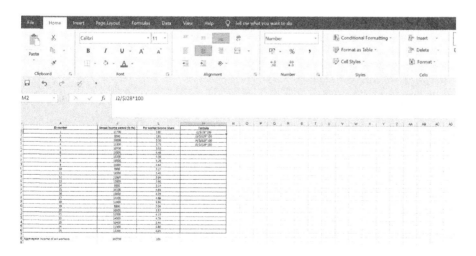

FIGURE 2.8 Absolute Cell Reference

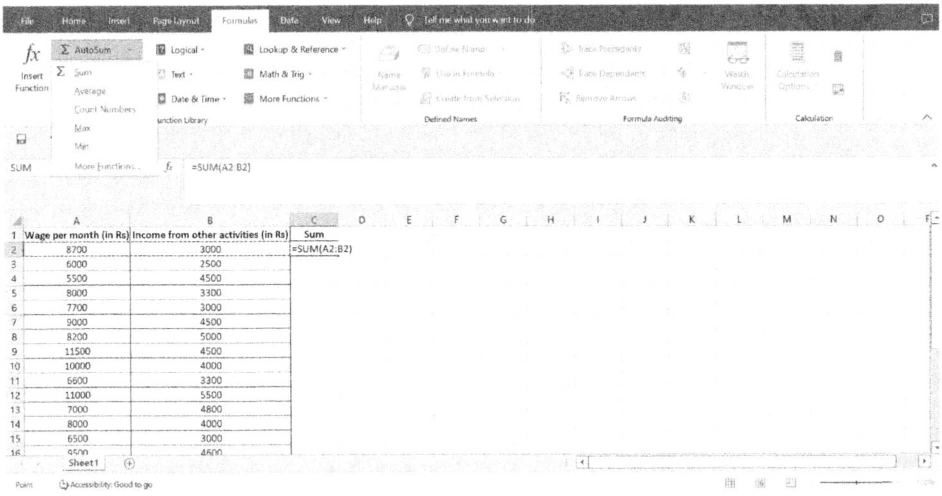

FIGURE 2.9   Usage of the AutoSum Function

and press **Enter**. This function automatically selects the cells to be added. It may be appropriate to note here that the **AutoSum** function also suggests other functions such as **Average**, **Count Numbers**, **Max** and **Min** numbers in the data range.

2.7   SUMIF Function

We can now calculate the total aggregate annual income earned by all the workers using the **Sum** function. In our dataset, this figure turns out to be ₹3,02,700. Our example categorically also specifies gender-related data.

We now want to determine the aggregate income of male and female workers separately. To do this, we use the **SUMIF** function. The **SUMIF function** adds all the numbers in a range of cells based on criteria (e.g., male workers). To carry this out, we type **=SUMIF** in the cell where we want our result. This command in parenthesis requires three inputs, as seen in Figure 2.10.

- The first one is the **Range** of cells we want to evaluate. Our example is column B (from B2 to B26), as shown in Figure 2.10
- Next is the **Criteria**. It is the condition or criterion in the form of a number, expression, or text that defines which cells will be added. We define **Criteria** m for males (and f for female workers). Notice that if the **Criteria** is text, it automatically is taken in *double quotation marks* (or if we have to write a formula directly, we need to put the **Criteria** in *double quotation marks*). However, numbers need not be wrapped in quotes but can be
- The last input is **Sum_range**, which are the data cells to be summed. In our example, Sum_range is J2 to J26 (J2: J26). This results in ₹1,99,900, which is the aggregate annual income of male workers. The same exercise can be undertaken for female workers, which according to our data, sums up to ₹1,02,800. Adding male and female annual income wages will aggregate to ₹3,02,700. It is the exact figure obtained by summing that of both male and female workers.

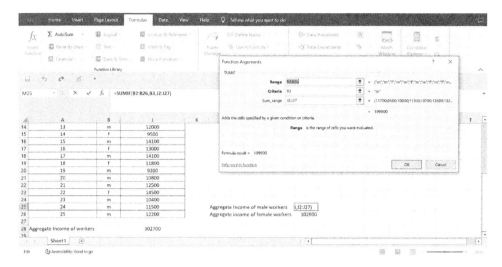

FIGURE 2.10 Usage of SUMIF Function

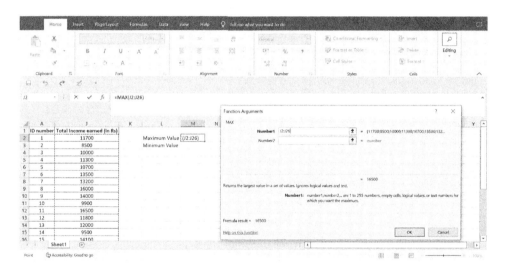

FIGURE 2.11 The MAX Function

2.8 MAX and MIN Function

There are many functions in Excel which can be found helpful in research and business statistics. Two such functions are **MAX** and **MIN** functions. The **MAX** function gives the largest
value in the set of data. Similarly, the **MIN** function provides the minimum value in a dataset.
The syntax (which is the layout and order of the function and its arguments) is =**MAX** and
the data range. In our dataset of annual income earned, the maximum yearly income earned
is ₹16,500 (Figure 2.11), and the minimum figure is ₹8,500 (Figure 2.12).

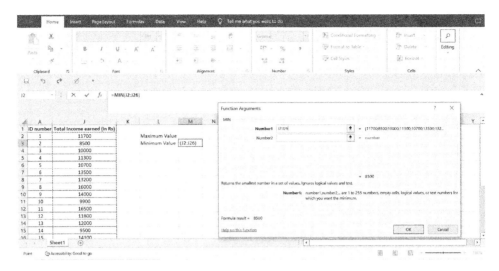

FIGURE 2.12 The MIN Function

FIGURE 2.13 The COUNT Function

2.9 COUNT and COUNTIF Function

As the name suggests, the **COUNT** function only counts the number of cells in the data range consisting of *numeral figures only*. The function starts with **=COUNT** and then it requires the data range to be selected, which then provides us with the count of numeral figures. In Figure 2.13, the income information of three workers is unknown (given in the text). After applying the formula, we can see that the output turns out to be 22. The output has not considered text values.

The **COUNTIF** function is an extension of the **COUNT** function and is of considerable use. It counts the numbers based on the **criteria**. For example, we want to find out numbers

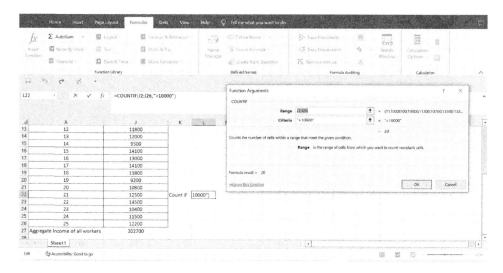

FIGURE 2.14   The COUNTIF Function

greater than 10,000. We apply **=COUNTIF**, select the data range, and the **criteria** is fixed as greater (>) than 10000. The answer we get is 20. That means, in a given range, there are 20 numbers greater than 10000 (Figure 2.14).

2.10   Power Function

The **Power** function computes and returns the result of a number raised to a power. **Power Excel function** takes two arguments. The first is a base (any real number), and the second is the exponent (power, which signifies how many times the given number will be multiplied by itself). For example, 3 raised to the power of 10 is explained in Figure 2.15. The answer is arrived by typing **=Power,** writing 3 in **Number box** and 10 in **Power box** which is equal to 59,049. Alternatively, it can also be done by typing =3^ (called hat) and typing 10, that is, to the number to which it is raised. Hence, we get the same result by using these two approaches.

2.11   Pivot Tables

We now introduce a **Pivot Table**, a potent tool for summing up data. We will understand here what a **Pivot Table** is, its uses, and how to construct one.

Pivot Table is a data summarization tool that helps summarize the data more comprehensively. In this, we can view data summaries in various formats as per our requirements. **Pivot Tables** are easy to create and use. **Pivot Tables** are also dynamic. It is dynamic because as data changes in the data file, the summary in the **Pivot Tables** automatically gets updated.

We illustrate it with an example of a fictitious company that supplies various articles through various representatives in different regions in the year 2019–2020. It may be noted that the size of the currently used data is a limited one, whereas real-life data may be a big file running into scores of **rows** and **columns**. The data presented in Figure 2.16 does not

FIGURE 2.15 The Power Function

convey any meaning *per se*. We may draw some useful information from the data, such as a summary of all items dispatched in various regions in the year mentioned using the **Pivot Table**. For this summary table, which needs to be drawn, the columns may represent the items dispatched, and the rows represent the regions. We will now use **Pivot Tables** to create such a summary.

We begin by inserting a **Pivot Table** template given in the **Insert** Tab. Excel asks for the data for which we wish to create a **Pivot Table**. We select the data from cell A1 through cell G26 (Figure 2.17). Then Excel also asks us where we want the **Pivot Table Report** to be placed – New Worksheet or Existing Worksheet – and then we press **OK** after selecting it. We, for example, select our data to be placed in a New Worksheet (Figure 2.18). We may rename the New Worksheet as a **Pivot Table**.

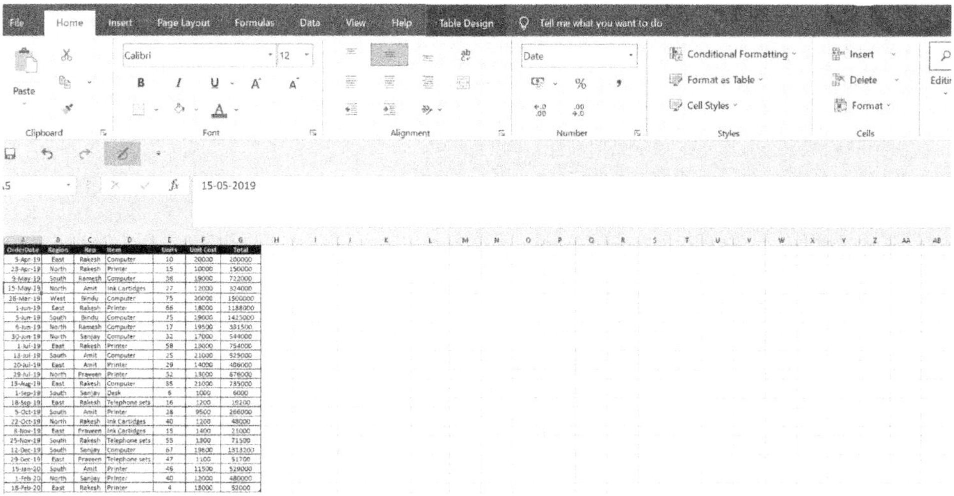

FIGURE 2.16 Sales Data of a Company

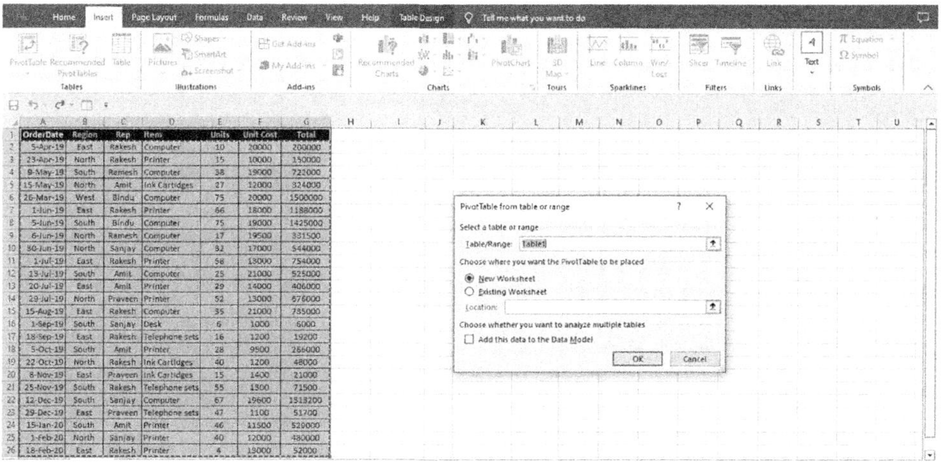

FIGURE 2.17 Inserting of a Pivot Table

In the left-hand side area, Excel has a template of the **Pivot Table**. We may notice that fields of the various columns in the data table are also given on the right-hand side. However, if we place the cursor anywhere outside the **Pivot Table**, the fields disappear but appear again as soon as we are back in the **Pivot Table** area. At the bottom, we have certain tools to organize our **Pivot Table Report**. Since we wish to find the data summary of items dispatched in various regions, we select the items and drag them to the **column box**. Similarly, we select the region and drag it to the **rows**. Since we wish to analyze the Items dispatched, we again drag the Items to the **Values** field. Excel has now categorized the data. We can now make it out that in the

- East region, 9 items were dispatched
- North Region, 7 items were dispatched
- South Region, 8 items were dispatched
- West Region, 1 item was dispatched

and the other details can be figured out from the given Pivot Table (Figure 2.19).

We can further process the summarized data reported in the **Pivot Table**. For instance, we may only wish to see the details of items dispatched region-wise for the first quarter. We can

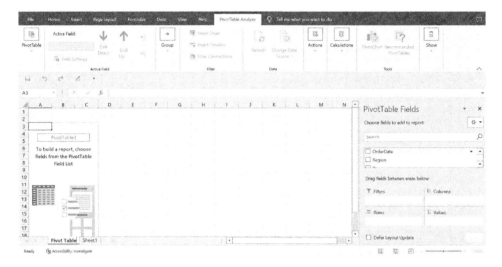

FIGURE 2.18 Illustration of a Pivot Table Template

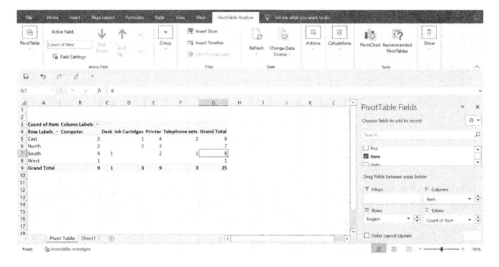

FIGURE 2.19 Summary of Results

achieve this by dragging the order date, in the **Pivot Table Fields,** to the **Filter** box. This gives the option of **Filter** on the top of the **Pivot Table**. Check the box **Select Multiple Items** first and uncheck the boxes mentioning dates not falling in the first quarter. Click **OK**. The **Pivot Table** report has now been filtered and only reports the figures for the first quarter (Figure 2.20).

We can add another filter to the report by placing it in the **Report Filter area,** as in Figure 2.21. Further, suppose we wish a **Pivot Table** to report sales figures by the representative's name. In that case, we can drag the variable *representative* from the **Pivot Table Field** to the **Filter** field. Another filter box appears below the former **Filter** and we select the representative's name in whose sales figures we are interested in following the same procedure just mentioned. The **Filter** can also be removed by selecting and dragging the variable from the

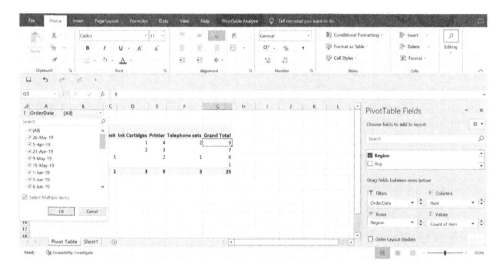

FIGURE 2.20 Step 1 in Data Filtering in Pivot Table

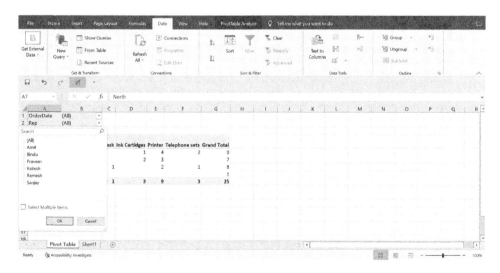

FIGURE 2.21 Step 2 in Data Filtering in Pivot Table

Column field back to the **Pivot Table Fields.** Likewise, dragging the representative field to the **Rows** area will show the region-wise sales by different representatives. The **Pivot Table** also shows both, the total of the sales and the individual sales by the respective representative.

We can also evoke arithmetic operations in the study of **Pivot Tables.** The numeric data allows us to do a lot of arithmetic calculations in the **Pivot Table,** such as Sum, Count, Average, Product, and many more.

In the ongoing example, to find the **Sum** of the number of dispatched items region-wise, we drag the region **Field** to the **Row** box and the units **Field** to the **Values** box. It automatically shows the sum of the items dispatched region-wise (Figure 2.22). If we again wish to see the number of maximum units dispatched in the same function, we click anywhere on the **Sum of Units** column, right-click and select **Summarize Values By** option and at last select Max. We can also choose Count, Average, or any such option from the **Summarized Value Fields** by drop-down box as per our purpose.

There is a further option of **Show Values As**. Figure 2.23 shows that this option offers several features: the percentage of Grand Total, percentage of Column Total and percentage of Row Total. For better data visualization, we can **group** and **ungroup** dates in our data in months, quarters, and years as per our requirement.

To recap, in this chapter, we have learned to perform basic arithmetic manipulations such as addition, subtraction, multiplication, and division. Besides, we have gone through the following basic functions:

- AutoSum
  (To find aggregates of all numbers in our dataset)
- SUMIF
  (To sum up the data with one or more conditions attached)
- MAX and MIN
  (To find the maximum and the minimum value(s) in the data)

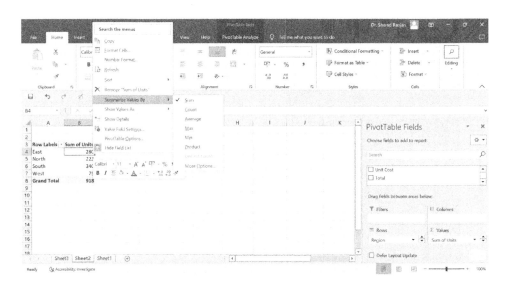

FIGURE 2.22 Summarizing of Values

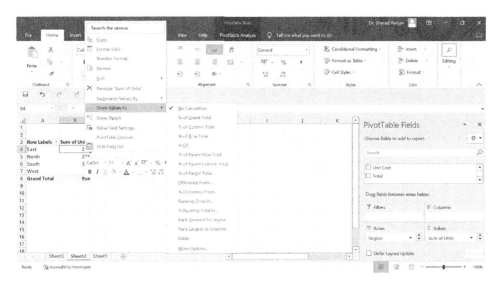

FIGURE 2.23   Forms of Summarized Values

- COUNT and COUNTIF
  (To find the count of numerals in our data with or without conditions)
- Power function
  (To get the result of a number raised to an exponential power)

Finally, we have been trained on how to summarize data using Pivot Tables. We have also explored the operation of arithmetic functions on the summarized data.

PRACTICE QUESTIONS

This table shows the marks secured in Physics of class X[th] students. Read the information given and answer the questions given afterward.

Roll No	Name	Physics		
		Theory (out of 70)	Practical (out of 30)	Total (out of 100)
1	Neetu	65	27	
2	Harshit	53	25	
3	Kashish	45	29	
4	Riya	55	26	
5	Tannu	48	28	
6	Khushi	55	25	
7	Vaibhav	60	29	
8	Archit		27	81
9	Sonia	43		90
10	Shruti		28	78

Roll No	Name	Physics		
		Theory (out of 70)	Practical (out of 30)	Total (out of 100)
11	Mannu		22	57
12	Aastha		27	85
13	Shubham	57		79
14	Amit	68	27	
15	Atul	55	22	

1. Complete the table.

2. If the total marks are increased to 300, compute the new table showing the combined upgraded marks.

3. Using the AutoSum function, calculate the aggregate marks of all students in theory and practical.

4. What average marks did the class obtain in theory and practical?

5. Using the SUMIF function, calculate the aggregate marks obtained by students scoring more than 80.

6. How many students scored more than 80 marks (use COUNTIF function)?

7. Name the students who topped the class and who scored the least marks.

8. Summarize the class results by using the Pivot Table.

3

DATA

Input Into Excel and Sources

Learning Objectives

After reading this chapter, the readers will be able to understand:

- Qualitative and quantitative data
- Meaning of primary and secondary data
- Methods of entering data in Excel
- Importing data from other sources
- Sources of data – Datasets available in the public domain such as RBI, Census, MOSPI, Directorate of Statistics and Economics, NSE, BSE, World Bank, and UN data and how to download them into Excel

---

Data is one of the most essential and key aspects of any study. Data is a collection of numbers, facts, figures, texts, words, or descriptions of things. A collection of data is known as datasets, usually organized in a tabular form. Datasets are then used to analyze and draw conclusions to understand a phenomenon better and/or to make informed decisions. In this chapter, we will learn data entry into an Excel sheet. This chapter also acquaints the readers with the freely available data resources on the various sectors of our economy that can be imported to an Excel spreadsheet.

3.1 Understanding Data

Data can be categorized into qualitative data and quantitative data. *Qualitative data* is non-numerical and based on categorical variables to describe, classify, or categorize things based on characteristics, properties, quality, or labels. For instance, information related to gender, marital status, suggestions, and customer service feedback are qualitative data examples. On the other hand, *quantitative data* is expressed in numerical terms and can be counted or measured. Information about the height, weight, age, size, area, scores, income, revenues, or prices illustrates quantitative data.

DOI: 10.4324/9781003398127-3

Based on the sources used to collect the data, the data can be classified into two types – *primary* and *secondary*. When the data is collected for the first time for a specific purpose of analysis, it is known as the primary data. Primary data, therefore, is the first-hand information collected. It is collected using surveys, questionnaires, or personal interviews. Examples are data collected by an organization from its customers to conduct market research or the census data collected by the government.

Secondary data refers to the information already collected. Examples of sources on secondary data are either reports published by government departments and organizations or their websites. Since collecting primary data is usually time-consuming and expensive, secondary data is used by many as it is less expensive, quick, and easy to collect. The information collected from either of these data sources can be analyzed using various techniques.

3.2 Data Entry in Excel

Excel has many features when it comes to data entry. We can enter both numbers and the alphabet in Excel. Usually, the following are the methods adopted to do the same.

The first method to enter the data in Excel is to type the data directly into the cell by using a keyboard. Alternately, select the cell where the data is required to appear and use **Formula Bar** to enter the data. For example, if we want to enter 350 in cell B1, select the cell B1 and go to the **Formula Bar**, enter 350, and press **Enter** button. The same can be done by entering the data in the cell itself. Nevertheless, this method to enter data manually, one by one, is difficult and not practical, if the data size is large. Moreover, manual data entry is time-consuming and the probability of error occurrence is also high.

The second method is by the use of *copy* and *paste* option. Select the cell that we would like to copy, right-click and select **copy** or press **Ctrl+C**. Then select the cell where we want to **paste** the data, right-click and select **paste** or press **Ctrl+V**. In case we want to copy the *same* data available in the cell to the subsequent cells, the method is to use the *Autofill* option. Select the data cell that we want to copy, bring the cursor bottom right corner of the cell to the + icon and drag up to the cell where we want the data to be copied. We can also fill other types of data series in the same manner. Select the first two data cells, bring the cursor to the same + icon, and drag it to the last cell where we want data to appear. The numbers in selected cells are filled orderly. Like numbers, one can also add months.

In case of any mistake in the data, like a spelling error or a number error, select the cell and double click into the cell and correct it or you can use **Formula Bar** and press **Enter**. Excel also provides *Auto Prompt*. If we type any name and want to repeat it in any other cell, select the cell where data is to be entered and type the first letter of the same name. Excel will auto prompt it and press **Enter** to confirm. In addition, it is important to understand the character of fractions here. To illustrate, if 2¼ is typed in a cell and **Enter** is pressed, the **Formula Bar** displays 2.25. But if we type fraction ¼, Excel automatically reads it in a date format. These mistakes can be easily avoided by just adding zero in front of the fraction (e.g., 0¼).

The third method is using the data entry form. In this utility, data can be entered up to 32 fields per record. This is a useful feature of Excel doing the process of data entry faster with fewer errors. Typically, the option of data is not available on the **Quick Access Toolbar** but can be added in the following manner:

- Right-click on any of the existing icons or click the down arrow in the **Quick Access Toolbar**
- Click on Customize Quick Access Toolbar
- From the drop-down list, select More Commands
- Select All commands and choose Forms from the list shown
- Click Add and enter OK
- The **Form** icon will be displayed in **Quick Access Toolbar** as shown in Figure 3.1.

To make a new form, we have to add headings in the column and adjust the width of each column. The form will use this width as the default size for all form fields. Select all the cells containing the headings and click **OK**. For example, if we want to create a form of consumer satisfaction with seven fields, then enter the headings such as name of the customer, quantity of apple purchased, income of the customer, price of apple, price of its substitutes, taste and preference, and the number of family members. Verify that all the columns have headings. Highlight your data range, including column headings, by clicking the cell from where the data starts and press **Ctrl+shift+** $\rightarrow$ in case the headings are in columns. Similarly, press **Ctrl+shift+** $\downarrow$ in case the headings are in rows. Then select **Forms** from the **Quick Access Toolbar**. Click **OK**. A new window will appear as shown next (Figure 3.2), with the heading of the column as fields.

Enter the data in the **Form** Fields. Press **Enter** or **New** button to enter the record in the table and get a blank form for the next record. This data form can be created to enter the primary data.

A data entry form in Excel has many different buttons as shown in Figure 3.2.

- **New**: This will clear the existing data in the form and allows it to create a new record
- **Delete**: This will allow deleting an existing record

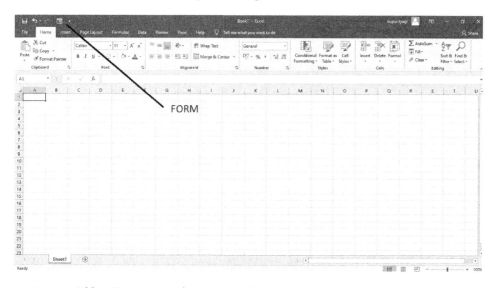

FIGURE 3.1   Adding Form to Quick Access Toolbar

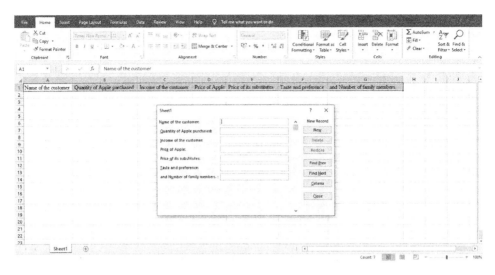

FIGURE 3.2 Adding Form to Quick Access Toolbar

- **Restore**: If editing an existing entry, one can restore the previous data in the form
- **Find Prev**: This will find the previous entry
- **Find Next**: This will find the next entry
- **Criteria**: This allows us to find specific records
- **Close**: This will close the form
- **Scroll Bar**: Use the **Scroll Bar** to go through the records.

Select any cell in the Excel table to navigate existing records and click on the **Form** icon in the **Quick Access Toolbar**. A new window will appear. To go to the next entry, click on the **Find Next** button. To go to the previous entry, click the **Find Prev** button. To edit an entry, simply make the change and press **Enter**.

3.3   Importing Data in Excel

In Excel, data can be imported from text file, web query, and comma-separated values (CSV) files. This is very useful and saves time. Through this feature, one can directly import the data from other sources and analyze it using Excel tools. The steps involved in importing data from the text are explained next:

- Select **Data** from the tabs
- Select **From Text** from the Get external data group
- From the new window, select **Text Files** from the bottom right-hand corner if your file does not have CSV. Otherwise, you can directly choose the CSV file that you want to import to Excel and select **Import**
- Select **Delimited** from Original Data Type of the newly appeared Text Import Wizard if your text data is in split form. Select **Next**

- If your text is split with a comma, then select **Comma** command from the Delimiters list. Like this, you can also select **Tab**, **Semicolon**, **Space**, and others according to your data format and press **Next**
- Select **General** from the newly displayed window, but there are cases when the data starts with zero. If **General** is selected, then Excel will not consider the zero. So to avoid this, one has to be more vigilant and select/highlight the column where zero starts and then select **Text** from the Column Data Format list
- In the same window, we can also control decimal (.) and thousand separator (,) by selecting **Advanced Key** on the right-hand side. After all these steps, select **Finish**.

A new dialogue box will appear. Data can be imported in the existing sheet or a new sheet. To convert the imported text into a table, press **Ctrl+T**. A table with filters will be displayed.

Excel can also import data directly from the websites. This feature makes Excel user-friendly and can import any data from any website. For this, first copy the URL of the site which contains the data that you want to import, and then follow the steps:

- Select **Data** from tabs
- Select **From Web** from the get external data groups
- A new web query window appears, then paste the URL that is already copied in the Address box given and click **Go**
- From the website opened, one can select the arrow near the table one want to add and select **Import** and **OK**.

3.4   Datasets Available in the Public Domain

Nowadays, secondary data is easily accessible online or from public and university libraries. It is economical to collect such secondary data as a wide range of datasets can be downloaded either free of cost or by paying nominal charges. Since the datasets are usually available in Excel format, there is no need to prepare an Excel data sheet for given parameters. Here is the list of a few important sources of publicly available data widely used.

3.4.1   Database for Indian Economy (DBIE)

The Reserve Bank of India (RBI) is the central bank of India which prepares and furnishes a large volume of economic and financial data through data publication and reports. The Department of Statistics and Information Management of RBI has set up a public website (*http://dbie.rbi.org.in*) for the database for the Indian economy, referred to as the RBI's data warehouse. This website provides quick access to a wide range of real-time economic and financial data. Data on the Database on Indian Economy (DBIE) website can be downloaded and saved as Excel files for analysis. The website has four parts – *Home* , *Statistics* , *Time-Series Publications* , and *Unit Level Data* (Figure 3.3).

The **home page** has some important INDICATORS like Reserve Money, GDP, Money Market, G–Sec Turnover, Business of Scheduled Banks, Monthly WPI and IIP, RBI Balance Sheet, and Foreign Exchange Reserves on the left-hand side. The SAARCFINANCE

Database dispenses time-series data on macroeconomic and socio-economic variables of SAARC countries that can be downloaded and saved in different formats, including Excel. The home page contains a dashboard that shows the economy at a glance. The new data or publication released on the website is notified below the dashboard. On the right-hand side, there are certain useful links such as Brochure on DBIE (English), Downloading Data into Excel, DBIE Data Release Calendar, RBI Main Site.

The second part, **Statistics,** has been divided into *seven subject areas* (Figure 3.3). The data series related to the *subject areas* and their various *sub-sectors* are compiled periodically. The subject areas are as follows:

1. **Real sector** comprises Agriculture, Industry, National Income, and Price and wages consisting of information mentioned in Figure 3.4.

    *   Agriculture such as production and area under cultivation data for major food grains and commercial crops, indices on area under cultivation, yield per hectare, and state-wise production of foodgrains
    *   Industrial statistics such as the production of select industries, Index of Industrial Production (IIP), production and imports of crude oil and petroleum products
    *   National Income includes quarterly estimates of gross domestic products, private final consumption expenditure, government final consumption expenditure, exports, and imports
    *   Prices and wages, such as consumer price indices.

FIGURE 3.3 DBIE Website: Statistics

FIGURE 3.4 Data on Real Sector in DBIE Website

2. **Corporate sector** includes data on finances of FDI companies, listed non-government non-financial companies, non-government non-banking financial and investment companies, non-government non-financial private limited companies, and non-governmental non-financial public limited companies.

3. **Financial sector** provides information on the following:

   • Banking – assets and liabilities such as capital, liabilities, and assets of scheduled commercial banks

   • Banking – branch statistics such as number of banks, branches, newly opened branches, and closed branches

   • Banking – performance indicators such as profitability, gross and net non-performing assets of scheduled commercial banks and so on

   • Banking – sectoral statistics, financial institutions such as assets and liabilities of Deposit Insurance and Credit Guarantee and Corporation, Industrial Financial Corporation of India, EXIM Bank, National Bank for Agriculture and Rural Development, National Housing Bank, Small Industrial Development Bank of India, and other financial institutions

   • Key rates such as bank rate, cash reserve ratio, and statutory liquidity ratio

   • Monetary statistics, non-banking financial companies, payment systems.

4. **Financial market** furnishes data on:

   • Equity and corporate debt market such as data series on Bombay Stock Exchange (BSE) and National Stock Exchange (NSE) indices

   • Forex market such as data series on exchange rates for four major currencies, that is, USD ($), Euro, GBP, and Japanese Yen against the domestic currency (INR)

   • Government securities market and money market.

5. **External sector** disseminates data on:

   • External debt such as government borrowing

   • External sector indices, forex reserve

   • International finance such as foreign investment inflows and international trade such as commodity-wise export and import

   • Components of the balance of payments such as current and capital account balance, merchandise trade, and service income.

6. **Public finance** segment supplies data on central and state government finance (combined), such as direct and indirect tax revenues of central and state governments and market borrowings of central and state governments.

7. **Socio-economic indicators** provide information on the employment situation in India and the population below the poverty line up to 2012.

To extract the data from the website, one can simply access the reports available in the STATISTICS tab. To do this, first, choose the sector and the sub-sector for which the data is required (Figure 3.4). The reports (daily, fortnight, monthly, quarterly, yearly) will be displayed and then click on the required report. The period for which the data is available is mentioned next to each report. The data will appear as shown in Figure 3.5. Click on the **Export** option, then select **Export Document As** to export the report to Excel, PDF, Text, and CSV.

FIGURE 3.5   Exporting Data (Sector-wise)

The third part is **Time-Series Publications** which includes numerous tables incorporated in various bank publications. They are organized under the respective publication tabs such as *Bank Branch Statistics, Data on International Banking Statistics of India, Handbook of Statistics on the Indian Economy, Monthly RBI Bulletin, Primary (Urban) Co-operative Banks' Outlook, Public Debt Statistics, Quarterly Statistics on Deposits and Credit of Scheduled Commercial Banks, Statistical Tables Relating to Banks in India,* and *Weekly Statistical Supplement, etc.* Reports under **Time-Series Publications** are real-time as they are continuously updated without waiting for the annual printed versions of the publication giving access to the latest data to the users. It is important to note that the time-series data available in these publications can be downloaded in Excel/Pdf/ text format. The steps to export data remain the same as mentioned previously.

The fourth and the last part, **Unit Level Data**, contains the reports related to the household surveys conducted by RBI such as *Inflation Expectations Survey of Household* to record households' expectations of change in price level and inflation rate and *Consumer Confidence Survey* to collect data on the consumer current perception and future expectations on five parameters – economic condition, employment scenario, general price levels, income, and spending of the households. The data can be downloaded in the same manner as the aforementioned.

3.4.2   Census of India

Census is the official count of the population of a country. The data collected in the census is of utmost importance in the assessment of the social, economic, and demographic conditions of a country. It is also the largest source of primary data for researchers, providing them with a necessary framework for their research work. In addition, the structured data vitally helps formulate, evaluate, and manage the various macro-economic policies and programs. The first complete Census of India was taken in the year 1871. Since then, the Census has been conducted continuously once every ten years. Post-1949, the census is conducted by the *Registrar General and Census Commissioner of India* under the Ministry of Home Affairs, Government of India. The data is generally collected in two phases. The *first* phase, that is, house listing operations, is regarding identifying and recording information related to the household. The *second* phase, population enumeration, is related to collecting information about individuals residing in the country. The last Census was conducted in 2011 and the process for the latest census, 2021 has been delayed due to the ongoing covid-19 pandemic.

Census collects a broad set of data on a wide range of parameters. The tabulation plan (*along with their table categories*) covers:

- Tables on Houses, Household Amenities, and Assets
- Tables on Houses, Household Amenities, and Assets – Female-Headed Households
- Tables on Houses, Household Amenities and Assets – Slum Households
- Household Tables (HH-Series)
- Final Population Totals
- Primary Census Abstracts
- General Population Tables (A-Series)
- General Economic Tables (B-Series)
- Social and Cultural Tables (C-Series)
- Migration Tables (D-Series)
- Fertility Tables (F-Series)
- Special Tables for Scheduled Castes (SC-Series)
- Special Tables for Scheduled Tables (ST-Series)
- Town Directory
- Village Directory

The Office of the Registrar General & Census Commissioner, India, publishes the afore-mentioned tables starting from the national level to state, district, town, and village level. The tables for 1991 to 2011 are also available online through its official web portal – **Census of India**. The website can be accessed through URL *https://censusindia.gov.in/*. A glimpse of the website's home page is shown in Figure 3.6.

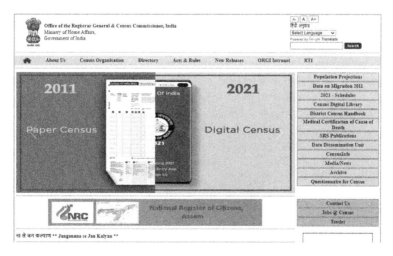

FIGURE 3.6 Census of India Website: Home Page

FIGURE 3.7   Downloading Census Data

Source: https://censusindia.gov.in/DigitalLibrary/Tables.aspx accessed on 26 May 2021

The process of downloading the data involves the following steps. First, we click on the **Census Digital Library** option on the right-hand side of the website's home page. This will direct the user to the home page of Central Digital Library (*https://censusindia.gov.in/ DigitalLibrary/Archive_home.aspx*). The Census digital library presently consists of Census tables from 1991 to 2011 only. Next, we click on the option **TABLES** from the tabs given at the top of the site. Then, select the *Census Year* under the *Census* option for which data is required from the drop-down menu (Figure 3.7). Data tables from 1991 to 2011 are freely downloadable and can be saved as Excel and CSV files for analysis.

Tabulation plans like tables on houses, household amenities and assets, final population totals, general population tables, general economic tables, migration tables, town directory, and village directory get displayed once the Census year is selected. If we click on one of these options, it shows a series of *tables categories* available under it, and one can choose from these multiple categories as per one's requirement.

For instance, if we were to download the data table for India's district and state-wise population for the census year 2001, we would choose the option of *General Population Tables*, as shown in Figure 3.8. One can then select from the multiple table categories provided under individual heads as per their requirement. We select the first option, *A1 tables: Area, households, and populations.*

Several tables available under the table category will be displayed as displayed in Figure 3.9. We will choose the required option, and an Excel file will be automatically downloaded. For example, in our case, we will select the Excel (.xls) file for the *number of villages, towns, households, population, and area.* An Excel file with the state and district-wise population will get downloaded.

Alike, we may need to download another data table relating to the population of *main workers* (worked for six months or more) in the state of Delhi, classified by Industry category, Education level, and sex from the Census year 2001. To do this, we choose the option of

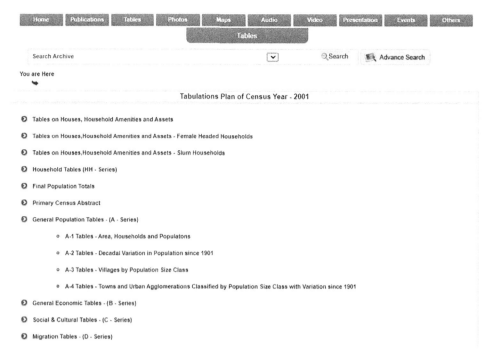

FIGURE 3.8   Downloading Census Data

Source: https://censusindia.gov.in/DigitalLibrary/TablesSeries2001.aspx accessed on 26 May 2021

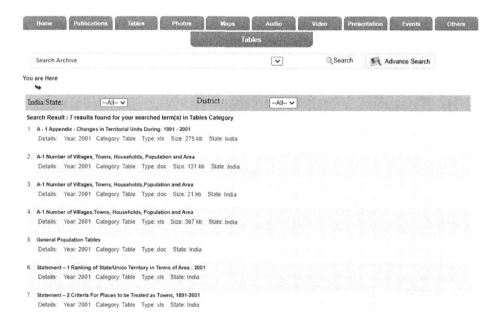

FIGURE 3.9   Downloading Census Data

Source: https://censusindia.gov.in/DigitalLibrary/MFTableSeries.aspx accessed on 26 May 2021

- Household Tables (HH - Series)
- Final Population Totals
- Primary Census Abstract
- General Population Tables - (A - Series)
- General Economic Tables - (B - Series)
  - B-1 to B-10
    - B-1 : Main Workers,Marginal Workers,Non-Workers and those Marginal Workers,Non-Workers Seeking/ Available for Work Classified by Age and Sex
    - B-1 City : Main Workers,Marginal Workers,Non-Workers and those Marginal Workers,Non-Workers Seeking/ Available for Work Classified by Age and Sex
    - B-1 SC : Main Workers,Marginal Workers,Non-Workers and those Marginal Workers,Non-Workers Seeking/ Available for Work Classified by Age and Sex for Scheduled Castes
    - B-1 ST : Main Workers,Marginal Workers,Non-Workers and those Marginal Workers,Non-Workers Seeking/ Available for Work Classified by Age and Sex for Scheduled Tribes
    - B-2 : Main Workers,Marginal Workers,Non-Workers and Those Marginal Workers,Non-Workers Seeking/ Available for Work Classified By Age, Sex and Religious Community

FIGURE 3.10   Downloading Census Data

Source: https://censusindia.gov.in/DigitalLibrary/TablesSeries2001.aspx accessed on 26 May 2021

FIGURE 3.11   Downloading Census Data

Source: https://censusindia.gov.in/DigitalLibrary/MFTableSeries.aspx accessed on 26 May 2021

General Economic Tables. A series of categories will be displayed, such as economic tables on the population of main workers, marginal workers, and non-workers classified by industry category, age, sex, education level, and caste (Figure 3.10).

We select the table category *B-7: Main Workers Classified By Industrial Category, Educational Level, and Sex.* The website lists down the tables found in that particular table category by clicking it. Then we select the state for which the data is required from the drop-down menu given on the top. Finally, we click on the required option, and an Excel file will be automatically downloaded (Figure 3.11). Likewise, other data tables can also be downloaded accordingly.

3.4.3   *Ministry of Statistics and Programme Implementation (MoSPI)*

MoSPI was established as an Independent Ministry on the 15th of October 1999 after the merger of the Department of Statistics and the Department of Programme Implementation. The Ministry has two wings, one relating to statistics called the National Statistical Office

FIGURE 3.12   The MoSPI Website

(NSO) and the other Programme Implementation (PI) wing. The Ministry focuses a substantial amount of importance on the coverage and quality of the statistics released in the country. MoSPI plays a vital role in preparing and maintaining a comprehensive economic and social statistics database. The statistics are usually based on administrative sources and surveys conducted by the central and state governments. The ministry releases the data in both printed form and on its website *www.mospi.gov.in/*. Figure 3.12 provides an overview of its website.

The website's home page contains all the latest press releases, recent reports, and announcements. A key performance indicator dashboard is also displayed. To download the reports issued by the ministry, click on the **Download Reports** option on the home page. The list of all the reports will be displayed. We can also search for the required reports in the **Search Reports** drop-down menu (Figure 3.13).

The statistics wing of ministry prepares *National Accounts Statistics*. It publishes consolidated sets of accounts for various macro-economic aggregates, non-financial corporations, government, households, the rest of the world, and industry-wise aggregates. These statements can be directly downloaded as Excel files for analysis. The latest national accounts statistics are available in the **Recent Reports** on the home page.

To download the previous national accounts statistics and other statistical publication click on the **Download Reports** on the home page and choose Statistical Publication from the drop-down menu in **Search Reports** and then select the desired publication from the given options, that is, Social Statistics, Economic Statistical, and National accounts. An example is shown in Figure 3.14.

The Ministry also furnishes *Quarterly GDP Data* and *Annual Estimates* of national products, government and private final consumption expenditure, savings, and capital formation. The

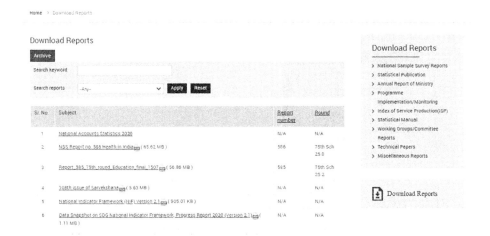

FIGURE 3.13 The Downloading of Reports at MoSPI

FIGURE 3.14 Statistical Publications Provided by MoSPI

Ministry gathers and reports the *Monthly Estimates Of Index Of Industrial Production*, releases *Consumer Price Index*, and annual inflation rates. The latest and previous estimates can be downloaded from the Ministry's list of the 'Press release' (Figure 3.15). We can choose the desired estimate from the drop-down menu in the search button and fill up the period (**Start date** and **End date**) for which we need to download the data.

To download a wide range of the Tables data, select the options of **Download Tables Data** on the home page. The list of tables data will be displayed as shown in Figure 3.16. It consists of

1. Unit level data for varied parameters
2. National accounts data
3. Statistical Year Book contains a large volume of data on various subject matters such as area, population, agriculture and other significant primary sectors, industries, trade, education, banks, insurance, prices, exchange rates, railways, and rainfall
4. Annual survey of industries data
5. Consumer price index

FIGURE 3.15   Press Release

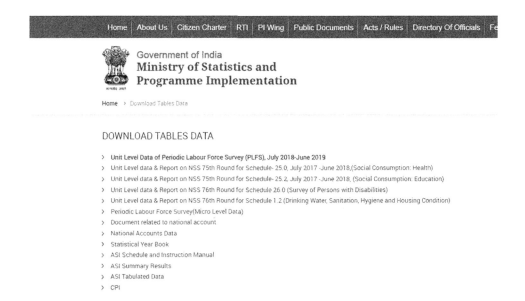

FIGURE 3.16   Downloading of Tables Data on MoSPI Website

MoSPI carries out the *Annual Survey of Industries* and publishes statistical information to estimate and analyze the manufacturing sector's growth, composition, and structure. It also conducts *Economic Censuses* periodically and *Large-Scale All-India Sample Surveys*. National Sample Survey program studies the impact of specific parameters such as employment, consumer expenditure, housing conditions, environment, literacy levels, health, nutrition, and family welfare on different population groups. It also disseminates the microdata from these surveys and censuses. To browse, search, and download relevant census or survey documents and metadata, click on **Micro Data Catalogue** (Figure 3.17) on the home page. The person will be redirected to an external website powered by the National Data Archive that provides web-based access to the entire metadata (Figure 3.18).

To view and download the data, click on the **Visit Catalogue** tab. The list of catalogues will be displayed (*free data available for public use as well as data not freely available to the users*), then choose the desired study (Figure 3.19). Once we choose the desired study, select the option get microdata. If the user is already registered, enter the username and password; otherwise, click on Register for the registration. After login, fill out the application and click on Submit. Then download from the given datasets.

FIGURE 3.17 Step 1 in Microdata Catalogue

FIGURE 3.18 Step 2 in Microdata Catalogue (NADA)

Data on various aspects of the socio-economic life of the population falling into different social and religious groups categories can also be downloaded from the National Data Bank. It is available as a link on the website's home page under Quick Links (Figure 3.20). The information sought can be found as per the requirement.

3.4.4 Directorate of Economics and Statistics

The Directorate of Economics and Statistics, Ministry of Agriculture and Farmers Welfare, Government of India (*https://eands.dacnet.nic.in/Default.htm*) is an important data source of information pertaining to the agricultural sector. It provides links to various reports related

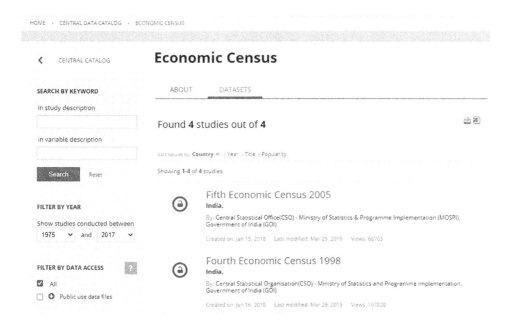

FIGURE 3.19   Step 3 in Microdata Catalogue (National Data Archive)

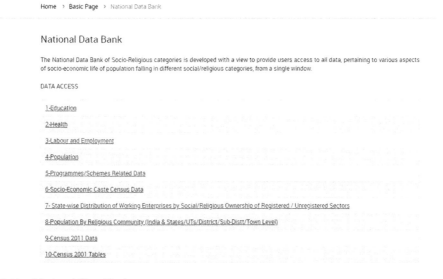

FIGURE 3.20   National Data Bank

to the agricultural sector such as *All India Crop Situation, Agricultural Statistics at a Glance,* and *Pocket Book of Agricultural Statistics.* These reports provide information in a pdf format like *socio-economic indicators, labour force, poverty and unemployment, land use statistics* and *livestock statistics,* amongst many, mainly at the all India level. It is important to note that every state has its Directorate of Economics and Statistics, which provides most of the economic data pertaining to the state and its district levels.

3.4.5 National Stock Exchange (NSE)

NSE is a leading stock exchange in India. It was incorporated in 1992 and commenced with advanced and automated electronic-based trading in 1994. It provides a platform for the companies to list themselves and raise capital and also allows the investors to trade in various investments and securities. A large volume of data and statistics related to equity, market, indices, mutual funds, equity derivatives, currency derivatives, commodity derivatives, interest rate derivatives, fixed income and debt, and public issues is provided on the website of NSE. The website's home page includes all the essential statistics, information, announcements, and a dashboard that shows a chart demonstrating the real-time value of Nifty 50. The new website can be accessed through URL *www.nseindia.com/* (new website). The link to the old website is *www1.nseindia.com*. A glimpse of the new website is shown in Figure 3.21.

The process of downloading the historical data involves the following steps. First, select the **Resources** tab and choose **Historical Reports** from the Downloads menu (Figure 3.22). The historical reports of Capital, Derivative, and Debt Market will appear (Figure 3.23). We can then select the required report from the numerous reports listed under different heads, for instance, Historical Index Data under the head Index in Capital Market reports (Figure 3.24). After filling up the relevant details like the Index Type and the period for which the data is to be extracted, that is, **start Date** and **end Date**, the data will be displayed. Finally, click on the **download option** on the right-hand side to export the data in Excel as a CSV file.

FIGURE 3.21 The New NSE Website

FIGURE 3.22 Step 1 in Downloading Historical Reports – NSE

FIGURE 3.23   Step 2 in Downloading Historical Reports – NSE

FIGURE 3.24   Step 3 in Downloading Historical Reports – NSE

FIGURE 3.25   Step 1 in Historical Data of a Company – NSE

Almost all the notable companies are listed on the stock exchange. To download data for a specific company listed on NSE, we can directly search the company's name in the Search option given on the top of the website (Figure 3.25). The information about the company will be displayed (Figure 3.26). Scroll down and select the option of Historical Data, and the desired data will appear (Figure 3.27). We can fill up the dates for which the data is to be extracted, that is, the **start date** and **end date** as per our requirements. Finally, click on the **download option** on the right-hand side to export the data in Excel as a CSV file.

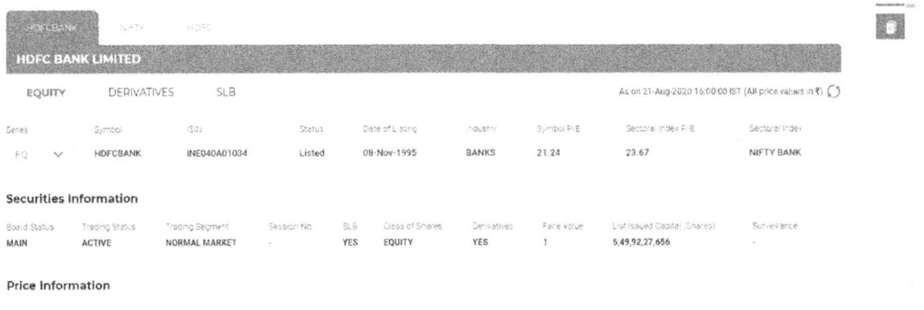

FIGURE 3.26 Step 2 in Historical Data of a Company – NSE

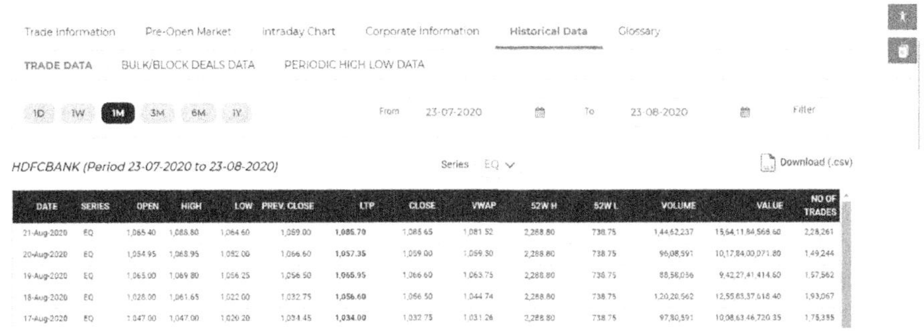

FIGURE 3.27 Step 3 in Historical Data of a Company – NSE

3.4.6 Bombay Stock Exchange (BSE)

BSE is the first Indian stock exchange which was established in 1875. It is Asia's oldest stock exchange. Similar to NSE, the website of BSE equally provides access to quick and accurate market data (real-time and historical) about the equity, equity derivatives, currency derivatives (including interest rate derivatives), commodity derivatives, and debt as well as corporate data to analyze and evaluate the performance of a company or the market as a whole and make informed decisions. The website's home page includes all the important statistics, information, announcements, and a dashboard that shows a chart demonstrating the real-time value of BSE SENSEX. Its website URL is *https://www.bseindia.com/*.

To export the market data available from the website into Excel, first select the Markets option from the menu as shown in Figure 3.28. Then select the Market Data option in the Markets menu (Figure 3.29).

The historical information with equity, indices, public issues/OFS/buybacks, listing, derivatives, currency derivatives, Indian depository receipts, debt, securities lending and borrowing, exchange-traded funds, mutual funds, commodity derivatives, foreign institutional investors, and so on will be displayed. Choose the required data from the list. For instance, the Indices Historical Prices under the head Indices (Figure 3.30).

Next, fill up the required historical data details such as the **Index Type** from the dropdown menu and the **period** for which the data is to be extracted, that is, *Daily*, *Monthly*, or *Yearly*, and the **start date**. Click on the **Submit** button (Figure 3.31). The desired data will

FIGURE 3.28   Step 1 in Downloading Historical Data – BSE

FIGURE 3.29   Step 2 in Downloading Historical Data – BSE

FIGURE 3.30   Step 3 in Downloading Historical Data – BSE

be displayed. Finally, click on the **download option** below the data on the left-hand side to export the data in Excel as a CSV file (Figure 3.32).

3.4.7   World Bank

The World Bank is an international organization, formerly known as the International Bank for Reconstruction and Development, which was founded in 1944 out of the Bretton Woods Agreement. It offers financial and technical assistance such as loans, grants, policy advice, training, research, and analysis to the developing countries with a motive to eradicate poverty, support economic advancement, and ensure a sustainable increase in the quality of life of the people in these developing countries.

The Development Data Group at the World Bank coordinates statistical and data work. It collects and maintains several macroeconomic, financial, and sectoral databases. Statistics

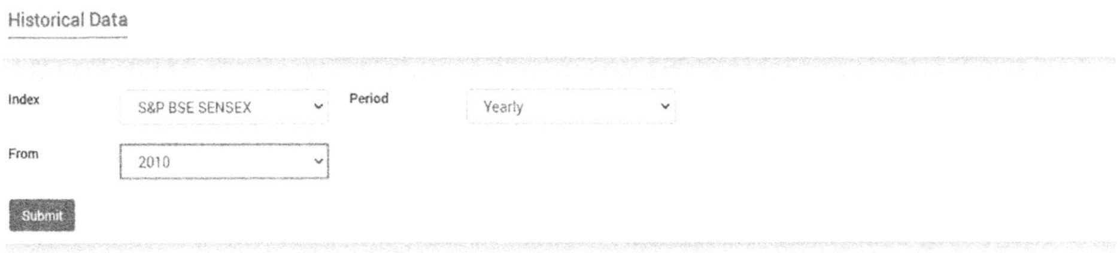

Historical Data

| Index | S&P BSE SENSEX ∨ | Period | Yearly ∨ |
| From | 2010 ∨ | | |

Submit

FIGURE 3.31   Step 4 in Downloading Historical Data – BSE

Indices : S&P BSE SENSEX
Period : Year 2010 to Year 2020

Year	Open	High	Low	Close
2010	17,473.45	21,108.64	15,651.99	20,509.09
2011	20,621.61	20,664.80	15,135.86	15,454.92
2012	15,534.67	19,612.18	15,358.02	19,426.71
2013	19,513.45	21,483.74	17,448.71	21,170.68
2014	21,222.19	28,822.37	19,963.12	27,499.42
2015	27,485.77	30,024.74	24,833.54	26,117.54
2016	26,101.50	29,077.28	22,494.61	26,626.46
2017	26,711.15	34,137.97	26,447.06	34,056.83
2018	34,059.99	38,989.65	32,483.84	36,068.33
2019	36,161.80	41,809.96	35,287.16	41,253.74
2020	41,349.36	42,273.87	26,638.90	38,434.72

Note: Kindly download the csv file to view all records ⬇

FIGURE 3.32   Step 5 in Downloading Historical Data – BSE

New to this site? Start Here   🏠 DataBank Microdata Data Catalog ▦

World Bank Open Data
Free and open access to global development data

·

Browse by Country or Indicator

FIGURE 3.33   World Bank Open Data

and data can be easily accessed on the **World Bank Open Data portal** (*https://data.worldbank.org*) by all users. The World Bank provides free and open access to a comprehensive set of high-quality data about development in countries around the globe. Its site facilitates easy access, download, and usage of the data. The data can be used free of cost with minimum restrictions. To obtain the data from the site, use the search box on the top of the page as shown in Figure 3.33. We can search for data for an indicator, country, or any topic (Figure 3.33).

The search box shows a list of matching results as we enter the text. We can select one option and the results will be displayed using graphs and a data table. Click on the **Download** button on the right-hand side to download the data into Excel, CSV, or XML format. If one selects a specific indicator, the data downloaded will contain the data for *all countries* for *all years* with respect to the chosen indicator (Figure 3.34). Similarly, if data is

FIGURE 3.34   Downloading Data: Indicator-wise

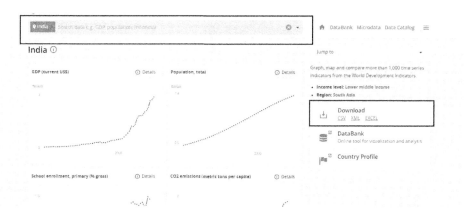

FIGURE 3.35   Downloading Data: Country-wise

downloaded for a country, then it will provide *all data* for *all years* for that particular country (Figure 3.35).

To download the data for *combinations of indicators and countries* (Figure 3.36) or *multiple countries* (Figure 3.37), we can insert additional items in the search box. However, we can only search for one indicator at a time.

The site provides open access to the data on the World Development Indicators, which dispense a variety of relevant, high-quality, and internationally comparable indicators such as population, Gross Domestic Product (GDP), CO_2 emissions, literacy rate, consumption, income, stock markets, and tourism. The database contains 1,600 time-series indicators for 217 economies and more than 40 country groups, with data for most of the indicators going back more than 50 years. These datasets can be found in several main themes: poverty and inequality, people, environment, economy, states and markets, and global links.

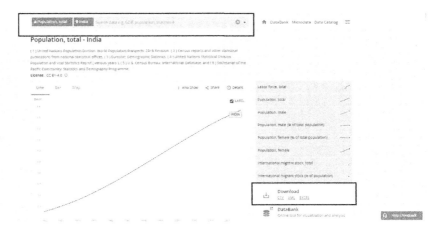

FIGURE 3.36 Downloading Data: Combination of an Indicator and Country

FIGURE 3.37 Downloading Data: Combination of an Indicator and Multiple Countries

The site also covers diverse collections and databases including **data bank**. The data available on the World Bank Open Data site are a subset of those available in the World Bank's data bank, which contains substantial collections of time-series data. One can access data bank as either a registered or an unregistered user and download the data to your system in either Excel, CSV, or Text format. A complete list of datasets published by the World Bank is available in the Data Catalogue. It contains all the datasets in the data bank, along with many other useful datasets covering data from surveys. The World Bank's Microdata Library provides access to microdata collected through sample surveys of households and business enterprises.

3.4.8 UNdata

UNdata is a web-based data service for the worldwide users maintained by the Statistics Division of the Department of Economic and Social Affairs of the *UN Secretariat*. It was launched in 2005 as part of a project, called 'Statistics as a Public Good'. The main objective of UNdata is to provide free access to global data and to educate users about the significance of statistics for the purpose of policy and decision-making. Users around the globe can search as well as download a large volume of statistical resources and data compiled by the United Nations and other international agencies. The website to download data is *https://data.un.org/*.

Plenty of databases and tables collectively known as *Datamarts* contain *millions of data points*. They cover a broad range of subjects, including population and migration, national accounts, education, labour, price and production indices, international trade, energy, crime, gender, nutrition and health, agriculture, science and technology, finance environment, communication, transport and tourism, and development assistance (Figure 3.38).

To download the data, one needs to simply type the keywords in the search box at the top of the page as shown in Figure 3.39 and click the **Search** button.

The search box recognizes countries, regions, subjects/indicators, and years. For instance, data series of 'Gdp Per Capita' matches the keywords shown in Figure 3.40. One can click on the desired series to view the entire record. As shown in Figure 3.41, the GDP per capita for all the countries and all years will be displayed. Click on the **Download** button above the data to Download the data series into XML, Excel, or text format. We can also apply filters to download the data series for one or more desired countries and years. However, we can only search for one indicator at a time (Figure 3.42).

The data from the sources discussed earlier are made available freely for its users with minimal restrictions on specific databases. However, some websites provide access to databases

Other UNSD Databases:

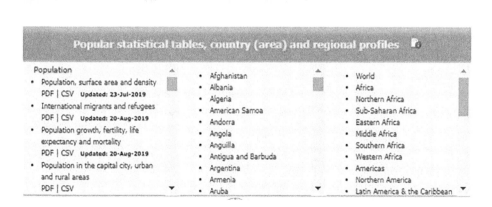

FIGURE 3.38 UNdata Website

FIGURE 3.39   Step 1 in Downloading of Data Series

FIGURE 3.40   Step 2 in Downloading of Data Series

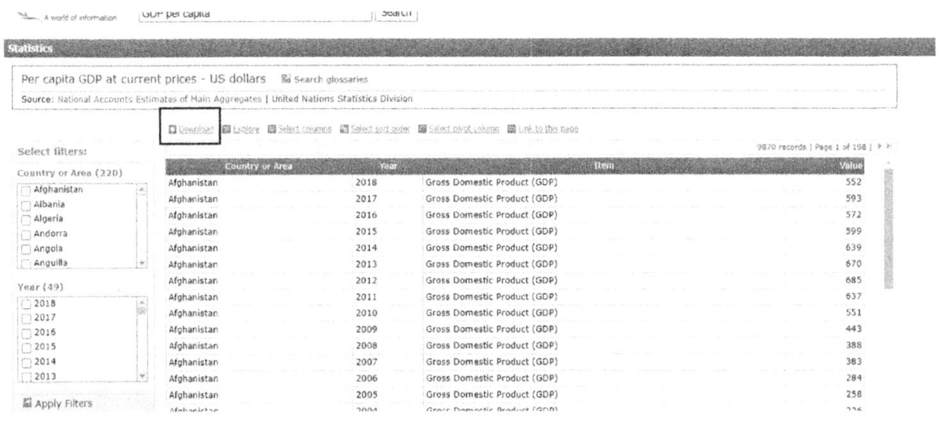

FIGURE 3.41   Step 3 in Downloading of Data Series

after paying a subscription charge. One of such examples is the EPWRF India Times Series. It provides access to reliable, up-to-date, and high-quality time-series data to assist in research across various sectors of the Indian economy. This online database comprises over 50,000 variables compressed in 20 modules and continuous time-series from 1950 based on availability. To access the data from a module, the user (individual, universities, institutes) can either pay annual subscription rates, which enables unlimited download from the subscribed module or pay per use service (pay uniform rates each time they use the service) based on the

FIGURE 3.42 Step 4 in Downloading of Data Series

number of rows and columns to be accessed. Likewise, Indiastat.com is a subscription-based website that comprehensively composes socio-economic data at the national and state levels.

To sum up, this chapter provides a broad understanding of data, various ways to input data into an Excel and various data sources from where the data can be downloaded, particularly in an Excel format. The downloaded data can be analyzed and interpreted based on different statistical techniques used in the book.

4

VISUALIZATION OF DATA USING CHARTS IN EXCEL

Learning Objectives

After reading this chapter, the readers will be able to understand

- Popular charts provided by Excel
- Plotting and interpreting the data using a line graph
- Plotting and interpreting the data using a column chart
- Plotting and interpreting the data using a histogram
- Representing the data using a pie chart
- Plotting and interpreting the scatter plot

Charts (also known as graphs) provide us with the easiest method for visualization of data. Not only they display data at a glance, but they also facilitate comparison and unveil trends and relationships. Raw data, if numerous, do not convey any information per se. The data needs to be summarized, processed, and presented to obtain information. Communicating information quickly is, therefore, an essential purpose of drawing graphs. In this background, the present chapter explores the charting features of Excel. We will introduce the popular charts this software provides and learn how to plot them. Some popular charts we will study are the line chart, column chart, pie chart, and scatter plot. The data we have exercised for this task is per capita gross domestic product for SAARC countries for the period 2010–2018, as shown in Figure 4.1. The data is expressed in dollars using purchasing power parity rates in 2011.

4.1 Line Graph

The line graph consists of a horizontal X-axis (independent variable) and a vertical Y-axis (dependent variable). The independent axis is called so because the values of the variable on this axis do not depend on the other variable taken. On the other hand, the values of the variable on the Y-axis depend on the independent variable taken on X-axis. The line graphs are appropriate when the values on both the axes are *numerally ordered* (instead of qualitative

DOI: 10.4324/9781003398127-4

Year	Country							
	Afghanistan	Bangladesh	Bhutan	India	Maldives	Nepal	Pakistan	Sri Lanka
2010	1672	2518	6814	4451	11965	1987	4072	8503
2011	1627	2651	7269	4625	12486	2053	4095	9156
2012	1773	2791	7548	4817	12261	2155	4149	9980
2013	1808	2925	7616	5065	12573	2250	4241	10239
2014	1796	3067	7954	5378	12892	2385	4348	10647
2015	1767	3232	8380	5743	12684	2455	4459	11078
2016	1757	3424	8944	6145	13019	2447	4609	11447
2017	1758	3634	9247	6516	13333	2606	4771	11706
2018	1735	3879	9348	6899	13611	2724	4928	11956

FIGURE 4.1   Per Capita Gross Domestic Product (2011 PPP $)

Source: UNDPHumanDevelepmentReports.2018. Statistical Update: Human Development Indices and Indicators. New York, available at *http://hdr.undp.org/en/content/human-development-indices-indicators-2018* (accessed 29 April 2020)

variables). We generally use this graph when we want to measure the values of a variable over a time period. Conventionally, time (expressed in days, weeks, quarters, years, and so on) is usually placed on the X-axis. We may now illustrate the preparation of the line graph using the data given in Figure 4.1 in Excel. To start with, note that the cursor is placed on an empty cell in Excel and follow these steps:

- In the **Insert** tab, select the **Insert Line** or **Area Chart** in the **Charts** option. Usually, the first option of **Line** is chosen, which is a more commonly used option among the options granted. Another similar way can be to select data first and then click on the **Insert** tab to choose the type of graph
- The blank slate that appears is the Format Chart Area. Right-click and choose the **Select Data** option. In the pop-up window, named *Select Data Source*, choose the **Chart data range**, which in our case is **A2 to I11** (note that the data range also includes an Excel name sheet along with it)
- The Legend Entries column (in the pop-up window) shows different data series for which we want the data to be presented, as shown in Figure 4.2. In our example, different data series include data from different countries. Note that the Legend entries column also shows 'Year' which is a *variable* and not a separate data series. Hence, the Year box may be unchecked
- The Horizontal Axis Labels need to be edited because, as mentioned before, the horizontal axis represents the time variable (in our case, Years). After clicking on **Edit**, select the data range, which is the year column (**A3 to A11**). Click **OK** and another **OK**
- The chart is ready, as shown in Figure 4.2.

4.1.1   How to Put Labels?

This chart is not self-explanatory. We, therefore, need to label this chart further. This can be done in two ways.

1. We may select the **Design** tab and then choose the **Add Chart Element,** as shown in Figure 4.3
2. We may click on the **+** sign given on the top right corner of the chart

FIGURE 4.2 Line Graph in Excel

FIGURE 4.3 Labelling of Chart

Different options displayed in the methods mentioned previously have been elaborated here.

- **Axis:** It helps us to show the two-primary axes (*horizontal* and *vertical*) on the graph. Generally, we show these two axes while preparing our chart
- **Axis Title:** It enables us to name the axes according to the variables we choose or select We may click on the **Axis title** which appears next to both the axes, and then rename it
- **Chart Title:** We can name or give the title to our chart by using it
- **Data Labels:** It displays the values of different data points in our graph. The values can be placed around the data points in different ways like centre, left, right, above, and below

- **Data Table:** In case we wish to show our entire dataset right below the chart, we may use this option
- **Error Bars:** It represents the variation graphically in data using standard error, percentage, and standard deviation. Statisticians more often use this option
- **Gridlines:** These are the horizontal and vertical lines displayed in the graph for better data readability
- **Legend:** It labels the different series of data presented in our graph. These labels can be placed on either right, top left, or bottom of the chart. It is an essential tool for differentiating the different data groups in the graph
- **Trendline:** It shows the general pattern or direction of the data in a linear, exponential, or linear forecast manner. At our level, it is not of much use
- **Up/down Bars:** It is used to connect the first and the last series of the data. Again, it is not of much importance at this stage.

4.1.2   Formatting the Axes

We can format the axes as well. Let us format the vertical value axis by right-clicking on the values of the Y-axis.

- Select **Format Axis** and a format axis box will appear, which offers various options
- The first two options that are minimum and maximum indicate the starting and ending values on Y-axis, which can be adjusted according to one's requirement
- Next, the spacing between the values on the Y-axis under the **Units** can also be changed in the **Major** box
- Another feature that can be used is **Display units** that adjust the units of the values shown.

Using the aforementioned features, the chart shown in Figure 4.3 is labelled, which looks much more informative in Figure 4.4 now. We can say just by looking at the graph that per-capita GDP is consistently the highest in Maldives and lowest in Afghanistan. It can also be observed that, for example, the per-capita GDP for India increased from $4,451 in 2010 to $6,899 in 2018.

4.2   Column Chart

Unlike the line graph, which displays continuous data over a time period, column chart (graph) is used to compare values *across categories* like years, countries, and movie genres, where the data is discrete. The data is displayed in rectangular bars. The height of rectangular bars is commensurate with data values. It provides a visual representation for comparing quantities, leading to an immediate clear vision of the data. One may sometimes get confused between a bar graph and a column graph; hence, creating a line of difference may be important. The significant difference lies in their orientation. The bar graph is oriented *horizontally*, while the column graph is *vertically* oriented.

Let us now look at the preparation and interpretation of the column graph in Excel.

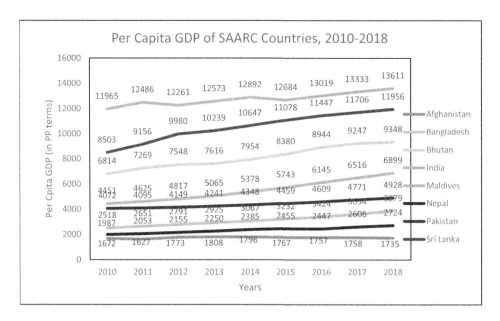

FIGURE 4.4 Per Capita GDP of SAARC Countries, 2010–2018

Source: UNDPHumanDevelepmentReports.2018. Statistical Update: Human Development Indices and Indicators. New York, Available at *http://hdr.undp.org/en/content/human-development-indices-indicators-2018* (accessed 29 April 2020)

We continue with the previous example of the GDP of SAARC countries. Most of the steps for drawing column charts are similar to the line graph. In the Excel file containing the data,

- Click on **Insert** Tab
- Move the cursor to **Insert Column or Bar Chart**. Choose the first Graph option, usually used, among the various available options. We again get to see a blank slate.
- Right-click in the slate area and choose **Select Data**
- In the dialogue box, click on **Add** under **Legend Entries**. Suppose we want to represent Afghanistan first. We select the cell named Afghanistan in the Series name. In Series values, we choose the data values of Afghanistan, that is, **B3: B11**
- Click **OK**
- In **Horizontal (Category) Axis Labels**, edit the category and select the data values of years as it is the *category* we wish to present
- Click **OK**, and we get our column graph ready for Afghanistan (Figure 4.5).

We can further add more series to our existing column chart. For example, if we click **Add** under Legend Entries and choose Bhutan as our second series, we will have to add the data values of Bhutan in the same way as we did for Afghanistan. Click **OK**, and we get the same column graph, now a combined representation of both countries. A similar practice can be followed for the remaining countries. If we want all the countries to be presented in our column graph, then following the aforesaid procedure of adding individual countries may be cumbersome. In that case, an alternative approach can be followed. In the dialogue box, we may select the entire data of the countries in the **Chart data range**, that is, **B2: I11**.

To make this chart more informative, we can make use of different chart element options discussed in the line graph. We get the following graph representing the same information as derived in the line graph as shown in Figure 4.6.

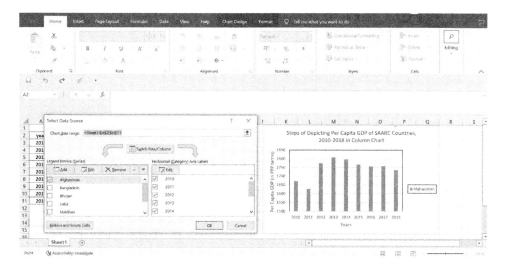

FIGURE 4.5   Steps of Depicting Per Capita GDP of SAARC Countries, 2010–2018 in Column Chart

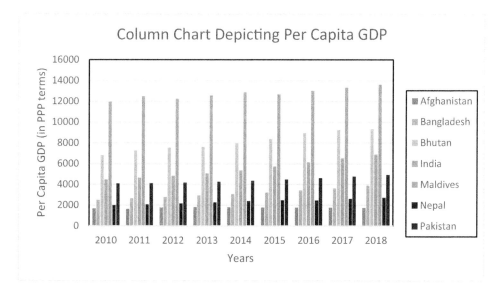

FIGURE 4.6   Column Chart Depicting Per Capita GDP

Source: Human Development Report, 2018.

4.3 Histogram

A histogram is essential as it helps study many statistical distributions, which we will discuss in the subsequent chapter. A histogram is a bar graph that represents a frequency distribution. The nature of data demarcates the main difference between a bar graph and a histogram. Whereas the bar chart plots *categorical data*, the histogram represents *quantitative data*, divided into equal parts, known as *bins* or *class intervals*. In other words, a histogram shows frequencies of data points that fall into different bins. Also, since there are no gaps between the data intervals, the histogram bars do not have spaces between them. The width of the bar represents the interval, and the height corresponds to the frequency.

Let us say; the intervals are 0–20, 20–30, 30–40, and so on. The limits 0, 20, and 30 become the lower limits and 20, 30, and 40 become the upper limits of the aforementioned class intervals. The data is continuous in the sense that the lower limit is included in a given interval, but the upper limit is included in the next range. For example, in the aforementioned intervals, 20 will be included in the 20–30 class interval, but 30 will be taken in the next class interval, 30–40.

We now take a look at the steps for constructing a histogram. Excel 2016 and higher versions provide a direct function for preparing a histogram of a given data. We use the hypothetical data given in the next table as an example to learn how to construct it. This data pertains to the educational background of 35 workers.

Number	Studied up to Which Class
1	9
2	18
3	15
4	9
5	10
6	8
7	3
8	8
9	15
10	8
11	10
12	18
13	10
14	9
15	0
16	10
17	9
18	9
19	8
20	10
21	5
22	10
23	15
24	10
25	9
26	9

Number	Studied up to Which Class
27	15
28	6
29	6
30	12
31	11
32	8
33	10
34	12
35	9

We, here, take up a few ways of preparing it. The first method is the one which is the most direct and easiest one. In our example, select the data we want to represent in the histogram, the column entitled 'Studied up to Which Class'.

• Go to **Insert** tab
• Click the first graph option in the **Insert Chart Statistic**, next to **Insert Line or Area Chart.** We have the histogram ready, as shown in Figure 4.7.

It may be noticed that Excel automatically selects the bin size but can be altered according to the requirement. To do this, right-click on the horizontal axis, and select the **format axis.** Various bin alterations can be made from the following options in the format axis box.

• **Bin Width:** It can be used for changing the class-interval size
• **Number of bins:** This option allows us to change the number of rectangular bars, which may better represent the data

FIGURE 4.7   The Histogram: Direct Method

- **Overflow bin:** If there are many scattered observations above a particular bin, then this option comprises all those observations in a single bin
- **Underflow bin:** If there are many scattered observations below a particular bin, then this option comprises all those observations in a single bin.

It may be remarked that Excel is programmed in such a way that the class intervals are exclusive, which means that the upper limit (and not the lower limit) is included in the class intervals. For example, class interval 3–6 contains numbers between 4 and 6. On the preparation of histogram, like other charts, this chart can also be labelled, by clicking using the chart elements on the **+** sign on the top right corner of the graph, such as **Axis, Axis Titles, Chart Title, Data Labels, and Legend** which serve the same functions as discussed earlier.

In the second method, we follow similar steps developed for the graphs prepared earlier.

- Click on the **Insert** tab and choose the first graph option from **Insert Statistic Chart**
- Right-click in the blank slate and choose **Select data**
- We select the data range in the **Chart data range** and click **OK**.

The graph we get has gaps between the bars. To make it look like a histogram, right-click on any bar and choose **Format Data Series**. A gap width option can be seen in **Series Options** with a three rectangular bar icon from where we can reduce the width to zero. All options discussed in the previous method can now be applied in the same way.

The next method we will discuss now is also being used in the earlier versions of Excel. This method can be followed by clicking on the **Data** tab and choosing **Data Analysis** which can be found in the right corner. It might be possible that this option may not be available in the **Data** tab. So, first, we need to add this by clicking on the **File** option and choosing *Options*. Go to **Add-Ins**, click **Go** next to the **Manage** option and select **Analysis ToolPak** and **Analysis ToolPak-VBA**. Click **OK** and reopen the Excel file. The option is now added.

Before starting this method, we need to explicitly make an additional column for class intervals. In our ongoing example, we have created class intervals of 3.

- In the *Data Analysis* dialogue box, select **Histogram** and click **OK**
- In the next dialogue box created, select **Input Range** which is the data range of the variable that needs to be shown. The class interval column is then selected as the **Bin-Range**.

It is a good practice to click on the checkbox named **Labels** if the given data series have them. To get the desired graph in the existing or new sheet, we also need to check **Chart Output.**

- Click **OK,** and Excel will create a chart and frequency table

We need to reduce the space between the bars to convert it into a histogram. To do this, right-click in the chart window but not in the area where the chart is made. Select **Format Chart Area** and click on the arrow next to **Chart Options**. Select **Series Frequency**, then click on the icon with three bars and reduce the gap width to zero.

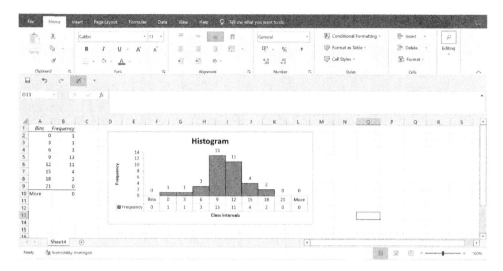

FIGURE 4.8   The Histogram: Another Method

We now get the desired histogram as in Figure 4.8. The bins here are not in the traditional form, so they need to be interpreted according to the frequency table created. The bin column shows the upper limit of the group. For example, in the frequency table, the cell with an upper limit of 6 is representative of the frequency of numbers lying between 4 and 6. This means it excludes the lower limit and includes the upper limit.

However, as mentioned earlier, the *first method* is favoured as it is an improvement over the methods described previously as latter methods go through a longer route.

4.4   Pie Chart

A pie chart is used to show a single series data *only* in a pictorial form. It is a circular chart divided into different parts. Each part represents a proportion of the variable taken into account. The quantity represented in pie chart can either be expressed in absolute numbers or percentages. The pie's total value is 100 per cent when expressed in percentages. We may also note that these charts are useful only when there are few categories to display as a large number of categories may not be very comprehensive and easy to interpret. For example, in our previous example, we can only represent, say, data on Afghanistan using a pie chart with years as our category. We cannot combine the data from other countries in the same pie chart. To illustrate it, let us move to a different example given below. The data considered represents the category-wise production of motor vehicles in India in the years 2008–2009 and 2009–2010.

Category	2008–09	2009–10
Total Commercial Vehicles	416,870	567,556
Cars	1,516,967	1,932,620
Multi-Utility Vehicles	321,626	424,791
Total Two-Wheelers	8,419,792	10,512,903
Three-Wheelers	497,020	619,194
GRAND TOTAL	**11,172,275**	**14,057,064**

First, we represent 2008–2009 data using a pie chart. Once the procedure of constructing the line and column chart explained earlier is clearly understood, then the formation of other charts can be similarly understood to a large extent. To begin with,

- Click on the **Insert** tab and select the pie chart icon right next to the **Recommended Charts**. We usually select the very first chart
- We again see a blank slate where we right-click and choose **Select Data**. As usual, we **Add** the Legend Entries by selecting the series name as **Category** (of motor vehicles) and series values as the data of 2008–2009, that is, **B2: B6**
- Now, **Edit** the Horizontal Axis Labels by selecting the different category names, **A2: A6** in our example
- Click **OK,** and the basic pie chart is ready to interpret (Figure 4.9). A similar pie chart can be drawn for the next data series of the year 2009–2010 as shown in Figure 4.10.

To explain the chart further, we can use some features by clicking on the **+** sign on the top right corner of the chart or click on **Add Chart Element** as done previously. The different options are elaborated as follows:

- **Chart Title:** We can give a title to our chart using a proper name (e.g. Production of Motor Vehicles 2008–09)
- **Data Labels:** It enables us to label different slices of the chart and contains some handy features. When we click on the arrow in Data Labels, the first three options help in depicting the values, the different parts of the pie chart represent. These values can be placed in the centre, inside the circle, or outside the circle, depending on the structure of the chart. The last option, **More Options**, contains the following Label Options
- **Series Name:** It displays the series that we are representing
- **Category Name:** It helps us to identify the different categories shown by the different parts of the chart

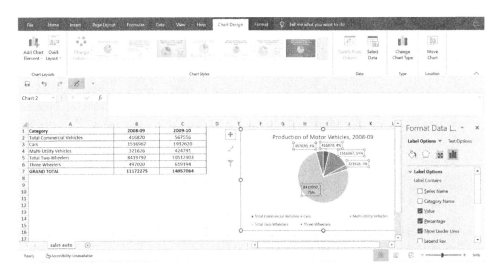

FIGURE 4.9 Steps in Labelling Pie Chart, Motor Vehicle Production 2008–2009

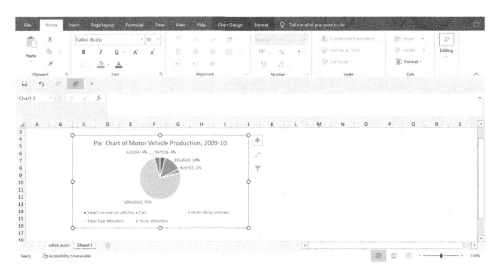

FIGURE 4.10   Pie Chart of Motor Vehicle Production 2009–2010

- **Value:** It depicts the absolute values of different categories of the data
- **Percentage:** It shows how much proportion a particular slice constitutes of the total proportion, expressed in percentage
- **Legend Key:** Along with the values, the represented key of different categories is shown.

Based on the chart drawn, we can make inferences by looking at the graph, which is one of the primary purposes of drawing a pie chart. We can say that 75 per cent of the total production of motor vehicles is of two-wheeler categories. Multi-utility vehicles contributed the least in the production in 2008–2009. We can also draw a comparison between the two series, that is, 2008–2009 and 2009–2010, using separate pie charts. By looking at both the graphs, we observe that the trend has not changed much as the two-wheeler category continues to contribute the largest proportion of the total production in 2009–2010.

4.5   Scatter Plot

The scatter plot, also known as the XY plot, helps us identify the relationship between two variables. This relationship may either be positive, negative, or null. Both X-axis and Y-axis in a scatter plot represent the two variables of interest. The coordinates of every point on the chart are the values of the two variables. For example, a coordinate (3,2) implies that the variable on the X-axis has a value 3, while 2 represents the value of the variable on the Y-axis. The x coordinate of a point is called *abscissa*, and y coordinate of a point is called *ordinate*.

We will now learn how to plot and interpret scatter plots in Excel. We start with a hypothetical example of a firm detailing its items sold in different months and the advertising cost incurred. The data is presented below. We are interested in finding out how the advertising cost and sales of the firm are related. We may keep in mind that if there is a priori relationship between the variables, or if one variable is dependent on the other variable, then the data may be organized by keeping the data of the independent variable first followed by the dependent variable data. Otherwise, we will have to correct the graph by clicking **Switch Rows/Column** from the **Select Data** option and removing all the series except the series of interest. However, if the two variables taken are unrelated, then the series can be arranged either way.

Month	Advertising Cost (in ₹)	Items Sold
January	4000	12
February	5500	27
March	4700	17
April	7500	30
May	9000	39
June	10000	48
July	9800	49
August	9400	45
September	8700	36
October	5000	22
November	4400	19
December	5800	30

In Excel 2019, the process of creating a scatter graph is quite simple. To begin with, we select the data of the two variables between which we want to explore the relationship: advertising cost and items sold in our example. Click on the **Insert** tab in the charts area where we had earlier plotted charts like line, pie we also have a **Scatter** option. Choose the first graph icon from the **Insert Scatter** option next to **Pie Chart** option. The scatter plot is ready, as presented in Figure 4.11. To better visualize data, we can use chart elements explained earlier. One additional feature which may be applicable in this chart is the trendline.

- **Trendline:** It shows the nature of the trend between the two variables by a line that best fits the data points.

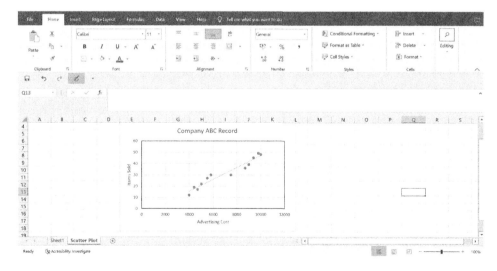

FIGURE 4.11 The Scatter Plot of Company ABC

The trendline we get in our example is upward sloping, indicating a positive relationship between advertising cost and items sold. With an increase in advertising costs, the company's sales also go up. However, if we look at this, the trendline does not tell us about the strength of the relationship. It is a subject matter of correlation to determine how strong a relationship is, which will be taken up in a later chapter. One critical practical application of scatter plot lies in simple linear regression, which will be discussed in the following chapter.

To recap, this lesson explored some essential tools of Excel, which helped us in the preparation of charts like line, column, pie, and scatter plots. We learned during the process of data analysis, how we can identify and make the correct choice of the graph. Deciding on the right chart type is a crucial step in data analysis.

PRACTICE QUESTIONS

1. The following table gives the data of age and number of persons corresponding to that age in a particular locality.

Age	Number of Persons
18	5
21	25
24	15
27	40
31	46
35	92
37	70
39	64
42	33
45	42
49	24
51	46
55	28
57	14
60	7

Identify the type of graph suitable for given data and prepare it in Excel. Also, interpret the results.

2. The following table presents the annual data of the sunshine company about its shoe sales.

Year	Pair of Shoes Sold
1990–91	20
1991–92	45
1992–93	110
1993–94	245
1994–95	290
1995–96	250
1996–97	503

Year	Pair of Shoes Sold
1997–98	483
1998–99	565
1999–2000	610

Choose the type of graph to be drawn for this firm and draw it in Excel.

3. The following data is about the household expenditure of families A and B per month (in ₹ 000).

Items of Expenditure	Family A	Family B
Food	50	70
Clothing	30	50
Rent	25	35
Education	10	25
Medical	9	20
Others	15	30

Draw a suitable graph. Which item did family A and B spend the most and the least?

4. Prepare a suitable graph from the following data of a firm.

Year	Exports (in ₹)	Imports (in ₹)
2010–11	459	305
2011–12	320	290
2012–13	350	340
2013–14	380	400
2014–15	300	280
2015–16	280	315
2016–17	350	370

5. The following table provides the birth rate (per thousand) of different countries.

Country	Birth Rate
India	35
Bangladesh	40
France	15
Australia	18
Brazil	25
Nigeria	42

Suggest and draw a suitable graph that can be drawn.

5

MEASURES OF CENTRAL TENDENCY

Learning Objectives

After reading this chapter, the readers will be able to understand

- Concept of descriptive statistics
- Measures of central tendency
- Meaning, calculation, and interpretation of arithmetic mean using Excel
- Meaning, calculation, and interpretation of median using Excel
- Meaning, calculation, and interpretation of mode using Excel
- Calculation and application of weighted mean, geometric mean, and harmonic mean using Excel

---

Descriptive statistics is the starting point of any data analysis. When working with a large volume of data, it becomes challenging to make sense of it. Therefore, it is important to identify a unique value that provides useful information capable of describing the data. Descriptive statistics describes the nature of the dataset. It helps us understand the characteristics of a large dataset more meaningfully. Descriptive statistics includes the two following categories of measurement of data:

1. Measures of central tendency or averages
2. Measures of dispersion or variability

This chapter introduces the first measure of descriptive statistics: measures of central tendency – their concept, their relevance, their application, and how to calculate them. The most commonly used measures of central tendency are mean, median, and mode.

A measure of central tendency *is a statistical measure* that summarizes the whole dataset by identifying the central position of the data or the distribution. It is a single value representing the centre or middle of a data group where most of the values lie. Three widely used measures of central tendency are

DOI: 10.4324/9781003398127-5

1. Mean
2. Median
3. Mode

Mean is further classified into the following categories based on the specific type of average required in different problems. We will explain these specific averages after we get through with the basic averages.

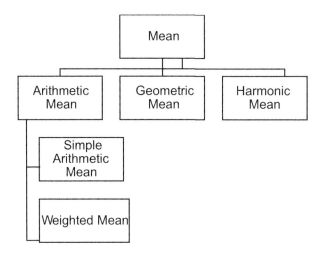

5.1 Arithmetic Mean

The arithmetic mean, popularly known as the *average* or the *expected value*, is one of the most common and frequently used measures of central tendency. It reflects the central location of the distribution and represents the data as a whole. For example, the mean height of a group of 50 students in a class is 1.62 meters, or the average time spent watching television per viewer in India is 4 hours a day.

The application of mean may include a company analyzing its performance or position by using averages like *average net profits* earned over a specific period by a company. Such data is available on the website of the respective company or the website of the NSE (*https://www1.nseindia.com/*). Similarly, the arithmetic mean can also be used to determine the average rating of apps on the Google play store. For example, 11,200 people rated the app between 1–5. Out of them, 3,000 rated 5, 2,500 rated 4, and so on. In this example, the average rating is 3.5625.

Rating	No. of People	Rating × no. of People
Good 5	3,000	15,000
4	2,500	10,000
3	4,000	12,000
2	1,200	2,400
Bad 1	500	500
Total	**11,200**	**39,900**
Mean	39,900/11,200	**3.5625**

The mean is calculated in two simple steps.

Step 1. We add all the values in our dataset called observations.
Step 2. We divide the sum by the number of observations.

The formula then becomes the following:

$$\overline{X} = \frac{Sum\ of\ all\ the\ observations}{Number\ of\ observations}$$

$$Or, \overline{X} = \frac{x_1 + x_2 + x_3 + \ldots + x_n}{n} = \frac{\sum_{i=1}^{n} x_i}{n}$$

where, $\overline{X}$ = symbol or notation for mean, x_i = ith observation in the distribution,
Σ = Sigma/operator for summation, n = number of observations

Illustration

The distribution of income of 20 employees working in an MNC is given next –

Employee ID	Monthly Income	Employee ID	Monthly Income
1	₹20,000	11	₹60,000
2	₹25,000	12	₹38,000
3	₹15,000	13	₹40,000
4	₹18,000	14	₹40,000
5	₹30,000	15	₹24,000
6	₹24,000	16	₹36,000
7	₹12,000	17	₹25,000
8	₹36,000	18	₹20,000
9	₹22,000	19	₹30,000
10	₹45,000	20	₹40,000

First Method (Direct Method)

Now we need to calculate the mean monthly income of these 20 employees.

Mean monthly income $(\overline{X})$ = ₹(20,000 + 25,000 + 15,000 + 18,000 + 30,000 + 2 4,000 + 12,000 + 36,000 + 22,000 + 45,000 + 60,000 + 38,000 + 40,000 + 40,000 + 24,000 + 36,000 + 25,000 + 20,000 + 30,000 + 40,000)/20
= ₹6,00,000/20
= ₹30,000

Here, the mean monthly income of ₹30,000 suggests that on average an employee working in this MNC earns ₹30,000 per month.

Second Method (Using Excel)

Step 1. Enter the employee ID and monthly income in an Excel sheet (Figure 5.1).
Step 2. Use the **AVERAGE** function to calculate the mean. Type the '=' (equal to) sign in the cell where the result is desired, say, 'B23' and enter the function name

AVERAGE and then select the range of numbers for which average is to be calculated, that is, **B2: B21** (Figure 5.2).

Step 3. Press **Enter**. The result will be displayed in cell B23 (Figure 5.3).

Merits of Mean

1. It is easy to calculate and simple to understand
2. It is reliable as it considers all the values in the distribution
3. It is widely used in various fields like mathematics, statistics, economics, and finance.

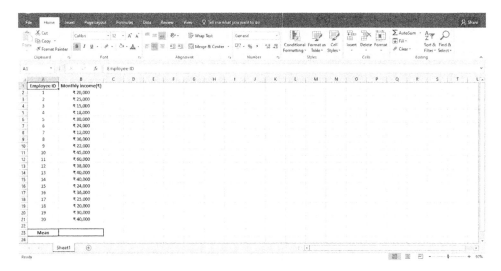

FIGURE 5.1 Step 1 in Calculating the Mean

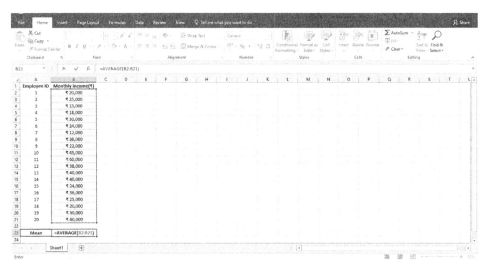

FIGURE 5.2 Step 2 in Calculating the Mean

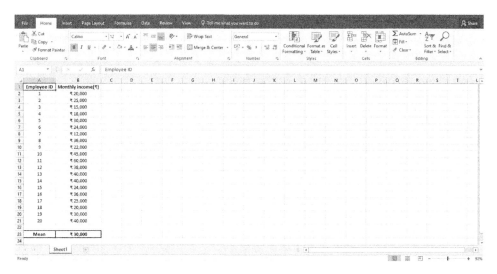

FIGURE 5.3   Step 3 in Calculating the Mean

Demerits of Mean

1. It is not possible to calculate the mean if any observation is missing
2. It cannot be calculated for qualitative or categorical data or data measured on a nominal and ordinal scale. For example,

    a. The mean honesty of employees working in a department cannot be calculated
    b. Similarly, the mean colour of balloons in a room cannot be calculated

3. Sometimes it may give an impossible or inconsistent result.

Let us see this with the help of an example. The table that follows shows the number of students in different years in a college.

Year	Number of students enrolled
First-year	560
Second-year	620
Third-year	550
Fourth-year	480
Total	**2,210**

The average number of students in all years are
= 2,210/4
= 552.5 people
This is impossible as the number of people cannot be in decimals or fractions.

4. If there are one or more extremely high or low values in the dataset, the results may be misleading as mean is affected by those extreme values or outliers and does not represent a true picture.

To understand this, let us consider the following example of the expenditure of Mr A for the year 2019.

He spends ₹50,000 per month.

In addition to this expense, he purchased a house worth ₹50,00,000 in August.

Now the average expenditure of Mr A for the year 2019 can be calculated as follows:

Months	Expenditure
January	₹50,000
February	₹50,000
March	₹50,000
April	₹50,000
May	₹50,000
June	₹50,000
July	₹50,000
August	₹50,50,000
September	₹50,000
October	₹50,000
November	₹50,000
December	₹50,000
Total	**₹56,00,000**

Total expenditure for the year = ₹56,00,000

Number of months in a year = 12

Mean expenditure = ₹56,00,000/12

= ₹4,66,666.67 per month

• In this example, the result leads to a misleading estimation of the amount spent by Mr A on an average in a month.

• Mr A spends exceptionally less than the mean expenditure in 11 out of the 12 months. The unusually high expenditure in August leads to a high mean value.

Thus, the mean may be a less effective measure of central tendency in the presence of extremely high or low values or outliers.

5.2 Median

The median is generally calculated to overcome the drawback of the mean. As noted in the preceding example, if one or more extraordinarily high or low values exist in the dataset, the results may be misleading as the mean is affected by those extreme values or outliers and does not represent a true picture.

Median refers to the middlemost number or the central value of the distribution when **Sorted** in ascending or descending order. The median divides the dataset into two halves, one which contains values more than the median and the other holding values less than the median. That is, 50 per cent of the values lie above the median, and 50 per cent of the values lie below the median. The median is generally used to estimate measuring the average property prices representing the general property market or the average per capita income. In India, the Ministry of Statistics and Program Implementation (*http://mospi.nic.in/data*) releases such summary statistics of GDP using the median.

The median is calculated with the help of the following steps:

Step 1.   Arrange the series of numbers in ascending or descending order.

Step 2.   Locate the middlemost number of the series.

- If there is an *odd number of observations*, then there will be one value in the middle, and that middlemost value is the median
- If there is an *even number of observations*, then there are two values in the middle, and the median is the average or the midpoint of those two values.

Formula

- If there is an odd number of observations

$$\text{Median} = \left(\frac{n+1}{2}\right)^{th} \text{term}$$

- If there is an even number of observations

$$\text{Median} = \text{Average of} \left(\frac{n}{2}\right)^{th} \text{term and} \left(\frac{n+1}{2}\right)^{th} \text{term}$$

$$= \frac{\left(\frac{n}{2}\right)^{th} term + \left(\frac{n+1}{2}\right)^{th} term}{2}$$

Where n = number of observations in the dataset.

Illustration

The daily sales figures (in ₹) of a clothing store in Delhi, Bombay, and Bangalore for the week are given in the following table. The store in Delhi and Bombay are open seven days a week, whereas the store in Bangalore remains closed on Sunday. Calculate the median weekly sale for each city.

City	Monday	Tuesday	Wednesday	Thursday	Friday	Saturday	Sunday
Delhi	₹6,500	₹8,600	₹7,800	₹9,700	₹5,900	₹10,500	₹6,750
Mumbai	₹12,000	₹8,250	₹9,000	₹7,400	₹9,450	₹6,800	₹5,500
Bangalore	₹4,500	₹9,650	₹8,700	₹8,650	₹5,900	₹9,200	–

Solution:

First Method (Direct Method)

Step 1. We arrange the series in ascending order

City							
Delhi	₹5,900	₹6,500	₹6,750	₹7,800	₹8,600	₹9,700	₹10,500
Mumbai	₹5,500	₹6,800	₹7,400	₹8,250	₹9,000	₹9,450	₹12,000
Bangalore	₹4,500	₹5,900	₹8,650	₹8,700	₹9,200	₹9,650	–

Step 2. Finding the middlemost value

City	Number of Observations	Median
Delhi	7	$\left(\dfrac{n+1}{2}\right)^{th} term = \left(\dfrac{7+1}{2}\right)^{th} term = 4^{th} term = ₹\mathbf{7,800}$
Mumbai	7	$\left(\dfrac{n+1}{2}\right)^{th} term = \left(\dfrac{7+1}{2}\right)^{th} term = 4^{th} term = ₹\mathbf{8,250}$
Bangalore	6	$\dfrac{\left(\dfrac{n}{2}\right)^{th} term + \left(\dfrac{n+1}{2}\right)^{th} term}{2} = \dfrac{3^{rd} term + 4^{th} term}{2}$ $= (₹8,650 + ₹8,700)/2$ $= ₹\mathbf{8,675}$

The median sale for Delhi is ₹7,800, that is, half of the sale values are less than ₹7,800, and another half are more than ₹7,800.

Similarly, the median sale for Mumbai and Bangalore is ₹8,250 and ₹8,675.

Second Method (Using Excel)

It is very easy to calculate the median using Excel.

Step 1. Enter the sales figures for each city in an Excel sheet. It is not necessary to sort the data in ascending order when calculating the median using Excel (Figure 5.4).

Step 2. Use the **MEDIAN** function to calculate the median. Type the '=' (equal to) sign in the cell where the result is desired, say, 'I2', for Delhi and enter the function name **MEDIAN** and then select the range of numbers for which median is to be calculated, that is, **B2: H2** for Delhi (Figure 5.5).

Step 3. Press Enter. The result will appear in cell I2 (Figure 5.6). Then click on the fill handle (the small black square in the bottom right corner when you select the cell) and drag it vertically to calculate the median for the next two cities automatically.

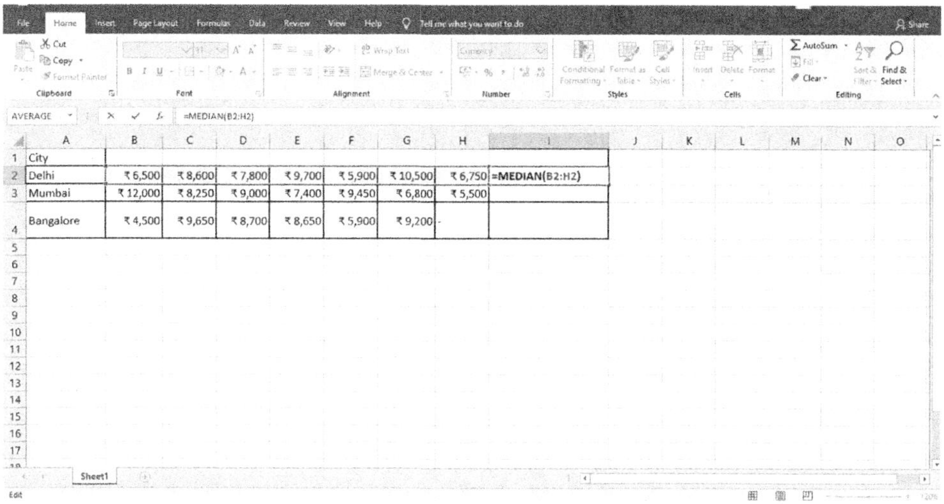

FIGURE 5.4 Step 1 in Calculating the Median

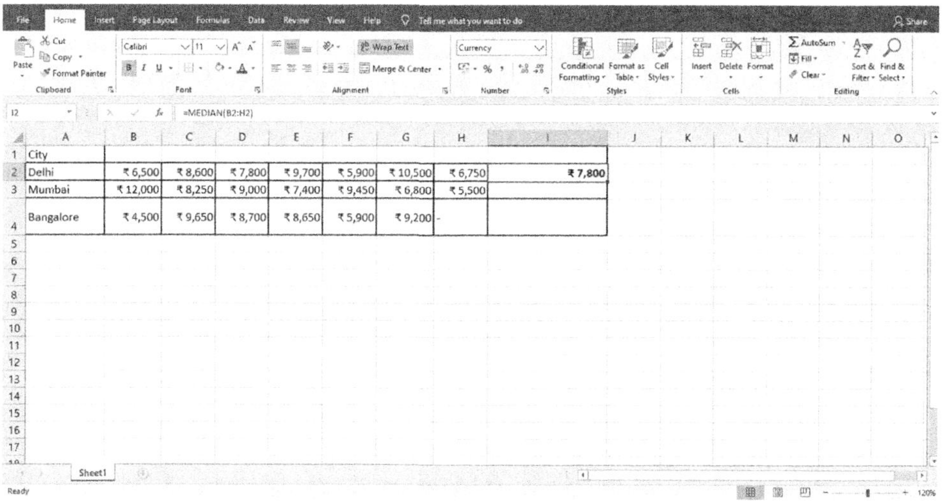

FIGURE 5.5 Step 2 in Calculating the Median

Merits of Median

1. It is simple to calculate and easy to understand
2. Unlike the mean, the median is not affected by the extreme values in the dataset. Thus, it is a better measure of central tendency in skewed distributions
3. The median can be calculated for data measured on both interval and ordinal scale
4. It can be determined graphically.

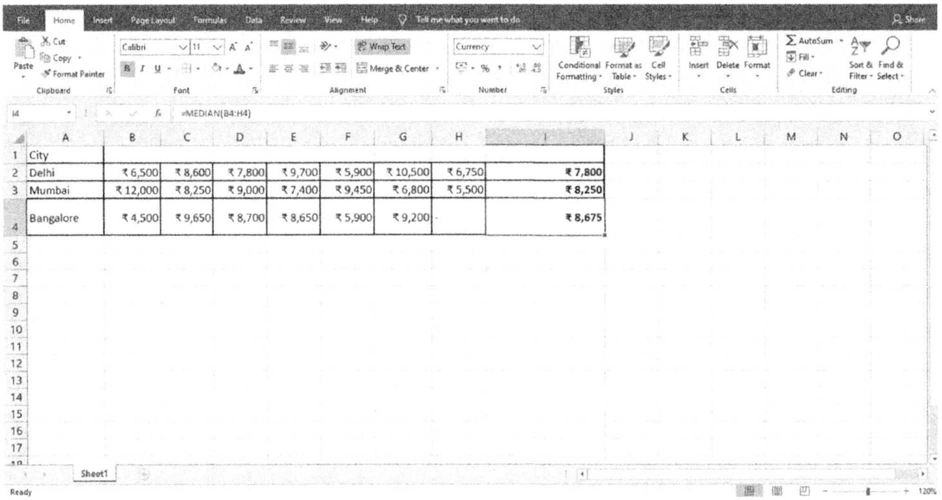

FIGURE 5.6 Step 3 in Calculating the Median

Demerits of Median

1. It is not based on all the values in the distribution as it does not utilize all the information in the dataset
2. To calculate the median, the data always needs to be arranged or sorted in order, that is, from least to greatest or vice versa
3. Sometimes it may give results that are not practically possible.

5.3 Mode

A mode is a measure of central tendency that helps identify the highest frequency value. It represents the most common and frequently occurring number in the dataset. The best thing about the mode is that it can be calculated for qualitative or categorical data.

The mode is generally useful and applied in situations that demand numbers. For example, we may be interested in popular YouTube videos – the one with the highest views/most downloaded. Similarly, in elections, the candidate seeking the maximum votes. The mode is also helpful for companies manufacturing popular products. The mode is calculated by counting the frequencies of all the values given in the dataset, that is, the number of times the value appears in the dataset. The value(s) having the highest frequency, or which is repeated the maximum number of times in the dataset is the mode. Thus, there is no mathematical formula to calculate the mode in the case of individual or discrete series.

Illustration

Compute the modal age from the following data of age (in years) for 30 people who attended the economics conference.

20	27	35	41	50
22	27	36	45	52
25	30	38	47	56
25	32	38	47	56
25	32	40	48	56
25	32	40	49	57

Solution:

First Method (Direct Method)

As we know, the mode is the value which repeats the maximum number of times in the dataset.

The age of 25 years appears four times in the dataset, which is the highest. Hence, the modal value is 25 years.

Second Method (Using Excel)

Step 1. Enter the data in the Excel sheet (Figure 5.7).

Step 2. Use the **MODE.SNGL** function to calculate the mode. Type the '=' (equal to) sign in the cell where the result is desired say, 'B9' and enter the function name **MODE.SNGL** and then select the range of numbers for which mode is to be calculated, **A2: E7,** as shown in Figure 5.8.

Step 3. Press **Enter**. The result will be displayed in cell B9 (Figure 5.9).

It may be noted that the function **MODE.MULT** was introduced in Excel 2010. This function may replace **MODE.SNGL** function. The limitation of **MODE.SNGL** function

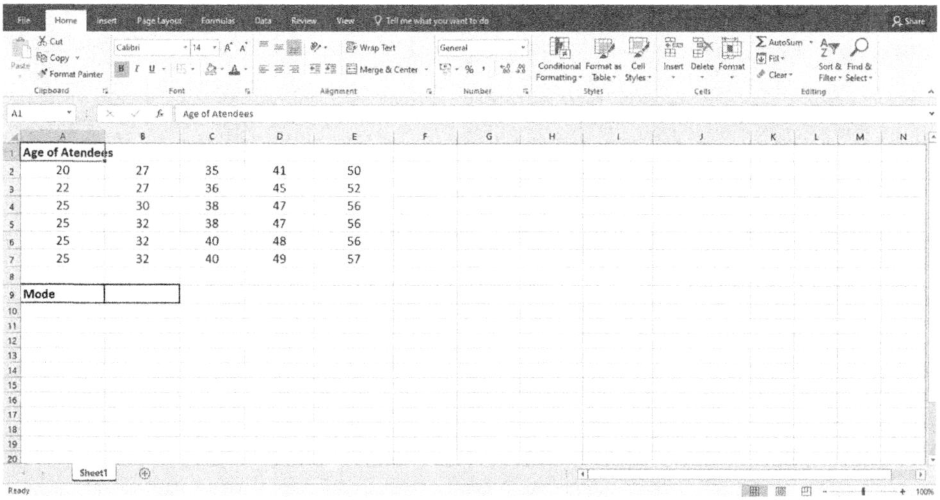

FIGURE 5.7 Step 1 in Calculating the Mode

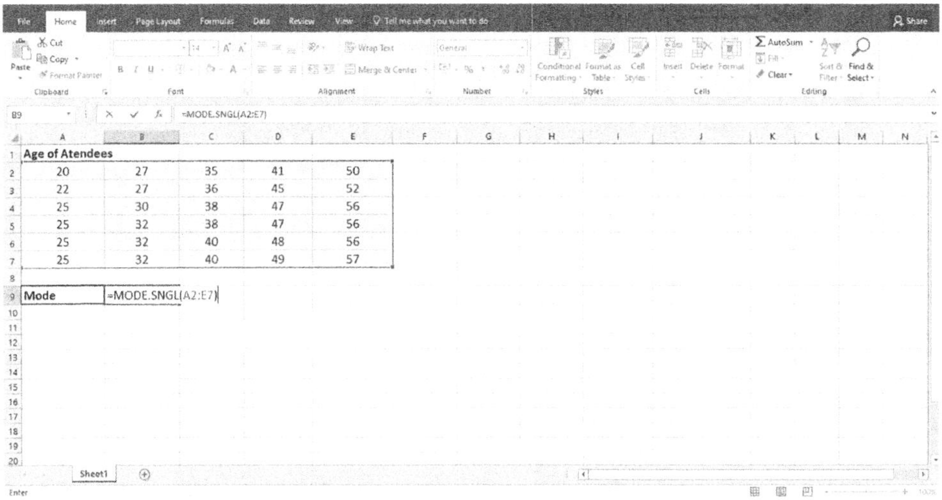

FIGURE 5.8 Step 2 in Calculating the Mode

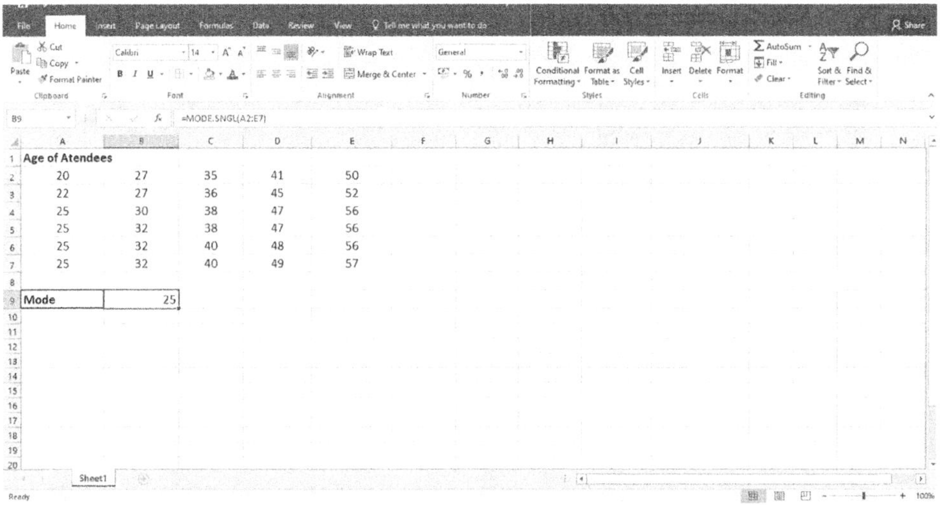

FIGURE 5.9 Step 3 in Calculating the Mode

is that it can be used only when there is a single-mode present in the dataset. However, the function **MODE.MULT** can be used both in the case of single and multiple modes. In case there is no mode, it will return #N/A.

5.3.1 Using Mode if the Data Is Given in Discrete Series (Frequency Distribution)

The marketing head of a multi-brand store is interested in finding the most popular shoe brand among the customers. The data of the purchases by customers from the store for the last week is summarized in the table as follows:

Brand	Frequency
Nike	67
Adidas	50
Reebok	36
Vans	46
Sketchers	58
New Balance	35
Puma	48
Total	**340**

Solution:

First Method (Direct Method)

- To determine the most popular shoe brand, we calculate the mode
- In the previous table, the brand 'Nike' has the highest frequency, 67
- This means that the brand 'Nike' appears the maximum number of times as the most purchased brand in the dataset
- So the marketing head can conclude that 'Nike' is the most popular shoe brand as it is the mode of distribution

Second Method (Graphical Method)

One of the best things about the mode is that it can be determined graphically. In Chapter 4, we discussed the various types of charts, their application, and how to insert them in Excel. To compute mode, we can insert a bar graph depicting the frequencies of the variables in the distribution.

    Step 1. Enter the data in Excel sheet.
    Step 2. Select the entire distribution, that is, **A1: B8.**

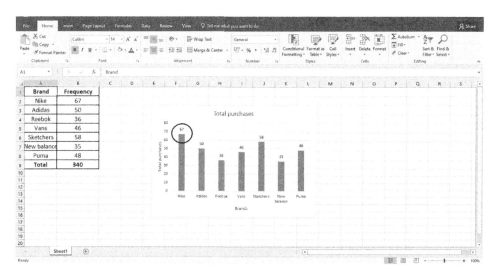

FIGURE 5.10   Calculating the Mode Using Graph

Step **3**. Click on the **Insert** tab, select **Insert Column** or **Bar Chart**, and choose the first graph. The graph is displayed. Add chart elements (Figure 5.10).

Step **4**. Identify the bar with the longest height depicting the highest frequency, that is, 67 for Nike.

Third Method (Using Excel)

We can compute mode in case of discrete series (frequency distribution of the variables is known) using Excel function **MAX** which returns the largest number in the dataset. This is useful in case of a huge volume of data.

Step **1**. Enter the data in Excel sheet.

Step **2**. Type '=**MAX (B2: B8)**' in the cell where the result is desired, say, B11 (Figure 5.11).

Step **3**. Press **Enter**. The maximum number will be displayed in the cell shown in Figure 5.12.

5.3.2 Merits of mode

1. It is simple to understand and sometimes can be computed easily with a single glimpse of data
2. It is not affected by the presence of extreme values in the dataset
3. It can be calculated for quantitative and categorical data or measured on a nominal scale
4. It can be determined graphically.

5.3.3 Demerits of Mode

1. It is not based on all the values in the dataset as it only considers the highest frequency
2. Results may be unclear or ill-defined as the dataset may have more than one mode in case two or more values have the same highest frequencies. Similarly, a distribution may have no mode if none of the values repeat.

Now, we take up the special averages referred to at the beginning of the chapter.

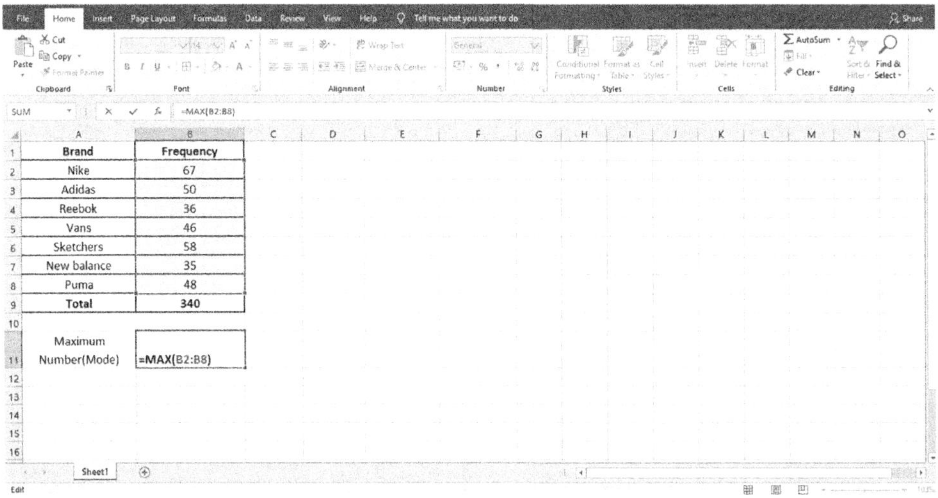

FIGURE 5.11 Step 1 in Calculating the Mode Using MAX

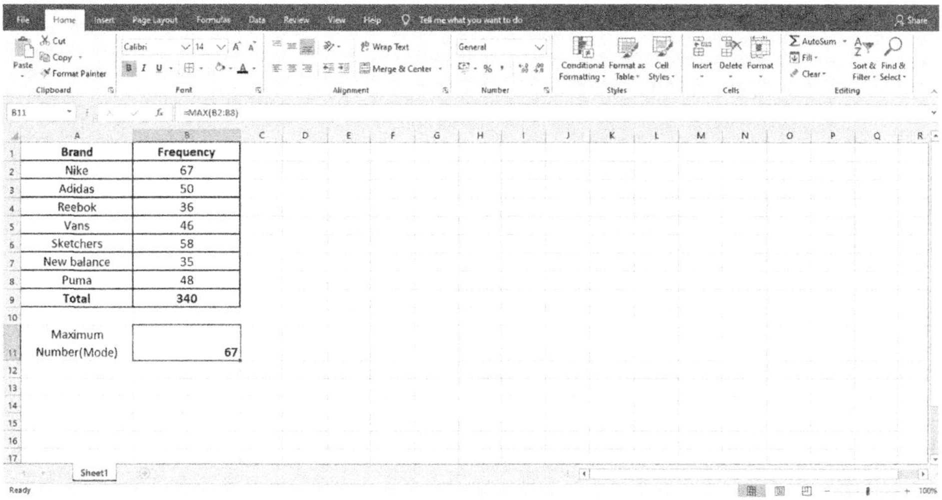

FIGURE 5.12 Step 2 in Calculating the Mode Using MAX

5.4 Weighted Arithmetic Mean

In scenarios when the observations do not contribute equally, the application of arithmetic mean in averaging is erroneous. The contribution in the calculation of the average, that is, value or importance of observation as compared to others, is given the term of *weights*. The weight given to observation is known as the *weighting factor*. Usually, the sum of all the weights is equal to 1 or 100 per cent.

Let us understand the argument with the help of an example of portfolio investment where weighted mean is widely used. Suppose an investor invests ₹1,00,000 in five different investment options. He invests ₹20,000, ₹15,000, ₹25,000, ₹16,000, ₹24,000 in investment options A, B, C, D, E, respectively. The returns are 5 per cent, 7.5 per cent, 6 per cent, 10 per cent, and 10 per cent from these investment options. In such cases, we cannot simply calculate the arithmetic mean to find the average return from this portfolio investment because we have invested different amounts in each investment category with different returns.

To arrive at an appropriate average, we first determine the proportion of funds invested in each type of investment. These are weights, that is, the proportion of funds invested by an investor in each type of investment. In this example, the weight for investment A is $20000/100000 = 0.2$ or 20 per cent (funds invested in investment Option A/Total funds invested). Similarly, weights are 0.15, 0.25, 0.16, and 0.24 in the rest of the schemes. The following steps are taken to proceed with the calculation:

Step 1. Multiply the observations with their corresponding weights.
Step 2. Add up all the products calculated in Step 1.
Step 3. Divide the sum calculated in Step 2 with the sum of all the weights.

$$\textbf{Formula} = \overline{X}_w = \frac{\textit{Sum of all the products of the values and their weight factor}}{\textit{Sum of all the weights}}$$

Or $\bar{X}_w = \dfrac{w_1 x_1 + w_2 x_2 + w_3 x_3 + \ldots + w_n x_n}{\sum w_i} = \dfrac{\sum_{i=1}^{n} w_i x_i}{\sum w_i}$

where $\bar{X}_w$ = symbol or notation for weighted mean

x_i = ith observation in the distribution

w_i = individual weight factor of ith observation

Σ = Sigma/operator for summation, n = number of observations

Putting values in the formula

$$\frac{0.2 * 5\% + 0.15 * 7.5\% + 0.25 * 6\% + 0.16 * 10\% + 0.24 * 10\%}{1}$$

$= 7.63\%$

The average return earned by this investor is 7.63 per cent, given his portfolio investment returns.

Illustration

Let us consider another example in detail to further clarify the concept and calculation along with the application of Excel. The college decided to grade the students for a competition based on the following criteria.

Criteria	Weightage
Round 1 (easy)	20%
Round 2 (medium)	30%
Round 3 (difficult)	50%

Marks obtained by four groups out of 100 marks are as follows:

Groups	A	B	C	D	Weights
Round 1 (easy)	95	75	85	60	**0.2**
Round 2 (medium)	60	65	70	55	**0.3**
Round 3 (difficult)	50	80	70	95	**0.5**

Calculate the weighted score and compare it with the simple arithmetic mean of group.

First Method

The difficulty levels of the rounds are different. Round 1 is easy (weightage 20%) so the score of Round 1 contributes least to the overall performance of the group. Similarly, Round 3 is Difficult (weightage 50%) so the score of Round 3 contributes the most to the group's overall performance. So, we calculate the weighted mean.

We use the formula

$$\overline{X}_w = \frac{w_1 x_1 + w_2 x_2 + w_3 x_3 + \ldots + w_n x_n}{\sum w_i} = \frac{\sum_{i=1}^{n} w_i x_i}{\sum w_i},$$

Groups	Sum of Products / Sum of Weights	Weighted Average	Ranking	Simple Average	Ranking
A	= (95 * 0.2 + 60 * 0.3 + 50 * 0.5)/1	62	IV	68.33	IV
B	= (75 * 0.2 + 65 * 0.3 + 80 * 0.5)/1	74.5	II	73.33	II
C	= (85 * 0.2 + 70 * 0.3 + 70 * 0.5)/1	73	III	75	I
D	= (60 * 0.2 + 55 * 0.3 + 95 * 0.5)/1	76	I	70	III

The weighted mean for Groups A, B, C, and D is 62, 74.5, 73, and 76, respectively. Compared to it, the simple averages are 68.33, 73.33, 75, and 70. In this example, according to the simple average, the first rank is given to group C as it has the highest mean score of 75. Comparing it with the weighted average, the first rank is given to group D as it has the highest score of 76.

Second Method (Using Excel)

Excel calculates weighted mean easily using the following steps.

Step 1. Enter the scores of all the groups for each round. Also, enter the corresponding weights for each round.

Step 2. Use the **SUMPRODUCT** function to calculate the weighted mean. Type the '=' (equal to) sign in the cell where the result is desired say, 'B7' and enter the function name **SUMPRODUCT** and then select the range for **Array 1,** that is, the scores of

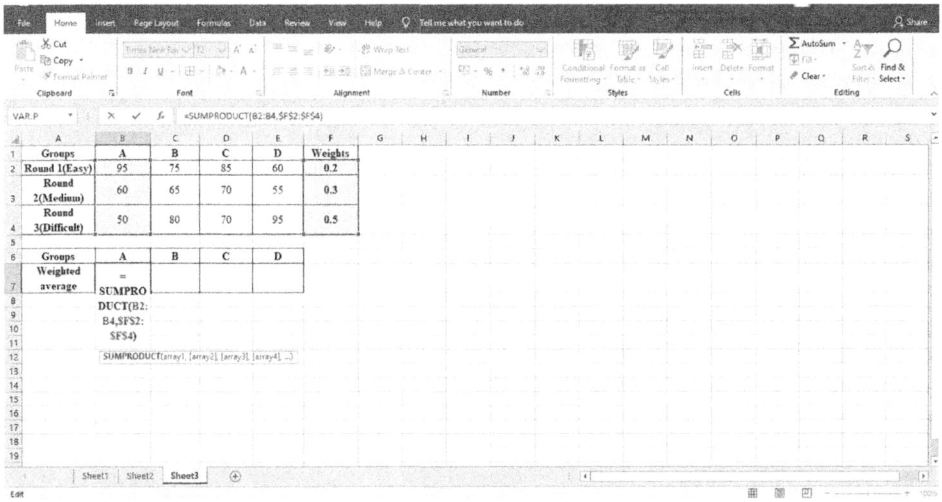

FIGURE 5.13 Step 1 in Calculating the Weighted Arithmetic Mean

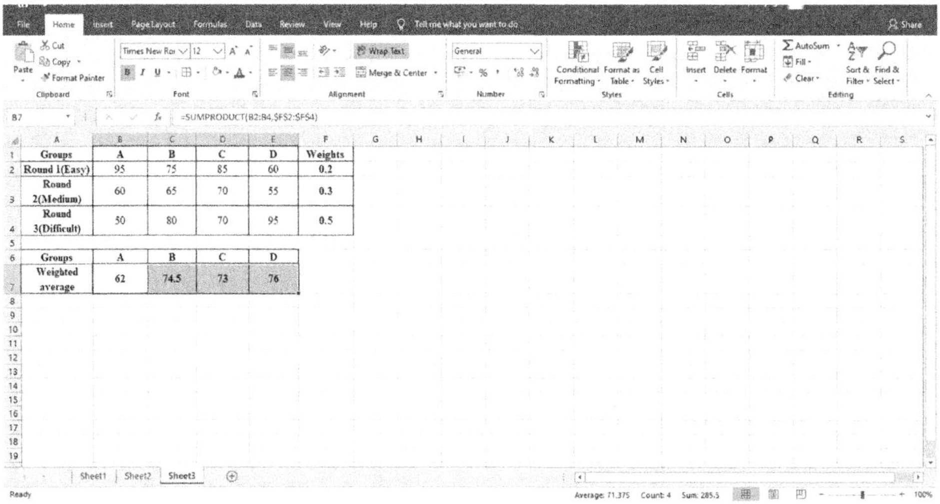

FIGURE 5.14   Step 2 in Calculating the Weighted Arithmetic Mean

group A for each round, that is, **B2: B4.** For **Array 2**, select the range of the weights for each round, that is, $F2: $F4[1] (Figure 5.13).

Step 3. Press **Enter.** The result will appear in cell B7. Then click on the **fill handle** (the small black square in the bottom right corner when you select the cell) and drag it horizontally to automatically calculate the weighted mean for Groups B, C, and D too (Figure 5.14).

5.5   Geometric Mean

It is a special type of mean and is commonly used to take into account the *effect of compounding*. Therefore, the geometric mean is used primarily in finance and demographic growth. In finance, it is used to calculate the average annual returns on investments over a specific period or average growth rate. Similarly, the population growth rate is calculated using this type of mean only. To calculate the geometric mean for 'n' numbers, we multiply all the numbers and take the nth root of the product.

Illustration

Let us understand its application in finance. For instance, the value of a firm increases from ₹1,00,000 to ₹1,10,000 in the first year and ₹1,65,000 in the second year. The growth rate in the first year thus will be 10 per cent and 50 per cent in the second year. The simple average of the growth rates will be 30 per cent.

Using simple average growth, the firm's value after 2nd year –

= 1,00,000 * (130% * 130%)

= ₹1,69,000

We can notice that this value is *more than the actual* value since the mean is additive. In contrast, the geometric mean is multiplicative and calculated as the nth root of the product of 'n' numbers. In our example, calculating $\sqrt[2]{110 \times 150}$ yields 128.45 (equivalent to 28.45% compound annual growth). Using geometric mean, the firm's value after second year will be

= $1,00,000 \times (128\% \times 128\%)$

= $1,65,000$

This is approximately equal to the actual value. Hence geometric mean is a better measure as it smooths the growth rates better. A generalized formula to calculate the geometric mean for n values is

= (Product of all the numbers)$^{1/n}$

$$= \sqrt[n]{x_1 * x_2 * x_3 * ..... * x_n} = \sqrt[n]{\prod_{t=1}^{n} x_i}$$

where

Π = Notation for the product,

x_i = i^{th} observation in the dataset,

n = number of observations

Calculating Geometric Mean Using Excel

It must be realized by now that it is difficult to calculate geometric mean manually, at least if the data size is large, due to extensive calculations involved. It can, however, be calculated using the Excel function **GEOMEAN** in a few simple steps.

Step 1. Enter the data in an Excel spreadsheet.

Step 2. Use the **GEOMEAN** function to calculate the geometric mean (Figure 5.15).

Type the '=' (equal to) sign in the cell where the result is desired, say, 'C7' and enter the function name **GEOMEAN** and then select the range for which geometric mean is to be calculated, C3: C4.

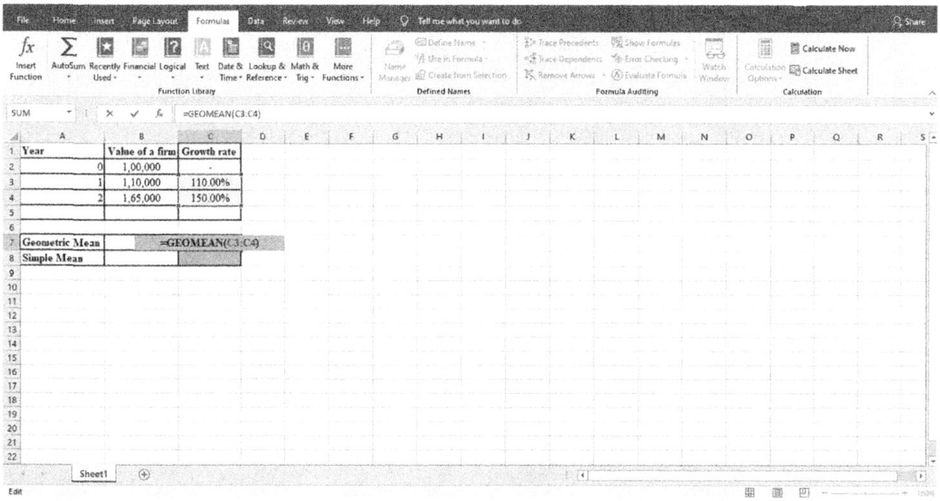

FIGURE 5.15   Step 1 in Calculating the Geometric Mean

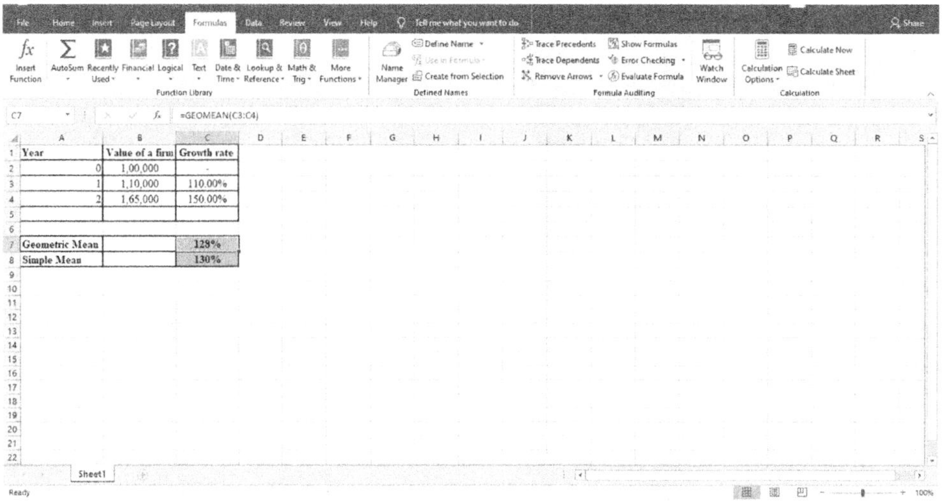

FIGURE 5.16   Step 2 in Calculating the Geometric Mean

Step 3. Press **Enter**. The result will appear in cell C7 (Figure 5.16).

A geometric mean of 128 per cent can be interpreted as the mean rate of growth of the firm value for two years which means if a firm value grew by 28.45 per cent uniformly over the two years, starting with 1,00,000 it would reach 1,65,000. The deduction of 100 is because the base value taken at the beginning of the period is 100. To derive the compound annual growth rate, the value of 100 taken initially is to be deducted from the value arrived at the end of the period. Therefore, whenever we talk of growth over a period, it is a geometric mean and not the arithmetic mean.

5.6   Harmonic Mean

Harmonic mean is another type of average which refers to the reciprocal of the simple average of the reciprocals of the observations. This type of mean gives large weightage to smaller values and smaller weightage to larger values. This mean is usually used with rates, and ratios (fractions) like average speed or price-earnings ratio. For example, a car travels at a speed of 30 km/hr from A to B and 45 km/hr from B to A. Then the *average speed is not the arithmetic mean*, that is $(30 + 45)/2$ km/hr $= 37.5$ km/hr.

The *average speed* is *harmonic mean*, that is $\dfrac{2}{1/30 + 1/45} = 36.36$ km/hr

Let us try to understand it by the following explanation.

• Speed = Distance/Time
• Time = Distance/Speed

Time (from A to B) = $D/30$
Time (from B to A) = $D/45$

Let us say the distance is D

Average speed = Total distance/Total time

$$= \frac{\text{Distance (from A to B)} + \text{Distance (from B to A)}}{\text{Time (from A to B)} + \text{Time (from B to A)}}$$

$$= \frac{2D}{\dfrac{D}{30} + \dfrac{D}{45}} = \frac{2D}{D\left(\dfrac{1}{30} + \dfrac{1}{45}\right)} = \frac{2}{1/30 + 1/45} = 36.36 \text{ km/hr}$$

A generalized formula of the harmonic mean is as follows:

$$\text{Harmonic mean} = \frac{\text{Number of observations}}{\text{Sum of reciprocals of given values}}$$

$$= \frac{n}{\dfrac{1}{x_1} + \dfrac{1}{x_2} + \dfrac{1}{x_3} + \cdots + \dfrac{1}{x_n}} = \frac{n}{\sum_{i=1}^{n} \dfrac{1}{x_n}}$$

where

x_i = i^{th} observation in the distribution

Σ = Sigma/operator for summation

n = number of observations

The steps involved are the following:

Step 1. Calculate the reciprocals of all the values in the dataset.

Step 2. Compute the simple arithmetic mean of the values calculated in Step 1.

Step 3. Calculate the reciprocal of the value obtained in Step 2.

Illustration

The test scores of 15 students in an examination are given next. Calculate the harmonic mean for scores.

Student	Scores
1	90
2	65
3	48
4	76
5	84
6	62
7	94
8	33
9	59
10	86
11	92
12	80
13	71
14	55
15	78

Solution:

First Method (Direct Method)

$$\text{Using harmonic mean} = \frac{\textit{number of observations}}{\textit{sum of reciprocals of given values}}$$

Scores
1/90
1/65
1/48
1/76
1/84
1/62
1/94
1/33
1/59
1/86
1/92
1/80
1/71
1/55
1/78
Sum = 0.2264955
n = 15

$$\sum_{i=1}^{n} \frac{1}{x_n} = .2264955$$

$$\text{Harmonic mean} = \frac{15}{.2264955}$$

$$= 66.2264$$

Second Method (Using Excel)

It is challenging to calculate the harmonic mean manually for large data. It can be calculated using the Excel function **HARMEAN** in the following steps.

Step 1. Enter the data in an Excel spreadsheet.

Step 2. Use the **HARMEAN** function to calculate the harmonic mean.

Type the '=' (equal to) sign in the cell where the result is desired, say, 'B18' and enter the function name **HARMEAN** and then select the range for which harmonic mean is to be calculated, that is, B2: B16 (Figure 5.17).

Step 3. Press **Enter**. The result will appear in cell B18 (Figure 5.18).

Student	Scores
1	90
2	65
3	48
4	76
5	84
6	62
7	94
8	33
9	59
10	86
11	92
12	80
13	71
14	55
15	78
Harmonic Mean	=HARMEAN(B2:B16)

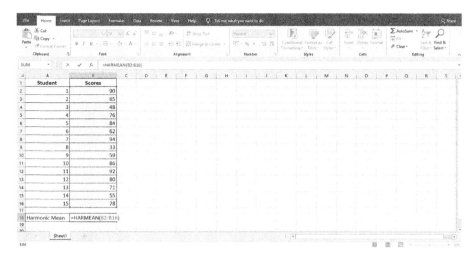

FIGURE 5.17 Step 1 in Calculating the Harmonic Mean

Student	Scores
1	90
2	65
3	48
4	76
5	84
6	62
7	94
8	33
9	59
10	86
11	92
12	80
13	71
14	55
15	78
Harmonic Mean	66.22646972

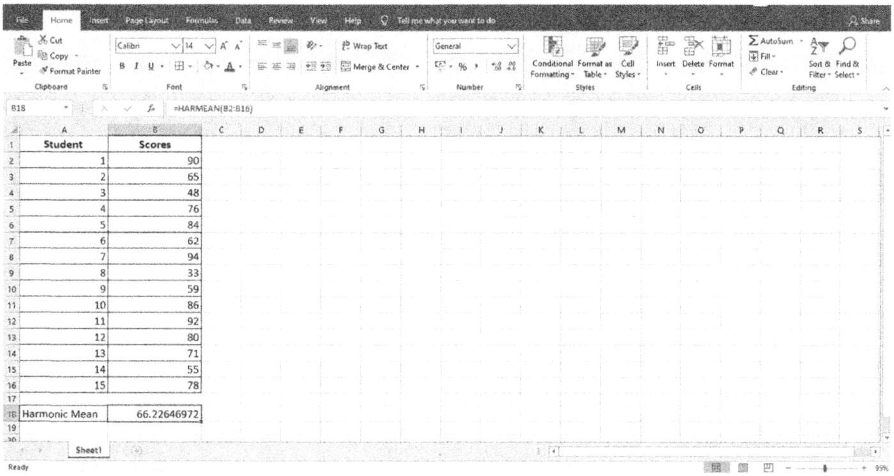

FIGURE 5.18 Step 2 in Calculating the Harmonic Mean

5.7 Relationship Between Arithmetic Mean, Geometric Mean, and Harmonic Mean

1. The value of the geometric mean is always less than or equal to the arithmetic mean.

The value of the harmonic mean is always less than or equal to the geometric mean
Therefore, we can conclude that

Arithmetic Mean ≥ Geometric Mean ≥ Harmonic Mean

2. Arithmetic mean, geometric mean, and harmonic mean are Pythagorean means, that is,

$(\text{Geometric Mean})^2 = \text{Arithmetic Mean} * \text{Harmonic Mean}$

To conclude, this chapter focused on the significance of the measures of the central tendency to reduce a large amount of data to a single value that represents and summarizes the data as a whole by identifying its central position. Further, we learned how to compute mean (arithmetic, geometric, and harmonic), median, and mode and apply them under different conditions. The question arises whether it is adequate or do we need to compute additional statistics to make the data more meaningful. We will find out the answer to this in our next chapter, where we will learn the computation and application of measures of dispersion or variability.

PRACTICE QUESTIONS

1. The sales targets achieved by 20 sales representatives of P Ltd are summarized next.

   Calculate mean and median for the data.

Sale Representative	Sales	Sale Representative	Sales
1	2,13,000	11	4,01,000
2	4,89,000	12	2,70,000
3	2,80,000	13	2,28,000
4	3,96,000	14	4,52,000
5	1,11,000	15	4,71,000
6	3,79,000	16	4,64,000
7	2,97,000	17	1,81,000
8	3,06,000	18	2,07,000
9	4,47,000	19	3,90,000
10	3,83,000	20	3,72,000

2. The maximum temperature recorded for November in Delhi is stated next. Calculate the median temperature and mode.

Day	Temperature (Celsius)	Day	Temperature (Celsius)	Day	Temperature (Celsius)
1	33	11	31	21	31
2	33	12	28	22	32
3	36	13	26	23	34
4	31	14	30	24	32
5	33	15	33	25	33
6	32	16	35	26	28
7	32	17	32	27	30
8	32	18	30	28	36
9	33	19	31	29	34
10	34	20	32	30	32

3. XYZ Ltd. earned Net Profit (million US $) as follows in the last ten years. Calculate the geometric mean.

Year	Net Profit (Million US $)
2019	67,160
2018	64,660
2017	63,500
2016	62,700
2015	63,050
2014	66,600
2013	66,400
2012	65,400
2011	57,830
2010	51,250

4. Ten cars travelled from Delhi to Chandigarh.

The table shows the petrol consumption for each car. Calculate the harmonic mean to estimate the average consumption of petrol per car.

Car	Petrol Consumption (km per litre)
1	20
2	18
3	15
4	21
5	18
6	17
7	19
8	12
9	19
10	24

5. The college decided to grade the students for a semester based on the following criteria.

Criteria	Weightage
Assignment	10%
Test	20%
Exam	60%
Viva	10%

Marks obtained by Shipra and Shraiya are as follows.

Groups	Shipra	Shraiya	Weights
Assignment	80	94	10%
Test	85	65	20%
Exam	92	70	60%
Viva	90	86	10%

Calculate the weighted score.

Note

1   We need to use absolute cell reference **$F2:$F4** in our formula so that it will not change when the formula is copied to other cells as the range **F2:F4** (weights for each round) remains constant for all the groups.

6

MEASURES OF DISPERSION

Learning Objectives

After reading this chapter, the readers will be able to understand

- Concept of measure of dispersion
- Meaning, calculation, and interpretation of range using Excel
- Meaning, calculation, and interpretation of standard deviation using Excel
- Meaning, calculation, and interpretation of variance using Excel
- Calculation and application of coefficient of variation
- Concept of symmetrical and asymmetrical distribution
- Computation of coefficient of skewness using Excel and its interpretation
- Concept and calculation of kurtosis using Excel
- Using data analysis tools to compute descriptive statistics

In the previous chapter, we discussed in detail the first measurement tool of descriptive statistics, measures of central tendency. This chapter will introduce the second category of descriptive statistics: measures of dispersion or variability. As the name suggests, it describes how spread out the dataset is. Commonly used statistical measures of dispersion are range, standard deviation, variance, and coefficient of variation. The extent to which the individual items vary or differ from the central value of the dataset is called *dispersion*. This chapter will also introduce the *skewness of distribution and kurtosis*.

The need to calculate the measures of dispersion can be understood with the help of the following table, which summarizes the test scores in two different sections of ten students each.

											Mean	Median
Class A	70	56	35	99	96	100	80	88	59	42	**72.5**	**75**
Class B	76	82	61	60	74	90	78	62	65	77	**72.5**	**75**

DOI: 10.4324/9781003398127-6

Here, both datasets have an exactly equal arithmetic mean of 72.5 and a median of 75. But we cannot say that the performance of both sections is the same. Looking closely, we find that in the first set, the numbers are *farther away from the mean score of 72.5* (the highest score being 100 and the lowest is 35), whereas the numbers in the second set are much *closer to the mean score* (90 being the highest score and lowest is 60). It implies that the values in the *first set of numbers are more dispersed* as the scores' differences are comparatively higher.

It is evident then that the measures of central tendency do not adequately summarize the data, and we need additional measures related to the amount of variation in the dataset. Plotting graphs of the preceding data provides a much clearer understanding of variability in the scores. The first set of Class A scores is largely scattered (Figure 6.1), whereas the scores in the second set have greater uniformity/concentration (Figure 6.2).

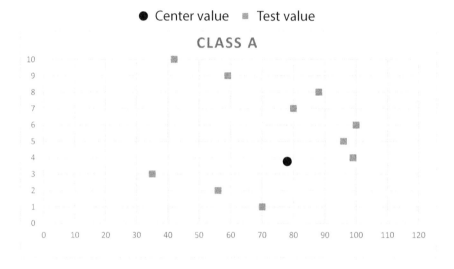

FIGURE 6.1   Scatter Plot for Scores of Class A

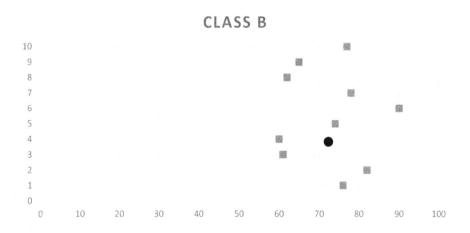

FIGURE 6.2   Scatter Plot for Scores of Class B

In light of the preceding, we explain next the aforesaid measures of the degree of variability present in the dataset. Any good measure of it should meet the following criteria:

1. It should be simple to calculate and easy to understand.
2. It should be based on all the values in the dataset, making it more reliable.
3. It should not be affected by the presence of extreme values or outliers.
4. It should facilitate further statistical analysis.
5. It should be able to depict true and accurate variability in the data.

6.1 Range

The range is the simplest measure of dispersion. A higher range implies higher variation or spreads in the data. It is the difference between the dataset's highest and lowest values. It is, therefore, calculated by subtracting the minimum value from the maximum value in the dataset.

Therefore, range = Maximum Value of data − Minimum Value of data

In the example cited earlier, the range of Class A score

= Maximum score − Minimum score

= 100 − 35 = 65

Correspondingly, the range of Class B score

= Maximum score − Minimum score

= 90 − 60 = 30

Illustration

Let us consider the historical data on the exchange rate for US Dollar (USD) to Indian Rupee (INR) for 12 months starting from Jan 2019 to December 2019. Calculate the range for the data follows.

Date	*USD/INR*
December	71.311
November	71.722
October	70.99
September	70.4987
August	71.6802
July	69.0775
June	69.325
May	69.98
April	69.8118
March	69.43
February	71.19
January	71.12

Source: The data can be accessed at https://finance.yahoo.com/quote/INR%3DX/history? period1 = 1563608203& period2 =1595230603&interval =1mo&filter=history&frequency=1mo

First Method (Direct Method)

Range of exchange rates
= Maximum Exchange rate − Minimum exchange rate
= 71.722 − 69.0775, which is equal to 2.6445

Second Method (Using Excel)

To calculate the range using Excel, follow these steps.

Step 1. Enter the exchange rates in the Excel sheet.
Step 2. Use the **MAX and MIN** functions to calculate the highest and lowest exchange rates. The range will be the difference between the highest and lowest values.

Type the '=' (equal to) sign in the cell where the result is desired, say, 'E4' and enter the function name **MAX** and then select the range of numbers to calculate the highest exchange rate, that is, **B2: B13,** Press **Enter**.

Step 3. Type the '=' (equal to) sign in the cell where the result is desired, say, 'E5' and enter the function name **MIN** and then select the same range of numbers to calculate the lowest exchange rate, that is, **B2: B13**. Press **Enter**.
Step 4. To calculate **Range**, Type the '=' (equal to) sign in the cell where the result is desired, say 'E6' then subtract the result in E5 from E4. Press **Enter** (Figures 6.3 and 6.4).

Merits of Range

1. It is very easy to compute
2. It is simple to understand even by a layman
3. It is less time-consuming.

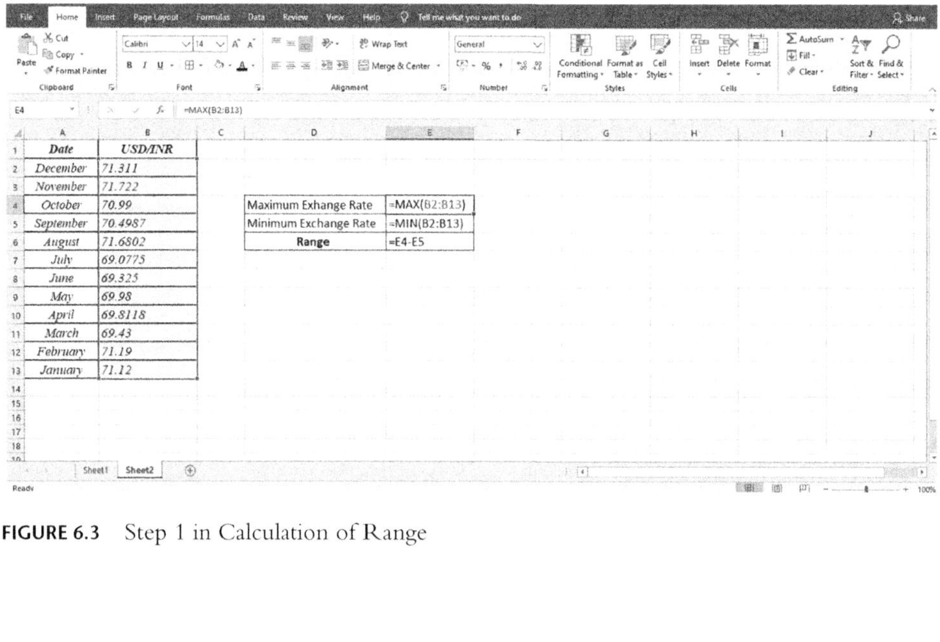

FIGURE 6.3   Step 1 in Calculation of Range

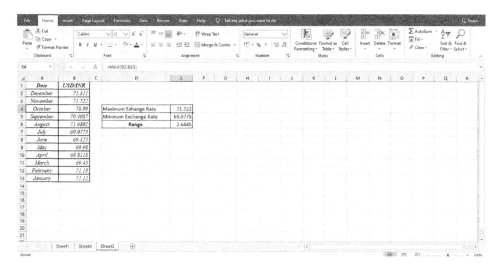

FIGURE 6.4   Step 2 in Calculation of Range

Demerits of Range

1. It is not based on all the values in a dataset
2. It does not facilitate further analysis
3. In the case of open-end continuous series, the upper limit of the highest class and the lower limit of the lowest class have to be estimated.

6.2   Standard Deviation

Standard deviation (denoted by the Greek letter sigma) is the square root of the sum of all the squared deviations of the observations from their mean divided by the number of observations in the dataset. Or in other words, the square root of the average of the squared deviations from the mean is the standard deviation. A large standard deviation indicates that the data has high variation or is widely spread. On the other hand, a low standard deviation means lower variation in the dataset. It is calculated with the help of the following steps.

Step 1. Calculate the arithmetic mean for a set of observations.
Step 2. Subtract the arithmetic mean calculated in Step 1 from each observation. The difference between each observation and the arithmetic mean is called a deviation from the mean.
Step 3. Square the deviations calculated earlier.
Step 4. Calculate the arithmetic mean of the squared deviations.
Step 5. Calculate the square root of the result obtained in Step 4.

Rule of Thumb (Assumes Normal Distribution)

*   We expect 68 per cent of our data to fall within the range + or −1 standard deviation of the mean. (± 1 * standard deviation).

- We expect 95 per cent of our data to fall within the range of + or −2 standard deviation of the mean. (± 2 * standard deviation).
- We expect 99.7 per cent of our data to fall within the range + or −3 standard deviation of the mean (± 3 * standard deviation).
- 0.3 per cent values falling beyond the third range are rare and unusual.

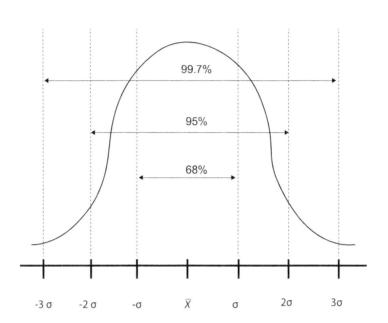

The steps described earlier of standard deviation for a series of numbers $x_1, x_2, x_3, \ldots x_n$ can be formalized as

$$\sigma = \sqrt{\frac{\sum_{i=1}^{n}\left(x_i - \bar{X}\right)^2}{n}}$$

Where σ = symbol for standard deviation
Σ = Sigma/operator for summation
$\bar{X}$ = arithmetic mean
$\left(x_i - \bar{X}\right)^2$ = squared deviation of ith observation from the arithmetic mean
n = number of observations

Important note: When we calculate the standard deviation for a sample to infer about the population from which it is drawn, we use $n - 1$ instead of n in the denominator, as it gives a better measure of standard deviation.

Population refers to the aggregate of all the items under study. The sample is the set of items taken out of the population as a representative.

Therefore, the population standard deviation is = $\sqrt{\dfrac{\sum_{i=1}^{N}\left(x_i - \mu\right)^2}{N}}$

and the sample standard deviation is $= \sqrt{\dfrac{\sum_{i=1}^{n}\left(x_i - \bar{x}\right)^2}{n-1}}$

Here, μ = population mean and $\bar{x}$ = sample mean, N = number of observations in the population, n = number of observations in a sample

Illustration

The following table presents the monthly salaries of CEOs of ten multinational companies. Calculate the standard deviation of salaries.

Company	Salary ('000)
A	100
B	120
C	400
D	280
E	90
F	250
G	340
H	170
I	300
J	600

First Method (Direct Method)

Company	Salary ('000) (X)	X − Mean	(X − Mean)²
A	100	−165	27,225
B	120	−145	21,025
C	400	135	18,225
D	280	15	225
E	90	−175	30,625
F	250	−15	225
G	340	75	5,625
H	170	−95	9,025
I	300	35	1,225
J	600	335	1,12,225
Total	**2,650**		**2,25,650**

Mean of salaries ('000) $= \dfrac{\sum_{i=1}^{n} x_i}{n} = 2650/10 = ₹265$

Standard deviation ('000) $= \sqrt{\dfrac{\sum_{i=1}^{n}\left(x_i - \bar{x}\right)^2}{n}} = \sqrt{\dfrac{225650}{10}} = ₹150.21651$

According to the rule of thumb, this means that the majority of the salaries (68 per cent) lie within the range of ₹2,65,000 – (1) * ₹1,50,216.5 and 2,65,000 + (1) * 1,50,216.5, that is, within ₹1,14,784 and ₹4,15,217.

Second Method (Using Excel)

Use the **STDEV.P** function to calculate the standard deviation of a population. If using the entire population is not possible, we can calculate the standard deviation of a sample drawn from the population using the Excel function **STDEV.S.**

To calculate the standard deviation using Excel, follow these steps as displayed in Figures 6.5 and 6.6.

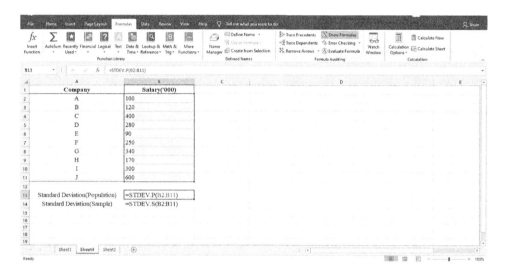

FIGURE 6.5   Step 1 in Calculation of Standard Deviation

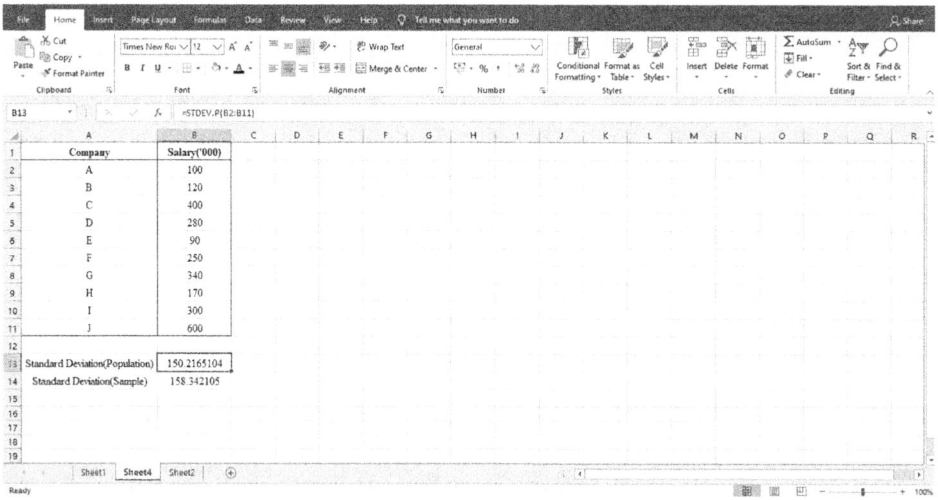

FIGURE 6.6   Step 2 in Calculation of Standard Deviation

Step 1. Enter the salaries in the Excel sheet.

Step 2. Use the **STDEV.P** function to calculate the standard deviation of the population.

Type the '=' (equal to) sign in the cell where the result is desired, say, 'B13' and enter the function name **STDEV.P** and then select the range of numbers, that is, **B2: B11.** Press **Enter**.

Step 3. Use the **STDEV.S** function to calculate the standard deviation of the sample.

Type the '=' (equal to) sign in the cell where the result is desired, say 'B14' and enter the function name **STDEV.S** and then select the range of numbers, that is, **B2: B11.** Press **Enter** (Figures 6.5 and 6.6).

Merits of Standard Deviation

1. It describes the spread or variation of the dataset from their average value
2. It is based on all the values of the dataset
3. It indicates the reliability of the measures of central tendency
4. It enables a comparative study of two or more datasets with respect to their consistency, stability or volatility
5. It is generally taken as an estimation of risk in an investment and helps to measure the market volatility
6. It facilitates further statistical analysis like skewness, correlation, regression, and hypothesis testing
7. It is expressed in the same units as the mean of the distribution; hence easier to interpret and more accurate.

Demerits of Standard Deviation

1. The calculation of standard deviation is difficult as it involves many steps
2. It cannot be easily understood
3. The standard deviation of two series cannot be added as it is a square root
4. It is affected by extreme values in the dataset because the deviations from mean are squared, due to which the larger deviation becomes proportionately bigger than the smaller deviations
5. Units of measurement do influence the value of the standard deviation. For example, if we measure some length in inches and measure the same in terms of centimetres, then the standard deviation in the latter will be 2.53 times the former.

6.3   Variance

Now let us look at another important measure of dispersion called variance. Variance refers to the average of the squared deviations from the mean. In simple words, it is the square of the standard deviation. It is denoted by (σ^2) referred to as sigma square. Mathematically, the variance for a series of numbers x_1, x_2, x_3, ..., x_n is expressed as

$$\sigma^2 = \frac{\sum_{i=1}^{n}\left(x_i - \overline{X}\right)^2}{n}$$

where

σ = symbol for standard deviation

$\sum$ = Sigma/operator for summation

$\overline{X}$ = arithmetic mean

$\left(x_i - \overline{X}\right)^2$ = squared deviation of ith observation from the arithmetic mean

n = number of observations

Illustration

Two teams played ten matches for the national level cricket tournament in Delhi. The scores of the two teams for all the matches in the tournament are given as follows.

Match	Team A	Team B
1	150	260
2	236	110
3	280	140
4	175	265
5	210	289
6	190	300
7	185	95
8	146	70
9	250	145
10	235	290

Calculate

1. Standard deviation
2. Variance
3. Which team has consistent performance?

First Method

Match	Team A	Team B	Team A (X − Mean)	Team B (X − Mean)	Team A (X − Mean)²	Team B (X − Mean)²
1	150	260	−55.7	63.6	3,102.49	4,044.96
2	236	110	30.3	−86.4	918.09	7,464.96
3	280	140	74.3	−56.4	5,520.49	3,180.96
4	175	265	−30.7	68.6	942.49	4,705.96
5	210	289	4.3	92.6	18.49	8,574.76

Match	Team A	Team B	Team A (X − Mean)	Team B (X − Mean)	Team A (X− Mean)²	Team B (X − Mean)²
6	190	300	−15.7	103.6	246.49	10,732.96
7	185	95	−20.7	−101.4	428.49	10,281.96
8	146	70	−59.7	−126.4	3,564.09	15,976.96
9	250	145	44.3	−51.4	1,962.49	2,641.96
10	235	290	29.3	93.6	858.49	8,760.96
Total	**2,057**	**1,964**			**17,562.1**	**76,366.4**

For Team A

Mean of scores $= \dfrac{\sum_{i=1}^{n} x_i}{n} = 2057/10 = 205.7$

a)   Standard deviation $= \sqrt{\dfrac{\sum_{i=1}^{n}\left(x_i - \bar{x}\right)^2}{n}} = \sqrt{\dfrac{17,562.1}{10}} = 41.90715929$

b)   Variance = (standard deviation)² = 1,756.21

For Team B

Mean of scores $= \dfrac{\sum_{i=1}^{n} x_i}{n} = 1,964/10 = 196.4$

a)   Standard deviation $= \sqrt{\dfrac{\sum_{i=1}^{n}\left(x_i - \bar{x}\right)^2}{n}} = \sqrt{\dfrac{76,366.4}{10}} = 87.38787$

b)   Variance = (standard deviation)² = 7,636.64

Based on the results, Team A performed consistently as their standard deviation, that is, total variation is less than that of Team B. However, variance describes the spread in the dataset, but no conclusions can be drawn from it. The standard deviation gives us a better picture of the variation in the dataset with the help of the rule of thumb (68–95–99.7 rule). For instance, in the preceding illustration

- The majority of the scores (68 per cent) of Team A lie within the range of 205.7 − 41.90 and 205.7 + 41.90, that is, *within* 163.8 to 247.6.
- The majority of Team B scores (68 per cent) lie within the range of 196.4 − 87.38 and 196.4 + 87.38, that is, *within* 109.02 to 283.78.

Second Method (Using Excel)

Use the **VAR.P** function to calculate the variance of a population. If using the entire population is not possible, we can calculate the variance of a sample drawn from the population using the Excel function **VAR.S**.

To calculate the variance using Excel, follow the steps as shown in Figures 6.7 and 6.8.

Step 1. Enter the scores in the Excel sheet.
Step 2. Use the **VAR.P** function to calculate the variance of the population.

Type the '=' (equal to) sign in the cell where the result is desired, say 'B13', enter the function name **VAR.P**, and then select the range of numbers, **B2: B11.** Press **Enter**.

Step 3. Use the **VAR.S** function to calculate the variance of the sample.

Type the '=' (equal to) sign in the cell where the result is desired, say 'B14', and enter the function name **VAR.S** and then select the range of numbers, that is, **B2: B11.** Press **Enter**.

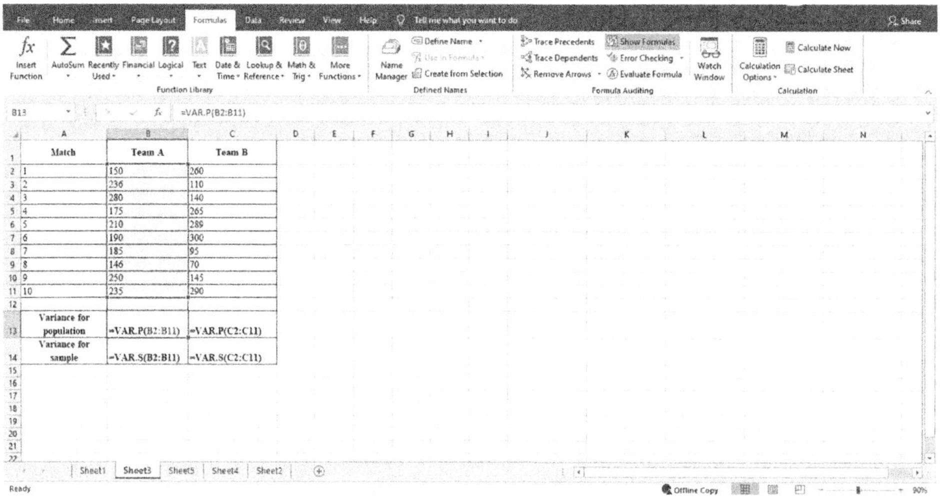

FIGURE 6.7   Step 1 in Calculation of Variance

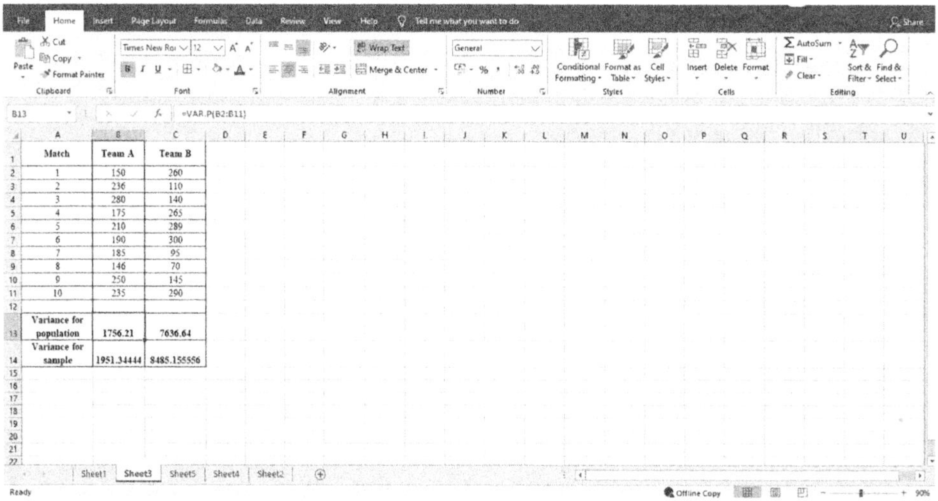

FIGURE 6.8   Step 2 in Calculation of Variance

Merits of Variance

1. It describes the spread or the variation in the data
2. It is a useful statistic used to draw insights from surveys
3. It is also used in accounting to determine the gap between the budgeted and actual amount of costs and revenues.

Demerits of Variance

1. It is difficult to calculate
2. It is not easy to interpret variance as it is expressed in square units and not in the same units as mean.

6.4   Coefficient of Variation

This statistical measure of dispersion measures relative variability. It is defined as the ratio of the standard deviation to the mean and is independent of the unit of measurement for which it is calculated. The coefficient of variation is expressed as:

$$= \frac{Standard\ Deviation}{Mean}$$

$$= \frac{\sigma}{\bar{X}}$$

It can be represented in terms of ratio or percentage. For percentage, we multiply the previous formula by 100 i.e. $\frac{\sigma}{\bar{X}} * 100$. Lower coefficient of variation suggests lesser variation than the mean. Similarly, a higher coefficient of variation signifies greater variation than the mean. That is, if set A has a coefficient of variation of 15 per cent and set B has a coefficient of variation of 20 per cent, then we can say that Set B has more variation relative to its mean.

The coefficient of variation is a useful statistic to compare two or more datasets having varied standard deviation and mean or different units of measurement. One should prefer the coefficient of variation for comparison instead of standard deviation. However, one problem with using the coefficient of variation is that when the mean is zero or negative, then the coefficient of variation can be misleading.

For example, let us consider two investment portfolios. We are given the mean of the returns earned and the standard deviation for the returns for each investment portfolio.

	Investment A	Investment B
Mean	0.48	0.53
Standard Deviation	0.110	0.149

Looking at the results, one might think that investment B provides comparatively higher average returns than A and that the risk is quite similar. But let us calculate the coefficient of variation to make a meaningful decision by using the formula of the coefficient of variation

$$= \frac{\sigma}{\overline{X}} * 100$$

	Investment A	Investment B
Mean	0.48	0.53
Standard Deviation	0.110	0.149
Coefficient of Variation	22.92%	28.11%

The calculation returns the coefficient of variation of 22.92 per cent in the case of Investment A and 28.11 per cent in the case of investment B. A higher degree of variability in Investment B makes it riskier than the alternative. In this case, Investment A is safer than that of Investment B.

Calculating the Coefficient of Variation Using Excel

There is no direct formula to calculate the coefficient of variation in Excel. Therefore,

1. We first calculate the simple arithmetic mean of the dataset using the **AVERAGE** function.
2. Then we calculate the standard deviation using the **STDEV.P** function.
3. Finally, for calculating the coefficient of variation, we divide the cell containing the standard deviation by the cell containing the mean.

6.5   Skewness

The distribution of the dataset may be symmetrical or asymmetrical. Whether the distribution is symmetrical or asymmetrical can be determined by the shape of the distribution when plotted.

Symmetrical distribution is the one that looks the same on the left side as on the right side, that is, the left side is identical to the right side. A *normal distribution* is a symmetrical distribution in which the value of the mean = median = mode and the skewness is zero. The frequency curve depicting such symmetrical distribution is known as a normal curve or perfectly bell-shaped curve as it looks similar to a bell. For symmetrical distributions, the mean = median = mode represented by the middle of the distribution.

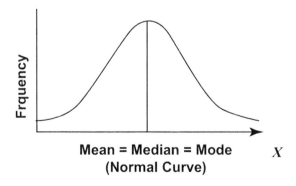

Mean = Median = Mode
(Normal Curve)

Asymmetrical distribution is a distribution whose left side is not identical to its right side. It has either a large number of extremely high values and fewer number of smaller values or a large number of smaller values and fewer number of high values. Skewness is a descriptive statistic that *measures the lack of symmetry*, that is, *asymmetry*. For an asymmetrical distribution, the mean ≠ median ≠ mode. The greater the differences between mean, median, and mode, the higher the skewness of the data. An asymmetrical distribution may be *positively skewed* or *negatively skewed*. A positively skewed distribution is skewed to the right, with a long tail towards the right. Also, mean > median > mode.

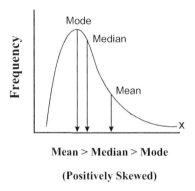

Mean > Median > Mode

(Positively Skewed)

Whereas a negatively skewed distribution is skewed to left. There is a long tail towards the left. Mean < median < mode.

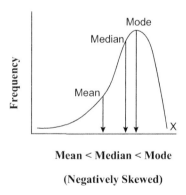

Mean < Median < Mode

(Negatively Skewed)

The measure to estimate the skewness as given by Karl Pearson is:

$$\text{Coefficient of Skewness (Skp)} = \frac{\text{Mean} - \text{Mode}}{\text{Standard Deviation}} = \frac{\overline{X} - M_o}{\sigma}$$

How to interpret the measure of skewness?

- If the coefficient of skewness = 0, then it is a *symmetric distribution* or *normal distribution*
- If the coefficient of skewness > 0, then it is a *positively skewed distribution*

- If the coefficient of skewness < 0, then it is a *negatively skewed distribution*
- If 0.5 > | coefficient of skewness | > 0, then the distribution is *comparatively symmetrical*
- If 1 > | coefficient of skewness | > 0.5, then the distribution is *moderately skewed*
- If | coefficient of skewness | > 1, then the distribution is *highly skewed*.

As we have noted earlier, the mode of a dataset may be ill-defined. A dataset may have more than one mode or may have no mode at all. In that case, we can use the median to compute the mode.

The mean, median, and mode relationship is known as the *empirical relationship*. According to which, for a skewed distribution the difference between mean and mode is three times the difference between mean and median.

$$\text{Mean} - \text{Mode} = 3\,(\text{Mean} - \text{Median})$$

$$\text{or Mode} = 3\text{Median} - 2\,\text{Mean}$$

Illustration

Rice production (in metric tonnes) by 30 farmers in India is summarized in the table that follows. Calculate the Karl Pearson coefficient of skewness.

Farmer	Rice Production	$(X - Mean)^2$	Farmer	Rice Production	$(X - Mean)^2$
1	29	3.61	16	35	62.41
2	20	50.41	17	15	146.41
3	24	9.61	18	25	4.41
4	30	8.41	19	35	62.41
5	34	47.61	20	33	34.81
6	26	1.21	21	26	1.21
7	19	65.61	22	25	4.41
8	10	292.41	23	40	166.41
9	40	166.41	24	50	524.41
10	40	166.41	25	45	320.41
11	5	488.41	26	15	146.41
12	20	50.41	27	28	0.81
13	24	9.61	28	26	1.21
14	10	292.41	29	35	62.41
15	26	1.21	30	23	16.81
Total	**357**	**1,653.75**	**Total**	**456**	**1,554.95**

$$\text{Mean} = \frac{\sum_{i=1}^{n} x_i}{n} = 27.1$$

$$\text{Median} = \frac{\left(\frac{n}{2}\right)^{th}\text{term} + \left(\frac{n}{2}+1\right)^{th}\text{term}}{2} = 26$$

Mode = highest frequency in the dataset = 26

$$\text{Standard deviation} = \sqrt{\frac{\sum_{i=1}^{n}(x_i - \bar{x})^2}{n}} = \sqrt{\frac{1,653.75 + 1,554.95}{30}} = 10.342$$

$$\text{Karl Pearson coefficient of skewness} = \frac{\text{Mean} - \text{Mode}}{\text{Standard Deviation}} = \frac{\bar{X} - M_o}{\sigma}$$

$$= \frac{27.1 - 26}{10.342} = 0.106$$

Answer and interpretation of result:

$0.5 > |$ coefficient of skewness $| > 0$, the data is comparatively *symmetrical distribution*.

Second Method (Using Excel)

To calculate the skewness using Excel, follow these steps:

Step 1. Enter the data in the Excel sheet.

Step 2. Use the **SKEW function** to calculate the skewness.

Type the '=' (equal to) sign in the cell where the result is desired, say, 'E6' and enter the function name **SKEW** and then select the range of numbers, **B2: B31.**

Step 3. Press **Enter**, the result will be displayed in the cell (Figures 6.9 and 6.10).

The *histogram* is an effective graphical representation of skewness. Let us plot a histogram for the data related to rice production. Looking at the graph, it can be concluded that the distribution is approximately symmetrical (Figure 6.11).

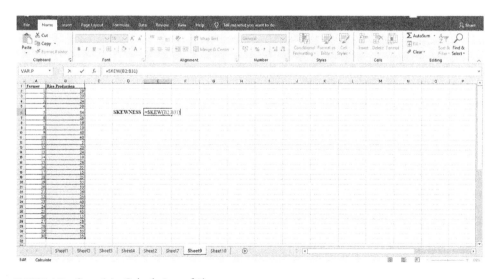

FIGURE 6.9   Step 1 in Calculation of Skewness

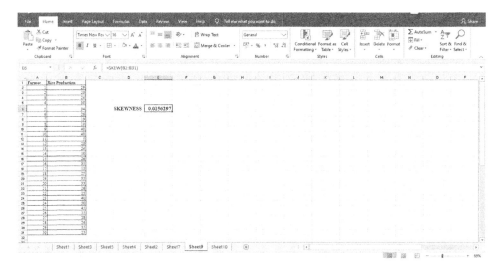

FIGURE 6.10 Step 2 in Calculation of Skewness

Note: Excel uses a different formula to calculate the skewness, due to which there can be a slight difference in the results as compared to the results using the Karl Pearson method.

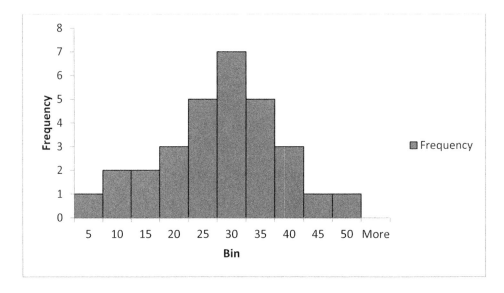

FIGURE 6.11 Histogram

6.6 Kurtosis

Another measure of descriptive statistics, 'kurtosis' defines the shape of a distribution's tail in relation to or in comparison with the normal distribution.[1] It is a measure of 'tailedness' of a distribution. It is denoted by β_2. The value of kurtosis is always compared to that of a normal distribution. It helps to identify whether the tails of the distribution include extreme values or outliers.

A heavy-tailed distribution has greater extreme values and high kurtosis. In other words, the heavier the tails, the higher the kurtosis. On the other hand, a light-tailed distribution has fewer extreme values and a low kurtosis or in other words, the lighter the tails, the lower the kurtosis. There are the following three categories of Kurtosis:

1. Mesokurtic
2. Leptokurtic
3. Platykurtic

6.6.1 Mesokurtic Distribution

A mesokurtic distribution refers to the distribution having kurtosis similar to that of normal distribution. The tails of such distribution are normal. It has a kurtosis equal to 3. There is equal distribution of items around the mean.

6.6.2 Leptokurtic Distribution

A leptokurtic distribution refers to the distribution having kurtosis greater than a mesokurtic distribution. 'Lepto' means thin or narrow which describes the long and narrow looking peak of the distribution. Such distributions have heavy tails on either side, indicating the presence of more extreme values than that of normal distribution. It has a kurtosis of greater than 3. There is too much concentration of items near the mean.

6.6.3 Platykurtic Distribution

A platykurtic distribution refers to the distribution having kurtosis lesser than a mesokurtic distribution. 'Platy' means flat or wide which describes the short and broad looking peak of the distribution. Such distributions have light tails on either side, indicating fewer or less extreme values than a normal distribution. It has a kurtosis of less than 3. There is less concentration of items near the mean.

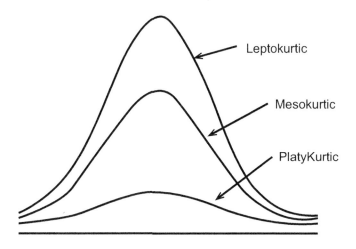

6.6.4 Excess Kurtosis

Kurtosis is sometimes described as excess kurtosis. Excess kurtosis is calculated by subtracting 3 from the kurtosis

Excess kurtosis = Kurtosis − 3

The table that follows summarizes the excess kurtosis in different distributions

Distribution	Kurtosis β_2	Excess kurtosis	Tails	Extreme value/Outliers
Mesokurtic/Normal distribution	3	3 − 3 = 0	Normal	Normal
Leptokurtic distribution	> 3	more than 0/ positive	Heavy	Greater than the normal distribution
Platykurtic distribution	< 3	less than 0/negative	Light	Less than the normal distribution

Point to Remember: Excel reports 'excess kurtosis'. Hence, the kurtosis of a normal distribution computed in Excel will equal 0.

Illustration

Fifteen contestants were asked to solve a puzzle. Time taken by each contestant is given next. Calculate the kurtosis and comment.

Contestants	Time Taken (in Minutes)
1	10
2	40
3	25
4	20
5	44
6	10
7	36
8	26
9	11
10	50
11	27
12	42
13	43
14	32
15	24

To calculate the kurtosis using Excel, follow these steps:

Step 1. Enter the data in the Excel sheet.
Step 2. Use the **KURT** function to calculate the kurtosis.

Type the '=' (equal to) sign in the cell where the result is desired say, 'E5' and enter the function name **KURT** and then select the range of numbers, that is, **B2: B16** (Figure 6.12).

Step 3. Press **Enter**, the result will be displayed in the cell (Figure 6.13).

Comment: Since excess kurtosis is less than 0, it is a platykurtic distribution. Such a distribution has light tails on either side, indicating fewer or less extreme values than of a normal distribution.

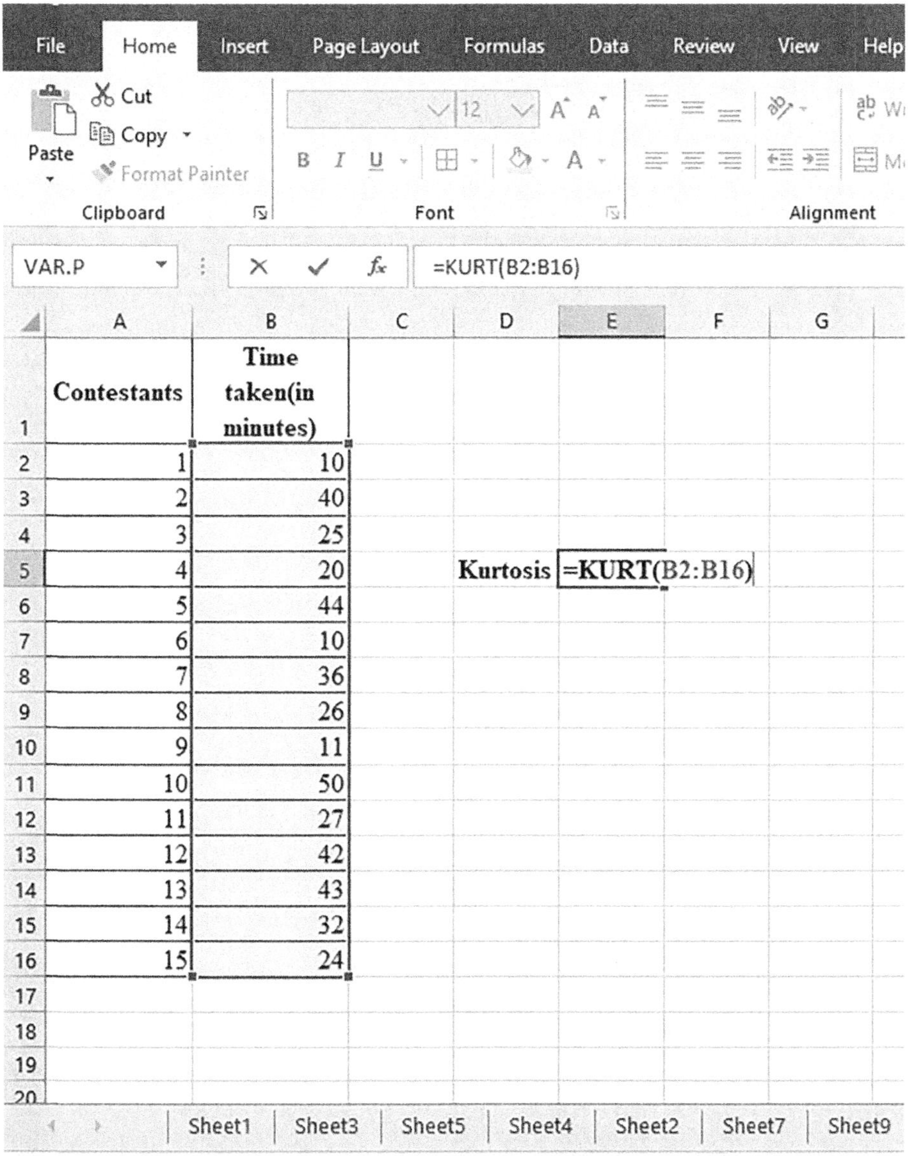

FIGURE 6.12   Step 1 in Calculation of Kurtosis

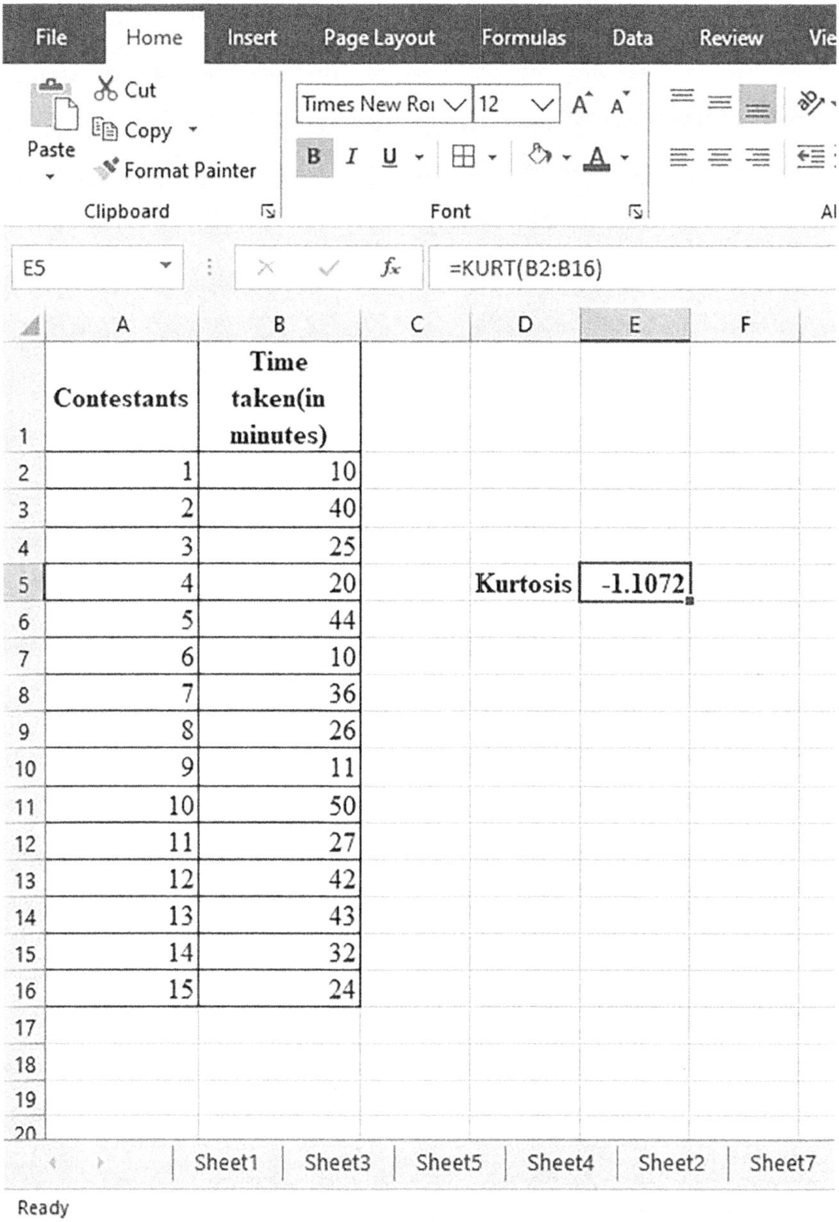

FIGURE 6.13 Step 2 in Calculation of Kurtosis

6.7 Data Analysis Using Excel

Another method to compute descriptive statistics using Excel is to use the data analysis option. It is one of the important and widely used tools to perform various financial, statistical, engineering, and mathematical functions to analyze data.

Illustration

The ratings for a movie given by 50 people between 1 and 5 (1 being the lowest and 5 being the highest) are given next. Calculate the descriptive statistics for the data.

Viewer	Rating	Viewer	Rating
1	5	26	5
2	3	27	1
3	5	28	5
4	4	29	1
5	2	30	3
6	2	31	3
7	2	32	5
8	3	33	4
9	1	34	2
10	3	35	3
11	3	36	1
12	5	37	4
13	3	38	4
14	1	39	1
15	3	40	1
16	3	41	4
17	1	42	1
18	1	43	4
19	4	44	3
20	4	45	3
21	1	46	1
22	3	47	5
23	3	48	2
24	2	49	4
25	2	50	4

To calculate the descriptive statistics using Excel, follow the steps shown in Figures 6.14 and 6.15.

Step 1. Enter the data in an Excel sheet.
Step 2. Go to the **Data** tab, and click on the option of **Data Analysis** in the analysis group on the right. (If you cannot find the **Data Analysis** button, follow the steps discussed in chapter 4 to load *Analysis ToolPak* in Excel.)
Step 3. A dialogue box will appear. Select the option of **Descriptive Statistics** from the list and click **OK.**
Step 4. A descriptive statistics dialogue box will appear.

• Fill in the following details

  Input range: The range of numbers for which the statistics are to be calculated is B2: B51.

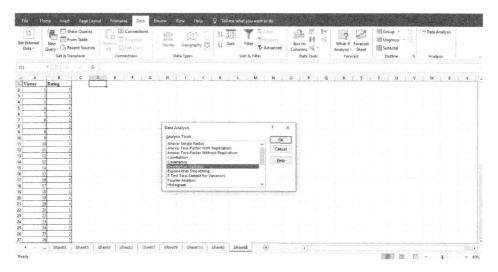

FIGURE 6.14   Step 1 in Data Analysis (Descriptive Statistics)

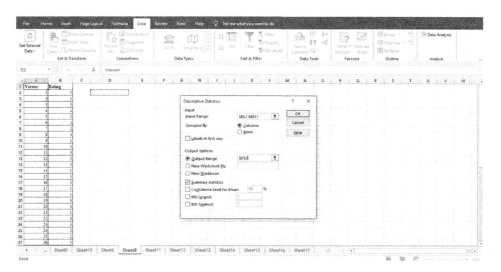

FIGURE 6.15   Step 2 in Data Analysis (Descriptive Statistics)

Output Range: The cell reference where the result is desired. Say, D1.

- Check on Summary statistics
- Click **OK**. The result will be displayed in the cell (Figure 6.16).

To recapitulate, this chapter delved into the common measures of dispersion which quantifies the variability in the dataset. The common measures covered were range, standard deviation, variance, and coefficient of variation. Besides, it also discussed the concept of skewness that measures asymmetry in the dataset determined by the shape of the distribution.

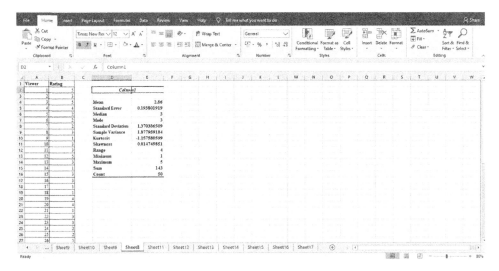

FIGURE 6.16 Step 3 in Data Analysis (Descriptive Statistics)

Likewise, kurtosis was also explained as a measure of tailedness in a distribution. Computations in general as well as using Excel functions of the measures discussed along with the interpretation of their results, remained the focal point. Chapters 5 and 6 combined introduced all the significant measures of descriptive statistics and covered all the basics needed to summarize any dataset.[2]

PRACTICE QUESTIONS

1. The table that follows summarizes the temperature (in Celsius) recorded for a month. Calculate range for the data.

Day	Temperature	Day	Temperature
1	31	16	29
2	28	17	28
3	24	18	30
4	33	19	25
5	28	20	28
6	27	21	28
7	33	22	27
8	29	23	31
9	29	24	30
10	26	25	29
11	32	26	27
12	29	27	33
13	33	28	26
14	32	29	24
15	33	30	27

2. The share prices for the last ten days of two firms, A and B, are next.

Share Prices (A) (₹)	Share Prices (B) (₹)
3,325	2,657
1,248	529
3,131	2,237
673	2,300
787	1,057
1,345	1,736
1,544	1,863
3,247	1,728
2,583	819

a) Calculate range for Firm A.
b) Calculate range for Firm B.
c) Which firm has comparatively stable prices?
d) Which firm has comparatively volatile prices?

3. The following table summarizes the GDP (in billion US Dollars) of 20 countries. Calculate the standard deviation and interpret the result.

Country	GDP (in Billion US Dollars)
1	740
2	9,600
3	95,400
4	15,500
5	8,000
6	3,200
7	8,600
8	9,700
9	12,600
10	7,850
11	9,600
12	3,800
13	1,120
14	9,200
15	12,400
16	7,500
17	4,800
18	13,400
19	8,300
20	2,060

4. The annual household income of ten individuals is given next:

Individual	Household Income (₹)
A	80,000
B	1,20,000
C	3,60,000
D	1,10,000
E	2,40,000
F	1,00,000
G	60,000
H	55,000
I	2,50,000
J	69,000

Calculate the standard deviation and variance for the data.

5. Calculate the standard deviation and coefficient of variation for the following data

Height (cm)	Weight (kg)
160	54
172	66
165	59
150	55
182	74
175	69

6. The ratings given by 40 people for a new feature on social media app are given next.

Ratings	
4	5
1	2
5	4
1	3
5	4
5	2
4	1
3	2
2	4
3	3
1	5
3	3
1	2
3	3
2	4

Ratings	
5	1
4	3
4	1
1	2
2	5

Is the data skewed? Calculate the skewness and comment.

7. The number of taxpayers in 30 different cities is given next. Calculate the skewness and kurtosis and comment.

City	No. of Taxpayers	City	No. of Taxpayers
1	1,93,764	16	4,37,250
2	2,55,622	17	2,16,456
3	3,93,160	18	2,48,884
4	3,91,913	19	2,44,819
5	2,08,184	20	2,00,691
6	1,47,657	21	2,20,692
7	3,66,196	22	1,98,851
8	1,95,910	23	2,89,528
9	1,10,765	24	2,05,525
10	3,32,423	25	1,35,678
11	2,68,776	26	2,09,044
12	2,46,520	27	1,91,041
13	1,62,412	28	3,15,933
14	2,07,902	29	4,96,468
15	3,47,370	30	1,90,576

8. The sales (₹) by a showroom in a month are given next. Calculate descriptive statistics using the data analysis option.

Sales (₹)		
30,000	68,300	31,800
78,000	28,400	43,900
34,500	89,100	64,400
11,700	12,500	1,02,000
2,31,000	45,000	68,900
84,200	22,400	14,900
51,300	33,400	53,500
29,900	68,700	30,200
56,300	32,000	25,900
28,400	81,800	84,000

Notes

1 Originally the kurtosis has been defined as a measure of peakedness or flatness. This interpretation was settled to be incorrect and proved wrong by Dr Peter Westfall in his article Kurtosis as Peakedness, 1905–2014. R.I.P, The American Statistician, Vol 68, Issue 3, 2014. In his article, Westfall argued that Kurtosis tells virtually nothing about the shape of the peak – its only unambiguous interpretation is in terms of tail extremity; i.e., either existing outliers (for the sample kurtosis) or propensity to produce outliers (for the kurtosis of a probability distribution). He also laid down numerous examples proving why kurtosis should never be defined in terms of peakedness. The new definition states that the kurtosis is the measure of the combined sizes of the tails of the distribution relative to the normal distribution.

2 The summary statistics presented in Figure 6.16 has an entry called standard error which will be explained in a later chapter on regression.

7

CORRELATION COEFFICIENT

Learning Objectives

After reading this chapter, the readers will be able to understand

- The two measures of association – covariance and correlation
- The concept of covariance
- The concept of correlation and how it is different from covariance
- Methods to estimate correlation coefficients – Pearson's and Spearman's methods
- The use of Excel in calculating correlation coefficients

In this chapter, we will introduce the concept, application, and computation of another set of descriptive measures that relate to an association between two or more variables. To illustrate, we might be interested in finding out the sales of ice creams as the temperature rises. The measures that attempt to quantify such a relationship between the variables and further help to answer the strength of the relationship are called *measures of association*. In this chapter, we will be studying two such measures, which are closely related to each other. These are *covariance* and *correlation*.

7.1 Covariance

Covariance is a statistical measure that analyzes the *linear relationship* between two random variables. It evaluates how the two variables vary together or covary. For instance, what happens to the other variable if one variable goes up, down, or remains constant? Accordingly, we can have the following types of linear relationships or covariances:

- A *positive covariance* indicates a direct relationship between the variables; the two variables tend to move together in the same direction, either upward or downward. So, when one

DOI: 10.4324/9781003398127-7

variable increases, the other variable increases or when one variable decreases, the other variable decreases.

- A *negative covariance* indicates an inverse relationship between variables; the two variables tend to move away or in the opposite direction from each other. So, when one variable increases, the other one decreases or vice versa.
- A *zero covariance* indicates that if the two variables are independent or unrelated, the covariance will be zero (0). However, a zero covariance does not necessarily imply that the variables are independent. A zero covariance means no linear relationship between the two variables and does not exhibit any pattern.

It may be reiterated that the covariance measures the directional relationship only, and we are, therefore, interested merely in the sign of the covariance value and thus ignore the size of the number. We cannot interpret anything about the strength of the relationship from the computations arrived.

For two random variables X and Y, the covariance (denoted by Cov (X, Y) or σ_{xy}) is calculated using the following formula. The unit of measurement of covariance, nevertheless, is the product of the units of individual variables. For instance, the unit of covariance measurement between height (in cm) and weight (in kg) will be cm $\times$ kg.

$$\mathrm{Cov}(X,Y) = \frac{\sum_{i=1}^{N}\left(x_i - \bar{X}\right)\left(y_i - \bar{Y}\right)}{N}$$

Here,

Σ = Sigma/operator for summation
$\bar{X}$ = Arithmetic mean of random variable X
$\bar{Y}$ = Arithmetic mean of random variable Y
N = Number of observations

Important note: When we calculate the covariance for a sample to infer about the population as a whole from which it is drawn, we use $n - 1$ instead of n in the denominator.

Therefore, the population covariance (σ_{xy}) is = $\dfrac{\sum_{i=1}^{N}\left(x_i - \mu_x\right)\left(y_i - \mu_y\right)}{N}$

And the sample covariance (s_{xy}) is = $\dfrac{\sum_{i=1}^{n}\left(x_i - \bar{x}\right)\left(y_i - \bar{y}\right)}{n - 1}$

Here, μ_x = population mean of random variable X, μ_y = population mean of random variable Y, $\bar{x}$ = sample mean of random variable X, $\bar{y}$ = sample mean of a random variable Y, N = number of observations in the population, n = number of observations in a sample.

Illustration

Sensex and Nifty 50 are the two benchmark stock market indices used in India. Both indices measure the stock market's overall performance and are indicators of the strength of the Indian economy. The following table summarizes the monthly rates of return on Sensex (X) and Nifty 50 (Y) for the year 2019. Calculate covariance and interpret the results.

| Time Period (2019) | Rates of Return (in Percentages) | |
	Sensex	Nifty 50
January	0.52%	0.35%
February	−1.07%	0.32%
March	7.82%	4.58%
April	0.93%	3.13%
May	1.75%	−0.58%
June	−0.80%	2.34%
July	−4.86%	−2.47%
August	−0.40%	−4.46%
September	3.57%	1.41%
October	3.78%	3.37%
November	1.66%	4.23%
December	1.13%	1.11%

Source: www.bseindia.com/, https://www1.nseindia.com/

First Method (Direct Method)

Time	Sensex (X)	Nifty 50 (Y)	$X - \bar{X}$	$Y - \bar{Y}$	$\left(X - \bar{X}\right) \times \left(Y - \bar{Y}\right)$
January	0.52	0.35	−0.65	−0.76	0.00494
February	−1.07	0.32	−2.24	−0.79	0.017696
March	7.82	4.58	6.65	3.47	0.230755
April	0.93	3.13	−0.24	2.02	−0.00485
May	1.75	−0.58	0.58	−1.69	−0.0098
June	−0.8	2.34	−1.97	1.23	−0.02423
July	−4.86	−2.47	−6.03	−3.58	0.215874
August	−0.4	−4.46	−1.57	−5.57	0.087449
September	3.57	1.41	2.4	0.3	0.0072
October	3.78	3.37	2.61	2.26	0.058986
November	1.66	4.23	0.49	3.12	0.015288
December	1.13	1.11	−0.04	0	0
Total	14.03	13.33			0.5993

$$\mathrm{Cov}(X,Y) = \frac{\sum_{i=1}^{N}\left(x_i - \bar{X}\right)\left(y_i - \bar{Y}\right)}{N}$$

Here, $\bar{X} = 14.03/12 = 1.169$ per cent

$\bar{Y} = 13.33/12 = 1.111$ per cent

$\sum_{i=1}^{N}\left(x_i - \bar{X}\right)\left(y_i - \bar{Y}\right) = 0.5993$ per cent

$N = 12$

$\mathrm{Cov}\,(X,\,Y) = \dfrac{0.5993\%}{12}$

$= 0.04994$ per cent

Second Method (Using Excel)

Use the **COVARIANCE.P** function to calculate the covariance of a population. If using the entire population is not possible, we can calculate the covariance of a sample drawn from the population using the Excel function **COVARIANCE.S.** To calculate the covariance using Excel, follow the stated steps:

Step 1. Enter the returns on Sensex (X) and Nifty 50 (Y) in the Excel sheet.

Step 2. Use the **COVARIANCE.P** function to calculate the covariance of the population. Type the '=' (equal to) sign in the cell where the result is desired, say, 'C15', and enter the function name **COVARIANCE.P** and then select the cell range of numbers (data points of variable X), that is, **B2:B13** for **Array 1** and the cell range of numbers (data points of variable Y), that is, **C2:C13** for **Array 2**. The formula will be =**COVARIANCE.P (B2:B13, C2:C13)** for the covariance of population and =**COVARIANCE.S (B2:B13, C2:C13)** for the covariance of a sample, as remarked in Figures 7.1 and 7.2.

Step 3. Press **Enter** for the result.

Interpretation of Results

* A positive covariance of 0.04994 per cent indicates a direct linear relationship between the variables, that is, returns on Sensex (X) and Nifty (Y)
* As the returns on Sensex rise, the returns on Nifty rise and vice versa
* As the returns on Sensex decrease, so do Nifty's returns and vice versa
* The returns tend to move in the same direction, upward or downward.

As mentioned earlier, the limitation of using covariance is that it does not tell anything about the strength of the relationship between the variables. Thus, covariance is not an appropriate measure when it comes to assessing the strength of the relationship. To overcome this limitation, we study correlation which deals with the strength of the relationship.

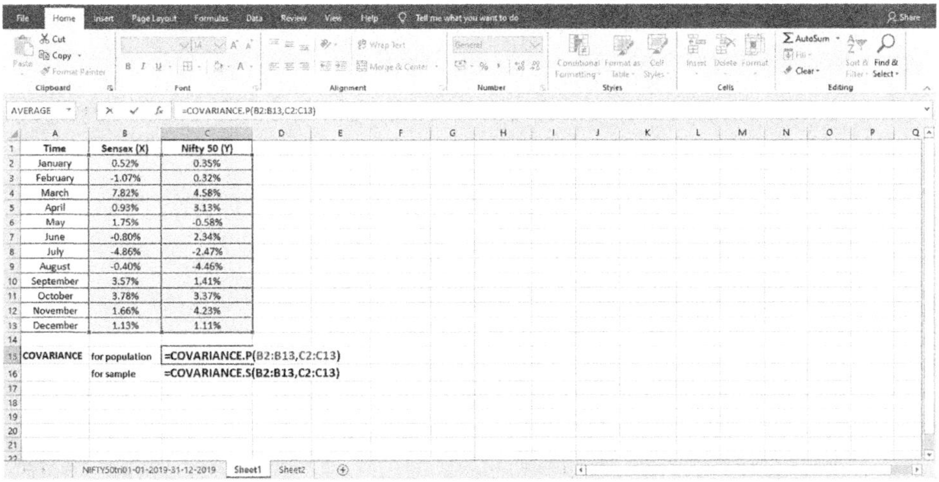

FIGURE 7.1 Step 1 in Calculation of Covariance

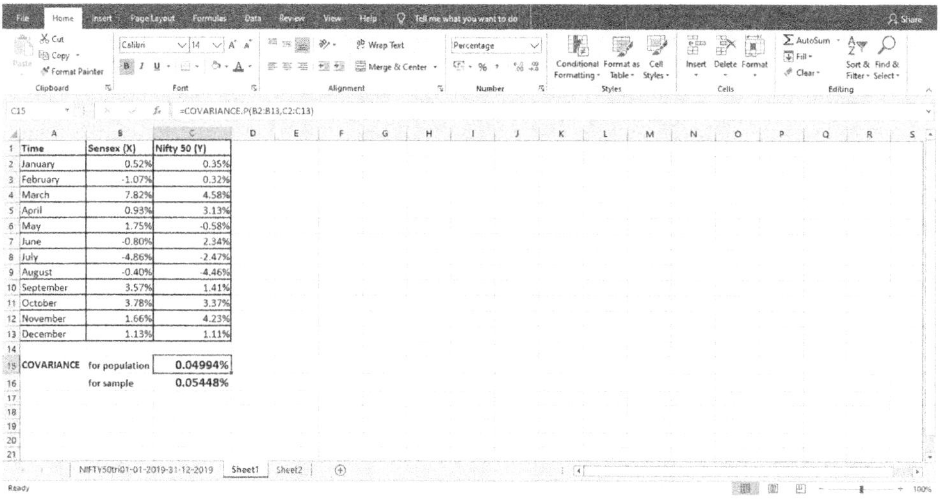

FIGURE 7.2   Step 2 in Calculation of Covariance

7.2   Correlation

Correlation is a statistical technique that measures the direction and the strength of the linear relationship between the variables. The study of correlation is important as it quantifies the degree of association between the variables and shows how strongly the variables are related. If two variables are correlated it means that if one variable increases or decreases, then the other variable also changes in the same or opposite direction besides assessing the strength of the relationship. An example of correlation may be the increase in the price of a stock of a company and an increase in the company's profitability and revenue.

However, *correlation does not necessarily mean causation*. That is, correlation in no way confirms that variable X causes variable Y to vary or vice versa. For example, we may observe that when ice cream sales increase during summers, the groundwater level reduces. Does that mean the consumption of ice cream causes depletion in the groundwater level or vice versa? In reality, this does not make any sense. It is the third factor, that is, summer season, which influences the movement in both variables. As it may be possible that due to the increase in temperature during summer, people tend to eat more ice cream, and the groundwater begins to evaporate due to hot temperature, leading to depletion of water level. Therefore, correlation does not imply any causal relationship or cause and effect relationship between the variables.

There can be both linear and non-linear relationships that can exist between two variables, but in this chapter, we restrict ourselves mainly to the linear one. Correlation can be categorized as follows:

- A *positive correlation* indicates a direct relationship between the variables. The two variables tend to move upward or downward in the same direction. So, when one variable increases, the other variable increases, or when one variable decreases, the other variable decreases. It is shown as an upward sloping line indicating the movement of the variables in the same direction (Figure 7.3).

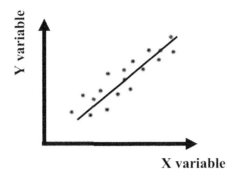

FIGURE 7.3 Positive Correlation

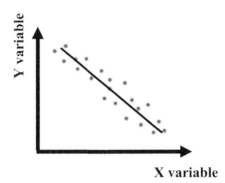

FIGURE 7.4 Negative Correlation

• A *negative correlation* indicates an inverse relationship between variables; the two variables tend to move away or in the opposite direction from each other. So, when one variable increases, the other one decreases. It is shown as a downward sloping line indicating the movement of the variables in the opposite direction (Figure 7.4).

• A *zero correlation* indicates no correlation between the datasets at all. However, a zero correlation does not necessarily imply that the variables are independent. A zero correlation will suggest that there is *no linear relationship* between the two variables, and they do not exhibit any pattern. The widely scattered points show it, and there is no upward rising or downward sloping line (Figure 7.5).

The *correlation coefficient* determines the degree of association between datasets. A correlation coefficient expresses or defines the strength of the association between variables, whether it is strong or weak or non-existent. The value of the coefficient of correlation lies between +1 and −1. The positive and negative signs will indicate the direction of the relationship, that is, direct or inverse. The closer the value of the coefficient is to 1 (+ve or −ve), the stronger the direct or inverse relationship.

If the value of the correlation coefficient attains the value of +1, it indicates a *perfect positive correlation*. It means when one variable increases by some percentage, the other variable also increases at the same percentage, or if one variable decreases by some percentage, the other variable also decreases at the same percentage. The correlation coefficient value between 0

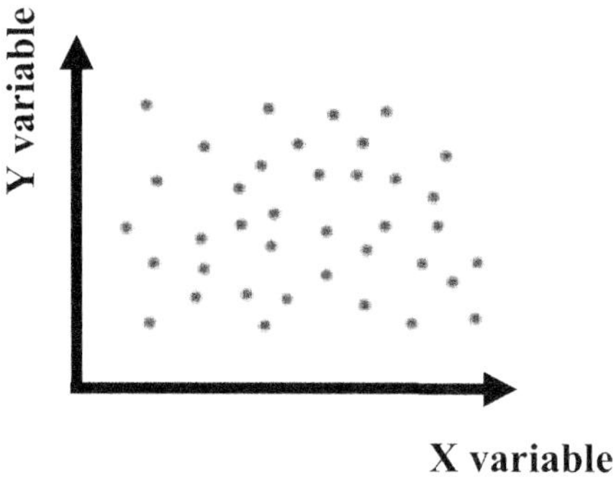

FIGURE 7.5 No Correlation

and 1 also indicates a *positive correlation*, although the change is not identical between the variables. Contrarily, the closer the value of the coefficient is to 0, the weaker is the relationship. If the coefficient of correlation is equal to 0, it indicates that the variables are uncorrelated or have no linear relationship. Generally, the coefficient of correlation of | 0.5 | and above shows a strong relationship between variables.

Correspondingly, the correlation coefficient of −1 indicates a *perfect negative correlation*. It means when one variable increases by some percentage, the other variable decreases identically. The values between 0 and −1 indicate a *negative correlation*. It means when one variable increases by some percentage, the other variable decreases but with lesser percentage, or if one variable decreases by some percentage, the other variable increases but with a lesser percentage.

As mentioned before, the correlation coefficient of 0 indicates *no correlation between the variables*. It means that the change in one variable is not linked to another variable. The correlation coefficient can be estimated with the help of the following methods.

7.3 Karl Pearson's Coefficient of Correlation

Karl Pearson's correlation coefficient is the most widely used method to measure the correlation between two variables. It is also referred to as the *Pearson product-moment correlation coefficient* denoted by 'r'. Pearson correlation coefficient has no unit of measurement. Thus, relationships across the variables can be measured regardless of the unit of measurement they are in. For example, the correlation coefficient between height (in cm) and weight (in kg) is neither expressed in cm nor kg. It is a number independent of the unit of measurement.

It may be noted that the Pearson Coefficient is also independent of the change in the scale and the origin of the variables. Thus, the magnitude of the coefficient is not affected by the change in the unit of measurement of the variables. For example, the correlation coefficient between height (in cm) and weight (in kg) will be equal to the correlation coefficient between height (in m) and weight (in g).

Karl Pearson's coefficient of correlation between two variables, X and Y, is calculated using the formula given next:

$$r_{xy} = \frac{\textit{Covariance between } X \textit{ and } Y}{\textit{Product of standard deviation of } X \textit{ and standard deviation of } Y} = \frac{\sigma_{xy}}{\sigma_x \sigma_y}$$

or, $r_{xy} = \dfrac{\sum_{i=1}^{N}\left(x_i - \bar{X}\right)\left(y_i - \bar{Y}\right)}{\sqrt{\sum_{i=1}^{N}\left(x_i - \bar{X}\right)^2 * \sum_{i=1}^{n}\left(y_i - \bar{Y}\right)^2}}$

Here,

x_i = i[th] observation of X variable
y_i = i[th] observation of Y variable
Σ = Sigma/operator for summation
$\bar{X}$ = arithmetic mean of random variable X
$\bar{Y}$ = arithmetic mean of random variable Y
N = no. of observations

or, $r_{xy} = \dfrac{N\left(\sum x_i y_i\right) - \left(\sum x_i\right)\left(\sum y_i\right)}{\sqrt{\left[N\sum x_i^2 - \left(\sum x_i\right)^2\right]\left[N\sum y_i^2 - \left(\sum y_i\right)^2\right]}}$

Here,

$\sum x_i$ = Sum of all observations of X variable
$\sum y_i$ = Sum of all observations of Y variable
$\sum x_i y_i$ = Sum of the product of X and Y
$\sum x_i^2$ = Sum of squares of X variable
$\sum y_i^2$ = Sum of the square of Y variable,
N = number of observations

Illustration

In the previous illustration of the monthly rates of return on Sensex (X) and Nifty 50 (Y) for the year 2019, we found out that there is a direct linear relationship between the variables, that is, returns on Sensex (X) and returns on Nifty (Y). But we could not interpret how strong is the relation between the variables. Now let us compute the correlation coefficient to determine the strength of this relationship.

First Method (Direct Method)

Time	Sensex (X)	Nifty 50 (Y)	X^2	Y^2	XY
January	0.52%	0.35%	0.0027%	0.0012%	0.0018%
February	−1.07%	0.32%	0.0114%	0.0010%	−0.0034%
March	7.82%	4.58%	0.6115%	0.2098%	0.3582%
April	0.93%	3.13%	0.0086%	0.0980%	0.0291%
May	1.75%	−0.58%	0.0306%	0.0034%	−0.0102%
June	−0.80%	2.34%	0.0064%	0.0548%	−0.0187%
July	−4.86%	−2.47%	0.2362%	0.0610%	0.1200%
August	−0.40%	−4.46%	0.0016%	0.1989%	0.0178%
September	3.57%	1.41%	0.1274%	0.0199%	0.0503%
October	3.78%	3.37%	0.1429%	0.1136%	0.1274%
November	1.66%	4.23%	0.0276%	0.1789%	0.0702%
December	1.13%	1.11%	0.0128%	0.0123%	0.0125%
Total	**14.03%**	**13.33%**	**1.219%**	**0.952%**	**0.755%**

Now, $\Sigma x = 0.1403$, $\Sigma y = 0.1333$, $\Sigma xy = 0.00755$, $\Sigma x^2 = 0.01219$, $\Sigma y^2 = 0.00952$

Substituting these values in the following formula:

$$r = \frac{N(\Sigma xy) - (\Sigma x)(\Sigma y)}{\sqrt{[N\Sigma x^2 - (\Sigma x)^2][N\Sigma y2 - (\Sigma x)^2]}}$$

$$\text{we get} = \frac{12 * 0.00755 - 0.1403 * 0.1333}{\sqrt{\left[12 * 0.01219 - (0.1403)^2\right]\left[12 * 0.00952 - (0.1333)^2\right]}}$$

$$= \frac{0.0906 - 0.01870}{\sqrt{[0.14628 - 0.01968][0.11424 - 0.017769]}}$$

$$= \frac{0.0719}{\sqrt{[0.1266][0.09647]}}$$

$$= \frac{0.0719}{\sqrt{0.012213}}$$

$$= \frac{0.0719}{0.1105} = 0.650$$

Second Method (Using Excel)

Use the **CORREL** function to calculate the correlation between the two datasets. To calculate the correlation using Excel, follow these steps:

Step 1. Enter the returns on Sensex (X) and Nifty 50 (Y) in the Excel sheet.
Step 2. Use the **CORREL** function to calculate the correlation. Type the '=' (equal to) sign in the cell where the result is desired, say, 'C15' and enter the function name '**CORREL**' and then select the cell range of numbers (data points of variable X), that is, **B2: B13** for **Array 1** and the cell range of numbers (data points of variable Y), that is, **C2: C13** for **Array 2**. **The formula will be =CORREL (B2: B13, C2: C13),** as shown in Figure 7.6.
Step 3. Press **Enter**. The result will be displayed in the cell as exhibited in Figure 7.7.

Third Method (Using Different Function in Excel)

Use the **PEARSON** function to calculate the Pearson product-moment correlation coefficient between the two datasets. The steps are as follows:

Step 1. Enter the returns on Sensex (X) and Nifty 50 (Y) in the Excel sheet.
Step 2. Use the **PEARSON** function to calculate the correlation.
Type the '=' (equal to) sign in the cell where the result is desired, say, 'C15' and enter the function name **PEARSON** and then select the cell range of numbers (data points of variable X), that is, **B2: B13** for **Array 1** and the cell range of numbers (data points of variable Y), that is, **C2: C13** for **Array 2**.
The formula will be =**PEARSON (B2: B13, C2: C13),** as shown in Figure 7.8.
Step 3. Press **Enter** for the results in the cell (Figure 7.9).

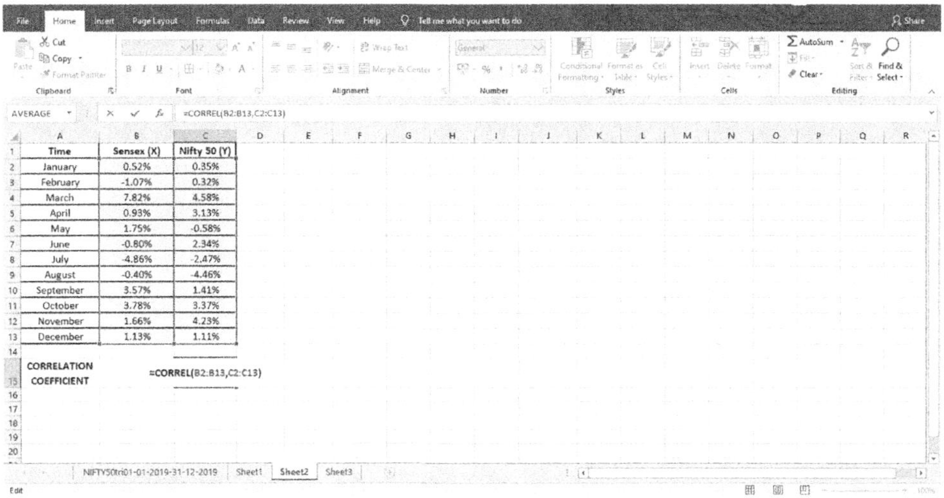

FIGURE 7.6   Step 1 in Calculation of Correlation

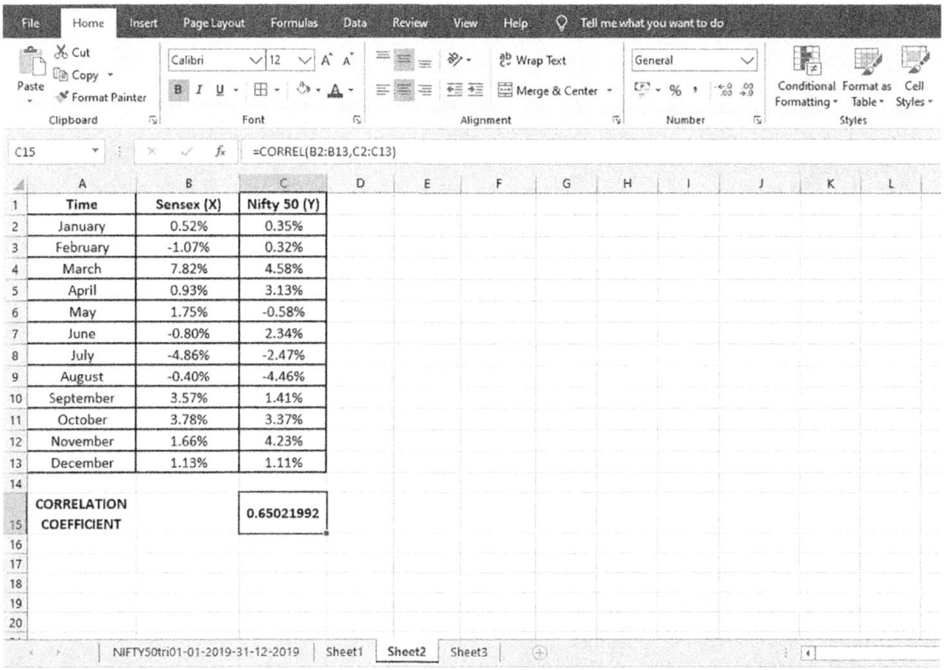

FIGURE 7.7   Step 2 in Calculation of Correlation

Fourth Method (Using Data Analysis in Excel)

There is another method to compute the correlation coefficient using Excel by clicking the option of data analysis. To calculate the correlation using **Data Analysis**, follow these steps:

Step 1. Enter the returns on Sensex (*X*) and Nifty 50 (*Y*) in the Excel sheet.

Step 2. Go to the **Data** tab, and click on the option of **Data Analysis** in the **Analysis** group on the right side.

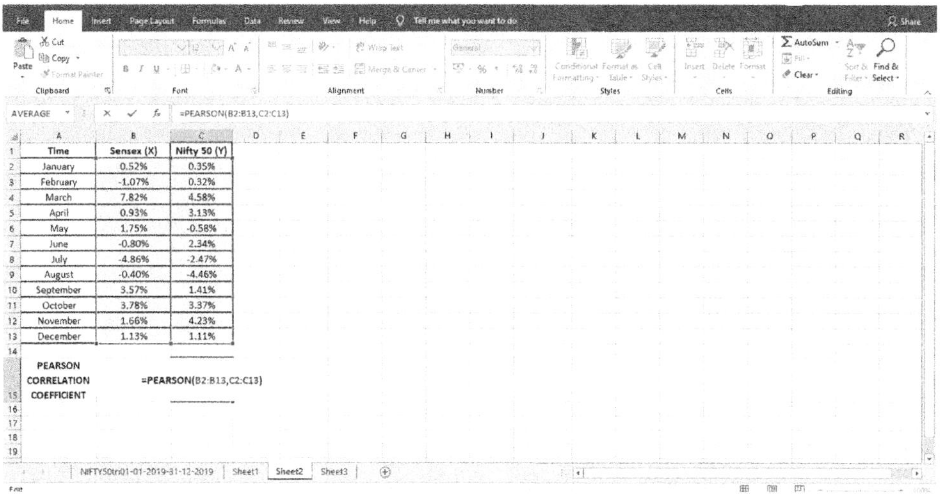

FIGURE 7.8   Step 1 in Calculation of the Pearson Correlation Coefficient

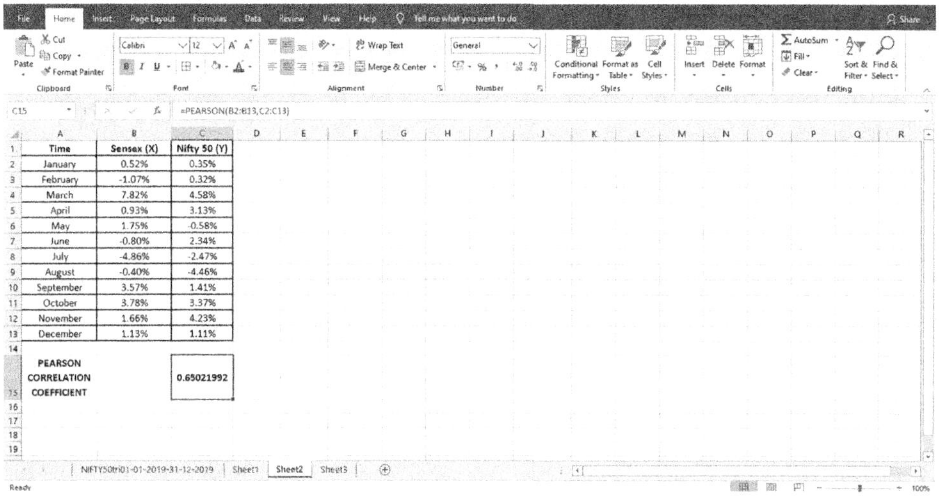

FIGURE 7.9   Step 2 in Calculation of Pearson Correlation Coefficient

Step 3. A dialogue box will appear. Select the **Correlation** option from the list and click **OK** (Figure 7.10).

Step 4. A **Correlation** dialogue box will appear. Fill in the following details

- **Input range**: The cell range of numbers for which the correlation is to be calculated, that is, B1: C13
- **Labels in the first row:** Check on **Labels in the first row.** Remember if you choose the label/name of the variables, that is, Sensex and Nifty 50, in the input range, then check the box **Labels in the first row**
- **Output Range**: The cell reference where the result is desired, say, E1, as in Figure 7.11

Step 5. Click **OK**. The result will be displayed in the cell (Figure 7.12).

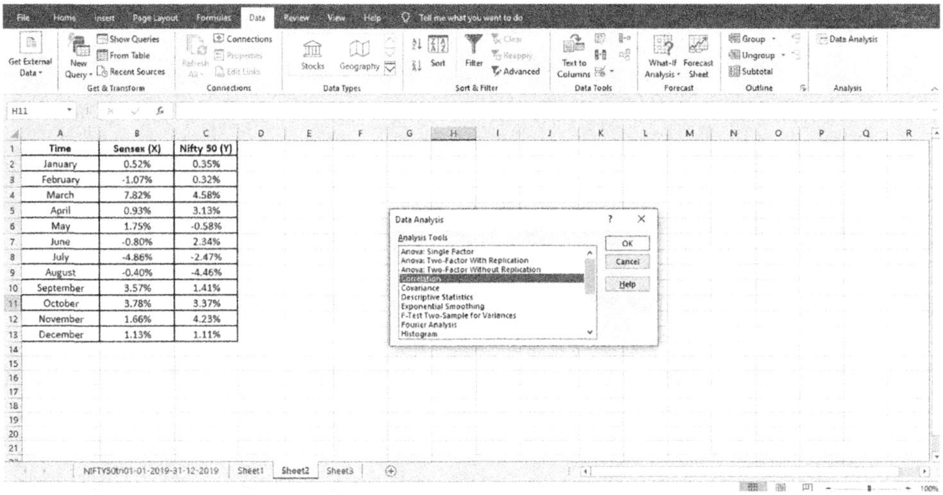

FIGURE 7.10   Step 1 in Calculation of Correlation

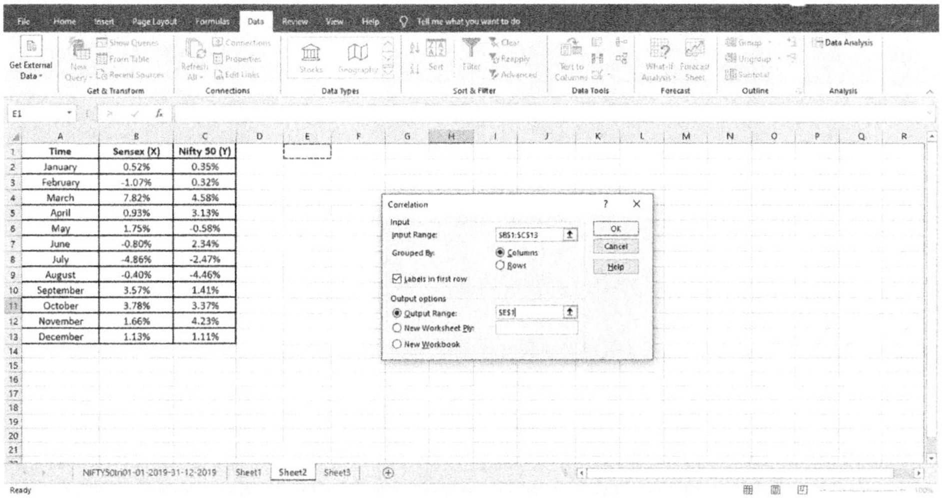

FIGURE 7.11   Step 2 in Calculation of Correlation Using Data Analysis

Interpretation of Results

We can see that the calculated correlation coefficient is the same irrespective of the method chosen. The calculated estimate of **+0.650** suggests:

- The **+** sign describes a *direct or positive linear relationship* between the variables: returns on Sensex (*X*) and Returns on Nifty (*Y*). It signifies that the indices returns tend to move in the same direction, upward or downward

- Correlation coefficient of *0.650 (r > 0.5) indicates strong positive correlation between the datasets.* It means that when the returns on one index *increase* by 100 per cent, then the returns on another index *also increase* but by a lesser percentage, that is, by 65 per cent or

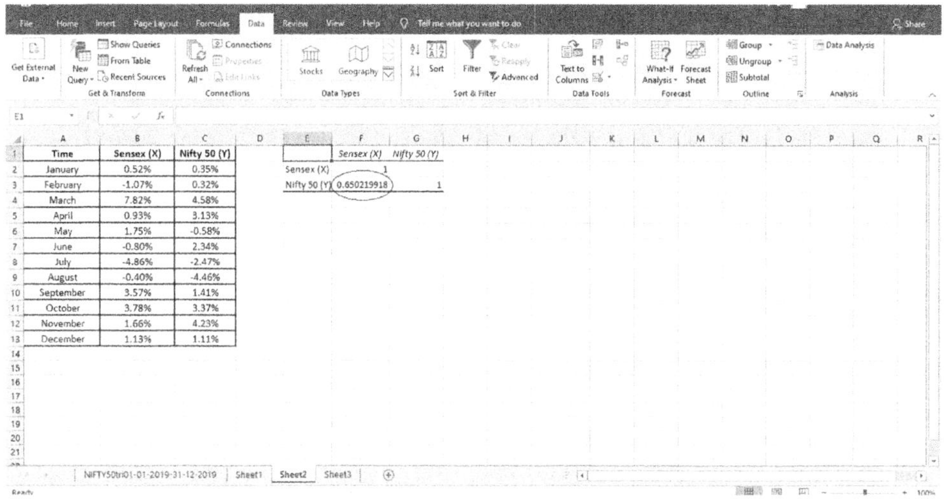

FIGURE 7.12 Step 3 in Calculation of Correlation Using Data Analysis

when the return on one index *decreases* by 100 per cent, then the returns on other *also decreases* but by lesser percentage, that is, 65 per cent.

We can also get an idea of the relationship between two variables with the help of a scatter plot in Excel, the preparation of which has already been explained earlier (Chapter 4). The *direction of the data points* helps to determine in what direction the variables change together or covary.

- An *upward sloping straight line* indicates a *positive or direct linear relationship*. The two variables tend to move in the same direction
- A *downward sloping straight line* indicates a *negative or inverse linear relationship*. The two variables tend to move away or in the opposite direction.

The *degree of the data points closeness* helps us to examine the strength of the relationship between variables, which is given next:

- If the data points lie on a straight line, there is a perfect correlation between the variables
- If the data points are close or near to the line, then there is a strong relationship between the variables
- There is a low correlation between the variables if the data points are widely scattered or dispersed around the line
- If the data points are widely scattered, and there is no upward rising or downward sloping line, the datasets are said to have no linear relationship.

The following scatter plot, as in Figure 7.13, illustrates the direction and strength of the relationship between the monthly rate of returns on Sensex (*X*) and Nifty 50 (*Y*). A perusal of the fitted trendline suggests the following:

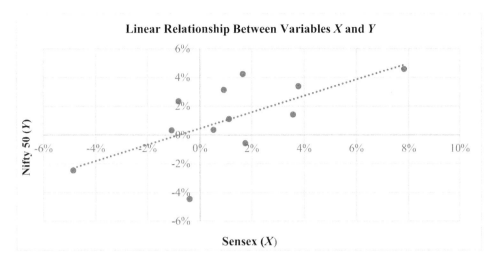

FIGURE 7.13 Scatter Plot Showing Linear Relationship Between the Monthly Rate of Returns on Sensex (X) and Nifty 50 (Y)

- The shape or the pattern of the data points follows a linear pattern
- The *trendline* which exhibits the nature of the trend that exists between the two variables is upward sloping to the right, indicating a direct relationship or positive correlation
- It shows that when returns on one index move in a specific direction, the returns on the other index tend to move in the same direction
- The data points scattered around the upward sloping line show the variables have a strong positive relationship.

Check Your Understanding

Does the strong positive correlation mean that the increase in the returns in Nifty 50 causes the increase in the returns of BSE Sensex, or the increase in returns of BSE Sensex causes the increase in the returns of Nifty 50?

   Ans. No. Correlation does not imply any cause-effect relationship.

7.4   Spearman's Coefficient of Correlation

The Spearman correlation coefficient, unlike Pearson's correlation coefficient method, is calculated for the data measured on ordinal or rank scale. Denoted by 'r_s' or Greek letter rho 'ρ', this method measures both the direction and strength of the monotonic relationship between the rankings in the two datasets. It is a non-parametric measure of correlation, giving a numerical value between +1 and −1. As discussed before,

- $r_s = +1$ shows perfect positive relationship
- $r_s = -1$ shows perfect negative relationship
- $r_s = 0$ no correlation

- The closer the value of the coefficient is to 1 (+ve or −ve), the higher the similarity in rankings of the two datasets
- The closer the value of the coefficient is to 0, the lower the similarity in the rankings of the two datasets.

The steps to calculate the Spearman coefficient of correlation are:

Step 1. The ranks are assigned to all the values in both datasets in the specified manner as shown. The first rank (1st) is given either to the highest value in both the datasets or to the lowest value in both the datasets. The following ranks are given accordingly in the same manner. In an example of marks of seven students in an exam, the assigned ranks are shown next.

Student	Scores	Rank
A	80	2
B	70	3
C	40	5
D	60	4
E	10	7
F	20	6
G	90	1

However, if two or more observations are identical, and there is a tie for the same rank, then the rank assigned is the *mean of the ranks that they occupy*. In the example given next, ranks are assigned to the scores of seven students in an exam out of which two students obtained the same score of 80.

Student	Scores	Rank
A	80	2.5
B	70	4
C	80	2.5
D	60	6
E	50	7
F	65	5
G	90	1

In this case, there is a tie between student A and student C for the second rank, with a score of 80 in both cases. Here, each of them with identical scores will be assigned the mean of the ranks $\dfrac{\left(2^{nd} + 3^{rd}\right)}{2} = \mathbf{2.5^{th}}$ rank. Now, the next highest score will be assigned the 4th rank, as student A and C together occupy the mean of 2nd and 3rd rank.

Step 2. The difference between the ranks of the two values in each dataset is then calculated, denoted by *d*.

Step 3. The square of the differences (d^2) is computed, and then, the sum of all the squared values is obtained.

Step 4. The Spearman coefficient of correlation is calculated using the following formula:

$$r_s = 1 - \frac{6\sum d_i^2}{n(n^2 - 1)}$$

Here,

d_i = Difference between ranks of the ith pair of the two variables,
$\sum d_i^2$ = Sum of the squares of the difference between ranks,
n = number of observations in each dataset

Illustration

Final year students of a college got placed in different companies. The following table summarizes students' marks (in percentages) at the graduate level and their first salary (per annum). Calculate the Spearman coefficient of correlation to find out the association between the two variables.

Result in % (Graduation)	First Salary (Per Annum; ₹)
76	5,65,000
44	5,70,000
80	6,50,000
87	9,20,000
90	8,60,000
92	7,80,000
66	6,30,000
57	4,00,000
97	8,20,000
88	9,50,000

First Method (Direct Method)

Result (Graduation; X)	First Salary (Y; ₹)	Rank (X)	Rank (Y)	d	d^2
76	5,65,000	7	9	−2	4
44	5,70,000	10	8	2	4
80	6,50,000	6	6	0	0
87	9,20,000	5	2	3	9
90	8,60,000	3	3	0	0
92	7,80,000	2	5	−3	9

Result (Graduation; X)	First Salary (Y; ₹)	Rank (X)	Rank (Y)	d	d²
66	6,30,000	8	7	1	1
57	4,00,000	9	10	−1	1
97	8,20,000	1	4	−3	9
88	9,50,000	4	1	3	9
					46

$\Sigma d^2 = 46$, $n = 10$

Substituting these values in the following formula:

$$r_s = 1 - \frac{6\Sigma d^2}{n\left(n^2 - 1\right)}$$

$$r_s = 1 - \frac{6 * 46}{10\left(10^2 - 1\right)}$$

$$= 1 - \frac{276}{990}$$

$$= 1 - 0.27878$$

$$= 0.7212$$

Second Method (Using Excel)

There is no direct or inbuilt function to calculate the Spearman coefficient of correlation using Excel. To compute the coefficient, we will first rank the values in each dataset and then calculate the simple correlation between the ranks of the data. To do this, we will use the **RANK** and **CORREL** function to calculate the Spearman correlation coefficient between the two datasets.
To calculate the spearman coefficient, follow these steps:

Step 1. Enter the result score and amount of the first salary in columns in the Excel sheet.
Step 2. Use the **RANK** function to rank the data.

1. To rank the variable X (Scores)

    a) Type the '=' (equal to) sign in the cell where the result is desired, say, 'C2', and enter the function name **RANK**.
    b) Select the cell number of the first value in variable X, that is, A2, and then select the cell range of numbers (all data points of variable X), that is, absolute reference, **$A$2: $A$11** as a reference of the list of numbers against which the rank is to be assigned.
    c) Type '**0**' to assign the first rank to the highest value, that is, to rank in descending order.

The formula will be =RANK (A2, $A$2: $A$11,0)

    d) Press **Enter** (see Figures 7.14 and 7.15).

The result will appear in cell C2. Then click on the fill handle (the small black square in the bottom right corner when you select the cell) and drag it vertically to rank for the other values automatically.

2. Similarly, to rank the variable Y (first salary):

a) Type the '=' (equal to) sign in the cell where the result is desired, say 'D2', and enter the function name **RANK**.

b) Select the cell number of the first value in variable X, that is, **B2,** and then select the cell range of numbers (all data points of variable X), that is, absolute reference **$B$2: $B$11** as a reference of the list of numbers against which the rank is to be assigned.

c) Type **0** to assign the first rank to the highest value, that is, to rank in descending order.

The formula will be =RANK (B2, $B$2: $B$11,0).

d) Press **Enter** (see Figures 7.14 and 7.15).

The result will appear in cell D2. Then click on the fill handle (the small black square in the bottom right corner when you select the cell) and drag it vertically to rank for the other values automatically.

Step 3. Finally, to compute the Spearman correlation, follow the mentioned steps:

1. Type the '=' (equal to) sign in the cell where the result is desired say, 'C15' and enter the function name **CORREL**.

2. Then select the cell range of numbers (data points of variable X), that is, **C2: C13** for **Array 1** and the cell range of numbers (data points of variable Y), that is, **D2: D13** for **Array 2.** The formula will be **=CORREL (C2: C13, D2: D13).**

Step 4. Press **Enter**. The result will be displayed in the cell (see Figures 7.16 and 7.17).

IMPORTANT POINTS

1. We need to use absolute cell reference **$A$2: $A$11** in our formula so that it won't change when the formula is copied down to cells below as the **range A2: A11 (**reference of the list of numbers against which the ranks is assigned) *remains constant for all the values.*

2. The 'order' argument (to rank in either descending or ascending order) in the formula is optional.

   • Choose 0 or leave the argument empty to rank the numbers in descending order (the largest number gets a rank of 1)

   • Choose 1 to rank the numbers in ascending order (the lowest number gets a rank of 1)

3. If two or more observations are identical, there is a tie for the same rank.

We use the **RANK.AVG** function to assign the average rank to more than one value having the same rank.

| C2 | ▼ | ⋮ | ✕ | ✓ | *fx* | =RANK(A2,$A$2:$A$11,0) |

▲	A	B	C	D
1	Result (Graduation)	First salary	Rank (X)	Rank (Y)
2	76	565000	=RANK(A2,$A$2:$A$11,0)	=RANK(B2,$B$2:$B$11,0)
3	44	570000		
4	80	650000		
5	87	920000		
6	90	860000		
7	92	780000		
8	66	630000		
9	57	400000		
10	97	820000		
11	88	950000		
12				

FIGURE 7.14   Step 1 in Calculation of the Spearman Correlation Coefficient

| C2 | ▼ | ⋮ | ✕ | ✓ | *fx* | =RANK(A2,$A$2:$A$11,0) |

▲	A	B	C	D	E	F	G
1	Result (Graduation)	First salary	Rank (X)	Rank (Y)			
2	76	₹ 5,65,000	7	9			
3	44	₹ 5,70,000	10	8			
4	80	₹ 6,50,000	6	6			
5	87	₹ 9,20,000	5	2			
6	90	₹ 8,60,000	3	3			
7	92	₹ 7,80,000	2	5			
8	66	₹ 6,30,000	8	7			
9	57	₹ 4,00,000	9	10			
10	97	₹ 8,20,000	1	4			
11	88	₹ 9,50,000	4	1			
12							

FIGURE 7.15   Step 2 in Calculation of the Spearman Correlation Coefficient

	A	B	C	D	E	F	G
	AVERAGE ▾ : × ✓ ƒx	=CORREL(C2:C11,D2:D11)					
1	Result (Graduation)	First salary	Rank (X)	Rank (Y)			
2	76	₹ 5,65,000	7	9			
3	44	₹ 5,70,000	10	8			
4	80	₹ 6,50,000	6	6			
5	87	₹ 9,20,000	5	2			
6	90	₹ 8,60,000	3	3			
7	92	₹ 7,80,000	2	5			
8	66	₹ 6,30,000	8	7			
9	57	₹ 4,00,000	9	10			
10	97	₹ 8,20,000	1	4			
11	88	₹ 9,50,000	4	1			
12							
13	CORRELATION (between the ranks)			=CORREL(C2:C11,D2:D11)			
14							
15							

FIGURE 7.16 Step 3 in Calculation of the Spearman Correlation Coefficient

	A	B	C	D	E	F	G
	D13 ▾ : × ✓ ƒx	=CORREL(C2:C11,D2:D11)					
1	Result (Graduation)	First salary	Rank (X)	Rank (Y)			
2	76	₹ 5,65,000	7	9			
3	44	₹ 5,70,000	10	8			
4	80	₹ 6,50,000	6	6			
5	87	₹ 9,20,000	5	2			
6	90	₹ 8,60,000	3	3			
7	92	₹ 7,80,000	2	5			
8	66	₹ 6,30,000	8	7			
9	57	₹ 4,00,000	9	10			
10	97	₹ 8,20,000	1	4			
11	88	₹ 9,50,000	4	1			
12							
13	CORRELATION (between the ranks)			0.72121212			
14							

FIGURE 7.17 Step 4 in Calculation of the Spearman Correlation Coefficient

The correlation coefficient of + 0.7212 suggests

- There is a *direct or positive linear relationship* between the ranks of the variables. The result score and amount of the first salary tend to *move in the same direction*, either upward or downward
- Correlation coefficient of 0.7212 ($r_s > 0.5$) suggests strong positive correlation between the datasets
- Therefore, we can conclude that the student who scores a high percentage is likely to get a higher amount of the first salary.

So far, the discussion has been centred around *linear relationships*. Correlation can, on the other hand, be negligible in two cases. First, when the variables are **independent** of each other and secondly, when there is *no linear relationship* between the two variables. Suppose the two variables are independent, and when one does not change with change in another variable, the correlation will be zero (0). The correlation coefficient having a zero (0) value does not imply that the variables are independent. We can only conclude that there is no linear relationship between them. Nonetheless, the two variables may have a *strong non-linear relationship*.

A *non-linear relationship* refers to the relationship between the variables where the other variable changes at varying rates if one variable changes. When the data points of two variables having a non-linear relationship are plotted on a graph and connected, it does not form a straight line but rather a curved line. Many relationships in economics are non-linear relationships. A few examples of non-linear relationships are quadratic polynomial, cubic polynomial, or logarithm relationships.

Consider the following hypothetical illustration, exhibiting the data related to the hours of work, output, and the average cost per unit of production level in a firm, assuming a fixed cost of ₹500 and a variable cost of ₹1 per unit. Note that both fixed and variable costs rise after 18 hours. The data indicates that, as hours of work increase, output increases uniformly, but the average cost does not come down uniformly as fixed costs get distributed over progressively.

Hours of Work	Output	Cost
5	10	51.00
6	12	42.67
7	14	36.71
8	16	32.25
9	18	28.78
10	20	26.00
11	22	23.73
12	24	21.83
13	26	20.23
14	28	18.86
15	30	17.67
16	32	16.63
17	34	15.71
18	36	14.89

Hours of Work	Output	Cost
19	38	16.47
20	40	17.00
21	42	17.20
22	44	17.50
23	46	18.00
24	48	18.50

A systematic approach before establishing any correlation between two variables is to plot the data points and have a graphical look at the data. For instance, Figure 7.18 endeavours to establish a correlation between the number of hours worked and average cost. It may be seen in the graph plotted below a non-linear relationship between the variables. However, calculating the correlation coefficient between the two variables yields $r = -0.8225$. *It is important to note here that the correlation coefficient value on the non-linear relationship is not meaningful. Correlation itself does not reveal anything on either linear or non-linear relationship. Although, if a relationship is linear, then correlation measures the strength of the relationship.*

To recap, this chapter principally discussed some techniques attempting to quantify the linear relationship between the variables. Although covariance analyses advise us on the directional relationship between two variables, an insight into the strength of relationships is important in statistical analysis. The study of the correlation coefficient helps to determine the strength of the relationship between variables. In particular, we focused on Karl Pearson's and Spearman's methods to estimate the correlation coefficient. It was clearly understood that these measures suggest no cause-and-effect relationship. To establish any relationship among variables and along with finding out the change in a (dependent) variable caused by the change in other (independent) variables, we will study regression analysis in the next chapter.

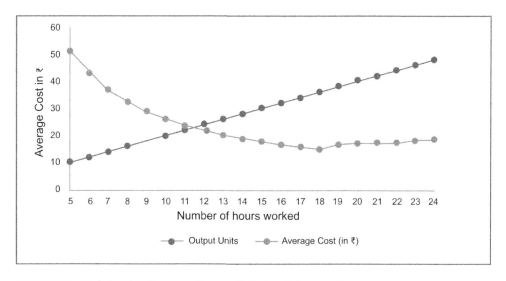

FIGURE 7.18 Relationship Between Hours of Work and Average Cost

PRACTICE QUESTIONS

1. Zero correlation implies that X and Y variables are independent. Comment.
2. The following table summarizes India's export and import values (in the US $ Million) for ten years starting from 2009–2010 to 2018–2019. Calculate the covariance and Pearson's correlation coefficient and comment on the relationship.

Period (2018)	Export	Import
2009–10	1,78,751	2,88,373
2010–11	2,49,816	3,69,769
2011–12	3,05,764	4,89,319
2012–13	3,00,401	4,90,737
2013–14	3,14,405	4,50,200
2014–15	3,10,338	4,48,033
2015–16	2,62,291	3,81,008
2016–17	2,75,852	3,84,357
2017–18	3,03,526	4,65,581
2018–19	3,31,020	5,07,436

Source: Department of Commerce, Ministry of Commerce and Industry, Government of India. Annual Report 2018–19. Retrieved from *https://commerce.gov.in/writereaddata/uploaded file/MOC_637036322182074251_Annual%20Report%202018–19%20English.pdf.*

3. Calculate the Karl Pearson coefficient of correlation between the net profits (in crores) and Non-performing assets (in crores) of the State Bank of India for ten years starting from 2009–2010 to 2018–2019.

Financial Year	Net Profits	NPA
2009–10	12,020.54	10,870.17
2010–11	11,179.94	12,346.89
2011–12	15,829.45	15,828.85
2012–13	18,322.99	21,956.48
2013–14	14,489.47	31,096.07
2014–15	17,517.37	27,590.58
2015–16	12,743.29	55,807.02
2016–17	−390.67	58,277.38
2017–18	−4,187.41	11,0854.7
2018–19	3,069.07	65,894.74

Source: Data retrieved from www.moneycontrol.com/financialstatebankindia/balance-sheetVI/sbi

4. The exam scores of 15 students in an Economics and Statistics class are given in the following table. Calculate the Spearman correlation coefficient to estimate the relationship between the scores.

Student ID	Economics	Statistics
1	94	88
2	95	60
3	35	84
4	75	100
5	100	80
6	46	90
7	93	70
8	81	75
9	60	84
10	45	54
11	92	77
12	76	86
13	44	78
14	87	65
15	84	52

5. The following are the marks of eight students in the Physics and Chemistry test. Find Karl Pearson's and Spearman's coefficient of correlation.

Based on correlation coefficients, it can be concluded that an increase in 10 marks in one subject will lead to an increase in 5.9 and 6.3 marks respectively in other subject, according to Pearson and Spearman estimations.

8

REGRESSION ANALYSIS

Learning Outcomes

After reading this chapter, the readers will be able to understand

- The concept of regression analysis
- Developing a linear regression model
- Estimation and interpretation of the regression coefficients
- Predicting the values of the dependent variable
- Derivation and interpretation of the coefficient of determination (R^2)
- Least squares method to obtain the best fitting line
- Performing the regression analysis using Data Analysis in Excel

In the previous chapter, we studied the measures of association that help estimate the degree of relationship between two datasets. It was pointed out that correlation analysis does not suggest any causal relationship between the variables. In regression analysis, the theory postulates a relationship between the variables, and analysis is performed to estimate the influence of one or more variables on the other.

Regression analysis can be linear or non-linear based on the relationship between variables. An important assumption of linear regression is that the relationship between the variables must be linear, which follows a straight-line relationship. On the other hand, a non-linear regression model studies variables having no linear relationship. That is, the curve of regression is not a straight line. The present chapter focuses on the linear regression model throughout the analysis. In addition to understanding the concept of regression analysis, its relevance, and applicability, we will also learn how to develop, estimate, and interpret a linear regression model. Based on this, we will make predictions and determine the fit of the model.

DOI: 10.4324/9781003398127-8

8.1 Regression Analysis

Regression analysis is a statistical technique that quantifies the relationship between the variables and predicts the value of one variable from another set of variables. The variable that predicts the other variable's value is known as the *independent variable*, the *explanatory variable*, the *predictor*, or simply the *X variable*. Likewise, the variable whose value is predicted is known as the *dependent variable*, or *variable of interest* or the *Y variable*. Linear regression analysis models the relationship between a dependent and an independent variable by fitting a linear equation. Let us look at the steps involved in developing a complete linear regression model.

8.2 Developing a Linear Regression Model

To create a regression model, we first identify and establish the relationship between the dependent and independent variables. The *simple* linear regression equation can be written in the form of:

$$Y = \beta_0 + \beta_1 X$$

Here,
  Y = Dependent variable
  X = Independent variable
  β_0 = Y-Intercept
  β_1 = Slope coefficient of Y with respect to X
  Correspondingly, the *multiple* linear regression equation for 'n' number of independent variables can be written in the form of:

$$Y = \beta_0 + \beta_1 X_1 + \beta_2 X_2 + \ldots\ldots\ldots + \beta_n X_n$$

Here,
  Y = Dependent variable
  X_i = i^{th} independent variable, $i \in \{1, 2 \ldots n\}$
  β_0 = Y-Intercept
  β_i = Slope coefficient of Y on X_i

The regression coefficient, denoted as β_i, is known as the regression coefficient of Y on X (when the value of variable Y depends on X). The β_0 known as the constant or the Y-intercept, estimates the value of Y when the value of X is zero. The magnitude of β_i signifies the change in Y due to a change in X_i by one unit, provided all the other explanatory variables are held constant. Together β_0 and β_1 are the parameters of the regression model that mathematically describe the relationship between dependent and independent variables. The regression model can be shown graphically as in Figure 8.1, where the Y-axis (vertical axis) depicts the dependent variable, and the X-axis (horizontal axis) shows the independent variable.

In this figure, the upward sloping straight line, from the lower left to the upper right, is the regression line represented by the equation of $Y = \beta_0 + \beta_1 X$. β_0 is the intercept of the line, crossing from the Y-axis, which indicates the value of the dependent variable when the

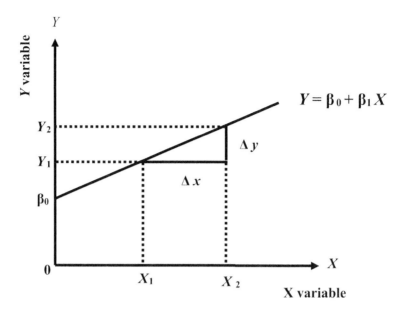

FIGURE 8.1   Graphical Representation of Regression Line

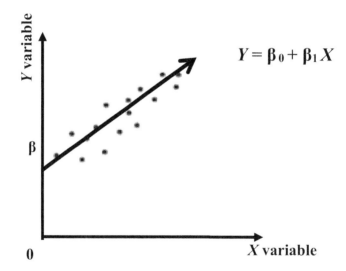

FIGURE 8.2   Regression Line With Positive Slope ($\beta_1 > 0$)

explanatory variable is zero. β_1 is the *slope* of the regression line, which measures *the rate of change in the Y corresponding to the unit change in the value of X*, that is:

$$\frac{\Delta y}{\Delta x} \ or \ \frac{Y_2 - Y_1}{X_2 - X_1}$$

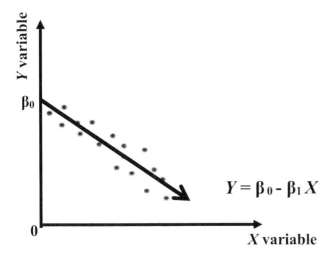

FIGURE 8.3   Regression Line With Negative Slope ($\beta_1 < 0$)

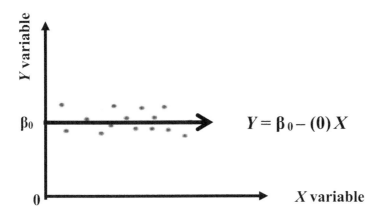

FIGURE 8.4   Regression Line With Constant Slope ($\beta_1 = 0$)

The slope coefficients may either be *positive, negative or zero* indicating the direction of change. The positive slope means for any given change in the value of X, the change in the value of Y is in the same direction. That is, a positive change in X is accompanied by a positive change in Y, and a negative change in X is followed by a negative change in Y (Figure 8.2). The negative slope implies that for any given change in the value of X, the change in the value of Y is in the opposite direction, an increase in X accompanied by a decrease in Y and a decrease in X by an increase in Y (Figure 8.3). However, if the slope is 0, the value of the Y remains constant for any value of X. It is represented by a straight line horizontal to the X-axis as shown in Figure 8.4.

8.3 Estimation of the Coefficients in the Regression Model

The second step is estimating the coefficient values in the regression model. For a dependent (Y) and independent variable (X), we have already developed a regression model and established the relationship between them in the form of an equation, $Y = \beta_0 + \beta_1 X$. The formula[1] for the slope coefficient is given by the ratio of the *covariance* of X and Y to the *variance* of X, that is:

$$\beta_1 = \frac{Cov(X, Y)}{\sigma_x^2}$$

$$\text{Or, } \beta_1 = \frac{\sum_{i=1}^{n}(x_i - \bar{X})(y_i - \bar{Y})}{\sum_{i=1}^{n}(x_i - \bar{X})^2}$$

$$\beta_1 = \frac{\sum x_i y_i}{\sum x_i^2}$$

Here,

$\sum$ = Sigma/operator for summation
$\bar{X}$ = arithmetic mean of the independent variable
$\bar{Y}$ = arithmetic mean of the dependent variable
x_i = value of the independent variable
y_i = value of the dependent variable

$$\text{Alternatively, } \beta_1 = \frac{n(\sum xy) - \sum x * \sum y}{n \sum x^2 - (\sum x)^2}$$

$$\text{Or, } \beta_1 = r * \frac{\sigma_y}{\sigma_x}$$

Here,

r = correlation coefficient
σ_x = standard deviation of the independent variable,
σ_y = standard deviation of the dependent variable

The value of parameter β_0 has no economic interpretation practically but can be calculated as follows:

$$\beta_0 = \bar{Y} - \beta_1 \bar{X}$$

Illustration

A company incurs promotion expenses to boost its revenue. The following table summarizes the company's monthly promotional expenses and total revenue for the last two years. The sales manager wants to examine how the company's total revenue depends on promotion expenses. Develop a regression model and estimate the regression coefficients.

Months	Promotion Expenses (X; ₹ Crores)	Revenue (Y; ₹ Crores)
1	400	5,500
2	410	5,540
3	430	5,550
4	450	5,600
5	480	5,600
6	510	5,600
7	530	5,700
8	540	5,700
9	550	5,800
10	560	5,800
11	560	5,900
12	570	5,900
13	570	5,950
14	580	6,000
15	620	6,040
16	630	6,050
17	640	6,100
18	640	6,200
19	660	6,300
20	590	6,600
21	630	6,850
22	640	6,800
23	680	7,000
24	690	7,500

First Method (Direct Method)

Months	Promotion Expenses (X)	Revenue (Y)	$x - \bar{X}$	$(x - \bar{X})^2$	$y - \bar{Y}$	$x - \bar{X} * y - \bar{Y}$
1	400	5,500	−165	27,225	−565.83	93,362.50
2	410	5,540	−155	24,025	−525.83	81,504.17
3	430	5,550	−135	18,225	−515.83	69,637.50
4	450	5,600	−115	13,225	−465.83	53,570.83
5	480	5,600	−85	7,225	−465.83	39,595.83
6	510	5,600	−55	3,025	−465.83	25,620.83
7	530	5,700	−35	1,225	−365.83	12,804.17
8	540	5,700	−25	625	−365.83	9,145.83
9	550	5,800	−15	225	−265.83	3,987.50
10	560	5,800	−5	25	−265.83	1,329.17
11	560	5,900	−5	25	−165.83	829.17

Months	Promotion Expenses (X)	Revenue (Y)	$x - \bar{X}$	$(x - \bar{X})^2$	$y - \bar{Y}$	$x - \bar{X} * y - \bar{Y}$
12	570	5,900	5	25	−165.83	−829.17
13	570	5,950	5	25	−115.83	−579.17
14	580	6,000	15	225	−65.83	−987.50
15	620	6,040	55	3,025	−25.83	−1,420.83
16	630	6,050	65	4,225	−15.83	−1,029.17
17	640	6,100	75	5,625	34.17	2,562.50
18	640	6,200	75	5,625	134.17	10,062.50
19	660	6,300	95	9,025	234.17	22,245.83
20	590	6,600	25	625	534.17	13,354.17
21	630	6,850	65	4,225	784.17	50,970.83
22	640	6,800	75	5,625	734.17	55,062.50
23	680	7,000	115	13,225	934.17	1,07,429.17
24	690	7,500	125	15,625	1,434.17	1,79,270.83
Total	**13,560**	**1,45,580**		**1,62,200**		**8,27,500**

Mean of independent variable $(\bar{X})$ = 13,560/24 = 565
Mean of dependent variable $(\bar{Y})$ = 1,45,580/24 = 6,065.8333

We already know that $\beta_1 = \dfrac{\sum_{i=1}^{n}(x_i - \bar{X})(y_i - \bar{Y})}{\sum_{i=1}^{n}(x_i - \bar{X})^2}$

Substituting the values in the previous formula, we get:

$$\beta_1 = \dfrac{\sum_{i=1}^{n}(x_i - \bar{X})(y_i - \bar{Y})}{\sum_{i=1}^{n}(x_i - \bar{X})^2}$$

$$= \dfrac{827,500}{162,200}$$

$$= 5.101726264$$

Similarly, $\beta_0 = \bar{Y} - \beta_1\bar{X}$

= 6,065.8333 − 5.101726264 * 565
= 6,065.8333 − 2,882.47533916
= 3,183.357994

As discussed, we first need to identify the dependent variable (Y) and independent variables in a regression model. In the present example, revenue depends on promotional expenses. Hence, revenue is a dependent variable and promotional expense is an independent or explanatory variable. In a mathematical or statistics parlance, revenue is a function of the promotional expenses. The linear equation is written as follows:

$Y = \beta_0 + \beta_1 X$

or Revenue = $\beta_0 + \beta_1$ * Promotion Expenses

We rewrite the regression equation by substituting the value of beta coefficients, that is, β_1 and β_0 calculated earlier:

Revenue = 3183.3579 + 5.101726 * Promotion Expenses

Second Method of Calculating Parameters (Using Excel)[2]

To estimate the Regression Model using Excel, we use the option of **Data Analysis** and follow the stated steps:

Step 1. Enter the promotion expenses (*X*) and Revenue (*Y*) in the Excel sheet (Figure 8.5).

Step 2. Go to the **Data** tab, and click on the option of **Data Analysis** in the **Analysis** group on the right side (Figure 8.5).

Step 3. A dialogue box will appear. Select the option of **Regression** from the list and click **OK** (Figure 8.6).

Step 4. A **Regression** dialogue box will appear. Fill in the following details (Figure 8.7).

- **Input *Y* range**: The cell range of the values of the dependent variable (revenue) for which the Regression Model is developed, that is, **C1: C25**
- **Input *X* range**: The cell range of the values of the independent variable (promotion expenses), that is, **B1: B25**
- **Check on Labels:** Remember if you choose the label/name of the variables, that is, promotion expenses and revenue in the **Input Range**, then check the box **Labels**
- Check on the **Confidence Level** and set it at **95 per cent**, which is also the default value
- **Output Range:** Under the output options, choose the cell reference where the result is desired in the existing worksheet. Say, **E2.**

Step 5. Click **OK**.

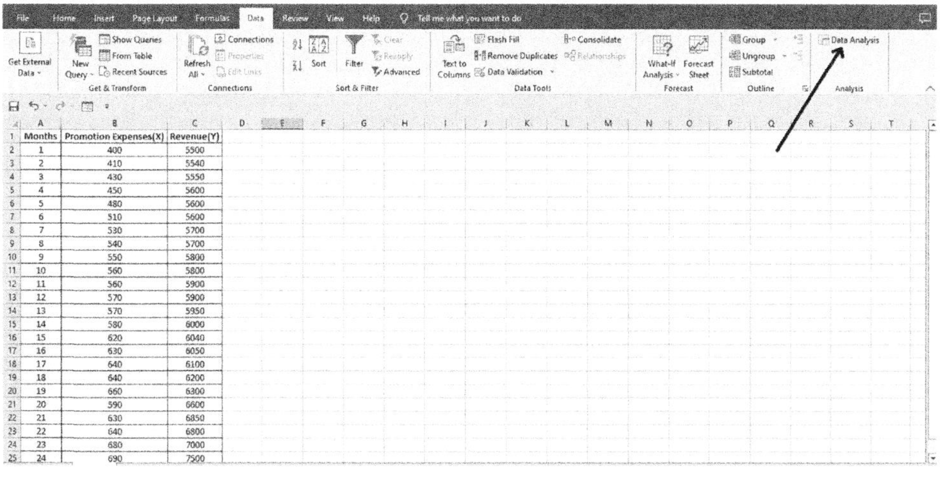

FIGURE 8.5 Step 1 in Calculating Regression Parameters

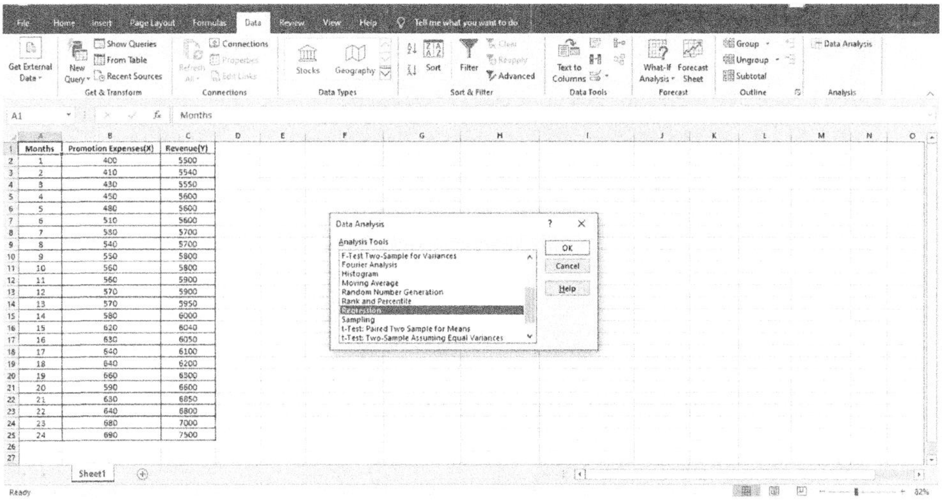

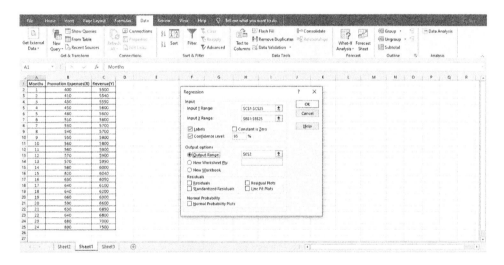

FIGURE 8.6 Step 2 in Calculating Regression Parameters

FIGURE 8.7 Step 3 in Calculating Regression Parameters

The regression result is displayed as a summary output table (Figure 8.8). The calculated values of parameters are identical in both methods.

8.4 Interpretation of the Estimated Coefficients in the Regression Model

In a regression model, interpretation of the analysis is very important. It is indeed one of the primary objectives. As mentioned before, β_0 and β_1 are the parameters with their respective meanings. Let us interpret the values of the coefficients estimated.

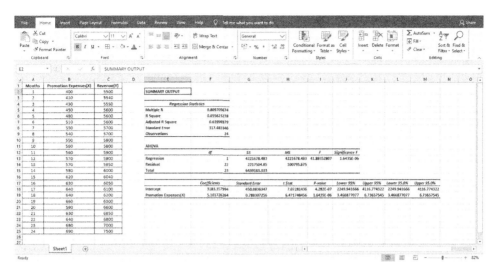

FIGURE 8.8   Step 4 in Calculating Regression Parameters

- $\beta_0 = 3{,}183.3579$ shows that the total revenue earned by the company is ₹3,183.3579 crore when the amount spent on promotion expenses is ₹0, that is if the company does not spend any money on promotional activities for the product. From a technical point of view, the amount of revenue earned with no promotion expenses is correct. But in managerial terms, this value is unrealistic or irrational as the company is expected to spend some amount on its promotional activities or sales strategies. Therefore, we tend to ignore the value of β_0 in economic analysis.
- The positive sign of β_1 indicates that as the promotion expenses increase, the revenue of the company also tends to increase. The value of β_1 as 5.10 demonstrates that the promotional expenditure of one crore rupees (a unit of the independent variable) will boost the revenues by ₹5.10 crore (dependent variable). The statistical significance of these values and the model will be examined later in the ensuing sections.

8.5   Forecast the Values of the Dependent Variable

Regression analysis is mostly used to make predictions. To predict the values of the dependent variable, we bring in the calculated values of parameters along with the values of the independent variable in the regression model. The predicted value of Y is customarily denoted by $\hat{y}$ known as y 'hat'.

Illustration

Let us clarify it with the ongoing illustration. The sales manager of the company has allocated the budget for the promotion expenditure of the company for the next five months. The budget amount for such expenses is tabled next. Based on these promotion expenditures, the sales manager wishes to determine the predicted sales revenue for the next five months.

Months	Budget for Promotion Expenses (₹ Crores)
1	650
2	700
3	760
4	720
5	800

First Method

The regression equation under discussion is:

Revenue = β_0 + β_1 * Promotion Expenses

Substituting the values of beta coefficients, that is, β_1 and β_0 calculated earlier, we get,

Revenue = 3,183.3579 + 5.101726 * Promotion Expenses

The predicted revenue (Y) when the promotion expenses are ₹650 crores, ₹700 crores, ₹760 crores, ₹720 crores, and ₹800 crores can be estimated as

Months	Budget for Promotions (X; ₹ Crores)	Estimated Revenue (in Crores)
1	650	3,183.3579 + 5.101726 * 650 = 6,499.48
2	700	3,183.3579 + 5.101726 * 700 = 6,754.57
3	760	3,183.3579 + 5.101726 * 760 = 7,060.67
4	720	3,183.3579 + 5.101726 * 720 = 6,856.60
5	800	3,183.3579 + 5.101726 * 800 = 7,264.74

The estimated revenue is ₹6,499.48 crores, ₹6,754.57 crores, ₹7,060.67 crores, ₹7,264.74 crores for the 1st, 2nd, 3rd, 4th and 5th months, respectively.

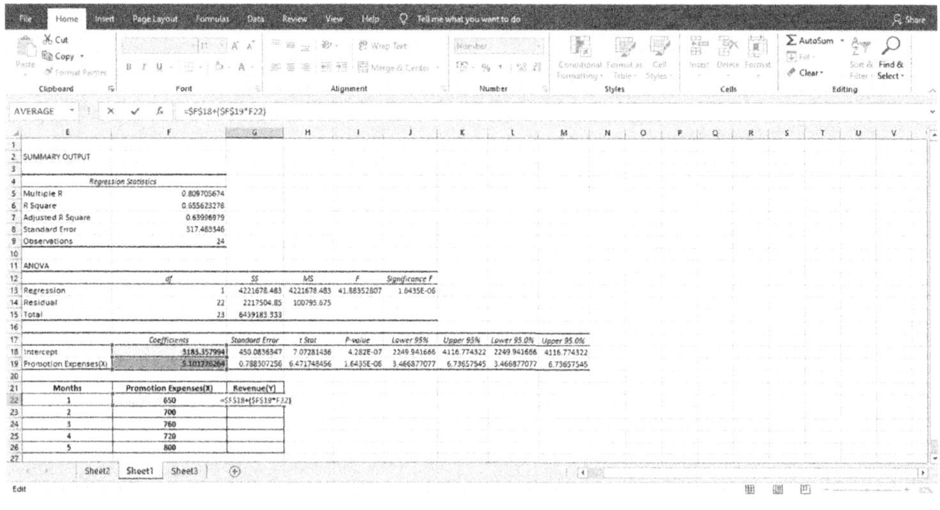

FIGURE 8.9 Step 1 Regression Analysis (Predicting the Dependent Variable)

G22	▾	:	>	✓	*fₓ*	=$F$18+($F$19*F22)

⊿	E	F	G	H	I	J	K	L	M
1									
2	SUMMARY OUTPUT								
3									
4	*Regression Statistics*								
5	Multiple R	0.809705674							
6	R Square	0.655623278							
7	Adjusted R Square	0.63996979							
8	Standard Error	317.483346							
9	Observations	24							
10									
11	ANOVA								
12		*df*	*SS*	*MS*	*F*	*Significance F*			
13	Regression	1	4221678.483	4221678.483	41.88352807	1.6435E-06			
14	Residual	22	2217504.85	100795.675					
15	Total	23	6439183.333						
16									
17		*Coefficients*	*Standard Error*	*t Stat*	*P-value*	*Lower 95%*	*Upper 95%*	*Lower 95.0%*	*Upper 95.0%*
18	Intercept	3183.357994	450.0836347	7.07281436	4.282E-07	2249.941666	4116.774322	2249.941666	4116.774322
19	Promotion Expenses(X)	5.101726264	0.788307256	6.471748456	1.6435E-06	3.466877077	6.73657545	3.466877077	6.73657545
20									

21	Months	Promotion Expenses(X)	Revenue(Y)
22	1	650	6499.48
23	2	700	6754.57
24	3	760	7060.67
25	4	720	6856.60
26	5	800	7264.74

FIGURE 8.10   Step 2 in Regression Analysis (Predicting the Dependent Variable)

Second Method (Using Excel)

Step 1. Enter the budgeted promotion expenses (X) in the Excel sheet as shown in Figure 8.9.

Step 2. Type the '=' (equal to) sign in the desired cell where the estimated revenue (Y) is to be calculated, say G22, and then select the cell number containing the value of the *constant* in the summary output, that is, F18, then insert a plus sign (+) to add the product of the value of coefficient (in summary output), that is, F19 and value of promotion expense (X) in the first month, that is, H22.

Step 3. Press **Enter**. The result will appear in cell G22. Then click on the fill handle (the small black square in the bottom right corner when you select the cell) and drag it vertically to automatically calculate the predicted revenue for the next months (Figure 8.10).

> We need to use absolute cell reference in our formula so that it will not change when the formula is copied down to cells below, as the *value of constant* and *slope coefficient* remains the same for all the values of the *Y* variable.

The regression coefficients which are estimated from the regression model are based on the sample data and are just the estimates for the population parameters and not the true regression coefficients. Figure 8.11 shows the population and the sample regression functions, PRF and SRF, respectively. $\hat{Y}$ is the estimated value of the actual value of the Y variable, that is, $E(Y|X_i)$. We observe that the $\hat{Y}$ overestimates the true value of Y, $E(Y|X_i)$ for a given value of X_i as shown. Similarly, for any value of X_i to the left of point A, the SRF underestimates the true PRF. Such a difference in the values is due to sampling fluctuations.

As we know, the SRF is an approximation of the PRF. We need to find out a mechanism to build the sample regression function so that the beta coefficients $(\hat{\beta}_0, \hat{\beta}_1)$ estimated from the regression model are as close as possible or near to the true value of the coefficients (β_0, β_1).

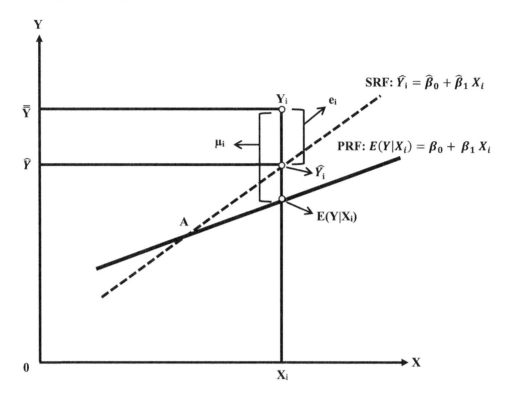

FIGURE 8.11 Population (PRF) and Sample Regression Functions (SRF)

The upcoming section addresses the concern about the OLS method or the least square criterion. The method reveals the procedures constructing the sample regression function, which is almost a counterpart of or a good estimator of the population regression function.

8.6 Residuals or Errors and OLS Method

The foregoing section brings about regression equation $Y = \beta_0 + \beta_1 X$ that has attempted to predict the values of the dependent variable, given the values of the independent variable. However, these predicted values may be different from the *actual* or the *observed* values of dependent variable Y. Based on the estimated regression model, we can then calculate the difference between the actual values of Y and the values predicted from the regression model. This difference is known as *errors* or *residuals* in the regression model. The residual is denoted by Greek small letter epsilon, 'ε'. Therefore, the regression equation showing the linear relationship between the dependent and independent variable can now be written as:

$$Y = \beta_0 + \beta_1 X + \varepsilon$$

Or, $\varepsilon = Y - \left(\beta_0 + \beta_1 X \right)$

That is, errors/residuals = Actual value (Y) – Predicted value $(\hat{Y})$

If the actual value is more than the predicted value, thus residual being positive, we can infer that the regression model *underpredicts* the value of the dependent variable. Equivalently, if the actual value is less than the predicted values, residual being negative, we construe that the regression model is *overpredicting* the value of the dependent variable. However, the model predicts accurately if the error or residual values are absent.

Drawing a scatter plot helps identify the residuals. The first step involved is plotting the *actual values* of the variable Y (dependent variable) for the given value of the X variable (independent variable) on a scatter plot. The line joining different data points does not necessarily fall on a straight line but fundamentally follows a linear pattern.

In the second step, based on the regression model followed, a *regression line* or the *line of best fit* is drawn based on the calculated parameters for the given dataset. The regression line obtained will seemingly be straight. It may be observed that some of the actual values of the Y variable *fall above* the regression line, and some *fall below* the regression line. The actual values plotted above the regression line (actual Y value > predicted Y value) are *positive residuals*. The residuals are negative if the actual values get plotted below the regression line (actual Y value < predicted Y value). Deviation of the dots (actual values) from the straight line (predicted or estimated values) are the residuals shown by a vertical bar, as displayed in Figure 8.12. The larger the deviation, the worse the model's fit to the data. Conversely, the closer the expected residual value to 0, the better the fit.

The error terms cancel out each other due to the positive and the negative signs. The objective of finding a best-fitted regression line is not to compensate the positive terms with the negative terms, but to minimize the error terms. To avoid the sign problem of error terms, we use the method of the *least-square criterion*, popularly known as the method of *Ordinary Least Squares* (OLS), which determines the equation of the straight line of best fit. This method creates a linear regression model that *minimizes the sum of squared errors (SS_E)* to obtain the regression line that best fits through the given set of data points and predicts the movement in the variable of interest. To find out the extent of fit of the regression model, another measurement called the coefficient of determination is exercised.

8.7 Coefficient of Determination

The coefficient of determination is a statistical tool of the goodness of fit of a regression model to the data. The coefficient of determination figures out the proportion of the variation in the Y variable explained by the X variable. Put differently, it tells us how many predicted data points would fall on the regression line. It is denoted by R^2 or R square. It is similar to the coefficient of correlation and simply is calculated by squaring the correlation coefficient between the two variables, $R^2 = (r)^2$. The value of the R^2 ranges between 0 and +1. For instance, $R^2 = 0.9$ indicates that the independent variable, *ceterus paribus* can explain 90 per cent of the variation in the dependent variable. On the other hand, a value closer to zero implies a poor fit model. That is, a smaller proportion of total variation in Y is explained by the explanatory variable.

Here, the *explained variation (SS_R)* or regression sum of squares is the variation in the Y variable due to the X variable. Whereas the variation in the Y variable due to the errors or the variation in the Y variable not accounted for by the X variable is known as the *unexplained variation or residual sum of squares (SS_E)*. *Total variation (SS_y)* in the dependent variable is the sum of the explained variation and unexplained variation, that is, $SS_y = SS_R + SS_E$.

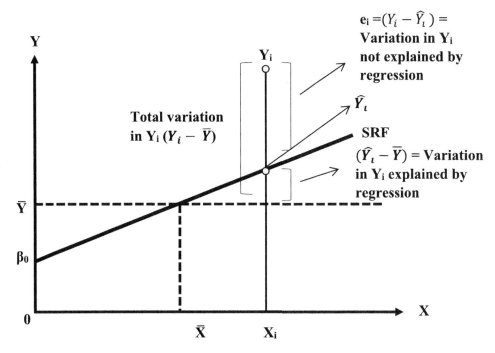

FIGURE 8.12 Graphical Representation of Three Types of Variations

Mathematically, these three types of variations are written as follows, which are derived from Figure 8.12:

Explained variation $\left(SS_R\right) = \sum_{i=1}^{n}\left(\hat{y} - \bar{Y}\right)^2$. It is the sum of the squares of the deviations of the predicted values from the mean value of the dependent variable.

Residual sum of squares $\left(SS_E\right) = \sum_{i=1}^{n}\left(Y_i - \hat{y}\right)^2$. This sum of squares is the divergence between the actual data and the estimated model.

Total variation $\left(SS_y\right) = \sum_{i=1}^{n}\left(Y_i - \bar{Y}\right)^2$. This sum of squares represents the difference between the actual Y value and its mean.

Here $\hat{y}$ = value estimated by the regression line

$\bar{Y}$ = mean of the dependent variable

Y_i = i^{th} observation of dependent variable

R^2 can now be expressed as the ratio between the explained variation to the total variation, that is:

$$R^2 = \frac{Explained\ Variation}{Total\ Variation}$$

$$= \frac{SS_x}{SS_y}$$

$$Or\ R^2 = 1 - \frac{Unexplained\ Variation}{Total\ Variation}$$

$$= 1 - \frac{SS_E}{SS_y}$$

$$= 1 - \frac{\sum u_t^2}{\sum_{i=1}^{n}(Y_i - \bar{Y})^2}$$

In the case of multiple regression, the coefficient of multiple determination (R^2) also represents the proportion of the variation in the Y variable explained by all the explanatory variables together. However, one problem with R^2 is that as we increase the number of X variables, the value of R^2 also increases even if there is no relationship between the additional X variable and Y variable, thus leading to an overfitting model. Therefore, we need to adjust the R^2 and instead use *Adjusted R^2* ($\overline{R^2}$). It can be computed as follows:

$$R^2_{adj} = 1 - \left\{ \frac{(1 - R^2)(N - 1)}{N - k - 1} \right\}$$

Here,

R^2 = coefficient of multiple determination

N = no. of observations in the variable or the sample size

k = no. of independent variables

It may be noted that the value of adjusted R^2 is always less than R^2. The reason is that as the number of explanatory variables (k) increases in the model, the denominator becomes smaller, and the value in parenthesis will become larger. Resultantly, $\overline{R^2}$ value will come out to be smaller than the R^2 value.

The adjusted R^2 increases or decreases depending on whether the additional variables improve the explanatory power of the model or not. Upon the addition of X variables, the adjusted R^2 will increase only if the additional independent variables contribute more to the model than what would have been expected by chance. On the other hand, it will decrease if the additional independent variables improve the model by less than expected by chance. Hence, adjusted R^2 should be used to compare the models having different numbers of independent variables. Therefore, adjusted R^2 determines the proportion of the Y variable variation explained by all the explanatory variables adjusted for the number of independent variables in the model.

Illustration

Calculate the value of the residuals or the errors for the previous illustration. Also, compute the value of the coefficient of determination and interpret the results.

First Method

The continuing regression equation can be written as:

$$\text{Revenue} = \beta_0 + \beta_1 * \text{Promotion Expenses}$$

Substituting the value beta coefficients, that is, $\beta_1 = 5.101726$ and $\beta_0 = 3,183.3579$, we get:

- Estimated/Predicted Revenue $= 3,183.3579 + 5.101726 *$ Promotion Expenses (Column 3)
- Residual/Errors $=$ Actual value of Y variable $-$ Predicted value of Y variable (Column 4)

(₹ *Crores*)

Months	Promotion Expenses (X) (1)	Revenue (Y) (2)	Predicted Revenue (ŷ) (3)	Residuals $(Y_i - \hat{y})$ (4)	$(Y_i - \bar{Y})^2$ (5)	$(Y_i - \hat{y})^2$ (6)
1	400	5,500	5,224.05	275.95	3,20,167.36	76,149.23
2	410	5,540	5,275.07	264.93	2,76,500.69	70,190.15
3	430	5,550	5,377.10	172.90	2,66,084.03	29,894.31
4	450	5,600	5,479.13	120.87	2,17,000.69	14,608.39
5	480	5,600	5,632.19	−32.19	2,17,000.69	1,035.98
6	510	5,600	5,785.24	−185.24	2,17,000.69	34,313.26
7	530	5,700	5,887.27	−187.27	1,33,834.03	35,071.14
8	540	5,700	5,938.29	−238.29	1,33,834.03	56,782.21
9	550	5,800	5,989.31	−189.31	70,667.36	35,837.31
10	560	5,800	6,040.32	−240.32	70,667.36	57,755.96
11	560	5,900	6,040.32	−140.32	27,500.69	19,691.02
12	570	5,900	6,091.34	−191.34	27,500.69	36,611.75
13	570	5,950	6,091.34	−141.34	13,417.36	19,977.55
14	580	6,000	6,142.36	−142.36	4,334.03	20,266.15
15	620	6,040	6,346.43	−306.43	667.36	93,898.29
16	630	6,050	6,397.45	−347.45	250.69	1,20,718.40
17	640	6,100	6,448.46	−348.46	1,167.36	1,21,426.33
18	640	6,200	6,448.46	−248.46	18,000.69	61,733.76
19	660	6,300	6,550.50	−250.50	54,834.03	62,748.91
20	590	6,600	6,193.38	406.62	2,85,334.03	1,65,342.68
21	630	6,850	6,397.45	452.55	6,14,917.36	2,04,805.54
22	640	6,800	6,448.46	351.54	5,39,000.69	1,23,578.40
23	680	7,000	6,652.53	347.47	8,72,667.36	1,20,734.11
24	690	7,500	6,703.55	796.45	20,56,834.03	6,34,334.01
Total	**13,560**	**1,45,580**			**64,39,183.33**	**22,17,504.85**

Mean of dependent variable $(Y) = 1,45,580/24 = 6,065.8333$

Total variation $= \sum_{i=1}^{n}(Y_i - \bar{Y})^2 = 6,439,183.33$

Unexplained variation $= \sum_{i=1}^{n}(Y_i - y)^2 = 2,217,504.85$

Explained variation $=$ Total variation $-$ Unexplained variation $= 4,221,678.48$

Coefficient of determination $(R^2) = \dfrac{\text{Explained Variation}}{\text{Total Variation}}$

$= \dfrac{4,221,678.48}{6,439,183.33} = 0.65562$

Second Method (Using Excel)

To estimate the residual and coefficient of determination in the regression model using Excel, we use the data analysis option to obtain the results in the form of a summary output and residual output. We create a new worksheet and follow similar steps for computing the coefficients and constant in the previous illustration.

Step 1. Enter the promotion expenses (X) and revenue (Y) in the Excel sheet.

Step 2. Go to the **Data** tab and click on the option of **Data Analysis** in the **Analysis** group on the right.

Step 3. A dialogue box will appear. Select the option of **Regression** from the list and click **OK.**

Step 4. A **Regression** dialogue box will appear. Fill in the following details (Figure 8.13)

- **Input Y range** – the cell range of the values of the dependent variable (revenue) for which the regression model is developed, that is, **C1: C25**
- **Input X range** – the cell range of the values of the independent variable (promotion expenses), that is, **B1: B25**
- Check on **Labels** – Remember if you choose the label/name of the variables, that is, promotion expenses and revenue in the input range, then check the box **Labels**
- Check on the **Confidence Level** and set it at **95 per cent**, which is also the default value
- Under the residuals options, select the **Residuals** checkbox to get the residual output as the results. Check on the **Line fit plots** (optional) to create a scatter plot of the line of best fit
- **Output Range** – Under the output options, choose the cell reference where the result is desired in the existing worksheet, say, **E2.**

Step 5. Click **OK.** The **Regression** result will be displayed in the form of a summary output (Figure 8.14), residual output table (Figure 8.15), and line fit plot in Figure 8.16.

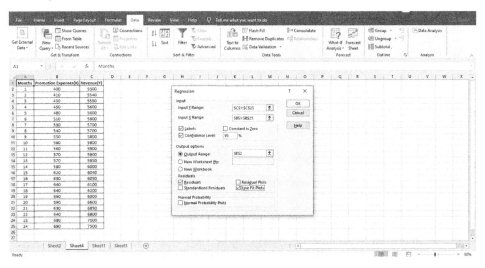

FIGURE 8.13   Regression Analysis Dialogue Box

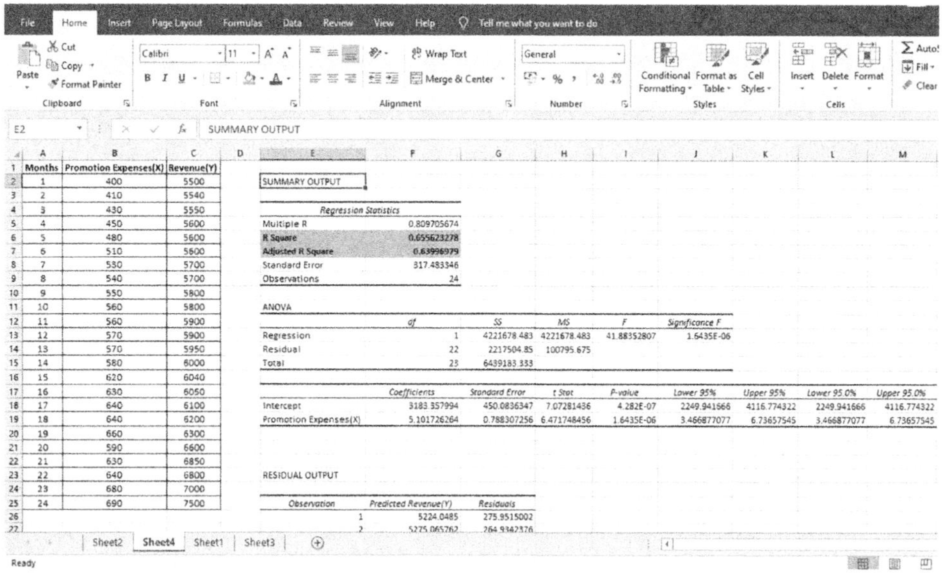

FIGURE 8.14 Regression Analysis (Summary Output)

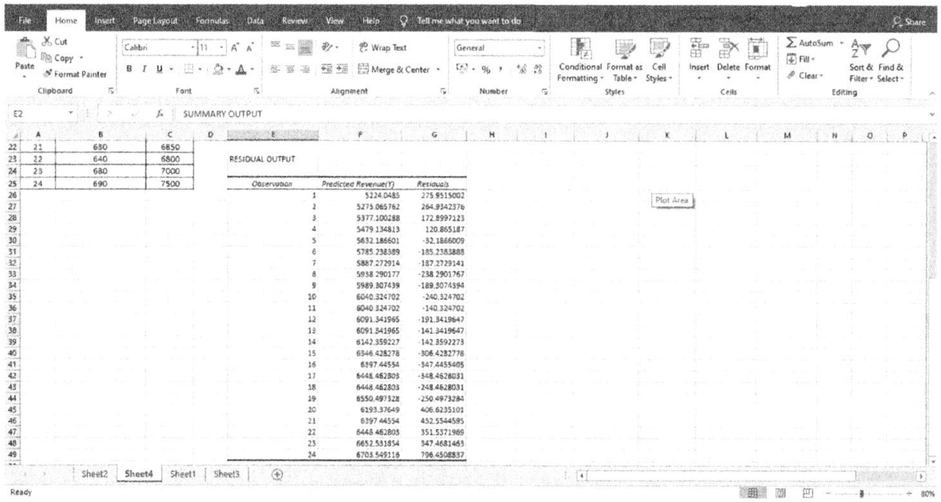

Months	Promotion Expenses(X)	Revenue(Y)
1	400	5500
2	410	5540
3	430	5550
4	450	5600
5	480	5600
6	510	5600
7	530	5700
8	540	5700
9	550	5800
10	560	5800
11	560	5900
12	570	5900
13	570	5950
14	580	6000
15	620	6040
16	630	6050
17	640	6100
18	640	6200
19	660	6300
20	590	6600
21	630	6850
22	640	6800
23	680	7000
24	690	7500

SUMMARY OUTPUT

Regression Statistics

Multiple R	0.809705674
R Square	0.655623278
Adjusted R Square	0.63996979
Standard Error	317.483346
Observations	24

ANOVA

	df	SS	MS	F	Significance F
Regression	1	4221678.483	4221678.483	41.88352807	1.6435E-06
Residual	22	2217504.85	100795.675		
Total	23	6439183.333			

	Coefficients	Standard Error	t Stat	P-value	Lower 95%	Upper 95%	Lower 95.0%	Upper 95.0%
Intercept	3183.357994	450.0836347	7.07281436	4.282E-07	2249.941666	4116.774322	2249.941666	4116.774322
Promotion Expenses(X)	5.101726264	0.788307256	6.471748456	1.6435E-06	3.466877077	6.73657545	3.466877077	6.73657545

RESIDUAL OUTPUT

Observation	Predicted Revenue(Y)	Residuals
1	5224.0485	275.9515002
2	5225.065762	264.9342376

FIGURE 8.15 Regression Analysis (Residual Output)

RESIDUAL OUTPUT

Observation	Predicted Revenue(Y)	Residuals
1	5224.0485	275.9515002
2	5275.065762	264.9342376
3	5377.100288	172.8997123
4	5479.134813	120.865187
5	5632.186601	-32.1866009
6	5785.238389	-185.2383888
7	5887.272914	-187.2729141
8	5938.290177	-238.2901767
9	5989.307439	-189.3074394
10	6040.324702	-240.324702
11	6040.324702	-140.324702
12	6091.341965	-191.3419647
13	6091.341965	-141.3419647
14	6142.359227	-142.3592273
15	6346.428278	-306.4282778
16	6397.44554	-347.4459405
17	6448.462803	-348.4628031
18	6448.462803	-248.4628031
19	6550.497528	-250.4973284
20	6193.37649	406.6235101
21	6397.44554	452.5344595
22	6448.462803	351.5371989
23	6652.531854	347.4681465
24	6703.549116	796.4508837

Interpretation of Results

Figure 8.14 shows the coefficient of determination or the R^2 produced as a part of the regression output. It comes out to be 0.65562. It means that the promotion expenses can explain 65.52 per cent of the variation in the revenue. The revenue earned by the company is strongly related to the amount spent on promotional activities, as these expenses account for 65.52 per cent of the variation in the sales revenue of the company. The remaining goes unexplained. The adjusted R^2 is equal to 0.6399.

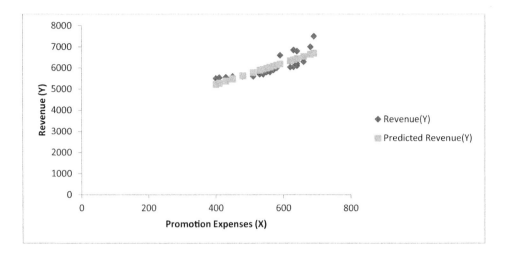

FIGURE 8.16   Regression Analysis: Promotional Expense Line Fit Plots

Interpretation of Results

Figure 8.15 shows the predicted values of revenue with the help of the regression equation and values of the residuals or errors the difference between the actual values of Y and the values predicted from the regression model. For instance, the residual of 275.95 in the 1st month implies that the regression model is *underpredicting* the revenue by 275.95 crore or the residual of (-32.1866) in the 5th month implies that the regression model is *overpredicting* the revenue by 32.1866 crore.

Interpretation of Results

Figure 8.16 displays the scatter plot of the line of best fit determined using the least square method obtained with regression output in Excel. The actual values of revenue plotted above the regression line are positive residuals whereas the actual values of revenue plotted below the regression line are negative residuals. Distance of the *actual values* (represented by grey colour) from the *predicted or estimated values* (represented by the straight line in grey colour) are the residuals.

Summing up, it can be concluded that regression analysis is one of the most important types of data analysis. In this chapter, we learned how to predict the value of a dependent variable from an independent one, for which we developed and estimated a regression model. The strength of the relationship, established by the value of R^2, describes the fit of the model. We used the *ordinary least squares* method to obtain the best fitting line, which attempts to minimize the sum of squared errors. Now the question arises about how we can determine whether the estimated coefficients are statistically significant. To figure it out, we will explain the process of conducting the hypothesis testing in the next chapter.

PRACTICE QUESTIONS

1. The working hours and the electricity consumption (in megawatts) in a factory are recorded for 20 days. Using an OLS method, estimate the values of the coefficients, and interpret the results.

Working Hours (X)	Electricity Consumption (Y)
14	920
8	730
10	840
9	850
5	700
5	720
8	760
8	790
9	820
7	710
6	710
7	750
7	790
13	900
8	870
12	930
11	910
5	650
13	870
14	970

2. The interest rate on loan charged by a bank and the demand for the loan (₹lacs) is given next. Estimate the values of the coefficients, and comment on the goodness of the fit of the model using the OLS method.

The Interest Rate on Loan (%; X)	Demand for Loans (₹ lacs; Y)
22	200
19	350
36	100
28	170
32	140
19	390
29	250
38	80
35	100
38	70
11	400
25	180

3. The rent (in ₹) and the area of the flats (in sq. ft.) for 20 houses in Delhi are given in the following table. Estimate the regression coefficients and find the rent value when the flat's area is 7500 sq. ft.

Area of the House (in sq. ft.; X)	Rent (Y)
2,000	16,000
2,600	18,000
2,800	20,000
3,300	21,000
4,000	25,000
4,000	27,000
4,000	31,000
4,300	32,500
4,800	33,000
6,000	37,000
6,500	39,000
6,600	42,000
7,200	43,000
7,200	44,000
7,400	51,000
8,400	51,000
8,400	52,000
8,500	55,000
8,700	56,000
8,800	59,000

4. The annual profits (in crores) for a company and its average annual share prices (₹) for the last 15 years are given next. Calculate the residuals and interpret the results.

Profits (in Crores; X)	Share Prices (Y)
600	7,800
560	6,000
540	6,800
460	6,800
400	5,900
360	5,700
330	5,500
330	4,500
280	4,300
270	2,800
220	2,500
220	2,600
200	2,100
170	1,000
120	1,800

5. The price of artificial jewellery (₹) and the orders placed (units) for the last 15 months are given next. You are required to interpret the regression output and the residual output obtained using Excel data analysis option.

Price (X)	Orders Placed (Y)
4,500	25,541
3,950	27,963
4,100	30,733
3,840	31,816
3,560	31,974
3,430	32,078
3,600	36,356
3,280	39,326
3,150	42,256
2,980	42,950
2,950	47,886
2,700	51,106
2,680	52,775
2,500	54,612
2,670	55,623

Notes

1 Summing up the given linear regression equation, we get

$$\Sigma Y = na + b\,\Sigma X \tag{1}$$
$$\Sigma XY = a\,\Sigma X + b\,\Sigma X^2 \tag{2}$$

Solving equations (1) and (2) simultaneously for a and b, we get

$$b = \frac{(\Sigma xy) - \dfrac{(\Sigma x)(\Sigma y)}{n}}{\Sigma x^2 - \dfrac{(\Sigma x)^2}{n}} \tag{3}$$

$$= \frac{n(\Sigma xy) - \Sigma x * \Sigma y}{n\Sigma x^2 - (\Sigma x)^2} \tag{4}$$

It may be recalled that the covariance between X and Y is given by

$$Cov(X, Y) = \frac{\Sigma XY}{n} - (\frac{\Sigma X}{n})(\frac{\Sigma Y}{n}) \tag{5}$$

Further, the variance of X is given by

$$\sigma_x^2 == \frac{\Sigma x^2}{n} - \left(\frac{\Sigma x}{n}\right)^2 \tag{6}$$

From (3), (5) and (6), we get

$$b = \frac{Cov(X,Y)}{\sigma_x^2}$$

2 Excel calculates parameters using ordinary least squares (OLS) method.

9

HYPOTHESIS TESTING IN REGRESSION ANALYSIS

Learning Objectives

After reading this chapter, the readers will be able to understand

- The concept of hypothesis testing
- Performing hypothesis testing to test the significance of the regression coefficients using:

  - The *t*-statistics approach
  - The *p*-value approach
  - Confidence interval approach

- Interpreting the statistical significance of the regression model and the coefficients with the help of regression results obtained in Excel

In the last chapter, we have observed that the population refers to the aggregate of all the items under study, but at times, it may not be possible to collect the data for the entire population. In that case, we select a sample from the population. The sample is the set of items taken from the population and is representative of it. The findings from this sample are generalized to the population as a whole and can infer about the population based on it.

The population parameters describe the characteristics of the entire population, while sample statistics describe the characteristics of the sample. The regression coefficients estimated from the regression model are based on the sample data and are the estimates for the population parameters (true values but unknown). Therefore, we use hypothesis testing to test the significance of the regression coefficients or to test whether the sample belongs to the population referred to. A regression output in Excel exhibits the following type of statistic. (a) *t*-statistics, (b) *p*-values, and (c) confidence intervals. The following sections attempt to understand the meaning of these tests so that they are interpreted aptly.

DOI: 10.4324/9781003398127-9

9.1 Hypothesis Testing Using the *t*-Statistics

In hypothesis testing, we make assumptions or statements about the population parameters. However, in reality, the assumptions made may not be true. Based on these assumptions, the hypothesis is formed, which can be tested using statistical tests wherein the validity of a belief, claim, or assumption made about the population based on the data is tested. The first approach is associated with the calculation of *t*-statistic, which tests the individual significance of the parameters estimated from the regression model. Hypothesis testing involves the following steps:

Step 1. Formulation of the Hypothesis

The first step involved is the formulation of the *null hypothesis* (H_0) and the *alternative hypothesis* (denoted by H_1 or H_A). The null hypothesis is assumed to be true, and the assumption is tested for rejection. With the rejection of the null hypothesis, we accept the alternative hypothesis. On the other hand, the alternative hypothesis is the opposite of the null hypothesis, which states that the population parameter is smaller or greater than the *null value (one-tailed)* or *non-directional (two-tailed)*. Note that the null hypothesis is only tested and not the alternative hypothesis.

H_0: $\mu = 0$
H_1: $\mu >$ or < 0 (One-tailed test)
H_1: $\mu \neq 0$ (Two-tailed test)

The null hypothesis always has strict equality. The following examples will help get a clear picture of the two tests. In the one-tailed test, for example, an Indian website claims that the average salary of finance managers is greater than 10 lacs per annum. The hypotheses can be stated as:

H_0: $\mu \leq 10$
(no change, that is, the average salary of finance managers is equal to or less than 10 lacs)

H_1: $\mu > 10$
(the average salary of finance managers is greater than 10 lacs)

On the other hand, in a two-tailed test, for example, if the objective is to examine the perception of the average typing speed of a student is 50 words per minute, the hypotheses for the study can be stated as:

H_0: $\mu = 50$
(no difference, that is, the average typing speed of a student is equal to 50 words per minute).

H_1: $\mu \neq 50$
(average typing speed of a student is not equal to 50 words per minute).

Step 2. Setting the significance level

Secondly, we set a significance level which is the probability at which we reject the null hypothesis when it is true. This is termed as the Type 1 Error, denoted by alpha (α). For instance, $\alpha = 0.05$ indicates that we are willing to take a 5 per cent chance that we may be wrong when we reject the null hypothesis when it is true. *Type 2 Error*, denoted by β (beta), is the probability of not rejecting the null hypothesis when it is false. The type 1 and type 2 errors are inversely related to each other, which means that as one of the errors increases, the other tends to decrease.

Power or $1 - \beta$ refers to the probability of rejecting a null hypothesis if it is false or the probability of not making a Type 2 error. Similarly, the *confidence level* or $1 - \alpha$ is the probability of not rejecting the null hypothesis when it is true or probability of not making a Type 1 error. Table 9.1 summarizes the type of errors and their significance.

Table 9.1 illustrates the significance level and the rejection region in a two-tailed test. The rejection area is on both sides of the distribution since the alternative hypothesis in this test is non-directional. Here, if $\alpha = 5$ per cent, then the distribution will have two rejection areas of 2.5 per cent ($\alpha/2$) on each side of the distribution (Figure 9.1). On the other hand, a one-tailed test (Figure 9.2) implies that there will be a single rejection region on either side of the

TABLE 9.1 Type 1 and Type 2 Errors

Statistical Decision \ True state of Null Hypothesis	Null Hypothesis is True	Null Hypothesis is False
Reject the null hypothesis	**TYPE 1 ERROR (α)** (Incorrect decision)	**POWER ($1 - \beta$)** (Correct decision)
Do not reject the null hypothesis	**CONFIDENCE LEVEL** **($1 - \alpha$)** (Correct decision)	**TYPE 2 ERROR (β)** (Incorrect decision)

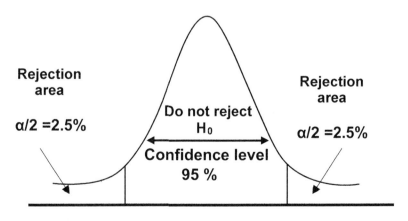

FIGURE 9.1 Rejection Areas for a Two-Tailed Test

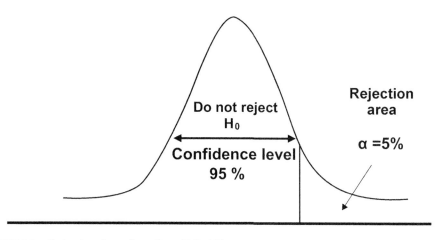

FIGURE 9.2 Rejection Areas for a One-Tailed Test

distribution. That is, if α = 5 per cent, then the distribution has one rejection region of 5 per cent on either side, left or right, depending on the sign of the null value in the alternative hypothesis. A significance level of 5 per cent is the most commonly used for making decisions in the field of finance, economics, or medicine. In Excel, the confidence level is set at 95 per cent by default, meaning a significance level of 5 per cent.

Step 3. Selecting the Suitable Test, Calculating the Test Statistic and Rejection Region

After considering several factors like population distribution or sample size, we choose the most appropriate statistical test to carry out the hypothesis testing. Based on the statistical test selected, we can calculate the test statistic value. Some common hypothesis tests are z-test, t-test, *chi-squared* test, and *ANOVA* and their test statistics are z statistics, t-statistics, *chi-square* statistics, and F-statistics respectively.

In the case of regression analysis, we translate our problem into t-distribution or z-distribution, based on sample size. A t-distribution is similar to a normal distribution with a bell-shaped curve but having relatively heavier tails. The t-test can be used to compare the means of population and sample means and determine whether the means of the two groups are significantly different from each other. The t-test is used for estimating the statistics when the sample size is small ($n < 30$) and the population standard deviation is unknown.

The formula for calculating the t-statistics is given by-

$$t = \frac{\text{Difference between the sample and the population mean}}{\text{Standard error}} = (\bar{x} - \mu) / (s/n)$$

Here,
    $\bar{x}$ = sample mean
    μ = population mean
    s = sample standard deviation
    n = sample size

It needs to be noted that many samples could be taken from the population. Each sample would have a mean and it is possible to think of a distribution of the sample mean and standard deviation of the sample mean. If the sample size is small, the variation would be high, and larger samples would have smaller variation. A measure of how different the sample mean is expected to be from the population mean is provided by the standard error of the mean, which is the standard deviation of the sample mean.

The t-test can also be used to conduct the hypothesis testing on the regression coefficients to determine if the slope coefficient is significantly different from zero. In the regression context, the t-statistic can be calculated as:

$$t = \frac{b_1 - \beta_1}{s_b}$$

Here,

b_1 = Estimated regression coefficient
β_1 = Slope coefficient against which we conduct the hypothesis test or the null value.
s_b = Standard error of β_1

The formula for standard error is: $\sqrt{\dfrac{\dfrac{SS_E}{n-2}}{\sum\left(X - \bar{X}\right)^2}}$

The following table summarizes the t-statistic and the rejection region.

Null Hypothesis: $H_0: \mu = \mu_0$

Test statistic value: $t = \dfrac{\bar{x} - \mu}{s / \sqrt{n}}$

Alternative Hypothesis	Rejection Region at level α
$H_1: \mu > \mu_0$	$t \geq t_{\alpha,\, n-1}$ (upper-tailed)
$H_1: \mu < \mu_0$	$t \leq -t_{\alpha,\, n-1}$ (lower-tailed)
$H_1: \mu \neq \mu_0$	either $t \geq t_{\alpha,\, n-1}$ or $t \leq -t_{\alpha,\, n-1}$ (two-tailed)

The cut-off value or the critical value $(t_{\alpha,\, n-1})$ for the rejection region is calculated for the given degrees of freedom and the significance level using the t-distribution table. We have already understood the concept of significance level in Step 2, so let us now go through the idea of the degrees of freedom. The *degrees of freedom* (*df*) represents how many values in a dataset are free to choose. It depends upon the number of parameters to be estimated, as we lose one degree of freedom for every parameter estimated. The degrees of freedom is calculated by subtracting the number of parameters to be estimated (k) from the sample size (n). Generally, for an ordinary t-test, the degrees of freedom is taken as $n - 1$. In the case of regression analysis, the degrees of freedom is taken as $n - k - 1$. For a simple linear regression (with one independent variable), the $df = n - 1 - 1 = n - 2$.

The degrees of freedom is given in the regression summary output obtained using the data analysis option in Excel as a residual degrees of freedom (*df*). As shown in Figure 9.3, the residual degrees of freedom (*df*) for $n = 28$ and one X variable is equal to **28 − 1 − 1 = 26**.

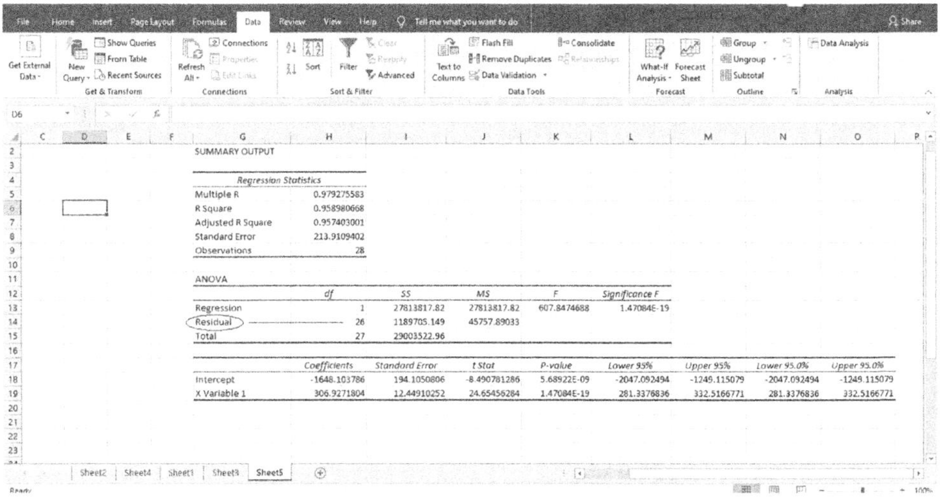

FIGURE 9.3 Regression Analysis Output: Residual Degrees of Freedom

Step 4. Check whether the t-statistic fall in the Rejection Region

If the t-statistic calculated in Step 3 fall in either of the rejection areas, we reject the null hypothesis. If the t-statistic fall outside the rejection area, we do not reject the null hypothesis. For example, the hypothesis stated as:

$H_0: \beta_1 = 0$ (no significant relationship between the dependent and independent variable)
$H_1: \beta_1 \neq 0$ (a significant relationship between the dependent and independent variable)

The cut-off value for say, $\alpha = 0.05$, and $df = 26$ comes out to be $\pm$ **2.056** as obtained from Table 9.2.[1] If the t-statistic calculated using the formula: $t = \dfrac{\overline{x} - \mu}{\dfrac{s}{n}}$ is more than $+2.056$ or

less than -2.056, that is, the value of the t-statistics falls to the left of the negative cut-off value or the right of the positive cut-off value, *we reject the null hypothesis* and conclude that there is a significant relationship between the dependent and independent variable. On the other hand, if the t-statistic does not fall in either of the rejection areas, *we do not reject the null hypothesis* and conclude that there is no significant relationship between the dependent and independent variables. It is important to note here that if a critical value is significant at 1 per cent, it must also be significant at 5 per cent. However, the converse is not true.

9.2 Hypothesis Testing Using the *p*-Value

The concept of *p*-value plays a vital role in interpreting the regression results and assessing the significance of the estimated regression coefficients. *The p-value is the probability that lies between 0 and 1 and is based on the assumption that the null hypothesis is true.* The *p*-values for every coefficient are automatically produced by Excel in the regression summary output obtained using the data analysis option. This means that Excel conducts hypothesis testing for every coefficient and produces the results in the form of *p*-values. To interpret the *p*-value,

TABLE 9.2 t-Distribution Table

t-test table

cum. prob	$t_{.50}$	$t_{.75}$	$t_{.80}$	$t_{.85}$	$t_{.90}$	$t_{.95}$	$t_{.975}$	$t_{.99}$	$t_{.995}$	$t_{.999}$	$t_{.9995}$
one-tail	0.50	0.25	0.20	0.15	0.10	0.05	0.025	0.01	0.005	0.001	0.0005
two-tails	1.00	0.50	0.40	0.30	0.20	0.10	0.05	0.02	0.01	0.002	0.001
df											
1	0.000	1.000	1.376	1.963	3.078	6.314	12.71	31.82	63.66	318.31	636.62
2	0.000	0.816	1.061	1.386	1.886	2.920	4.303	6.965	9.925	22.327	31.599
3	0.000	0.765	0.978	1.250	1.638	2.353	3.182	4.541	5.841	10.215	12.924
4	0.000	0.741	0.941	1.190	1.533	2.132	2.776	3.747	4.604	7.173	8.610
5	0.000	0.727	0.920	1.156	1.476	2.015	2.571	3.365	4.032	5.893	6.869
6	0.000	0.718	0.906	1.134	1.440	1.943	2.447	3.143	3.707	5.208	5.959
7	0.000	0.711	0.896	1.119	1.415	1.895	2.365	2.998	3.499	4.785	5.408
8	0.000	0.706	0.889	1.108	1.397	1.860	2.306	2.896	3.355	4.501	5.041
9	0.000	0.703	0.883	1.100	1.383	1.833	2.262	2.821	3.250	4.297	4.781
10	0.000	0.700	0.879	1.093	1.372	1.812	2.228	2.764	3.169	4.144	4.587
11	0.000	0.697	0.876	1.088	1.363	1.796	2.201	2.718	3.106	4.025	4.437
12	0.000	0.695	0.873	1.083	1.356	1.782	2.179	2.681	3.055	3.930	4.318
13	0.000	0.694	0.870	1.079	1.350	1.771	2.160	2.650	3.012	3.852	4.221
14	0.000	0.692	0.868	1.076	1.345	1.761	2.145	2.624	2.977	3.787	4.140
15	0.000	0.691	0.866	1.074	1.341	1.753	2.131	2.602	2.947	3.733	4.073
16	0.000	0.690	0.865	1.071	1.337	1.746	2.120	2.583	2.921	3.686	4.015
17	0.000	0.689	0.863	1.069	1.333	1.740	2.110	2.567	2.898	3.646	3.965
18	0.000	0.688	0.862	1.067	1.330	1.734	2.101	2.552	2.878	3.610	3.922
19	0.000	0.688	0.861	1.066	1.328	1.729	2.093	2.539	2.861	3.579	3.883
20	0.000	0.687	0.860	1.064	1.325	1.725	2.086	2.528	2.845	3.552	3.850
21	0.000	0.686	0.859	1.063	1.323	1.721	2.080	2.518	2.831	3.527	3.819
22	0.000	0.686	0.858	1.061	1.321	1.717	2.074	2.508	2.819	3.505	3.792
23	0.000	0.685	0.858	1.060	1.319	1.714	2.069	2.500	2.807	3.485	3.768
24	0.000	0.685	0.857	1.059	1.318	1.711	2.064	2.492	2.797	3.467	3.745
25	0.000	0.684	0.856	1.058	1.316	1.708	2.060	2.485	2.787	3.450	3.725
26	0.000	0.684	0.856	1.058	1.315	1.706	2.056	2.479	2.779	3.435	3.707
27	0.000	0.684	0.855	1.057	1.314	1.703	2.052	2.473	2.771	3.421	3.690
28	0.000	0.683	0.855	1.056	1.313	1.701	2.048	2.467	2.763	3.408	3.674
29	0.000	0.683	0.854	1.055	1.311	1.699	2.045	2.462	2.756	3.396	3.659
30	0.000	0.683	0.854	1.055	1.310	1.697	2.042	2.457	2.750	3.385	3.646
40	0.000	0.681	0.851	1.050	1.303	1.684	2.021	2.423	2.704	3.307	3.551
60	0.000	0.679	0.848	1.045	1.296	1.671	2.000	2.390	2.660	3.232	3.460
80	0.000	0.678	0.846	1.043	1.292	1.664	1.990	2.374	2.639	3.195	3.416
100	0.000	0.677	0.845	1.042	1.290	1.660	1.984	2.364	2.626	3.174	3.390
1000	0.000	0.675	0.842	1.037	1.282	1.646	1.962	2.330	2.581	3.098	3.300
z	0.000	0.674	0.842	1.036	1.282	1.645	1.960	2.326	2.576	3.090	3.291
	0%	50%	60%	70%	80%	90%	95%	98%	99%	99.8%	99.9%
					Confidence Level						

it is important to find out which test statistic is used. The first three steps for conducting the hypothesis testing, namely, formulating the hypothesis, setting the significance level, and selecting the suitable test, remain the same.

Suppose the given test statistic is t-statistic. The p-values can be interpreted as follows. In a two-tailed hypothesis test, the rejection region on both sides is calculated using $\alpha/2$. In Figure 9.4, if the p-value is greater than the significance level, it does not fall in the rejection region. In that case, we do not reject the null hypothesis when $p > \alpha$. Similarly, in Figure 9.5, the t-statistic falls in the rejection region as we observe that the p-value is less than the significance level. Thus, we reject the null hypothesis when $p < \alpha$.

For example, for a two-tail test, say, $\alpha = 0.05$, residual $df = 26$, and t-statistics = 24.6545, (Figure 9.6) the p-value is equal to **0.0001**. Since the p-value is less than α, that is, $0.0001 < 0.05$, *we reject the null hypothesis*. On the other hand, for another two-tail test, if the $\alpha = 0.05$, residual $df = 26$, and t-statistics is 0.85 then the p-value is equal to **0.40.** Since the p-value is greater than α, that is, $0.40 > 0.05$, *we do not reject the null hypothesis*.

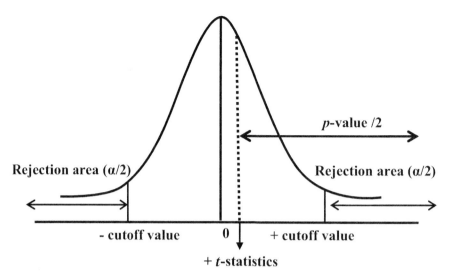

FIGURE 9.4   *t*-Distribution *p*-Value > alpha (α)

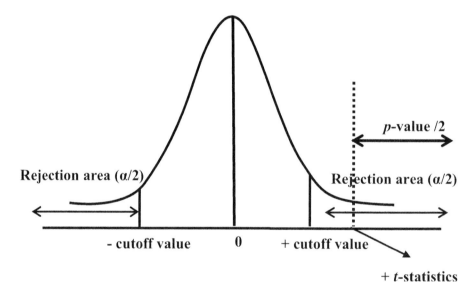

FIGURE 9.5   *t*-Distribution *p*-Value < alpha (α)

9.3   Hypothesis Testing Using the Confidence Interval

The third approach used for hypothesis testing is the *confidence interval approach*. It is the most simple and easiest approach to conduct hypothesis testing. It involves interpreting the confidence intervals obtained for the estimated regression coefficients in the regression output in Excel. The confidence level of 0.95 means that if we keep repeating the event, then in 95 per cent of the events, the true population parameter will lie in the confidence interval range.

The following steps need to be followed for conducting hypothesis testing using confidence intervals, Step 1 being the same as earlier.

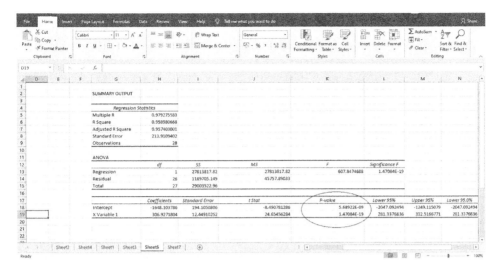

FIGURE 9.6 *t*-Distribution Computed *p*-Value < alpha (α)

Step 2. Consider the 95 Per Cent Confidence Interval as Produced for the Slope Coefficient of the *X* Variable by the Regression Output in Excel.

In this step, we check whether or not the null value falls in the 95 per cent confidence interval. The lower limit and the upper limit for the 95 per cent confidence interval is specified in the regression output. If the null value indeed falls within the confidence intervals, *we do not reject the null hypothesis*, or we may say that we do not reject the null hypothesis for any value between the two specified limits of the confidence interval. On the other hand, if the value in the null hypothesis does not fall in the confidence intervals, *we reject the null hypothesis*.

We can conclude that

- If the value specified in H_0 lies outside the interval, we can reject H_0.
- If the value specified in H_0 lies within the interval, we do not reject H_0.

Continuing on the previous example, we need to test the significance of the regression model and interpret the results obtained based on confidence intervals. The highlighted part in the regression output displays the upper and the lower limit for the 95 per cent confidence interval (Figure 9.7). We notice that the reference value in the null hypothesis, that is, 0 does not fall in the specified range; it falls outside the 95 per cent confidence interval. Hence, we reject the null hypothesis, which implies a significant relationship between the dependent and independent variables.

Illustration

The regression output realized in Chapter 8 example (A company incurring promotion expenses to boost their revenue) is reproduced in Figure 9.8.

We have already developed and estimated the regression model for the promotion expenses as the independent variable and the revenue as the dependent variable. The estimated regression model is:

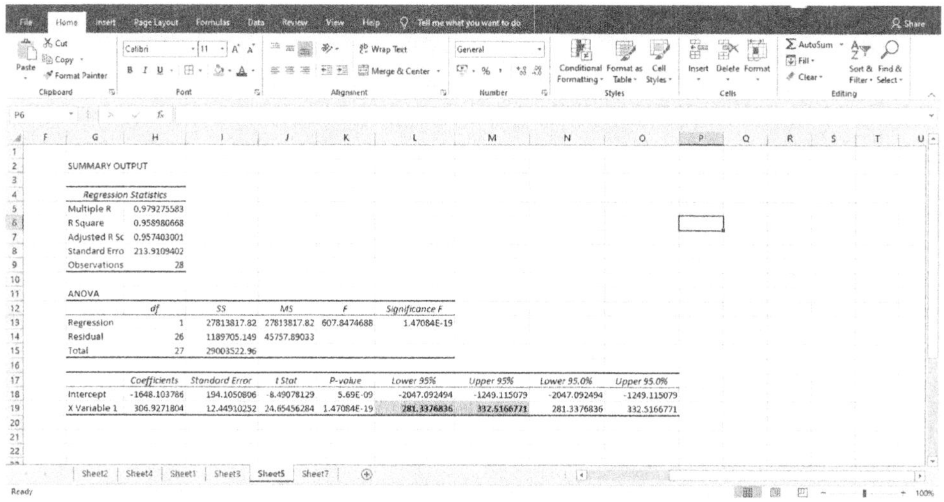

SUMMARY OUTPUT

Regression Statistics	
Multiple R	0.979275583
R Square	0.958980668
Adjusted R Sc	0.957403001
Standard Erro	213.9109402
Observations	28

ANOVA

	df	SS	MS	F	Significance F
Regression	1	27813817.82	27813817.82	607.8474688	1.47084E-19
Residual	26	1189705.149	45757.89033		
Total	27	29003522.96			

	Coefficients	Standard Error	t Stat	P-value	Lower 95%	Upper 95%	Lower 95.0%	Upper 95.0%
Intercept	-1648.103786	194.1050806	-8.49078129	5.69E-09	-2047.092494	-1249.115079	-2047.092494	-1249.115079
X Variable 1	306.9271804	12.44910252	24.65456284	1.47084E-19	281.3376836	332.5166771	281.3376836	332.5166771

FIGURE 9.7 Regression Analysis Output (95% Confidence Intervals)

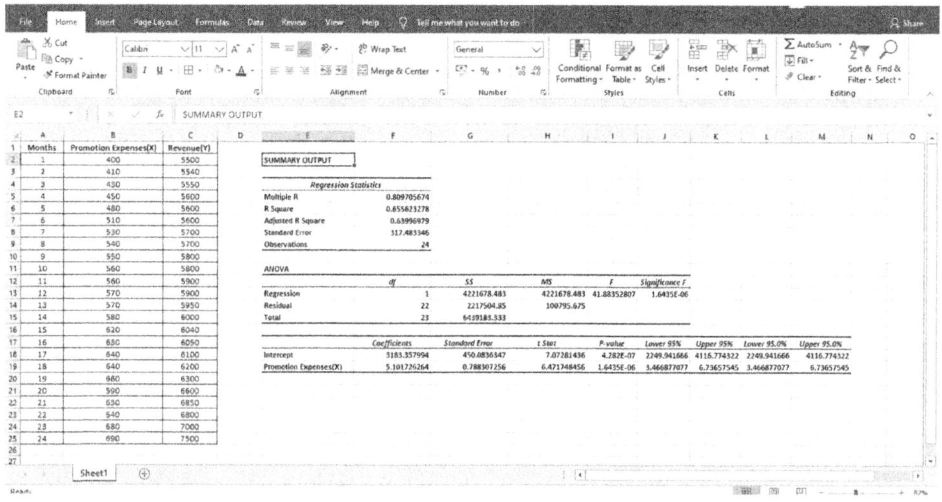

Months	Promotion Expenses(X)	Revenue(Y)
1	400	5500
2	410	5540
3	430	5550
4	450	5600
5	480	5600
6	510	5600
7	530	5700
8	540	5700
9	550	5800
10	560	5800
11	560	5900
12	570	5900
13	570	5950
14	580	6000
15	620	6040
16	630	6050
17	640	6100
18	640	6200
19	660	6300
20	590	6600
21	630	6850
22	640	6800
23	680	7000
24	690	7500

SUMMARY OUTPUT

Regression Statistics	
Multiple R	0.809705674
R Square	0.655623278
Adjusted R Square	0.63996979
Standard Error	317.483346
Observations	24

ANOVA

	df	SS	MS	F	Significance F
Regression	1	4221678.483	4221678.483	41.88352807	1.6435E-06
Residual	22	2217504.85	100795.675		
Total	23	6439183.333			

	Coefficients	Standard Error	t Stat	P-value	Lower 95%	Upper 95%	Lower 95.0%	Upper 95.0%
Intercept	3183.357994	450.0836347	7.07281436	4.282E-07	2249.941666	4116.774322	2249.941666	4116.774322
Promotion Expenses(X)	5.101726264	0.788307256	6.471748456	1.6435E-06	3.466877077	6.73657545	3.466877077	6.73657545

FIGURE 9.8 Test Results of the Regression Equation Displayed in the Excel Sheet

$$\text{Revenue} = 3{,}183.3579 + 5.101726 \times \text{Promotional Expenses}$$

Now, the sales manager wishes to test the significance of the developed regression model and assess the promotion expenses' importance in explaining the revenue variation.

Solution and interpretation:

First Method (*t*-Value Approach)

The null hypothesis assumes that the beta coefficient is equal to zero (null value) which means that there is no significant relationship between the promotion expenses and revenues. The hypotheses can be stated as:

$$H_0: \beta_1 = 0$$
$$H_1: \beta_1 \neq 0$$

The significance level (α) is set at **5%.**

Excel provides the t-statistic (t-value) as 6.4717.

The critical t-value is calculated using the table. The rejection region for this two-tailed test is either $t \geq t_{\alpha, n-2}$ or $t \leq -t_{\alpha, n-2}$. The table value of $t_{.05,22}$ is 2.074. Since $6.4717 > 2.074$, we reject the null hypothesis. This implies that there is a significant relationship between the revenue earned by the company (dependent variable) and promotion expense incurred (independent variable).

Second Method (p-Value Approach)

The p-value that Excel provides us is 1.6435E-06 which denotes a very small number equal to 0.000001643. We observe that this p-value is less than the significance level of 0.05, that is, $p < \alpha$, therefore, we *reject the null hypothesis* and conclude that there is a significant relationship between the revenues earned by the company (dependent variable) and promotion expense incurred (independent variable).

Third Method (Confidence Interval Approach)

The lower limit and the upper limit for the 95 per cent confidence interval are specified in the regression output as 3.466877 and 6.73657545, respectively (Figure 9.8). Since our null value $\beta_1 = 0$ does not fall within the confidence intervals, *we reject the null hypothesis*, which further implies a significant relationship between the revenues earned by the company (dependent variable) and promotion expense incurred (independent variable).

It is important to note that the outcomes in all these approaches remain the same, which is to reject the null hypothesis.

To sum up, this chapter introduced a very important concept of hypothesis testing, which plays a crucial role in making inferences about the true population estimates. The estimated coefficients are checked, whether there is a significant linear relationship between the dependent and independent variables, using different approaches.

PRACTICE QUESTIONS

1. The area of the house (in sq. ft.) and the electricity bill (₹) is given next. Test the significance of the regression coefficients estimated using the t-statistics approach. (Significance level = 5 per cent).

Area of the House (in sq. ft.) (X)	Electricity Bill (in ₹) (Y)
1,716	10,800
1,886	18,000
2,056	16,000
2,057	20,000
2,095	21,000
2,403	23,000
3,291	24,500
3,333	27,000
3,747	26,000
3,838	28,500

Area of the House (in sq. ft.) (X)	Electricity Bill (in ₹) (Y)
4,726	29,500
4,956	31,000
5,561	31,600
7,550	32,000
7,815	31,900
7,863	32,500
7,899	36,000
8,128	34,000
8,215	39,000
8,500	38,311

2. The average annual income of 25 people and the taxes paid by them in ₹ are given in the following table. Develop the regression model and test the significance of the regression model developed using the p-values approach. (Significance level = 5 per cent).

Individual Annual Income (X)	Taxes Paid (Y)
7,00,000	70,000
7,50,000	90,000
7,70,000	1,23,200
8,50,000	85,000
8,54,000	1,28,100
8,70,000	69,600
10,30,000	2,06,000
10,30,000	2,06,000
10,80,000	2,16,000
11,00,000	2,20,000
11,20,000	2,40,000
11,30,000	2,26,000
11,60,000	2,30,000
12,40,000	2,48,000
13,00,000	2,60,000
13,60,000	2,72,000
14,60,000	2,80,000
15,00,000	3,00,000
16,50,000	4,95,000
17,80,000	5,34,000
18,00,000	5,48,000
18,25,000	5,50,000
19,70,000	5,91,000
19,80,000	5,94,000
20,42,000	6,12,600

3. Abhinav uploads videos on YouTube on Statistics and Economics concepts. The views and likes on 20 of his videos are given next. Abhinav believes that the number of views

has a significant impact on the number of likes on the videos. Conduct the significance test to determine if the views (The X variable) are useful to explain the variation in the number of likes (Y variable) using the p-values approach. Is the belief of Abhinav correct? (Significance level = 5 per cent)

Views (X)	Likes (Y)
2,12,000	1,06,000
1,39,000	55,600
2,98,000	89,400
2,16,000	9,000
3,01,000	15,000
3,15,000	1,57,500
3,50,000	1,40,000
3,70,000	1,11,000
4,60,000	25,000
4,80,000	10,000
4,75,000	2,37,500
5,00,000	2,00,000
5,20,000	1,56,000
5,62,000	1,12,400
6,30,000	20,000
6,00,000	3,00,000
8,60,000	3,44,000
8,80,000	2,64,000
9,50,000	50,000
9,30,000	70,000

4. The literacy level (in percentage) and the number of people below the poverty line (as per cent of the total population) for 20 states are given next. Develop the regression model and test the significance of the regression model developed using a 95 per cent confidence interval approach. (Significance level = 5 per cent). Is your answer the same if the test the significance is done using a 99 per cent confidence interval approach (Significance level = 1 per cent)?

Literacy Level (%) (X)	People Below the Poverty Line (%) (Y)
94	5
92	7
89	8
86	9
82	9
81	12
78	15
78	17
76	19

Literacy Level (%) (X)	People Below the Poverty Line (%) (Y)
73	21
72	22
68	26
67	28
65	25
62	29
61	32
59	35
52	27
51	36
50	39

5. The rainfall (in inches) and production of rice (in thousand million tonnes) is given next. Interpret the regression output as provided by Excel to test the significance of the regression coefficients. The agriculture officer claims that when rainfall increases by 1 inch the rice production increases by 1400 thousand million tonnes. Check the validity of this claim. (Significance level = 5 per cent).

Rainfall (in Inches) (X)	Rice Production (in Thousand Million Tonnes) (Y)
30	1,17,939
28	1,16,480
29	1,12,760
25	1,09,698
23	1,06,646
16	1,05,482
22	1,05,301
20	1,05,241
17	1,04,408
15	99,172
13	96,682
12	95,970
11	93,345
12	91,785
14	89,083

Note

1   The t-distribution table has degrees of freedom in the rows and the significance level in the columns for both the one-tail and two-tail tests. The intersection cell, in a two-tail test, if the degree of freedom is 26 and the significance level is at 5 per cent, the critical value read from the table is **2.056.**

10

UNDERSTANDING GROWTH RATES

Learning Objectives

After reading this chapter, the readers will be able to understand

- Concept of growth and growth rate
- Meaning, calculation, and interpretation of average annual growth rate using Excel
- Meaning, calculation, and interpretation of compound annual growth rate using Excel

Growth refers to the increase or development of a specific variable from one form or stage to another. In business, the terminology could include estimating an increase in the revenue or an increase in the market share, amongst others. Similarly, economic growth could imply the ability of a country to produce more goods and services in successive years. It is measured in terms of the Gross Domestic Product (GDP), the aggregate value of all the goods and services produced within the country during a specified period, generally taken as a year. Nonetheless, growth may also be used to study the increase in population size, the measure of economic activity of a nation, corporate performance, and returns on investment.

10.1   Growth Rate

Measuring growth rate is of interest to various stakeholders. Growth rate usually refers to the percentage change in the value of a specific variable over a certain period. It is defined as the difference between the final (ending) and initial (beginning) value of the variable expressed as a percentage of the initial value. Growth rates are generally used by analysts, investors, management of a company, and others to assess past performance and also to predict future values. Various growth rates, such as industry growth rate, economic growth rate, company growth rate, or even investment returns, can be calculated. They depict the growth trends or trajectory for the company's performance, investment, or economy, etc., and give insights

DOI: 10.4324/9781003398127-10

into how it will perform in the future. Given its usefulness, in this chapter, we introduce the various types of growth rate, their application, and how to calculate them mainly using Excel.

10.2   Simple Growth Rate

To measure the simple growth rate, the following steps are taken:

Step 1. Calculate the difference between the final and initial value, that is, subtract the initial value from the final value. It may be positive or negative. A positive value means an increase in the variable's value, and a negative refers to a decrease in the variable's value.

Step 2. Divide the difference obtained in the previous step by the initial value.

Step 3. Multiply the value obtained in Step 2 by 100 to express it in percentage terms.

The formula used to calculate the simple growth rate, thus, is expressed as follows.

$$Simple\ Growth\ Rate = \frac{Final\ value - Initial\ value}{Initial\ value} * 100$$

$$Alternatively, \left(\frac{Final\ value}{Initial\ value} - 1\right) * 100$$

Illustration

A business is interested in finding out the simple growth rate of its revenue over the past five years. During their first year of business, the revenue was ₹5,50,000. After the fifth year, its yearly revenue turned out to be ₹19,50,000.

The simple growth rate can be easily calculated by using the formula mentioned earlier as follows:

$$Growth\ rate = \frac{Final\ value - Initial\ value}{Initial\ value} * 100$$

Where, final value = ₹19,50,000
Initial value = ₹5,50,000
Substituting this value in the formula, we get,

$$Growth\ rate = \frac{19,50,000 - 5,50,000}{5,50,000} * 100$$

$$= \frac{14,00,000}{550000} * 100$$

$$= 254.5454 \text{ per cent.}$$

It can be concluded that this business has grown at a rate of 254.5454 per cent over five years. However, the limitation of using the earlier formula for growth rate is that it does not account for the intermediary years. Also, the growth rate of two different companies or investments cannot be compared if the number of years is different. Therefore, to overcome it, we calculate the average annual growth rate to make the results more meaningful and comparable. The following section presents an exposition of the concept and calculation of the average annual growth rate.

10.3   Average Annual Growth Rate

The average annual growth rate over a period of time is the average of growth rate for each year. It refers to the average increase or decrease in the value of a variable over a specified period. The average annual growth rate is generally used to calculate the average investment returns over several years. It can also be used to study revenue growth, dividend growth, profit growth, and changes in economic activity (GDP growth rate). It helps determine long-term growth trends or trajectories. It is calculated using the simple arithmetic mean of year-on-year or periodic growth rates.

To compute the average return, we must first compute the growth rates for each year in the series. Once the growth rates for each period are calculated, we will add up all the values and divide them by the total number of years to compute the annual rate of return on an average.

The formula for average annual growth rate is as follows:

$$\text{Average annual growth rate} = \frac{g_1 + g_2 + \ldots g_n}{n}$$

Here, g_1 = Growth rate for the first year
g_2 = Growth rate for the second year
g_n = Growth rate for the nth year
n = number of years

$$\text{or, Average annual growth rate} = \frac{Sum\ of\ the\ growth\ rates\ for\ each\ year}{number\ of\ years}$$

Illustration

We try to understand the concept of the average annual growth rate with the following example. Suppose that the GDP increases from ₹1,000 crores to ₹1,100 crores in the first year, ₹1,400 crores in the second, ₹1,200 crores in the third year, ₹1,500 crores in the fourth year, and ₹1,800 crores in the fifth year. Calculate the average annual growth rate.

First Method (Direct Method)

As per the information available,

Initial value = ₹1,000 crores

GDP at the end of year 1 = ₹1,100 crores
GDP at the end of year 2 = ₹1,400 crores
GDP at the end of year 3 = ₹1,200 crores
GDP at the end of year 4 = ₹1,500 crores
GDP at the end of year 5 = ₹1,500 crores

Here, for the first year, the growth rate will be equal to

$$\frac{Final\ value - Initial\ value}{Initial\ value} * 100$$

i.e., $\dfrac{GDP\ in\ year\ 2 - GDP\ in\ year\ 1}{GDP\ in\ year\ 1} * 100$

$$= \frac{1100 - 1000}{1000} * 100 = 10\ \text{per cent.}$$

Similarly, using the preceding growth rate formula, the growth rates from years 1 to 5 can be computed as follows:

Year	GDP (in ₹Crores)	Growth Rate
0	₹1,000	–
1	₹1,100	10%
2	₹1,400	27.27%
3	₹1,200	(14.28%)
4	₹1,500	25%
5	₹1,800	20%

Looking at the different growth rates, it may not be straightforward for an analyst to interpret the overall growth in the economy over five years. Hence, an average annual growth rate is calculated.

$$\text{Average annual growth rate} = \frac{Sum\ of\ the\ growth\ rates\ for\ each\ year}{number\ of\ years}$$

Where, the sum of the growth rates = $10 + 27.27 - 14.28 + 25 + 20 = 67.99$
By substituting the value in the formula, we get,

$$\text{Average annual growth rate} = \frac{67.99}{5} = 13.598\ \text{per cent.}$$

Ans. The average annual growth rate for GDP is 13.598 or 13.6 per cent.

Second Method (Using Excel)

To calculate the average annual growth rate using Excel, follow these steps:

Step 1. Enter the GDP values for all five years in the Excel spreadsheet as shown in Figure 10.1.

Step 2. First, we calculate the growth rates for each year. For the first year, we calculate the growth rate with the formula $= \dfrac{\textbf{GDP in year 2} - \textbf{GDP in year 1}}{\textbf{GDP in year 1}}$.

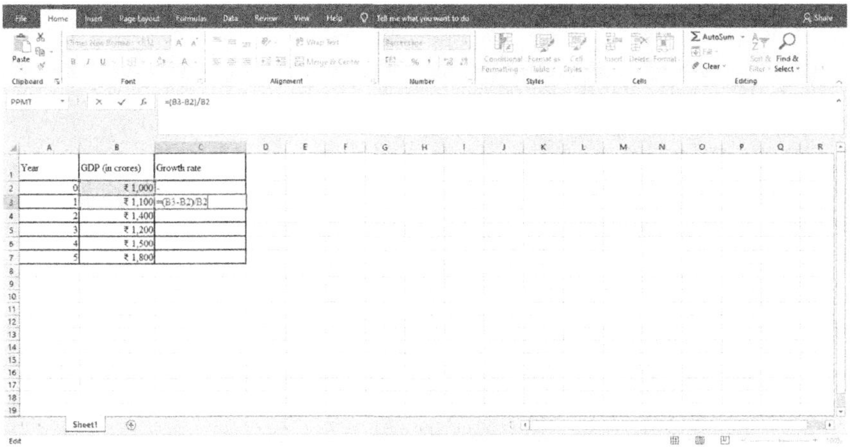

FIGURE 10.1 Step 1 in the Calculation of Average Annual Growth Rate

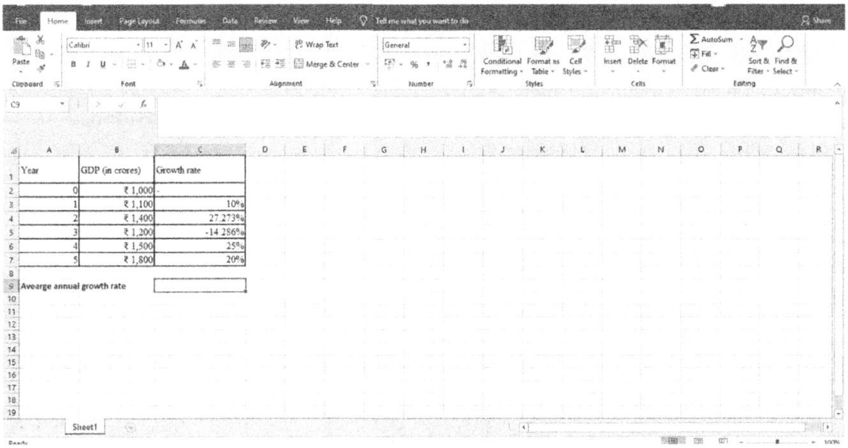

FIGURE 10.2 Step 2 in the Calculation of Average Annual Growth Rate

Type '=' (equal to) sign in the blank cell where the result is desired, say, 'C3' and then enter the preceding formula, '= (B3-B2)/B2'. Press **Enter**. The result will appear in cell C3 (Figure 10.1). Click the **Percent Style** button on the **Home** tab to format the results as a percentage.

Step 3. Click on the fill handle (the small black square in the bottom right corner when you select the cell) and drag it vertically to calculate the growth rate for all the years, as shown in Figure 10.2.

Step 4. Once the growth rates for each period are calculated, we will then calculate the simple average of the series of growth rates. We use the **AVERAGE** function to calculate the mean. Type the '=' (equal to) sign in the cell where the result is desired, say 'C9', and enter the function name **AVERAGE** and then select the range of numbers for which average is to be calculated, that is, **C3:C7**. Press **Enter**. The result will appear in cell C9 (Figure 10.3).

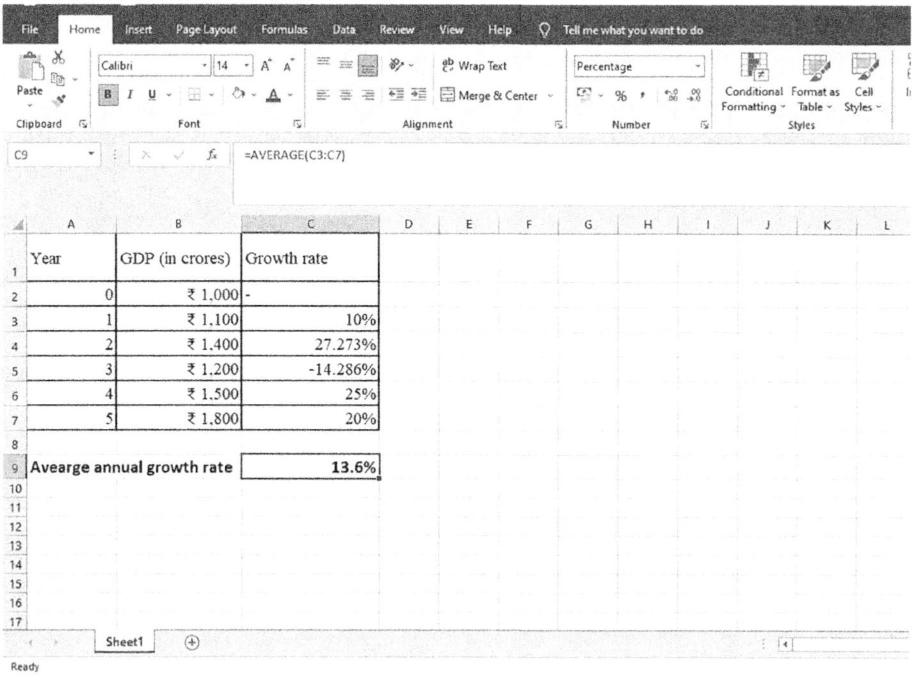

FIGURE 10.3 Step 3 in the Calculation of Average Annual Growth Rate

As we have noticed, an average annual growth rate is simply the average of a series of growth rates. Even though it is helpful to estimate the growth trend, it may be misleading as it ignores the degree of fluctuations or change occurring in the values in a given period. Investment grows at a rate of 40 per cent in the first year and 25 per cent in the second year. The average annual growth rate would be 32.5 per cent. Therefore, the fluctuations that occurred in the rate of return on the investments during that period have not been taken into account by the average annual growth rate. This may lead to an overestimation of the growth rate. We take one more example to understand this vital point. Let us assume that the revenue earned by a business over the past seven years is given in the following table.

Year	Revenue (₹)
0	3,50,000
1	6,00,000
2	7,00,000
3	10,50,000
4	9,00,000
5	7,50,000
6	4,00,000
7	3,50,000

We calculate the revenue growth rate for each year

Year	Revenue (₹)	Growth rate
0	3,50,000	—
1	6,00,000	71.43%
2	7,00,000	16.67%
3	10,50,000	50.00%
4	9,00,000	−14.29%
5	7,50,000	−16.67%
6	4,00,000	−46.67%
7	3,50,000	−12.50%
Total		47.98%

The average annual calculated growth rate is 47.98 per cent/7 = 6.8542 per cent. Yet, we notice that the overall revenue growth rate of the business over seven years is Nil as revenue for the first year is the same as the revenue generated in the seventh year, which is ₹3,50,000. Nevertheless, the calculated average annual growth rate turns out as 6.8542 per cent. As mentioned earlier, measuring the average annual growth rate when fluctuations characterize the data can be misleading and lead to overestimation.

Another major drawback with using the average annual growth rate is that since it is a linear measure, it does not consider or accommodate the compounding effects. This is where the compound annual growth rate becomes beneficial. The relevance, application, and calculation of compound annual growth rate (CAGR) are explained in the following section.

10.4   Compound Annual Growth Rate

An advantage of using CAGR in place of the average annual growth rate is that the fluctuating values do not affect the former. In addition, it also considers the compounding effect, that is, the accumulation of growth as in the case of population or when an additional sum earned on an investment is reinvested assuming the same growth rate. Compound annual growth rate also enables assessment of investment performance within the investment period. It allows a quick comparison between alternative investment schemes' performance or their expected future values.

Therefore, the compound annual growth rate is the annual rate that tells us how much a variable has grown over the period assuming that the income earned is reinvested at the end of each year during the whole period. The additional money earned is reinvested at the same growth rate. Let us understand it with an example. An investor invests ₹100 in a fixed deposit on which he earns an interest of 10 per cent per annum compounded annually. At the end of year one, the investor earns ₹10 as the interest. The interest earned is reinvested at the same rate along with the original amount for the next year; that is, the investment amount (Principal) for the second year will be ₹100 + ₹10 = ₹110. The interest is now paid on both the principal and accumulated interest. Therefore, the interest for the second year will be 10 per cent of ₹110 = ₹11. Finally, the value of the investment at the end of the second year is ₹100 + ₹10 + ₹11 = ₹121. This is similar to the compound interest concept explained in Chapter 12.

Nevertheless, a limitation of CAGR is that it assumes a constant growth rate throughout the period. This means that it ignores the volatility (of a variable) due to which the results may vary from the actual. Therefore, it is not an accurate estimate of the growth rate but a single representative annualized figure of the compounded occurrence.

To determine the formula for the compound annual growth rate (CAGR), let us begin with the general formula to calculate the compound rate of interest that we show in Chapter 12,

i.e., $FV_n = P(1+r)^n$

where FV_n = Future value

P = Principal or the value at the beginning

r = rate of interest compounded annually or compound annual growth rate

n = number of years

Now, we rearrange the preceding formula to calculate the compound annual growth rate (r)

We get $r = \left(\dfrac{FV_n}{P}\right)^{1/n} - 1$

Or, CAGR $= \left(\dfrac{Final\ value}{Initial\ value}\right)^{(1/n)} - 1$

Illustration

An investor invested ₹25,000 (10 units for ₹2,500 each) in a mutual fund for five years. The NAV of the fund for all the years is given in the following table:

Year	NAV of the Mutual Fund (₹)
0	2,500
1	3,000
2	3,200
3	1,500
4	2,800
5	3,600

First Method (Direct Method)

As per the information available,

Initial value = ₹2,500

NAV at the end of year 5 = ₹3,600

The compound annual growth rate will be calculated with the help of the formula given next

i.e., CAGR $= \left(\dfrac{Final\ value}{Initial\ value}\right)^{(1/n)} - 1$

Substituting the aforementioned values in the formula, we get,

$$\text{CAGR} = \left(\frac{3{,}600}{2{,}500}\right)^{1/5} - 1 = 1.075654 - 1$$

$$= 0.075654 \text{ or } 7.5654 \text{ per cent}$$

Thus, the NAV of the mutual fund grew at a CAGR of 7.5654 per cent for five years.

Second Method (Using Excel)

To calculate the compound annual growth rate using Excel, follow these steps:

Step 1. Enter the NAV values for all five years in the Excel spreadsheet (Figure 10.3).

Step 2. As shown in Figure 10.3, the final value is entered in **B7**, and the initial value is entered in cell **B2**. Type '=' (equal to sign) in the blank cell where the result is desired, say, 'B8' and then enter the formula for CAGR as given earlier, that is, $= (B7/B2)^{\wedge (1/5)} - 1$.

Step 3. Press **Enter.** The result will appear in cell **B8** (Figure 10.4). Click the **Percent Style** button on the **Home** tab to format the result as a percentage.

Note: '^' is the symbol that indicates 'power of the base value' in Excel.

Third Method (Using Excel)

To calculate the compound annual growth rate using Excel, follow these steps:

Step 1. Enter the NAV values for all five years in the Excel spreadsheet (Figure 10.5).

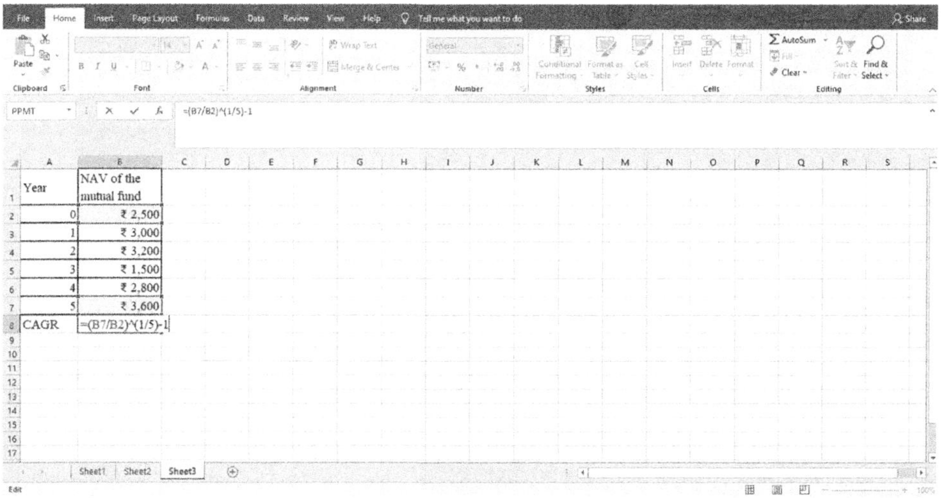

FIGURE 10.4   Calculation of Compound Annual Growth Rate

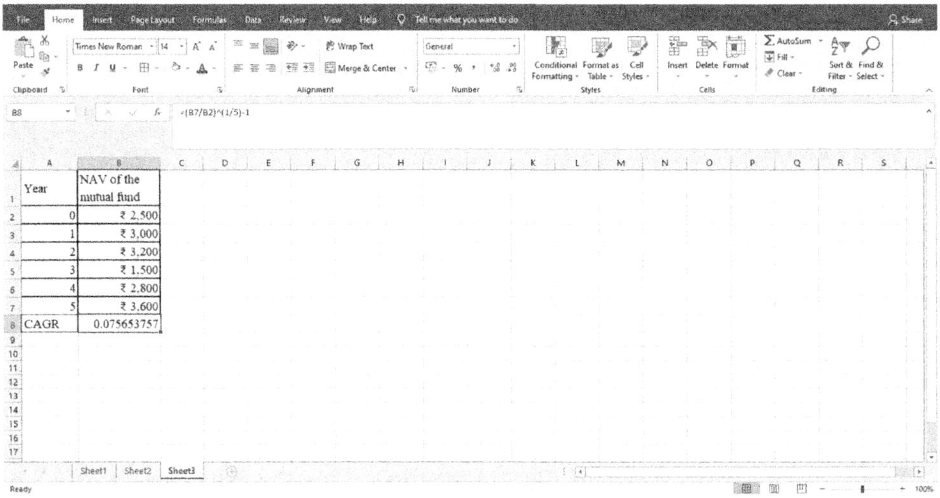

FIGURE 10.5 Calculation of Compound Annual Growth Rate

Step 2. We use the **RRI** function to calculate the Compound Annual Growth Rate (CAGR) in Excel. The function is available in Excel 2013 and later versions. The function returns an equivalent interest rate for the growth of an investment, and the result will be the same as the one obtained using the mathematical formula for CAGR. The syntax of the function is =RRI (nper, PV, *FV*).

Here,

nper = number of periods

PV = Present value of investment or value at the beginning of the investment period

FV = Future value of the investment or value at the end of an investment period

As shown in Figure 10.5, the ending value is entered in **B7,** and the beginning value is entered in cell **B2**. Therefore, in our case nper = 5, *FV* = 3,600 and PV = 2,500. Type the '=' (equal to) sign in the cell where the result is desired, say '**B8**', and the formula '=RRI (5, B2, B7)' and press **Enter.**

Step 3. The result will appear in cell **B8** (Figure 10.6). Click the **Percent Style** button on the **Home** tab to format the result as a percentage.

Let's take a slightly different example. In real life, we often face a situation when we need to know the CAGR to achieve a fixed amount in the future. Say, for instance, Mr X has ₹4,00,00 today, which he wants to invest for his retirement. He needs to know the CAGR at which he should invest this amount to create a corpus of ₹1,00,00,000 after 40 years using the RRI function. To calculate in Excel, the following are undertaken to conclude that he needs to invest the amount at a CAGR of 8.38 per cent.

Step 1. Enter the number of periods, present value, and future value in the Excel spreadsheet (Figure 10.7).

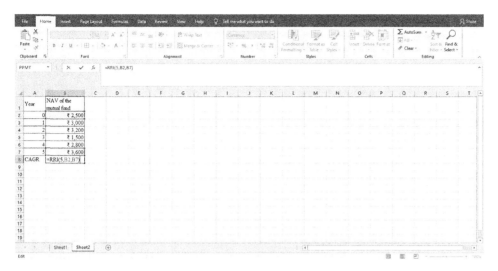

FIGURE 10.6   Calculation of Compound Annual Growth Rate Using RRI Function

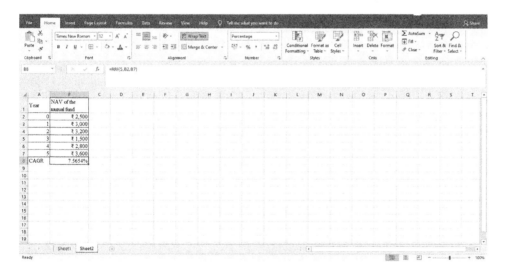

FIGURE 10.7   Calculation of Compound Annual Growth Rate Using RRI Function

    Step 2. We use the **RRI** function to calculate CAGR in Excel. As shown in Figure 10.7 the number of periods (nper) is entered in **B1,** initial value (present value) is entered in cell **B2** and final value (future value) is entered in **B2** Therefore, in our case nper = 40, FV = 1,00,00,000 and PV = 4,00,000. Type the '=' (equal to) sign in the cell where the result is desired, say '**B5**', and the formula '=RRI (B1, B2, B3)' and press **Enter.**

    Step 3. The result will appear in cell **B5** (Figure 10.8). Click the **Percent Style** button on the **Home** tab to format the result as a percentage (Figure 10.9).

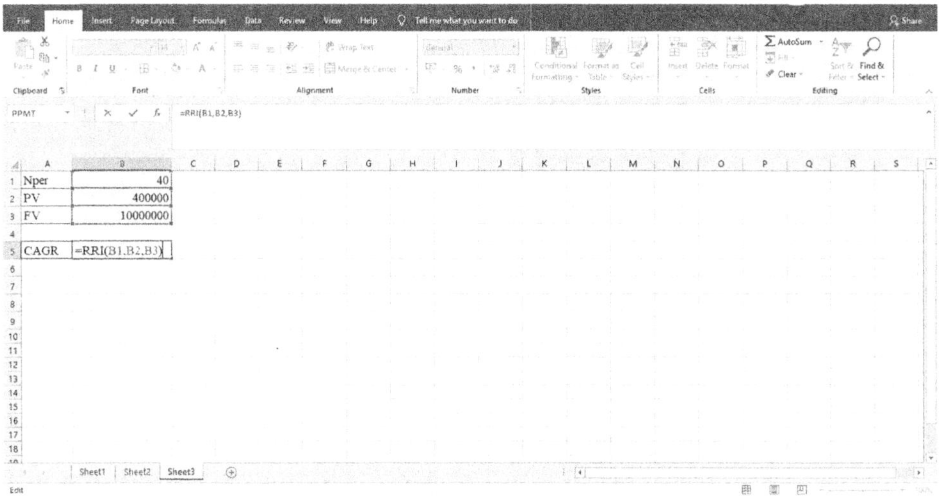

FIGURE 10.8 Calculation of Compound Annual Growth Rate Using RRI Function

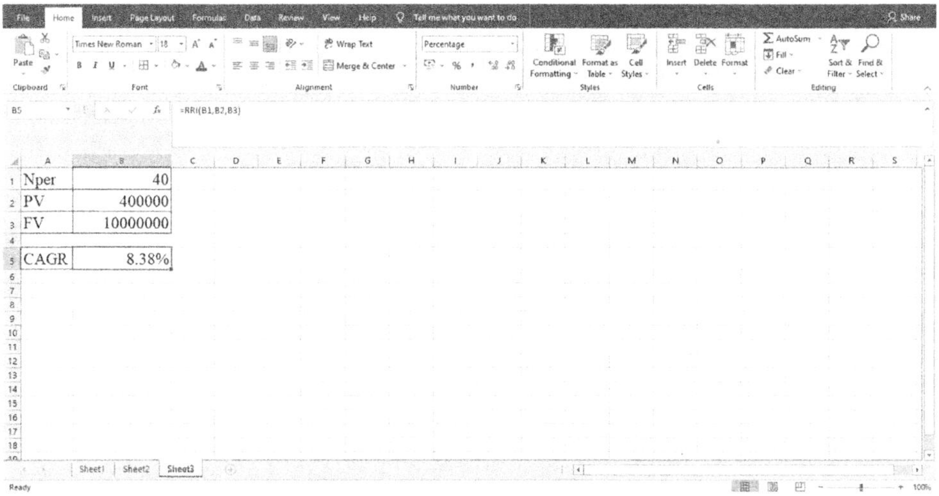

FIGURE 10.9 Calculation of Compound Annual Growth Rate Using RRI Function

In sum, this chapter discussed the methods that attempt to quantify and interpret an increase or decrease in the value of a variable over a period. We learned the application and the calculation of the growth rate, average annual growth rate, and compound annual growth rate. CAGR is the most reliable way of tracking the growth of an investment as it considers the compounding factor. The advantages and disadvantages of using each method have also been discussed in each section.

PRACTICE QUESTIONS

1. During their first year of business, their profit was ₹3,00,000. After the sixth year, their yearly profit is ₹15,75,000. Calculate the growth rate.
2. The population of India according to census 2001 and 2011 are 1,028,737,436 and 1,210,193,422 respectively. Calculate the population growth rate.
3. The country's GDP (in crores) for ten years is given in the following table. Calculate the average annual growth rate over ten years.

Year	GDP (₹ Crores)
0	1,500
1	1,650
2	1,390
3	1,180
4	1,450
5	1,680
6	1,800
7	2,000
8	2,200
9	2,700
10	2,500

4. An investor invested ₹10,00,00 in a debt fund for the next ten years. Calculate the compound annual growth rate of the investment if he will receive ₹25,00,000 at maturity.
5. Mr X has ₹1,00,000 today. He wants to invest this amount in his child's education. Calculate the rate (compound annual growth rate) at which he should invest this amount to create a corpus of ₹45,00,000 after 20 years.

11
GROWTH RATE USING REGRESSION ANALYSIS

Learning Objectives

After reading this chapter, the readers will be able to understand

- Concept of growth rate and natural logarithms
- Calculation of growth rate using regression analysis (OLS method)
- Calculation of simple growth using the LINEST function
- Calculation of exponential growth or CAGR using the LOGEST function

---

In the last chapter, we understood the concept of *growth* and *growth rate*, calculation and application of *average annual growth rate* and *compound annual growth rate*. This chapter will introduce some exciting ways of calculating the growth rate with the help of natural logarithms and regression analysis (semi-log model). Two Excel functions, namely the LINEST and LOGEST, have also been discussed in detail to determine the simple growth rate and compound annual growth rate, respectively.

11.1 Growth Rates and Logarithms

A logarithm is actually how many times a number is multiplied by itself to get another number. It gives the exponent as the output if the exponentiation result is given as the input. For instance, $4 * 4 = 16$. Here, 4 is multiplied 2 times to get 16; in other words, 4 raised to power 2 is 16. The number that we multiply is called 'base', that is, 4, the number of times it is multiplied, known as power or exponent, is equal to 2, which is the logarithm value, and 16 is the result which we want. We can write this as $\log_4 (16) = 2$ or logarithm of 16 with base 4 is 2. Here are some more examples of exponential equations and their logarithmic form:

- $5^4 = 625$ can be written as $\log_5 (625) = 4$
- $3^3 = 27$ can be written as $\log_3 (27) = 3$
- $10^2 = 100$ can be written as $\log_{10} (100) = 2$

DOI: 10.4324/9781003398127-11

A natural logarithm, denoted by 'ln' is a logarithm to the base e (log$_e$), where 'e', known as the Euler's number, is a mathematical constant approximately equal to 2.71828. The natural log of a number is equal to what e must be raised to get that number. So, for example, the value of ln (10) is equal to what e must be raised to, to get 10, that is, e^x = 10. We need to solve for x here. We get, $e^{2.30258}$ = 10. Therefore, ln (10) = 2.30258. Before we begin, let us understand a few basic rules of the logarithm.

1. The logarithm of the multiplication of a and b is the sum of the logarithm of a and logarithm of b, that is, $\ln(ab) = \ln(a) + \ln(b)$.
2. The logarithm of the division of a and b is the difference of the logarithm of a and logarithm of b, that is, $\ln(a/b) = \ln(a) - \ln(b)$.
3. ln $(1 + a)$ is approximately equal to a when a is a very small number.

Now, Suppose the GDP for the period n be Y_n

$$\text{The growth rate (g) for one year} = \frac{Y_{n+1} - Y_n}{Y_n}$$

$$\text{that is, } g = \frac{Y_{n+1}}{Y_n} - 1$$

$$\text{or, } 1 + g = \frac{Y_{n+1}}{Y_n} \tag{1}$$

Now, taking the natural log of both the sides in equation (1),

$$\text{we get, } \ln\left(1 + g\right) = \ln\left(\frac{Y_{n+1}}{Y_n}\right)$$

We apply the basic rules given earlier

$$g = \ln\left(Y_{n+1}\right) - \ln\left(Y_n\right) \tag{2}$$

Equation (2) can be interpreted as the difference between the two natural log numbers approximately equal to the growth rate or the percentage change between those numbers. For instance, if GDP increases from ₹40 crores to ₹42 crores. The percentage change or the growth rate will be $\frac{₹42 - ₹40}{₹40}$ = 0.05 or 5%; And the approximate percentage change can also be calculated as ln (42) − ln (40), which is equal to 3.73766 − 3.68887 = 0.4879 or 4.88 per cent.

11.2   Growth Rate Using Regression Analysis (OLS Method)

By now, we have understood the importance and usefulness of the growth rate along with different methods to calculate it. Another very interesting way of determining the growth rate is with the help of regression analysis.

As discussed in earlier chapters, regression analysis quantifies the relationship between the variables and estimates the influence of one or more variables on the other. The variable which predicts the other variable's value is known as the independent variable X. Likewise, the variable whose value is predicted is known as the dependent variable or Y variable.

Let us start by taking an example. The following table provides us with the hypothetical data related to the value of an investment at the end of each year for the last 15 years.

Years	Value of Investment (in ₹ Crores)
1	5,500
2	6,000
3	7,800
4	7,900
5	8,500
6	8,700
7	9,000
8	9,300
9	9,800
10	10,000
11	11,400
12	12,800
13	13,900
14	14,600
15	15,000

Now, we wish to determine the growth rate of the investment of this company. For this, we will consider the general formula to calculate the compound rate of interest (for detailed derivation, see Chapter 12):

$$FV_n = P(1 + r)^n$$

where FV_n = Future Value
P = Principal or the value at the beginning
r = rate of interest compounded annually or compound annual growth rate
n = number of years

Let's rearrange the previous formula by taking natural log of both the sides, we get
$\ln FV_n = \ln P(1 + r)^n$
or, $\ln FV_n = \ln P + \ln (1 + r)^n$ [Logarithm product rule: $\ln a.b = \ln (a) + \ln (b)$]
or, $\ln FV_n = \ln P + n \ln (1 + r)$ [Logarithm power rule: $\ln (a)^b = b. \ln (a)$]
Let, $\ln P = \beta_0$ and $\ln (1 + r) = \beta_1$

Adding an error term in the previous equation, we get:
$\ln FV_n = \beta_0 + n\beta_1 + \varepsilon$ If we closely observe the previous equation, we find that it looks similar to the simple linear regression model, that is, $Y = \beta_0 + \beta_1 X + \varepsilon$ where Y is the dependent variable, X is the independent variable, β_0 is known as the constant or the Y-intercept,

and the β_1 signifies the slope coefficient. Since only one of the variables in the equation is in the form of a logarithm, the previous model is also known as the semi-log model. *Semi-log models are widely used to compute the growth rates.*

In Chapter 8, we have understood how to estimate the values of the parameters, that is, β_0 and β_1 using Excel. One needs to remember that the values of the dependent variable are the natural logarithm of the value of an investment. Hence, we need to convert the investment value into their natural logs and proceed with the regression analysis. In case the period is given in the form of years like 1969, 1970, 1971, . . ., in that case, years can also be taken as 1, 2, 3, and so on for simplification. To further estimate the regression model using Excel, we use the option of **Data Analysis** and follow the stated steps:

Step 1. Enter the time (X) and the investment value (Y) in the Excel sheet.

Step 2. We use the **LN function** (*equivalent to natural log **ln** used earlier*) to convert investment values into their natural logarithms. Type '=' (equal to sign) in the blank cell where the result is desired, say, 'C2', then enter the function name **LN** and choose the value of an investment for the first year, that is, B2. Press **Enter**. The result will appear in cell C2 (Figure 11.1).

Click on the fill handle (the small black square in the bottom right corner when you select the cell) and drag it down to calculate the values of the natural logarithms for all the years, as shown in Figure 11.2.

Step 3. Next, go to the **Data** tab, and click on the option of **Data Analysis** in the **Analysis** group on the right side (Figure 11.2).

Step 4. A dialogue box will appear. Select the option of **Regression** from the list and click **OK**.

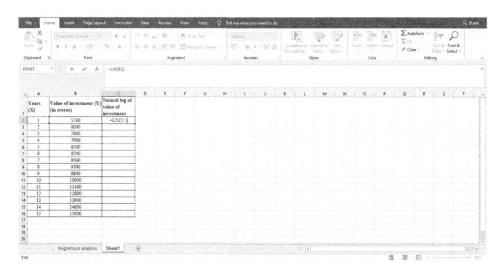

FIGURE 11.1   Step 1 in Calculation of Compound Annual Growth Rate

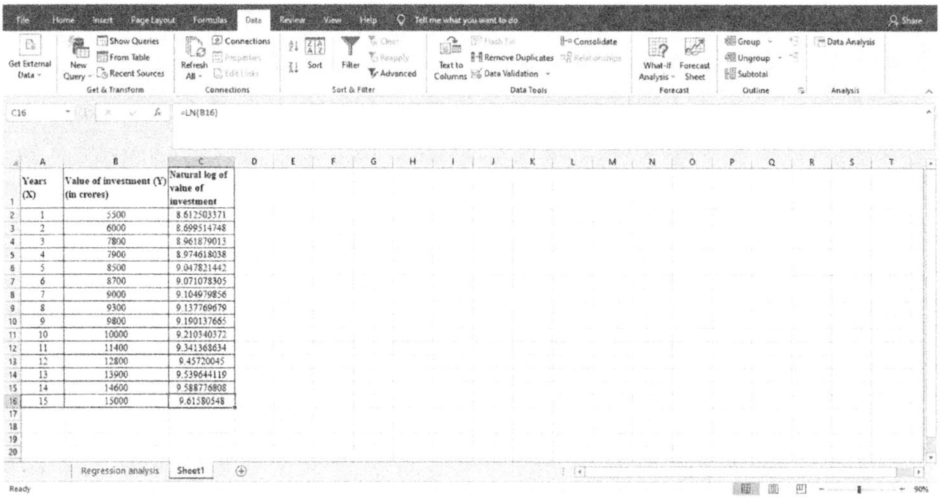

FIGURE 11.2 Step 2 in Calculation of Compound Annual Growth Rate

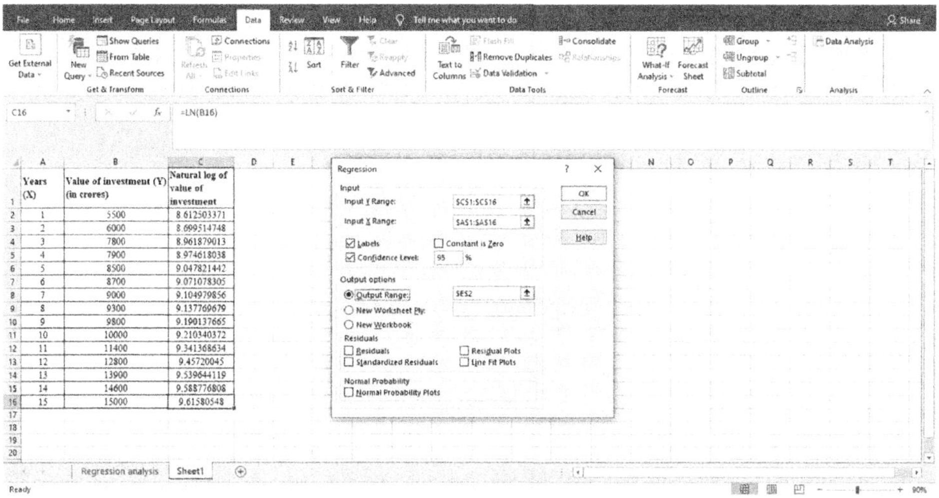

FIGURE 11.3 Steps 3, 4, and 5 in Calculation of Compound Annual Growth Rate

Step 5. A Regression dialogue box will appear. Fill in the following details (Figure 11.3).

- **Input Y Range:** The cell range of the dependent variable values (value of investment) for which the regression model is developed, that is, **C1:C16**
- **Input X Range:** The cell range of the values of the independent variable (time), that is, **A1:A16**
- **Check on Labels:** Remember if you choose the label/name of the variables, that is, time and value of an investment in the **Input Range**, then check the box **Labels**

FIGURE 11.4   Step 6 in Calculation of Compound Annual Growth Rate Using OLS Method (Summary Output)

- Check on the **Confidence Level** and set it at **95 percent**, which is also the default value
- **Output Range:** Under the output options, choose the cell reference where the result is desired in the existing worksheet, say E2

Step 6. Click **OK**. The regression result is displayed as a summary output table (Figure 11.4).

The summary output reports the following values:

$\beta_0 = 8.64388$
$\beta_1 = 0.06579$
and $R^2 = 0.95568$ or 95.568%

The regression equation can now be written as:

$\ln FVn = 8.64388 + n\ (0.06579) + \varepsilon$

Interpretation of the Parameters Estimated

- As we know, β_0 (constant or intercept) has been taken as an estimate of **ln P**. We can say that $\beta_0 = \ln P = 8.64388$. Therefore, we take the antilog of β_0, which is 5,675.27435. This means that the value of an investment when $t = 0$ at the beginning of the first year is ₹5,675.27435 crores approximately.
- β_1 is the slope of the regression line, which measures the rate of change in the Y corresponding to the unit change in the value of X. Therefore, in our case β_1 of 0.06579 means that on average, the log of value of the investment is increasing at the rate of 0.06579 or 6.58 per cent every year. This is nothing but the *instantaneous growth rate.*

- As we know, β_1 is taken as an estimate of **ln (1 + r).** We can say that, $\beta_1 = \ln (1 + r) = 0.06579$. Therefore, we take the antilog of β_1 and get the antilog of 0.06579 as 1.06801.
- That is 1.06801 $= 1 + r$.

or $r = 1.06801 - 1$ which equals to 0.06801. Since r is the compound annual growth rate, this means that the compound rate of growth in the value of the investment is 0.06801 or 6.801 per cent.

To summarize, the *instantaneous growth* rate (at a point in time) is 6.58 per cent and the *compound annual growth rate* (over the period) is 6.801 per cent. However, in practice, we generally refer to the instantaneous growth rate. Having understood this distinction, we now introduce two important functions provided in Excel, namely the Linest function and the Logest function, to calculate the growth rate.

11.3   Linest Function and Growth Rate

LINEST calculates simple or linear growth rates. This method creates a linear regression model that minimizes the sum of squared errors (SSE) to obtain the regression line that best fits through the specified set of X and Y values and predicts the movement in the variable of interest.

LINEST function in Excel is short for linear estimation and performs the linear regression analysis. It calculates the statistics and returns an array of values describing a line using the ordinary least square method, which determines the equation of the straight line of best fit. We already know that the regression equation showing the linear relationship between the dependent and independent variable can be written as:

$$Y = \beta_0 + \beta_1 X$$

Here, Y = Dependent variable or Y variable
X = Independent variable or X variable
β_0 = Y-intercept
β_1 = Slope coefficient of Y with respect to X
The Syntax of the function is **LINEST (known_y's, [known_x's], [const], [stats]).** The arguments given in the formula are as follows:

- **known_y's:** The cell range of the values of the dependent variable or the set of Y-values already known
- **known_x's:** The cell range of the values of the independent variable or the set of X-values already known
- **const:** A logical value that specifies whether to form a regression equation with the constant value equal to 0. This is an optional argument and TRUE by default.

    If const is **TRUE or left blank**, constant (β_0) is calculated normally, that is, to form an equation with a non-zero intercept.
    If const is **FALSE**, β_0 is set equal to 0 and the β_1 values (slope coefficients) are adjusted to fit $Y = \beta_1 X$.
    stats − A logical value that specifies whether to return additional regression statistics. This is an optional argument and FALSE by default.

If stats is **TRUE**, the LINEST function returns the additional regression statistics.

If stats is **FALSE** or left blank, the LINEST function returns only the slope coefficients (β_1) and the constant (β_0).

Apart from the slope coefficient and the constant, the additional statistics given by the function are:

1. The standard error values for the coefficients
2. The standard error value for the constant
3. The coefficient of determination
4. The standard error for the y-estimate
5. The F statistic
6. The degrees of freedom
7. The regression sum of squares or explained variation
8. The residual sum of squares or unexplained variation

The following table shows the order in which **LINEST** returns an array of statistics in the case of one independent variable in an Excel sheet:

Slope Coefficient	Constant or Intercept
Standard error values for the coefficients	Standard error value for the constant
Coefficient of determination	Standard error for the y-estimate
F statistic	Degrees of freedom
Regression sum of squares or explained variation	Residual sum of squares or unexplained variation

Illustrating the LINEST Function for Determining the Growth Rate

Let us take the previous example (value of the investment at the end of each year for 15 years) to understand the use of the **LINEST** function to determine the growth of a variable. As the **LINEST** function gives an array of values, that is, perform multiple calculations, it is entered as an *array formula*. The steps for which are as follows:

Step 1. Enter the time (X) and the investment value (Y) in the Excel sheet (Figure 11.5).

Step 2. Select the area where the result or the output is desired by dragging to form a 5-row by 2-column data array, that is, **D2:E6**. For **LINEST**, we need to select any ten cells (in case of one independent variable) consisting two columns (two cells horizontally) and five rows (Figure 11.5).

Step 3. Type '=' (equal to sign) and enter the function name **LINEST**. Select the cell range of the values of the dependent variable, **B2:B16**, then select the cell range of the values of the independent variable, that is, **A2:A16**, the third argument will be **TRUE** or can be left blank and the last argument is **TRUE** (Figure 11.6).

Step 4. Since **LINEST** is an array function and the output of the function will be shown in multiple cells, we have to press **CTRL+SHIFT+Enter**. Remember, if the **Enter** alone is pressed, the function returns only the first slope coefficient.

Step 5. The function will return an array of values comprising the various statistics. The values in the first two cells adjacent to each other will contain the value of slope coefficient and the constant of the regression equation, as shown in Figure 11.7.

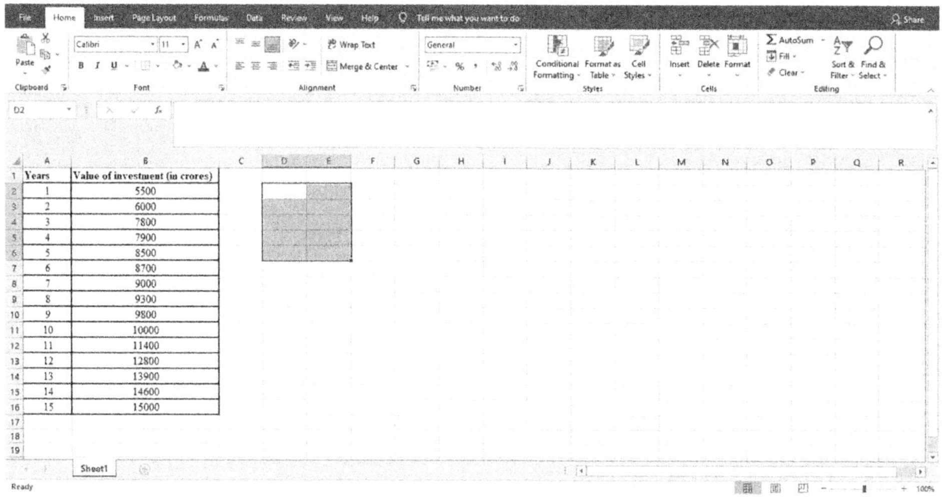

Years	Value of investment (in crores)
1	5500
2	6000
3	7800
4	7900
5	8500
6	8700
7	9000
8	9300
9	9800
10	10000
11	11400
12	12800
13	13900
14	14600
15	15000

FIGURE 11.5 Steps 1 and 2 in the Calculation of Regression Coefficients Using the LINEST Function

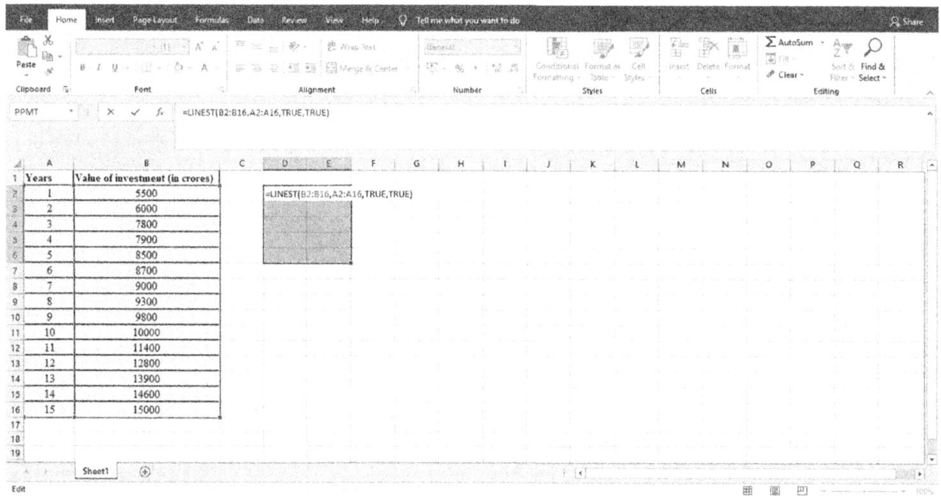

Years	Value of investment (in crores)
1	5500
2	6000
3	7800
4	7900
5	8500
6	8700
7	9000
8	9300
9	9800
10	10000
11	11400
12	12800
13	13900
14	14600
15	15000

FIGURE 11.6 Steps 3 and 4 in the Calculation of Regression Coefficients Using the LINEST Function

Interpretation: The **LINEST** function calculates the simple or linear growth that represents the change (increase or decrease) in the data points corresponding to each year. According to the result, the slope coefficient or β_1 is 643.928. This indicates that over 15 years the value of the investment has been increasing at an absolute rate of ₹643.928 crores per year. Since the slope coefficients are positive, it shows that there is an upward trend in the value of the investment.

Taking the equation of the line, it is possible to visualize $\beta_1/\beta_0 * 100$ as a simple growth rate. Further, the computation of β_1 and β_0 in Excel does not need entering the *X*-values or the years. LINEST (known_*y*'s) returns the results taking the time variable as default.

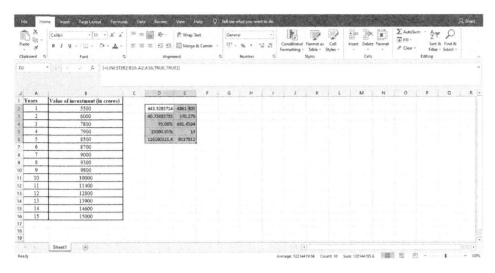

FIGURE 11.7   Step 5 in the Calculation of Regression Coefficients Using the LINEST Function

11.4   The Logest Function and Growth Rate

In the real world, variables exhibit growth, that is, not linear. The rate of change either increases or decreases over time, for example, growth of money deposited in a bank, population growth, value of investments, etc. In such cases, the growth is slow in the beginning and then speeds up rapidly. An exponential function is used to describe the exponential growth or exponential decrease in such variables.

LOGEST function in Excel is generally used to calculate the growth rate of the variable which grows exponentially due to compounding, that is, compound annual growth rate (CAGR). An advantage of using **LOGEST** is that it considers the yearly variations to calculate the CAGR instead of just the beginning and the ending values. The function computes the value of coefficients or statistics for an exponential function that causes the function to best fit for the given values of the X and Y variable and returns an array of values describing the exponential curve.

An exponential regression equation can be written in the following form:
Here,

Y = Dependent variable or Y variable

X = Independent variable or X variable or exponent

β_0 = Constant or base

β_1 = Slope coefficient of Y with respect to X

The Syntax of the function is **LOGEST (known_y's, [known_x's], [const], [stats]).** The arguments given in the formula are as follows:

- **known_y's:** The cell range of the values of the dependent variable or the set of Y-values already known
- **known_x's:** The cell range of the values of the independent variable or the set of X-values are already known
- **const:** A logical value that specifies whether to form a regression equation with the constant value equal to 1. This is an optional argument and TRUE by default.

If const is **TRUE or left blank**, constant (β_0) is calculated normally, that is, to form an equation with a non-zero intercept.

If const is **FALSE**, β_0 is set equal to 1, and the β_1-values (the slope coefficient) are adjusted to fit $Y = \beta_1{}^X$

stats: A logical value that specifies whether to return additional regression statistics. This is an optional argument, and FALSE by default.

If stats is **TRUE**, the LOGEST function returns the additional regression statistics.

If stats is **FALSE** or left blank LOGEST function returns only the slope coefficients (β_1) and the constant (β_0).

Apart from the slope coefficient and the constant, the additional statistics given by the function are:

1. The standard error values for the coefficients
2. The standard error value for the constant
3. The coefficient of determination
4. The standard error for the y estimate
5. The F statistic
6. The degrees of freedom
7. The regression sum of squares or explained variation
8. The residual sum of squares or unexplained variation

The following table shows the order in which **LOGEST** returns an array of statistics in the case of one independent variable in an Excel sheet:

Slope Coefficient	Constant or Intercept
Standard error values for the coefficients	Standard error value for the constant
Coefficient of determination	Standard error for the y estimate
F statistic	Degrees of freedom
Regression sum of squares or explained variation	Residual sum of squares or unexplained variation

Illustrating the LOGEST Function for Determining the Growth Rate

Now let us understand how **LOGEST** can be used to determine the compound annual growth rate. We begin with the general formula to calculate the compound rate of interest that we derived in Chapter 7,

i.e., $FV_n = P(1 + r)^n$

If we look closely, the previous equation is an exponential function

where $FV_n = Y$, that is, the dependent variable

$P = \beta_0$, that is, constant

$1 + r = \beta_1$, that is, slope coefficient

$n = X$, that is, independent variable

As discussed earlier the **LOGEST** function in Excel returns the value of the slope coefficient. So, we will use this function to calculate β_1. Also, from the previous equation, we know that

$\beta_1 = 1 + r$
or $r = \beta_1 - 1$

Therefore, we can say that the Excel formula for compound annual growth rate using **LOGEST** is

$= \text{LOGEST (known\_y's, known\_x's, const, stats)} - 1$

We continue with the previous example of the value of the investment at the end of each year for 15 years to understand the use of the **LOGEST** function to determine the CAGR. Since the **LOGEST** function gives an array of values, that is, performs multiple calculations, it is entered as an *array formula*. The steps for which are as follows:

Step 1. Enter the time (*X*) and value of investment (*Y*) in the Excel sheet (Figure 11.8).
Step 2. Select the area where the result or the output is desired by dragging to form a 5-row by a 2-column data array, that is, **D2:E6**. For **LOGEST**, we need to select any ten cells (in the case of one independent variable) comprising two columns (two cells horizontally) and five rows (Figure 11.8).
Step 3. Type '=' (equal to sign) and enter the function name **LOGEST.** Select the cell range of the values of the dependent variable, that is, **B2:B16**, then select the cell range of the values of the independent variable, that is, **A2:A16**, third argument will be **TRUE** or can be left blank and the last argument is **TRUE** (Figure 11.9).

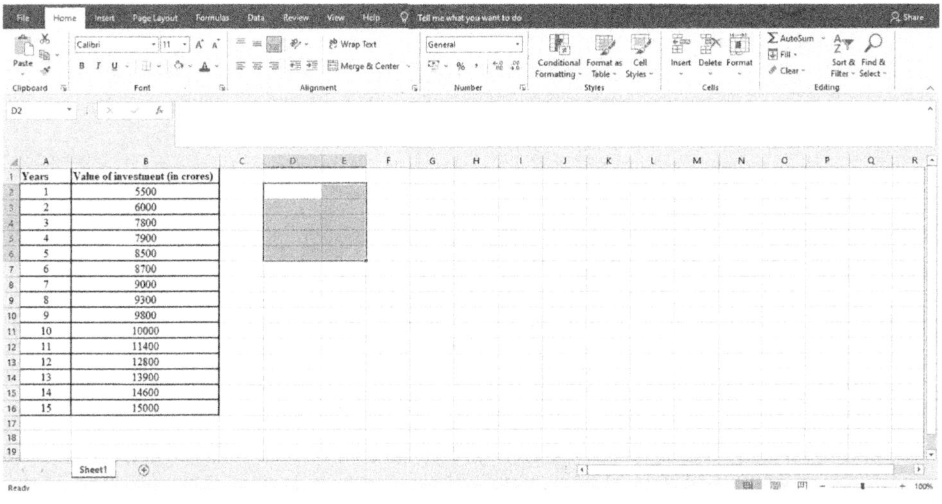

FIGURE 11.8   Step 1 in Calculation of Regression Coefficients Using LOGEST Function

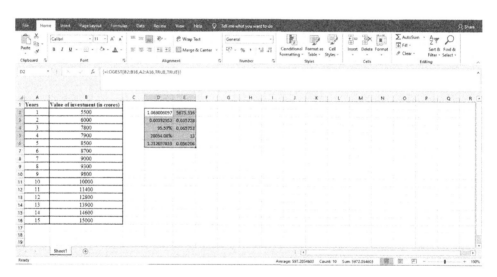

FIGURE 11.9   Steps 2 and 3 in Calculation of Regression Coefficients Using the LOGEST Function

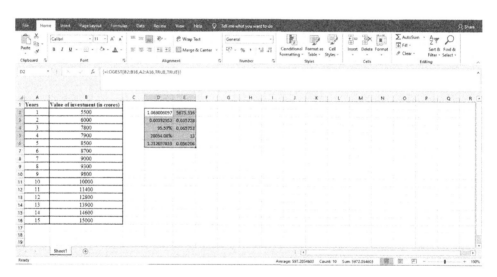

FIGURE 11.10   Steps 4 and 5 in Calculation of Regression Coefficients Using the LOGEST Function

Step 4. Since **LOGEST** is an array function and the output of the function will be shown in multiple cells, we have to press **CTRL+SHIFT+Enter**. Remember if **Enter** is pressed alone, the function returns only the first slope coefficient.

Step 5. The function will return an array of values comprising the various statistics. The values in the first two cells adjacent to each other will contain the value of slope coefficient and the constant of regression equation as shown in Figure 11.10.

Interpretation: The **LOGEST** function helps to calculate the compound annual growth rate. According to the results obtained, the slope coefficient or β_1 is 1.068006097 or 1.06801

approx. Since the slope coefficient is greater than 1, it shows exponential growth in the investment value, that is, as time (X) increases, the value of investment (Y) first increases slowly but then increases rapidly.

We know that the Excel formula for compound annual growth rate using **LOGEST** is

= LOGEST (known_y's, known_x's, const, stats) − 1

Therefore, CAGR = 1.06801 − 1

= 0.06801 or 6.801 per cent.

We note that the value of CAGR using the LOGEST function is identical to that obtained using the semi-log model. Exactly like LINEST, LOGEST also returns the growth rates even when you do not enter the X-values. It takes the default X as a time variable simplifying the computation greatly.

To conclude, this chapter explains a very interesting way of calculating the percentage change or growth rate using the natural logarithms, which states that the growth rate between two numbers can be determined by calculating the difference between the natural logarithms of those two numbers. Another fascinating way of calculating growth rate with the help of the regression model (known as the semi-log model) has been included. The highlight of this chapter is the introduction of the two useful functions of Excel, LINEST and LOGEST, which compute simple and exponential growth rates respectively, which have been discussed in detail using application-based examples. All these concepts are of utmost importance in real life.

PRACTICE QUESTIONS

1. With the help of the given data, calculate

   a) The compound annual growth rate and instantaneous growth rate with the help of a regression model (semi-log mode)
   b) Simple growth rate using LINEST
   c) CAGR using LOGEST

Years	Revenue (Y; ₹) (in Crores)
1	1,100
2	1,500
3	2,000
4	2,400
5	2,700
6	3,500
7	3,000
8	4,000
9	4,600
10	5,000
11	5,900
12	6,200

12

COMPOUNDING: FUTURE VALUE OF MONEY

Learning Objectives

After reading this chapter, the readers will be able to understand

- The concept of the time value of money
- Simple interest and compound interest
- Calculation and interpretation of the future value of single cash flows using table and Excel
- Calculation and interpretation of the future value of an annuity using table and Excel

---

One of the most essential and basic concepts in finance is the *time value of money* . Most investment decisions in business revolve around the *value of money*, with the underlying assumption that money does not retain its value over time. In other words, the value of money does not remain constant over time as money's purchasing power would fall with the rise in prices.

12.1 Time Value of Money

In any discussion of money, it is said that *a rupee today is worth more than a rupee tomorrow*. The implication is that the value of a rupee *today* will not be the same as the value of the same rupee over a period, say *after one year*. Similarly, the value of a rupee after one year cannot be compared with its value today.

Let us understand this by taking a simple example. We have won ₹10,000 in a lottery, and we are given two options:

Option A: Take ₹10,000 today.
Option B: Take ₹10,000 after five years.

DOI: 10.4324/9781003398127-12

What would we like to choose? Being a rational individual, we would choose to receive the amount today instead of waiting for five years. Why? First, we can invest this money today and receive a higher amount tomorrow because of the interest received on the amount invested. Second, we might be uncertain that we may not get our money back after five years.

The *interest rate* (r) is used for translating money from one time period to another. It represents the *price of time* and the *price of risk*. The price of time is the *opportunity cost* of money, that is, we forego money that could have been used or invested elsewhere. The interest rate, thus, can also be understood as a reward for inflation and is generally positive. The price of risk involves the *risk* or *uncertainty* of not getting back the money in the future. The value of money over time with interest can thus be adjusted using the following two techniques.

- **Compounding**: It computes the worth of today's rupee in the future.
- **Discounting**: It refers to today's value of an amount we have in the future.

The focus in the present chapter, however, is on *compounding* only. The applications of discounting are discussed subsequently in the next chapter.

12.2   Simple Interest

Before learning about *compound interest* (i.e., compounding), which is commonly used in undertaking financial decisions, we need to distinguish it from *simple interest* (SI). While computing SI, interest is paid *only* on the principal amount and calculated using the following formula:

$SI = Prn$

Where

SI = Simple Interest
P = Principal amount
r = interest rate (per year)
n = time (in years or fraction of a year).

Example: Arun invested ₹1,000 in Bank A for two years. The bank promised him to pay the money at a simple interest rate of 10 per cent per annum. In this example, at the end of the first year, the amount Arun gets from the bank is

$$SI = 1,000 * \frac{10}{100} * 1, \text{ which is equal to } ₹100.$$

Similarly, at the end of the second year also, he will get the same amount of ₹100 as the simple interest rate is calculated on the basic principal amount, ₹1,000 in this case. At the end of two years, he will get a total of ₹1,000 plus ₹100 (interest amount of the first year) plus ₹100 (interest accrued in the second year), which equals ₹1,200.

12.3 Compound Interest

Interest is *compounded* if the interest is paid on both the *principal amount* and the *(accumulated) interest*. For example, if Arun now invests ₹1,000 in Bank A for two years and the interest rate is 10 per cent that is *compounded yearly*, then interest earned by him is as follows:

- At the end of the first year, the interest amount earned will be

$$(1,000 * \frac{10}{100}) \text{ or } ₹100.$$

Future Value (FV$_1$) after one year = ₹1,000 + (₹1,000 * $\frac{10}{100}$) = ₹1,100

- At the end of the second year, the interest amount earned now will be on the principal amount (₹1,000) plus the interest earned in the first year (₹100) which equals ₹1,100.

$$\rightarrow \quad (1,000 \quad + \quad 100) \quad \times \quad (\frac{10}{100}) \quad = \quad 110$$

(Principal amount)   (interest earned   (interest rate)   (interest earned
                 in the first year)   in the second year)

$$\rightarrow FV_2 \quad = \quad 1,100 \quad + \quad 110$$

(principal amount)   (interest earned
(in the second year)   in the second year)

$$FV_2 = FV_1 + FV_1 (\frac{10}{100}) = 1,210$$

Had he continued to invest in the third year, he would have earned an interest of 10 per cent on ₹1,210, which is ₹121. So, the total amount he would have received at the end of the third year is ₹1,210 + ₹121, which equals ₹1,331.

$$FV_3 = FV_2 + FV_2 (\frac{10}{100}) = ₹1,331$$

This leads us to a general formula to calculate the compound rate of interest.
After 1 year, $FV_1 = P + Pr = P(1 + r)$
After 2 years, $FV_2 = P(1 + r) (1 + r) = P(1 + r)^2$
After 3 years, $FV_3 = P(1 + r)^2 (1 + r) = P (1 + r)^3$
After n years, $FV_n = P(1 + r)^n$, where $(1 + r)$ is equal to the *future value factor*.

The compound amount depends on two factors, namely the interest rate (r) and compounding periods (n). Higher the interest rate (r) and the term of the investment (n), the higher the income that will be added to the principal amount. Time is the main driving force behind compounding. In finance, even if the interest rate is not changed much but the number of compounding periods is large, the increase in future returns will be substantial. Therefore, it is generally advised in financial planning to remain invested for a more extended period for better returns, compounding being the primary reason. Figure 12.1 shows the growth of the amount earned in subsequent years had Arun, in our preceding example, continued to invest for more than three years.

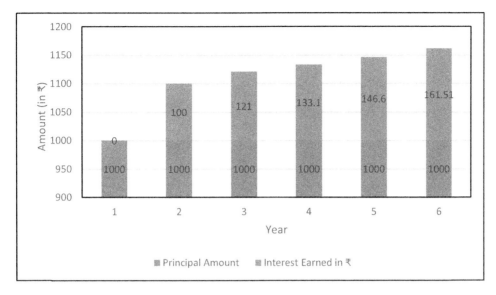

FIGURE 12.1 Impact of Compounding in Investment

The impact of compounding can also be ascertained as follows. If Arun had continued with the same investment for 50 years, the compounded amount would have turned out to be nearly ₹1,17,391. However, reducing the investment by a period of five years would have cost him an amount of ₹44,500. This is the power of compounding. Impressed by it, Albert Einstein famously said, '*compound interest is the eighth wonder of the world. He who understands it earns it; he who does not, pays it*'.

If the said investment amount is compounded, say, semi-annually, then the rate of interest, though it would reduce by half, the number of conversion periods would have increased to two, resulting in an even higher amount. Thus, the higher the n, the more the future value received, making the impact of compounding conspicuous. In this example, the formula becomes

$$FV_n = P\left(1 + \frac{r}{2}\right)^{n \times 2}$$

The interest amount earned in the first year, in the ongoing example would be 102.5 rather than 100 when the compounding was done semi-annually.

Illustration

Ravi deposits an amount of ₹50,000 in his bank for five years. The bank offers a 6 per cent interest rate compounded annually. How much would he get at the end of the fifth year?

Solution

There are three methods to solve such problems.

First (Direct) method:

In the previous section, we have arrived at the following formula.[1]

$$FV = PV\left(1+r\right)^{n}$$

$$= 50,000\left(1+0.06\right)^{5}$$

$$= 50,000\left(1.06\right)^{5}$$

$$= 50,000 \times 1.3382$$

$$= ₹66,910$$

Second Method (Using Future Value Interest Factor Table)

Another way to arrive at the future value of *single cash flows* is by using *future value interest factor (FVIF)* tables. The *FVIF* tables can be understood as ratios of the amount received in a year to the amount received in the preceding year.

For instance, depositing ₹50,000 in a bank at the rate of 6 per cent, the future values will be ₹53,000 in the first year, ₹56,180 in the second year, ₹59,550 in the third year, ₹63,125 in the fourth year, and ₹66,910 in the fifth year. Dividing the amount received in year 1, year 2, year 3, year 4, and year 5 by the principal amount in year 0, we get *quotients* as 1.06, 1.1236, 1.191, 1.2625, and 1.3382, respectively. These quotients obtained are called *future value interest factor* in the language of compounding. The quotient values for different combinations of n and r are readily available in the FVIF (given in Table 12.1) and therefore need not be calculated manually.[2] We can then easily obtain future values by multiplying these quotients by the principal amount (of year 0).

For example, the future value at the end of the second year at an interest rate of 6 per cent is read at the intersection point of r at 6 per cent and n of 2 periods. This number gives us the required quotient value. Similarly, the future value at the end of the fifth year at 6 per cent is 1.3382. Thus, multiplying the quotient value of 1.3382 by the principal amount of ₹50,000 straightaway gives the value of ₹66,910. Similarly, the future values of any principal amount can be obtained for any given combination of interest rate (r) and the number of periods (n) by just looking at the *FVIF* table.

Third Method (Using Excel)

Excel calculates compounding quickly. To arrive at the result, we take the following steps. We proceed by clicking on the **Insert** function f_{x} option adjacent to the **Formula Bar**, selecting category **Financial** and choosing *FV* as the function. Next, write the arguments.

- **Rate**, which we take as 6 per cent. The rate is written as either 0.06 or with a percentage sign, 6%
- The **Nper** argument is the number of periods. It is 5 years in our example
- **Pmt** refers to the payment made periodically, but since we take one-time investment in our example, we leave it blank

TABLE 12.1 Future Value Interest Factor Table

Future Value Interest Factors for One Rupee Compounded at r Percent for n Periods: $FVIF\ r_{,n} = (1 + r)$

Period	1%	2%	3%	4%	5%	6%	7%	8%	9%	10%	11%	12%	13%	14%	15%	16%	20%	24%	25%	30%
1	1.01	1.02	1.03	1.04	1.05	1.06	1.07	1.08	1.09	1.1	1.11	1.12	1.13	1.14	1.15	1.16	1.2	1.24	1.25	1.3
2	1.0201	1.0404	1.0609	1.0816	1.1025	1.1236	1.1449	1.1664	1.1881	1.21	1.2321	1.2544	1.2769	1.2996	1.3225	1.3456	1.44	1.5376	1.5625	1.69
3	1.0303	1.0612	1.0927	1.1249	1.1576	1.191	1.225	1.2597	1.295	1.331	1.3676	1.4049	1.4429	1.4815	1.5209	1.5609	1.728	1.9066	1.9531	2.197
4	1.0406	1.0824	1.1255	1.1699	1.2155	1.2625	1.3108	1.3605	1.4116	1.4641	1.5181	1.5735	1.6305	1.689	1.749	1.8106	2.0736	2.3642	2.4414	2.8561
5	1.051	1.1041	1.1593	1.2167	1.2763	1.3382	1.4026	1.4693	1.5386	1.6105	1.6851	1.7623	1.8424	1.9254	2.0114	2.1003	2.4883	2.9316	3.0518	3.7129
6	1.0615	1.1262	1.1941	1.2653	1.3401	1.4185	1.5007	1.5869	1.6771	1.7716	1.8704	1.9738	2.082	2.195	2.3131	2.4364	2.986	3.6352	3.8147	4.8268
7	1.0721	1.1487	1.2299	1.3159	1.4071	1.5036	1.6058	1.7138	1.828	1.9487	2.0762	2.2107	2.3526	2.5023	2.66	2.8262	3.5832	4.5077	4.7684	6.2749
8	1.0829	1.1717	1.2668	1.3686	1.4775	1.5938	1.7182	1.8509	1.9926	2.1436	2.3045	2.476	2.6584	2.8526	3.059	3.2784	4.2998	5.5895	5.9605	8.1573
9	1.0937	1.1951	1.3048	1.4233	1.5513	1.6895	1.8385	1.999	2.1719	2.3579	2.558	2.7731	3.004	3.2519	3.5179	3.803	5.1598	6.931	7.4506	10.604
10	1.1046	1.219	1.3439	1.4802	1.6289	1.7908	1.9672	2.1589	2.3674	2.5937	2.8394	3.1058	3.3946	3.7072	4.0456	4.4114	6.1917	8.5944	9.3132	13.786
11	1.1157	1.2434	1.3842	1.5395	1.7103	1.8983	2.1049	2.3316	2.5804	2.8531	3.1518	3.4785	3.8359	4.2262	4.6524	5.1173	7.4301	10.657	11.642	17.922
12	1.1268	1.2682	1.4258	1.601	1.7959	2.0122	2.2522	2.5182	2.8127	3.1384	3.4985	3.896	4.3345	4.8179	5.3503	5.936	8.9161	13.215	14.552	23.298
13	1.1381	1.2936	1.4685	1.6651	1.8856	2.1329	2.4098	2.7196	3.0658	3.4523	3.8833	4.3635	4.898	5.4924	6.1528	6.8858	10.699	16.386	18.19	30.288
14	1.1495	1.3195	1.5126	1.7317	1.9799	2.2609	2.5785	2.9372	3.3417	3.7975	4.3104	4.8871	5.5348	6.2613	7.0757	7.9875	12.839	20.319	22.737	39.374
15	1.161	1.3459	1.558	1.8009	2.0789	2.3966	2.759	3.1722	3.6425	4.1772	4.7846	5.4736	6.2543	7.1379	8.1371	9.2655	15.407	25.196	28.422	51.186
16	1.1726	1.3728	1.6047	1.873	2.1829	2.5404	2.9522	3.4259	3.9703	4.595	5.3109	6.1304	7.0673	8.1372	9.3576	10.748	18.488	31.243	35.527	66.542
17	1.1843	1.4002	1.6528	1.9479	2.292	2.6928	3.1588	3.7	4.3276	5.0545	5.8951	6.866	7.9861	9.2765	10.761	12.468	22.186	38.741	44.409	86.504
18	1.1961	1.4282	1.7024	2.0258	2.4066	2.8543	3.3799	3.996	4.7171	5.5599	6.5436	7.69	9.0243	10.575	12.375	14.463	26.623	48.039	55.511	112.46
19	1.2081	1.4568	1.7535	2.1068	2.527	3.0256	3.6165	4.3157	5.1417	6.1159	7.2633	8.6128	10.197	12.056	14.232	16.777	31.948	59.568	69.389	146.19
20	1.2202	1.4859	1.8061	2.1911	2.6533	3.2071	3.8697	4.661	5.6044	6.7275	8.0623	9.6463	11.523	13.743	16.367	19.461	38.338	73.864	86.736	190.05
21	1.2324	1.5157	1.8603	2.2788	2.786	3.3996	4.1406	5.0338	6.1088	7.4002	8.9492	10.804	13.021	15.668	18.822	22.574	46.005	91.592	108.42	247.07
22	1.2447	1.546	1.9161	2.3699	2.9253	3.6035	4.4304	5.4365	6.6586	8.1403	9.9336	12.1	14.714	17.861	21.645	26.186	55.206	113.57	135.53	321.18
23	1.2572	1.5769	1.9736	2.4647	3.0715	3.8197	4.7405	5.8715	7.2579	8.9543	11.026	13.552	16.627	20.362	24.891	30.376	66.247	140.83	169.41	417.54
24	1.2697	1.6084	2.0328	2.5633	3.2251	4.0489	5.0724	6.3412	7.9111	9.8497	12.239	15.179	18.788	23.212	28.625	35.236	79.497	174.63	211.76	542.8
25	1.2824	1.6406	2.0938	2.6658	3.3864	4.2919	5.4274	6.8485	8.6231	10.835	13.585	17	21.231	26.462	32.919	40.874	95.396	216.54	264.7	705.64
30	1.3478	1.8114	2.4273	3.2434	4.3219	5.7435	7.6123	10.063	13.268	17.449	22.892	29.96	39.116	50.95	66.212	85.85	237.38	634.82	807.79	x
35	1.4166	1.9999	2.8139	3.9461	5.516	7.6861	10.677	14.785	20.414	28.102	38.575	52.8	72.069	98.1	133.18	180.31	590.67	x	x	x
36	1.4308	2.0399	2.8983	4.1039	5.7918	8.1473	11.424	15.968	22.251	30.913	42.818	59.136	81.437	111.83	153.15	209.16	708.8	x	x	x
40	1.4889	2.208	3.262	4.801	7.04	10.286	14.974	21.725	31.409	45.259	65.001	93.051	132.78	188.88	267.86	378.72	x	x	x	x
50	1.6446	2.6916	4.3839	7.1067	11.467	18.42	29.457	46.902	74.358	117.39	184.57	289	450.74	700.23	x	x	x	x	x	x

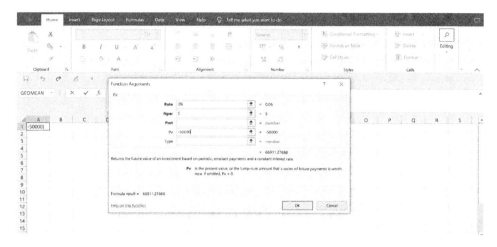

FIGURE 12.2   Calculating Future Value Using Excel

- **PV** is the principal amount (present value) invested. Remember that a (-) sign is written along with the principal amount as it is an *out-going* payment
- Leave **Type** as blank or write 0, implying payment is made at the end of the year/period
- Alternatively, the same calculation is done by writing = *FV* (**Rate, Nper, PMT, PV**) in the **Formula Bar**. These arguments appear automatically as soon as we write the '=*FV*'. We need to fill the values of these arguments accordingly
- We get the same result of ₹66,911 (Figure 12.2). A marginal difference that is arising is on account of rounding off errors.

Check Your Understanding

At an interest rate of 10 per cent, is it better to have ₹100 today than ₹121 in two years?
   Ans. True

12.4   Future Value of an Annuity

An *annuity* is a series of payments made at equal intervals. Examples are regular savings account deposits, monthly home mortgage payments, insurance payments, and pension payments. In practice, we seldom make any decision (say investment) based on a one-time payment but multiple payments. Hence, it is quite imperative to understand annuity calculations.

   The future value of an ordinary annuity is simply a sum of the future values of the individual cash flows. For example, Arun now decides to invest ₹10,000 each in year 0, year 1, and year 2 at the rate of 10 per cent. How much will he get after three years? A timeline is important to understand such calculations that are presented in Table 12.2.

   If we look carefully at this Table 12.2, we can notice the cash flow of year 0 is 0 as nothing is happening in year 0, which is today. The years 1, 2, and 3 represent the end of years 1, 2, and 3, respectively. *Years to end* refer to how many years are left. For example, in year 0, years to end are 3, as year 0 to 1 is counted as one year. Similarly, year 1–2 as the second year and year 2–3 as the third year. Remember, year 3 is the end of the period in this example.

TABLE 12.2 Timeline of a Cash Flow

Year	Cash Flow	Years to End	Future Value
0	0	3	0
1	C	2	$C(1 + r)^2$
2	C	1	$C(1 + r)^1$
3	C	0	C

To determine future values, let us consider one cash flow at a time. At point 0, the future value must be 0 because conventionally, we do not get cash flow in year 0. The first annuity occurs at the end of year 1 and the number of years to end is 2. Therefore, $C(1 + r)^2$ is the formula as derived before. Similarly, the future values of C in years 2 and 3 take the formula $C(1 + r)^1$ and C. Thus, having three C's at different points of time is different from having them at the same point of time because of the time value of money. The arguments discussed earlier can now be used to generalize the formula. The summation of future value for 3-period payments is expressed as $C(1+r)^2 + C(1+r)^1 + C$. Note that the *FV* with power 3 has not been considered due to the absence of cash flow in period 0.

$$FV_3 = C\left[(1+r)^2 + (1+r)^1 + 1\right]$$

Multiplying both sides by $(1 + r)$, we get

$$FV_3(1+r) = C\left[(1+r)^3 + (1+r)^2 + (1+r)\right]$$

Subtracting $FV_3(1 + r)$ from FV_3

$$= C\left[(1+r)^3 + (1+r)^2 + (1+r)\right] - C\left[(1+r)^2 + (1+r)^1 + 1\right]$$

$$= C\left[(1+r)^3 - 1)\right]$$

Solving for $FV_3 = C\left[\dfrac{(1+r)^3 - 1}{r}\right]$

For period *n*,

$$FV_n = C\left[\dfrac{(1+r)^n - 1}{r}\right]$$

Illustration

Kumar deposited ₹60,000 per year continuously for five years in his bank. The bank pays 8 per cent per annum interest compounded yearly. Find out the total amount available to Kumar at the end of five years.

Solution:

There can be three methods to solve such problems.

First (Direct) method:

$$FVA = C \times \left[\frac{(1+r)^n - 1}{r} \right]$$

$$= 60{,}000 \times \left[\frac{(1+.08)^5 - 1}{.08} \right]$$

$$= ₹3{,}51{,}996$$

Second Method (Using Future Value Annuity Table)

Similar to the formation of the FVIF table, a future value annuity table is drawn. It is an alternative way of calculating quotients manually. The quotient values are readily available in this table, as shown in Table 12.3. For example, in the ongoing illustration, we can see that the corresponding quotient value of r (at 8%) and n of 5 periods is 5.8666. Multiplying the PV amount of ₹60,000 by 5.8666 delivers an amount of ₹3,51,996. A simple and straightforward method if no financial calculator is available.

Third Method (Using Excel):

The steps in Excel are almost the same as those followed earlier. We proceed by clicking on the **Insert** function f_x option adjacent to the **Formula Bar** and choosing *FV* as the function. Next, we write the arguments as follows.

- **Rate**, which is taken as 8 per cent. The rate is written either as 0.08 or with a percentage sign, that is, 8%
- The **Nper** argument is the number of periods. It is 5 years in our example
- **Pmt** refers to the payment made periodically. In our example, we are paying an amount of ₹60,000 per year, hence we place this figure in **Pmt.** As noted, a (-) sign is written along with the principal amount as it is an *out-going* payment
- **Pv** is the present value of an investment. We leave it blank as this is not a single cash flow problem
- Leave **Type** as blank or write 0, implying payment is made at the end of the year/period
- Alternatively, the same calculation is done by writing '= *FV* (**Rate**, **Nper, Pmt, PV**)' in the **Formula Bar**. These arguments appear automatically as soon as we write the '=*FV*'. We need to fill the values of these arguments accordingly in the same order as required
- We can notice the calculated as ₹3,51,996 in Figure 12.3.

To sum up, this chapter enables us to calculate the future values of both single and multiple cash flows. This calculation helps in building asset creation as well as in financial planning. Various methodologies to calculate future values have been systematically explained to understand the concept behind these calculations. These concepts are of utmost importance in real life. The foundation of concepts that have been laid through in this chapter forms a base for subsequent topics.

TABLE 12.3 Future Annuity Value Table

Future Value Interest Factors for a One-Rupee Annuity Compounded at r Percent for n Periods: $FVIFA_{r,n} = [(1 + r)^n - 1] / r$

Period	1%	2%	3%	4%	5%	6%	7%	8%	9%	10%	11%	12%	13%	14%	15%	16%	20%	24%	25%	30%
1	1	1.02	1.03	1.04	1.05	1.06	1.07	1.08	1.09	1.1	1.11	1.12	1.13	1.14	1.15	1.16	1.2	1.24	1.25	1.3
2	2.01	2.02	2.03	2.04	2.05	2.06	2.07	2.08	2.09	2.1	2.11	2.12	2.13	2.14	2.15	2.16	2.2	2.24	2.25	2.3
3	3.0301	3.0604	3.0909	3.1216	3.1525	3.1836	3.2149	3.2464	3.2781	3.31	3.3421	3.3744	3.4069	3.4396	3.4725	3.5056	3.64	3.7776	3.8125	3.99
4	4.0604	4.1216	4.1836	4.2465	4.3101	4.3746	4.4399	4.5061	4.5731	4.641	4.7097	4.7793	4.8498	4.9211	4.9934	5.0665	5.368	5.6842	5.7656	6.187
5	5.101	5.204	5.3091	5.4163	5.5256	5.6371	5.7507	5.8666	5.9847	6.1051	6.2278	6.3528	6.4803	6.6101	6.7424	6.8771	7.4416	8.0484	8.207	9.0431
6	6.152	6.3081	6.4684	6.633	6.8019	6.9753	7.1533	7.3359	7.5233	7.7156	7.9129	8.1152	8.3227	8.5355	8.7537	8.9775	9.9299	10.98	11.259	12.756
7	7.2135	7.4343	7.6625	7.8983	8.142	8.3938	8.654	8.9228	9.2004	9.4872	9.7833	10.089	10.405	10.73	11.067	11.414	12.916	14.615	15.073	17.583
8	8.2857	8.583	8.8923	9.2142	9.5491	9.8975	10.26	10.637	11.028	11.436	11.859	12.3	12.757	13.233	13.727	14.24	16.499	19.123	19.842	23.858
9	9.3685	9.7546	10.159	10.583	11.027	11.491	11.978	12.488	13.021	13.579	14.164	14.776	15.416	16.085	16.786	17.519	20.799	24.712	25.802	32.015
10	10.462	10.95	11.464	12.006	12.578	13.181	13.816	14.487	15.193	15.937	16.722	17.549	18.42	19.337	20.304	21.321	25.959	31.643	33.253	42.619
11	11.567	12.169	12.808	13.486	14.207	14.972	15.784	16.645	17.56	18.531	19.561	20.655	21.814	23.045	24.349	25.733	32.15	40.238	42.566	56.405
12	12.683	13.412	14.192	15.026	15.917	16.87	17.888	18.977	20.141	21.384	22.713	24.133	25.65	27.271	29.002	30.85	39.581	50.895	54.208	74.327
13	13.809	14.68	15.618	16.627	17.713	18.882	20.141	21.495	22.953	24.523	26.212	28.029	29.985	32.089	34.352	36.786	48.497	64.11	68.76	97.625
14	14.947	15.974	17.086	18.292	19.599	21.015	22.55	24.215	26.019	27.975	30.095	32.393	34.883	37.581	40.505	43.672	59.196	80.496	86.949	127.91
15	16.097	17.293	18.599	20.024	21.579	23.276	25.129	27.152	29.361	31.772	34.405	37.28	40.417	43.842	47.58	51.66	72.035	100.82	109.69	167.29
16	17.258	18.639	20.157	21.825	23.657	25.673	27.888	30.324	33.003	35.95	39.19	42.753	46.672	50.98	55.717	60.925	87.442	126.01	138.11	218.47
17	18.43	20.012	21.762	23.698	25.84	28.213	30.84	33.75	36.974	40.545	44.501	48.884	53.739	59.118	65.075	71.673	105.93	157.25	173.64	285.01
18	19.615	21.412	23.414	25.645	28.132	30.906	33.999	37.45	41.301	45.599	50.396	55.75	61.725	68.394	75.836	84.141	128.12	195.99	218.05	371.52
19	20.811	22.841	25.117	27.671	30.539	33.76	37.379	41.446	46.018	51.159	56.939	63.44	70.749	78.969	88.212	98.603	154.74	244.03	273.56	483.97
20	22.019	24.297	26.87	29.778	33.066	36.786	40.995	45.762	51.16	57.275	64.203	72.052	80.947	91.025	102.44	115.38	186.69	303.6	342.95	630.17
21	23.239	25.783	28.676	31.969	35.719	39.993	44.865	50.423	56.765	64.002	72.265	81.699	92.47	104.77	118.81	134.84	225.03	377.47	429.68	820.22
22	24.472	27.299	30.537	34.248	38.505	43.392	49.006	55.457	62.873	71.403	81.214	92.503	105.49	120.44	137.63	157.42	271.03	469.06	538.1	*
23	25.716	28.845	32.453	36.618	41.43	46.996	53.436	60.893	69.532	79.543	91.148	104.6	120.21	138.3	159.28	183.6	326.24	582.63	673.63	*
24	26.973	30.422	34.426	39.083	44.502	50.816	58.177	66.765	76.79	88.497	102.17	118.16	136.83	158.66	184.17	213.98	392.48	723.46	843.03	*
25	28.243	32.03	36.459	41.646	47.727	54.865	63.249	73.106	84.701	98.347	114.41	133.33	155.62	181.87	212.79	249.21	471.98	898.09	*	*
30	34.785	40.568	47.575	56.085	66.439	79.058	94.461	113.28	136.31	164.49	199.02	241.33	293.2	356.79	434.75	530.31	*	*	*	*
35	41.66	49.994	60.462	73.652	90.32	111.44	138.24	172.32	215.71	271.02	341.59	431.66	546.68	693.57	881.17	*	*	*	*	*
36	43.077	51.994	63.276	77.598	95.836	119.12	148.91	187.1	236.13	299.13	380.16	484.46	618.75	791.67	*	*	*	*	*	*
40	48.886	60.402	75.401	95.026	120.8	154.76	199.64	259.06	337.88	442.59	581.83	767.09	*	*	*	*	*	*	*	*
50	64.463	84.579	112.8	152.67	209.35	290.34	406.53	573.77	815.08	*	*	*	*	*	*	*	*	*	*	*

FIGURE 12.3 Calculating Future Value of Annuity Using Excel

PRACTICE QUESTIONS

1. Rajesh has deposited ₹100 in an account that pays 3 per cent compounded yearly. What would be the balance amount in his account at the end of three years if he withdrew only the interest on the interest each year?

2. Ria decided to invest ₹15,000 in her savings account that pays 3 per cent interest, compounded quarterly. How much will she have in her account at the end of five years if she does not make any withdrawals?

3. Rohan has ₹1,000 that he will invest in a safe financial instrument expected to return 3 per cent annually. Ananya has ₹500 which she invests in a stock market that is expected to return 7 per cent annually. Who will have more money after 20 years? And how much do they have in *FV* terms?

4. Daksh has ₹1,00,000 to decide on two investment options. Option 1 returns 60 per cent annually for four years, but he can invest ₹10,000 at the most. The return on Option 2 is 12 per cent annually for four years, but it would require the entire investment of ₹1,00,000. Which option should Daksh choose, and what is the benefit over the alternate option? Assume that ₹90,000 not invested in Option 1 would be deposited safely but with no interest.

5. Rama is 35 years old and wants to plan for her retirement. She decides to save ₹4,800 starting at the end of this year until she is 65. She can make 7 per cent of returns on her account. How much money will she have at age 65 for her retirement?

6. Vanya's parents have been putting money in an account for her since she was 5 years old. She has now turned 21 and has access to this money. Her mother asks her to guess what her account is worth today after she gives her a hint that they have invested ₹1,000 every year since her 5th birthday and have again made an investment. The interest rate is 3.5 per cent annually. What is the worth of Vanya's account today?

Notes

1 P and PV are used interchangeably. PV means present value.
2 We can reverse this procedure and get PV factor. Dividing the principal amount by the subsequent future values gives the quotient values which are the *Present Value Interest Factor* (*PVIF*). For example, dividing 50,000 by the future values 53,000, 56,180, and 59550 yield 0.9434, 0,89, and 0.8396 respectively for the given combination of r (6%) and n = 1, 2, and 3.

13

INVESTMENT DECISION CRITERIA

NPV and IRR

Learning Objectives

After reading this chapter, the readers will be able to understand

- Meaning and decision rule of net present value (NPV) method
- Computation of NPV using Excel
- Meaning and decision rule of internal rate of return (IRR) method
- Calculation of IRR using Excel
- Application of IRR in endowment plans, moneyback policies, and pension plans
- IRR vs XIRR

In this chapter, the techniques which are used to decide whether the business project and investment are worth pursuing or not are introduced. An investor generally encounters a problem or challenge in deciding on the most economically viable project or a venture. He/she is confronted with several alternative options from which he/she will have to choose a particular investment opportunity. The investment may involve a considerable amount of money. Consequently, such an investment involves critical scrutiny; thus, a careful decision is essential.

According to the theory of decision-making, any right decision for a good investment must have the following properties:

- The benefits of the project are more than the cost incurred
- The criteria should have units of measurement
- It is simple to calculate
- It is easy to compare different ideas/projects

Based on the preceding criteria, two distinct techniques are generally used in deciding on business investment.

DOI: 10.4324/9781003398127-13

- Net Present Value (NPV)
- Internal Rate of Return (IRR)

These two methods act as a decision criterion to determine the idea of undertaking a good project. However, there are several advantages and disadvantages associated with each of these methods. The merits and demerits attributed to each of these methods will be discussed.

13.1   Net Present Value (NPV)

NPV refers to the *difference* between future cash-flow streams converted into present values at an appropriate discount rate and the initial investment. While considering the difference, the present values at an appropriate discount rate are regarded as positive entity, while the initial investment is considered a negative entity. Therefore, in calculating NPV, we consider all cash flows that are both positive and negative entities in nature.

NPV comprises two crucial components.

- The *cash flows* generated in the future. These are mainly the returns that are attributed to the project in the future. Therefore, the values of these returns should be forecasted based on realistic assumptions.
- The *discount rate* captures the opportunity cost of an idea or the investment opportunity that an investor comes across. Alternatively, it can be understood as the rate equivalent to the expected returns prevailing in the same businesses. Thus, one should be quite careful in applying a discount rate in practice.

13.1.1   *Decision Rule: Accept/Reject Criteria*

The accept/reject criteria of the NPV method works by comparing the present value of the future cash streams with the initial investment.

- If NPV is positive, then the project is worth accepting.
- If the project's NPV is negative, the project is not investment worthy. As a result of a higher discount rate, if NPV turns out to be negative, it is either on account of a higher cost of capital or higher expected returns.
- When NPV is equal to 0, the decision of accepting or rejecting the project becomes indifferent as there is neither a gain nor a loss.

In the case of mutually exclusive projects, when selecting one project leads to rejecting other projects, select the project with the highest NPV.

13.1.2   *Calculating NPV*

NPV is simply a difference between the present value of all future cash-flow streams and initial investments.

NPV = Present Value of all future cash-flow streams − Initial Investment

$$\text{NPV} = \left[\frac{C_1}{(1+r)} + \frac{C_2}{(1+r)^2} + \frac{C_3}{(1+r)^3} + \dots\dots \frac{C_n}{(1+r)^n} \right] - I_0 \tag{1}$$

Here,

C$_1$, C$_2$ . . . C$_n$ = Cash flows generated at different points of time in the future.

r = Discount rate

n = Estimated life of the project

t = time period

I$_0$ = Initial investment

Equation 1 can be summarized as the following formula

$$NPV = \sum_{t=1}^{n} \frac{C_t}{(1+r)^t} - I_0 \tag{2}$$

$$NPV = \sum_{t=1}^{n} C_t \times \frac{1}{(1+r)^t} - I_0,$$

$$NPV = \sum_{t=1}^{n} C_t \times PVF_{r,t} - I_0 \tag{3}$$

Where $PVF_{r,t}$ = Present value factor for the given discount rate and the given year.

The following illustrations will depict the detailed steps and calculations involved in computing NPV and the decision-making process for a particular project or investment.

Illustration

Tarun is considering buying a second-hand car to use it as a taxi. The cost of this car is ₹50,000. The car has a life expectancy of five years and no salvage value. The estimated cash inflows from year 1 to 5 are as follows: ₹10,000; ₹10,450; ₹11,800; ₹12,250, and ₹16,750. The appropriate discount rate is 10 per cent. State its NPV and if this investment is worth it.

Solution

There are three methods to solve such problems.

First Method (Direct Method)

NPV = Present Value of Cash Inflows − Present Value of Cash Outflows

$$NPV = \sum_{t=1}^{n} \frac{C_t}{(1+r)^t} - I_0$$

$$NPV = C_1 \times \frac{1}{(1+0.10)^1} + C_2 \times \frac{1}{(1+0.10)^2} + C_3 \times \frac{1}{(1+0.10)^3} + C_4 \times \frac{1}{(1+0.10)^4} +$$

$$C_5 \times \frac{1}{(1+0.10)^5} - I_0$$

$$NPV = 10,000 \times 0.909 + 10,450 \times 0.826 + 11,800 \times 0.751 + 12,250 \times 0.683$$
$$+ 16,750 \times 0.621 - 50,000$$

$$NPV = 9,090 + 8,632 + 8,862 + 8,367 + 10,402 - 50,000$$

$$NPV = 45,353 - 50,000$$

$$NPV = -(Rs.4,647)$$

The NPV is negative, so the investment is not good.

Second Method (Using PVF Table)

Year	Cash Flows	Present Value Factor at 10% (PVF$_{10\%, t}$)	Present Value of Cash Flows
1	10,000	0.909	9,090
2	10,450	0.826	8,632
3	11,800	0.751	8,862
4	12,250	0.683	8,367
5	16,750	0.621	10,402
Total Present Value			45,353
Less: Initial cash outlay			50,000
Net Present Value (NPV)			**−4,647**

Note: Present value factors can be calculated using the formula: $\dfrac{1}{(1+r)^t}$ and are readily obtainable from the PVF table.

$$PVF_{10\%,1} = \frac{1}{(1+0.10)^1} = 0.909 \qquad PVF_{10\%,2} = \frac{1}{(1+0.10)^2} = 0.826$$

$$PVF_{10\%,3} = \frac{1}{(1+0.10)^3} = 0.751$$

$$PVF_{10\%,4} = \frac{1}{(1+0.10)^4} = 0.683 \qquad PVF_{10\%,5} = \frac{1}{(1+0.10)^5} = 0.621$$

Third Method (using Excel)

NPV can be calculated using Excel as well.

Step 1. Enter the data of all the cash inflows and outflows.
Step 2. Use the formula NPV and fill in the required arguments, which are discount rate and values (of cash inflows).
Step 3. Subtract the result we get in Step 2 from the initial investment.

The calculations are shown in Figure 13.1. The difference between the results we get in methods 2 and 3 is due to rounding-off.

When manually computing NPV in the case of annuity streams, the methods mentioned earlier can be applied similarly but with the help of the PVAF table.

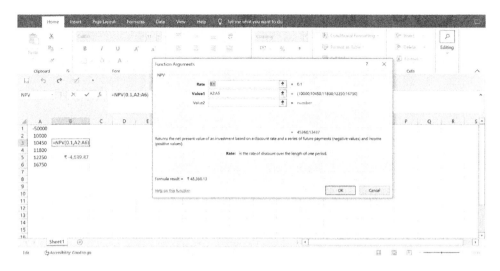

FIGURE 13.1   Calculating NPV Using Excel

Check Your Understanding

Consider an investment that has the following expected cash flows. The discount rate is 10 per cent. What is the NPV of this investment?

YEAR	Cash Flows A
TODAY	₹ − 10,000
1	₹1,000
2	₹1,000
3	₹9,000

Ans. ₹ − 1,503

The method is associated with several merits and demerits, as discussed next.

13.2   Merits and Demerits of the NPV Method

13.2.1. Merits of NPV

1.   It takes into account the time value of money
2.   It takes into consideration all the cash flows arising out of the project in its lifetime
3.   It is an absolute measure of profitability
4.   This method satisfies the value-additivity principle. It gives output in terms of the absolute amount so the NPVs of the project can be added, which is not possible with other methods
5.   It meets the firms/investment goals of wealth maximization.

13.2.2 Demerits of NPV

1. This method ignores uncertainties in cash flows that exist in the real world
2. The uncertainties are also involved in the calculation of the discount rate.

Another method considered in deciding whether a particular investment option is economically viable is *IRR*.

13.3 Internal Rate of Return (IRR)

IRR is the *discount rate* which equates the PV of the cash inflows with the PV of the cash outflows or at which NPV is zero. In other words, IRR is a modified compound annual growth rate and is used to calculate return over a holding period when the investments are multiple or in a varied frequency. IRR is also called the marginal efficiency of capital, the marginal productivity of capital, the yield on investment, time adjusted rate of return, a marginal rate of return, and so on.

The following condition must be true to arrive at IRR:

Present value of cash inflows = Present value of cash outflows

→ *Present value of cash inflows − Present value of cash outflows = 0*

→ $NPV = 0$

Symbolically,

$$\sum_{t=1}^{n} \frac{C_t}{(1+r)^t} = \sum_{t=1}^{n} \frac{CO_t}{(1+r)^t}$$

$$\rightarrow \sum_{t=1}^{n} \frac{C_t}{(1+r)^t} - \sum_{t=1}^{n} \frac{CO_t}{(1+r)^t} = 0$$

→ $NPV = 0$

Suppose we put 10 per cent in place of r and both sides become equal (or NPV = 0), then this 10 per cent is the internal rate of return.

Note: If cash outflows are in the zero years only (multiple cash outflows are not there), then there is no need to calculate the PV of the cash outflows.

For calculating IRR directly, we use the trial and error approach. We can either use the PVF table in the case of mixed streams or the PVAF table in the case of annuity streams.

- We take a percentage with a given n and compute the PV of the project's cash inflows. If the PV of cash inflows is equal to the PV of cash outflows (or cash outflows in the zero years), then the percentage taken is the IRR
- If the NPV is negative, then reduce the discount rate to get a positive NPV and
- If the NPV is positive, then increase the discount rate to get a negative NPV.

Now using the two percentages – one where NPV is positive and the other where NPV is negative, to arrive at IRR, we apply the following formula[1]:

$$IRR = LDR + \frac{NPV_{LDR}}{NPV_{LDR} - NPV_{HDR}} \times |Difference \ of \ Rates|$$

or

$$IRR = LDR + \frac{PV_{LDR} - PV \ of \ cash \ outflows \ or \ Initial \ outlay}{PV_{LDR} - PV_{HDR}} \times |Difference \ of \ Rates|$$

(The preceding formulae are for the linear interpolation)
Here, LDR = Lower Discount Rate, HDR = Higher Discount Rate
The difference in rates is taken after ignoring the signs.

Note:

1. We sometimes are not able to decide the discount rate with which to start working. For that, we take any discount rate and compute the PV of cash inflows or NPV. Now, the PV of cash inflows or NPV will give you the direction regarding the next discount rate.
2. The difference between the two percentages is usually taken as 5.

The IRR decision rule states that:

- If the asset's IRR is less than the standard rate of return, then do not select the asset.
- If the asset's IRR is greater than the standard rate of return, then select the asset.

To comprehend the detailed working of this technique, the following illustrations would be helpful both for computing IRR manually and by deploying Excel.

Illustration

The cost of a machine is ₹42,000. Cash inflows are as follows:

Year	Amount (₹)
1	12,000
2	12,000
3	14,000
4	15,000
5	16,000

Calculate IRR.

Solution:

There are two methods to solve such problems.

First Method

In the first method, the trial and error method is used. Let us calculate the NPV at the discount rate of 10 per cent.

Year	Cash Inflows	Present Value Factors at 10% ($PVF_{10\%,\ t}$)	Present Value at 10%
1	12,000	0.909	10,908
2	12,000	0.826	9,912
3	14,000	0.751	10,514
4	15,000	0.683	10,245
5	16,000	0.621	9,936
Total PV			51,515
Less: Initial cash outlay			− 42,000
NPV			**9,515**

NPV is positive, so we shall increase the discount rate; now let us calculate the NPV at the discount rate of 15 per cent.

Year	Cash Inflows	Present Value Factors at 15% ($PVF_{15\%,\ n}$)	Present Value at 15%
1	12,000	0.870	10,440
2	12,000	0.756	9,072
3	14,000	0.658	9,212
4	15,000	0.572	8,580
5	16,000	0.497	7,952
Total present Value			45,256
Less: Initial cash outlay			− 42,000
NPV			**3,256**

NPV is positive, so we shall increase the discount rate; now let us calculate the NPV at the discount rate of 20 per cent.

Year	Cash Inflows	Present Value Factors at 20% ($PVF_{20\%,\ n}$)	Present Value at 20%
1	12,000	0.833	9,996
2	12,000	0.694	8,328
3	14,000	0.579	8,106
4	15,000	0.482	7,230
5	16,000	0.402	6,432
Total PV			40,092
Less: Initial cash outlay			− 42,000
NPV			**(1,908)**

Now the NPV is negative at 20 per cent and positive at 15 per cent. It means that the IRR lies between 20 and 15 per cent. So, there is a need to apply the formula for interpolation.

$$IRR = LDR + \frac{NPV_{LDR}}{NPV_{LDR} - NPV_{HDR}} \times |Difference\ of\ Rates|$$

$$IRR = 15 + \frac{NPV_{15\%}}{NPV_{15\%} - NPV_{20\%}} \times 5$$

$$IRR = 15 + \frac{3256}{Rs.3,256 - (-Rs.1,908)} \times 5$$

$$IRR = 15 + 0.6305 * 5$$

$$IRR = 15 + 3.1525$$

$$IRR \cong 18.15$$

Or

$$IRR = LDR + \frac{PV_{LDR} - PV\ of\ cash\ outflows\ or\ Initial\ outlay}{PV_{LDR} - PV_{HDR}} \times |Difference\ of\ Rates|$$

$$IRR = 15 + \frac{PV_{15\%} - PV\ of\ cash\ outflows\ or\ Initial\ outlay}{PV_{15\%} - PV_{20\%}} \times 5$$

$$IRR = 15 + \frac{45,256 - 42,000}{45,256 - 40,092} \times 5$$

$$IRR = 15 + 0.6305 * 5$$

$$IRR = 15 + 3.1525$$

$$IRR \cong 18.15$$

Second Method (Using Excel)

Excel provides an easy way of computing IRR. Instead of going into the complicated manual calculations, we can simply use the IRR function in Excel. As shown in Figure 13.2, the IRR comes out to be 18.04.

- We first need to enter all the cash outflows and inflows values, respectively
- Choose the function IRR from the f_x function
- Fill the values arguments by selecting all the cells containing values
- Leave the **Guess** argument blank.

Check Your Understanding

Consider an investment decision that has the following expected cash flows. What is the IRR of this investment decision?

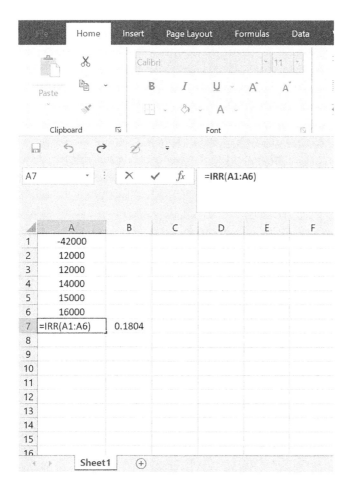

FIGURE 13.2   Calculating IRR Using Excel

Year	Amount
0	−₹1,00,000
1	₹45,000
2	₹45,000
3	₹45,000

Ans. 16.65 per cent

IRR is a widely used technique in our daily life for simple applications such as insurance policy and mutual fund investment. A detailed account of the steps involved in computing IRR-based decisions regarding the viability of investing in any project are explained as follows.

13.4   Common Applications of IRR

IRR is mostly used in investment decisions such as insurance policies and mutual fund investments. The methodology to calculate IRR remains the same in either of the investments. However, we take the case of calculating returns in insurance policies only which is a common form of investment. Insurance plans include endowment plans, money-back plans, pension plans, or any other plan in which we pay premiums. The three examples we consider here are:

13.4.1 Endowment Plans With Money Back at Maturity

Suppose we have to pay an annual premium of ₹30,000 for 20 years. At the end of the 21st year, we get ₹10 lakh, and the IRR (that is, the return on this investment) can be calculated as shown in Figure 13.3. Solving in Excel, using the IRR function, we get a return of 4.65 per cent. As indicated earlier, the minus sign represents the outgoing cash flow (premiums paid for 20 years in our example).

13.4.2 Moneyback Policies With Money Back in between

Suppose the premium is ₹25,000 per year for 20 years, but we get, say, at the end 4th, 8th, 12th, and 16th year an amount of ₹30,000, ₹30,000, ₹30,000, and ₹50,000 respectively. The sum assured at the time of maturity at the end of the 21st year is ₹5,00,000. In such a case,

Year 1	−3,00,000
Year 2	−3,00,000
Year 3	−3,00,000
Year 4	−3,00,000
Year 5	−3,00,000
Year 6	−3,00,000
Year 7	−3,00,000
Year 8	−3,00,000
Year 9	−3,00,000
Year 10	−3,00,000
Year 11	−3,00,000
Year 12	−3,00,000
Year 13	−3,00,000
Year 14	−3,00,000
Year 15	−3,00,000
Year 16	−3,00,000
Year 17	−3,00,000
Year 18	−3,00,000
Year 19	−3,00,000
Year 20	−3,00,000
Year 21	1,00,00,000
IRR	**0.0465**

FIGURE 13.3 Calculating IRR of Endowment Plans

Year 1	−25,000
Year 2	−25,000
Year 3	−25,000
Year 4	5,000
Year 5	−25,000
Year 6	−25,000
Year 7	−25,000
Year 8	5,000
Year 9	−25,000
Year 10	−25,000
Year 11	−25,000
Year 12	5,000
Year 13	−25,000
Year 14	−25,000
Year 15	−25,000
Year 16	25,000
Year 17	−25,000
Year 18	−25,000
Year 19	−25,000
Year 20	−25,000
Year 21	5,00,000
IRR	**0.029796**

FIGURE 13.4   Calculating IRR in a Money-Back Policy

we need to adjust the amount paid in 4th, 8th, 12th, and 16th years. Accordingly, we take the difference between the amount we pay and the amount we get. The adjusted amount will be ₹5000 (−25000 + 30000) in 4th, 8th, and 12th and ₹25000 (−25000 + 50000) in the 16th year. Calculating IRR in Excel will yield 2.98 per cent (Figure 13.4).

13.4.3. A Simple Pension Plan

Pension plans are quite popular now. Let us take an example to understand its return before considering an investment in it. We have been asked to pay a premium of ₹25,000 for ten years. For the next ten years, we do not get anything. However, for the next 40 years, the company promises us to pay a pension back at ₹25,000 each year. If we analyze it in absolute terms, we spend an amount at ₹2,50,000 and get in return ₹10,00,000. It sounds attractive, and a lot of investors may fall for it. To analyze it correctly, we have to consider the IRR application. IRR is a cruel tool as it makes us come to terms with reality. Calculating IRR in Excel, we enter −25,000 in the first ten cells, 0 in the next ten cells, and 25,000 in the next 40 cells. This will yield a return of 4.37 per cent. Now it is up to us whether we want to invest at this return rate.

13.5   IRR vs Extended Internal Rate of Return (XIRR)

The only difference between IRR and XIRR that the latter allows us to assign a date to each cash flow. Let us take an example. We make a payment of ₹1,000 each month for 13 months on *specific dates*, as shown in Figure 13.5. After the end of this period, its redemption value is ₹14,500. The XIRR formula in Excel additionally brings in the **Dates** argument. We generally leave the **Guess** argument blank. It can be seen in the formula result that this investment is yielding a return of 19.8 per cent. Note that we must be cautious about the format of the dates. Excel only recognizes the date format, which is given in Figure 13.5.

There are several advantages and disadvantages associated with the method of IRR as discussed in section 13.6.

13.6   Merits and Limitations of IRR

Merits of IRR

1. This method recognizes the time value of money, and all the cash flows over the life of the project/investment
2. This method itself determines a rate
3. It helps in achieving the objective of wealth maximization
4. This method gives a rate that can be compared with the standard rate of return to evaluate the project.

Limitations of IRR

1. The calculation is difficult and tedious
2. Sometimes this method gives more than one IRR, especially when the sign of cash flows changes. This leads to confusion. To understand it better, let us take the following example:

FIGURE 13.5   Calculating XIRR

Cash Flows	Years From Now
−100	0
230	1
−132	2

Calculating IRR in Excel yields 10 per cent. Let us start by guessing a random IRR, say .20. We get NPV as 0 even at 20 per cent, and our guess turns out to be correct. This clearly shows that more than one IRR is present in this case. So which IRR should be chosen? The solution lies in the following graphical representation. When $r = 0$, NPV is negative. As r tends to 10 per cent, NPV approaches 0. Between 10 and 20 per cent, NPV is positive, and at 20 per cent, NPV is again 0. Increasing r further makes NPV negative. We will undoubtedly prefer the rates with positive NPV. So we can choose any rate between 10 and 20 per cent comparable to similar businesses.

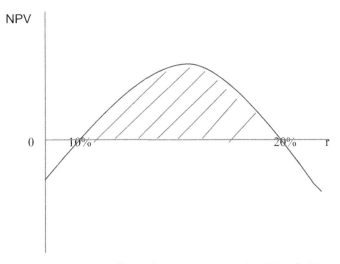

3. When we compare two mutually exclusive projects, an intuitive decision rule would be to accept the project with the highest IRR. This rule is unfortunately incorrect as we show in the following example.

Consider two projects, A and B, with the following cash flows. Which one would we choose?

Year	Project A	Project B
0	−2,000	−2,000
1	400	2,000
2	2,400	625
IRR	**20%**	**25%**
NPV (@5%)	558	472
NPV (@20%)	0	101
NPV (@11%)	308	309

Based on IRR, we will be inclined towards Project B as its IRR is higher. But IRR is plagued by short-term bias. Even though the two projects are of the same physical length, project A yields higher returns in the later years while project B yields a higher return in the earlier years. IRR favours project B because of earlier high returns. But comparing 20 per cent with 25 per cent directly is not the right thing to do. We are comparing this internally, *but we should compare it with a benchmark, for example, the cost of capital r.* We are more interested in knowing *how well we are doing relative to the competitors* and not in our internal rate of return.

We here calculate NPV using three rates – 5, 20, and 11 per cent as shown earlier. If $r =$ 5 per cent, we will choose project A (as its NPV is more). If $r = 20$ per cent, we would then select project B. However, at $r = 11$ per cent, we are indifferent between the two projects as the NPV is almost the same.

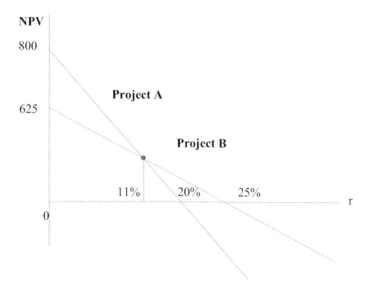

It is clear from the graph that if r is less than 11 per cent, we will choose project A, and if r is greater than 11 per cent, we will choose project B (because of higher NPV). In any case, we will not select any project if r is more than 25 per cent because of the negative NPV.

4. IRR also suffers from a small investment bias. Consider two projects, A and B, with the following cash flows.

Year	Project A (₹)	Project B (₹)
0	−5,000	−50,000
1	7,500	64,000
IRR	**50%**	**28%**

In Project A, since the investment is smaller (−₹5,000), the return will turn out to be higher because of the smaller denominator as compared to project B [Growth = $(FV - PV)/$ PV]. IRR is a percentage and favours little things over large. This shows there is a built-in bias of scale.

5. IRR implicitly assumes that the obtained positive cash flows are *re-invested at the rate at which they are generated*. This assumption, however, may not always hold. To get rid of this limitation, an alternative method, namely, *modified internal rate of return* (MIRR) is used. MIRR assumes the re-investment taking place at the rate of the cost of capital.

So, to summarize, this chapter is featured to explain two important criteria in decision-making in the selection of the project and/or investment. These criteria, NPV and IRR, are closely linked to each other and have their own sets of problems. However, IRR is a more prevalent and widely used method than NPV. This is because it is improper to calculate NPV unless the appropriate discount rate is known. Moreover, in investment decisions, individuals and analysts seem to prefer rates of return rather than absolute values. Similarly, IRR is a straightforward mode of disclosing information about a project.

PRACTICE QUESTIONS

1. Hariti needs ₹12,000 to purchase the mobile she wants to purchase. Her father offers to loan her the money but wants to teach her the time value of money. He offers to have her repay the loan in the future using pocket money. They agree that she will repay ₹4,500 in 3, 6, and 15 months from now. Assuming a 6 per cent cost of capital and that compounding is done monthly, what is the NPV of the loan?

2. Dolly runs a boutique. She decides to expand her business. The additional rental space will cost her ₹7,200 per year at the end of each year and an immediate one-time investment of ₹10,000 for other machines. The boutique will generate an extra income of ₹10,000 per year at the end of each year. The business is expected to last 20 years. The discount rate is 10 per cent. What is the NPV of the boutique project? (round off decimals).

3. Consider two investments, A and B

	Cash Flows	
YEAR	A (₹)	B (₹)
TODAY	−5,000	−5,000
1	1,000	0
2	2,000	0
3	2,000	4,000
4	1,500	1,000
5	1,000	2,500

Which investment is more profitable if the cost of capital of both investments is 7 per cent?

4. Which investment would you choose if you were offered the following two investments?

	Cash Flows	
YEAR	A (₹)	B (₹)
TODAY	₹ − 1,000	₹ − 1,000
1	₹700	₹0
2	₹1,200	₹2,100

The cost of capital for both investments is 10 per cent.

5. Varun owned a factory that got burned down in an accident. The worth of vacant land is ₹70,000. He also received ₹2,00,000 from his insurance company. Varun plans to build another factory on the same land which will cost ₹2,75,000. He expects that the value of the finished factory in the market will be ₹3,85,000 next year. The discount rate is 10 per cent. What are the NPV and IRR of this decision?

6. Sunshine technology is considering the following three projects, and it has to choose only one. Project A has an expense of ₹10,0000 today, and the cash flows over the next three years are ₹20,000, ₹40,000 and ₹70,000. Project B has an outflow of ₹1,10,000 and cash flows of ₹40,000, ₹80,000, and ₹20,000. The cost of Project C is ₹1,20,000, and cash inflows of ₹0, ₹20,000, and ₹1,41,500. Which project should this company choose if the capital cost for similar projects is 6 per cent?

Note

1   The derivation of this formula is beyond the scope of this book.

14

LOAN AMORTIZATION

Learning Objectives

After reading this chapter, the readers will be able to understand

- The difference between fixed and reducing balance types of loans
- The calculation of equated monthly instalment (EMI)
- Loan amortization schedule
- Calculating various components in loan schedule using Excel
- Effective annual rate

Loan amortization is one of the most basic applications used in the time value of money. A loan mainly involves a lending exercise. The lender lends money to the borrower to get back his money and interest on it. The calculation of a loan requires the following basic concepts.

1. **Equated Monthly Instalment (EMI):** It is a periodic payment made on a loan. It primarily depends upon the interest rate (r) and the number of periods (n) over which the amount is to be paid. The *higher* the number of periods and/or *lower* the r, the lesser the EMI will be and *vice versa*. The term is equivalent to **PMT** (short for payment) in Excel.
2. **Principal Payment:** It refers to the amount of money returned out of the principal amount borrowed.
3. **Interest Payment:** It is the amount of interest paid on loan to the lender.

14.1   Type of Loan: Fixed Interest vs Reducing Balance Method

Two common methods adopted to calculate the loan are fixed interest and reducing balance. The difference between the two is that in the fixed interest method, interest is calculated on the *principal amount borrowed through the loan period*. On the other hand, in the reducing balance

DOI: 10.4324/9781003398127-14

method, the interest rate is calculated on the remaining principal amount at any time. In this section, calculations based on the fixed rate method are elucidated.

One of the advantages of a fixed rate type of loan is its simplified computation of EMI and its components, namely interest amount and principal payment. Besides, even if there is an increase in the interest rate on loans, we continue to pay the same fixed amount as the interest rate on loan taken is already fixed. Yet, in practice, loans based on fixed rate are usually not favoured. We will understand this statement subsequently. The formula to calculate EMI is the following:

$$\frac{P+\left(P*r*n\right)}{n*12}$$

where

P = Principal amount

r = Rate of interest

n = Number of years (multiplied by 12 in case calculations are to be made monthly)

That is, the total of principal and total interest payable for the time for which the loan has been taken is divided by the number of instalments. Let us take an example to understand the calculations. We consider a loan of ₹1,00,000 to be paid off with three *annual payments* with a fixed rate of 10 per cent. Substituting the values in the stated formula, the EMI of this loan is:

$$=\frac{1,00,000+\left(1,00,000*.10*3\right)}{3}=₹43,333$$

Alternatively, using Excel, the syntax of the EMI amount is shown in Figure 14.1.

Given the calculation methodology, the repayment table showing interest and payment amount can be drawn as presented in the next table. During the tenure of the loan, the interest amount paid is ₹30,000, and the total repayment amount is ₹1,30,000.

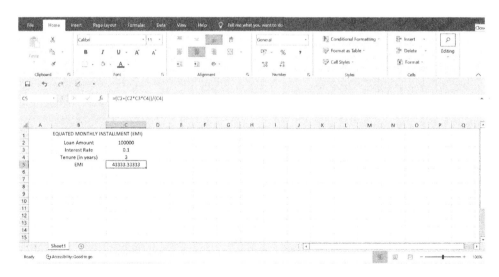

FIGURE 14.1   Calculating EMI Using the Fixed Rate Method

Year	EMI Amount (in ₹)	Interest Amount Paid (in ₹)	Principal Amount Paid (in ₹)
1	₹43,333	₹10,000	₹33,333
2	₹43,333	₹10,000	₹33,333
3	₹43,333	₹10,000	₹33,333

14.1.1 Arithmetic Derivation of Payment (PMT)/EMI in Reducing Balance Method

We can derive the payment factor mathematically in the following way:

Let us consider three years of timeline with r as the interest rate per annum.

The PV of a cash flow or payment (C) occurring after a year would be:

$$PV = \frac{C}{(1+r)}$$

The PV of a cash flow occurring after two years would be:

$$PV = \frac{C}{(1+r)^2}$$

Similarly, the PV of cash flow after three years:

$$PV = \frac{C}{(1+r)^3}$$

The PV of the annuity of these three years together will be:

$$PV = \frac{C}{(1+r)} + \frac{C}{(1+r)^2} + \frac{C}{(1+r)^3}$$

Or it can be rewritten as follows:

$$PV = C\left[\frac{1}{(1+r)} + \frac{1}{(1+r)^2} + \frac{1}{(1+r)^3}\right]$$

Multiplying (1+r) both the sides between two equations, we get

$$PV(1+r) = C\left[1 + \frac{1}{(1+r)} + \frac{1}{(1+r)^2}\right]$$

$$PV(1+r) - PV = C\left[1 + \frac{1}{(1+r)} + \frac{1}{(1+r)^2}\right] - C\left[\frac{1}{(1+r)} + \frac{1}{(1+r)^2} + \frac{1}{(1+r)^3}\right]$$

$$PVr = C\left[1 - \frac{1}{(1+r)^3}\right]$$

$$PV = \frac{C\left[1 - \frac{1}{(1+r)^3}\right]}{r}$$

$$\text{Or } C \text{ (or PMT)} = \frac{PV}{\left[\dfrac{1 - \dfrac{1}{(1+r)^3}}{r}\right]}$$

If the number of years = n, the generalized formula is:

$$\text{PMT} = \frac{PV}{\left[\dfrac{1 - \dfrac{1}{(1+r)^n}}{r}\right]}$$

If the loan amount (i.e., PV), interest rate, and the number of years for which loan are known, we can use the previous equation to calculate EMI. Assuming r as 10 per cent for n for three years, the following expression will turn out as 2.4869

$$\frac{\left[1 - \dfrac{1}{\left(1+r\right)^n}\right]}{r}$$

14.1.2   Calculating Payment or EMI Using Present Value Interest Factor of Annuity (PVIFA)

We can avoid the tedious denominator calculation and simply refer to the PVIFA table. For example, a loan amount of ₹100,000 is taken for three years at an interest rate of 10 per cent. We can quickly solve the denominator part by looking at the intersection of the 10 per cent interest rate and the number of periods equal to 3 in the PVIFA table.

* The interactive figure is 2.4869 (compare it with the expression calculated).
* Dividing PV by this value (that is, 100,000) gives us the EMI value of ₹40,211 (rounded off).

   Note that this EMI value is calculated yearly, which means each year a payment of ₹40,211 has to be made. For calculating *monthly* EMI payments, we know that the interest rate needs to be adjusted by the number of months and will be in decimals. *Since the PVIFA table does not contain the interest rate in decimals, we, therefore, cannot use the table when calculating the EMI amount monthly.*

Check Your Understanding

Consider a loan of ₹2,00,000 that is to be paid off with ten annual payments with a 10 per cent rate of interest. Calculate the amount of EMI per year.

   Ans. ₹32,549 (rounded off)

14.2   Loan Amortization With Table

Let us understand the loan amortization concept with the help of a table. We start by taking the same loan example in which we borrow ₹100,000 for three years at the rate of 10 per cent. The balance at the beginning of *first year* or *time 0* is ₹100,000, as it is the amount we are starting with. The first payment will occur at the end of the first year, which is ₹40,211 as calculated earlier. Since the interest rate is fixed, the yearly payments for all the years will be ₹40,211. At the end of the first year, we break the amount paid to the lender, that is, ₹40,211 into two components – *interest* and the *principal amount repaid.*

The interest amount paid at the rate of 10 per cent of the amount borrowed is ₹10,000. Subsequently, we need to determine how much the loan amount is paid. The loan repayment is the *difference* between the yearly annual payment (PMT) and the interest paid, that is, ₹40,211 – ₹10,000 = ₹30,211 in the first year. This means that a repayment of ₹30, 211 has been made out of the total loan amount. Payment of ₹30,211 implies that at the beginning of the second year, the amount of loan left for repayment is calculated by subtracting the principal amount repaid from the beginning balance, that is, ₹1,00,000 – ₹30,211, which is equal to ₹69,789.

Beginning Year	Balance at the Beginning of the Year	Yearly Payment	Interest Paid	Principal Amount Paid	Balance at the End of the Year
Today	–	–	–	–	100000
1	100000	40211	10000	30211	69789
2	69789	40211	6979	33232	36557
3	36557	40211	3656	36555	2[1]

Similarly, in the second year, the interest payment will be 10 per cent of the beginning amount of ₹69,789, which is ₹6,979. The principal amount repaid will be the difference between the annual payment of ₹40,211 and ₹6,979 (interest amount), which equals ₹33,232. Notice that for the third year, the EMI payment (₹40,211) is coming out to be more than the beginning balance of the third year. The reason behind this is that the outstanding balance of ₹36,557 at the beginning of the third year also has an interest payment due on it, that is of ₹3,656. In this manner, the entire loan gets paid off. A point of observation here is that the proportion of interest amount decreases, whereas the principal amount increases in the EMI component over time.

Check Your Understanding

Suppose you borrow ₹6,00,000 and pay it back over 20 years in annual payments. If the interest rate is 5 per cent, complete the information corresponding to the second- and third-year payments.

Likewise, this procedure can also be followed for calculating *monthly* EMI, as shown in the table. However, we cannot use the PVIFA table in this case because of the reason stated earlier. Hence, PMT needs to be calculated manually at this point in case of the unavailability of any financial calculator. In this case, the monthly EMI would turn out to be an amount of ₹3,227. This leads us to an important conclusion that as the number of periods increases, the EMI amount decreases.

14.3 Amount of Loan After *n* Periods

Suppose someone is interested in finding out the balance loan amount at the beginning of the 16th month; it would be very cumbersome to find it manually by following the procedure described earlier. *Here, we must understand that the answer to this question is equivalent to finding out the PV of the loan amount at the beginning of the 16th month.*

To find out the PV, we need the following:

- **r,** which is 0.1/12 (compounding monthly)
- **Pmt,** which is ₹ −3,227 (the amount is negative as it is an outgoing payment)
- Leave future value (*FV*) blank
- Write 0 as the **Type** argument (Type 0 implies payment at the end of the period)
- The most important thing is to decide what to take as the total number of periods (**Nper**). *We count Nper in such cases as the number of periods left of the loan amount.* For example, in this case, the number of periods left is 21 (by subtracting the number of periods in which we have repaid the loan amount, that is 15, from the total number of periods for which the loan is taken, that is, 36).

The balance of the loan amount at the beginning of the 16th month is ₹61,927. The figures can be realized from the calculations done underneath in Figure 14.2.

Check Your Understanding

Amit borrows ₹1,00,000 at 8 per cent compounded annually. Equal annual payments are to be made for six years. However, at the time of the fourth payment, he chose to pay off the loan. How much should be paid?

   Ans. ₹60,207

Beginning of the Month	Balance at the Beginning of the Year (₹)	Monthly Payment (₹)	Interest Paid (₹)	Principal Amount Paid (₹)	Balance at the End of the Year (₹)
1	1,00,000	3,227	833	2,393	97,607
2	97,607	3,227	813	2,413	95,193
3	95,193	3,227	793	2,433	92,760
4	92,760	3,227	773	2,454	90,306
5	90,306	3,227	753	2,474	87,832
6	87,832	3,227	732	2,495	85,337
7	85,337	3,227	711	2,516	82,822
8	82,822	3,227	690	2,537	80,285
9	80,285	3,227	669	2,558	77,727
10	77,727	3,227	648	2,579	75,148
11	75,148	3,227	626	2,600	72,548
12	72,548	3,227	605	2,622	69,926
13	69,926	3,227	583	2,644	67,282
14	67,282	3,227	561	2,666	64,616
15	64,616	3,227	538	2,688	61,927
16	**61,927**	3,227	516	2,711	59,217
17	59,217	3,227	493	2,733	56,484
18	56,484	3,227	471	2,756	53,728
19	53,728	3,227	448	2,779	50,949
20	50,949	3,227	425	2,802	48,146
21	48,146	3,227	401	2,825	45,321
22	45,321	3,227	378	2,849	42,472

Beginning of the Month	Balance at the Beginning of the Year (₹)	Monthly Payment (₹)	Interest Paid (₹)	Principal Amount Paid (₹)	Balance at the End of the Year (₹)
23	42,472	3,227	354	2,873	39,599
24	39,599	3,227	330	2,897	36,702
25	36,702	3,227	306	2,921	33,781
26	33,781	3,227	282	2,945	30,836
27	30,836	3,227	257	2,970	27,867
28	27,867	3,227	232	2,994	24,872
29	24,872	3,227	207	3,019	21,853
30	21,853	3,227	182	3,045	18,808
31	18,808	3,227	157	3,070	15,738
32	15,738	3,227	131	3,096	12,642
33	12,642	3,227	105	3,121	9,521
34	9,521	3,227	79	3,147	6,374
35	6,374	3,227	53	3,174	3,200
36	3,200	3,227	27	3,200	0

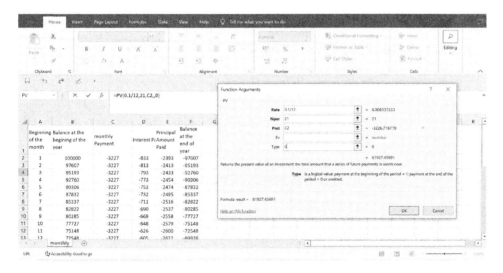

FIGURE 14.2   Calculating Outstanding Loan Amount Using PV Method

14.4   Payment or EMI Using Excel

There is a direct method for calculating EMI using Excel. This method allows us to avoid all the previous steps performed in the table. The **PMT** function directly helps us to calculate EMI. To perform this function, we click on the **Insert** function f_x. Select **PMT** from the dialogue box. In the **Function Arguments** dialogue box, we fill in the values of different parameters asked. The illustration of the same example discussed before is presented in Figure 14.3. In this example,

- **Rate** is taken as .1/12 (compounded monthly)

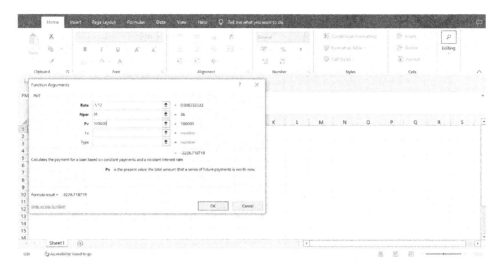

FIGURE 14.3   Calculating EMI Amount Using Excel

- **Nper** as 36 (total number of months are 36)
- **PV** (loan amount) as ₹1,00,000.

The corresponding value of EMI can be seen in Figure 14.3 as ₹3,227 (rounded off). The amount is the same as manually calculated earlier. Note that this function can also alternatively be written as '=PMT(.1/12,36,1,00,000)' in the **Formula Bar**.

14.5   Cumulative Principal and Interest Amount Using Excel

If we wish to find out how much of the total principal amount we have repaid at the end of the 15th period, we use the function **CUMPRINC**. Instead of finding the PV value as we did earlier, we can use this function. Select the function **CUMPRINC** after clicking on f_x. In the dialogue box, we start filling in the argument values.

- **Rate** is taken, as usual, that is, 0.1/12 as in our example
- **Nper** is 36, the total number of periods in the calculation
- **PV** (loan amount) is 1,00,000
- **Start_period** is taken as 1 since we want to calculate from the starting period. It is not always necessarily 1 as we may wish to calculate by taking any starting period
- **End_period** is taken as 15 as in our example, as the number of periods completed is 15
- **Type** is taken as 0 as type refers to the timing of the payment.

   Thus, at the end of the 15th period, the total principal amount that has been repaid is ₹38,073 (Figure 14.4). The balance remaining is ₹100,000-₹38,073 = ₹61,927. This amount can be cross-verified from Figure 14.2 as well. Note that the (-) sign represents the cash outflow or the payment made.

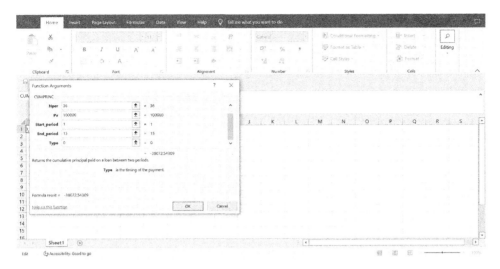

FIGURE 14.4   CUMPRINC Function in Excel

Check Your Understanding

Manisha takes a loan of ₹50,00,000 from a bank to buy a house for 20 years. The bank agrees to provide a loan at an interest rate of 8 per cent per annum compounded monthly. At the end of five years, Manisha is interested in knowing how much of the total principal amount she has paid in the last two years.

Ans. ₹2,79,628

Similarly, the total interest amount paid between any two periods can be found using the Excel function **CUMIPMT**. The dialogue box, after selecting this function, requires the following parameters.

- **Rate** is 0.1/12 as in our example
- **Nper** is 36, the total number of periods in the calculation
- **PV** (loan amount) is ₹1,00,000
- **Start_period** is taken as 1 since we want to calculate from the starting period. It is not always necessarily 1 as we may wish to calculate by taking any starting period
- **End_period** is taken as 15; as in our example, we want to determine the interest paid at the end of the 15th period
- **Type** is taken as 0 because the type refers to the timing of the payment

Thus, the total interest amount paid on the loan amount until the 15th period is ₹10,328. We can cross-check the result by adding the interest amounts paid up to the 15th period, exactly equal to the calculation shown in Figure 14.5.

Check Your Understanding

Now Manisha wants to know how much total interest amount she will pay in the first 15 years.

Ans. ₹4,590,556

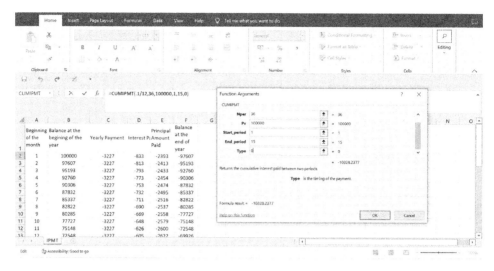

FIGURE 14.5 CUMIPMT Function in Excel

14.6 PPMT and IPMT

There are two more related functions besides those already discussed, often used in loan repayments.

- **PPMT** function: It helps us to find how much of the principal amount we have to repay in nth month
- **IPMT** function: It enables us to find how much of the interest amount we will have to repay in the nth month

14.6.1 PPMT Function

In the ongoing example, if we randomly want to find how much of the principal amount we will have to repay, say in the 5th month, we use this function. After selecting the **PPMT** function, the following parameters are required.

- **Rate** is 0.1/12
- **Per** is 5 as it is the period in which we want to find the principal repayment amount
- **Nper** is the total number of periods, that is, 36
- **PV** is the loan amount taken which is ₹1,00,000
- **FV** is the future value and is left blank
- **Type** is taken as 0.

Performing this task would have been time-consuming had we used the table procedure to find this. The **PPMT** function has simplified the work to a great extent as we have to insert the corresponding values. Both these methods lead to the same results, as shown in Figure 14.6.

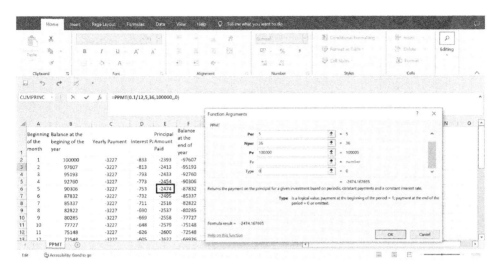

FIGURE 14.6 PPMT Function in Excel

Check Your Understanding

Mr X has taken a car loan of ₹50,000 at 6 per cent per annum compounded monthly for three years. Calculate the principal amount paid in his 25th instalment.

Ans. ₹1,433

14.6.2   IPMT Function

We may want to find out the interest payment on the loan amount, say in the 5th month. The IPMT function will help us carry out this task by requiring the values of the same arguments as in the **IPMT** function.

- **Rate** as 0.1/12
- **Per** is 5 as it is the period in which we want to find the principal amount of repayment
- **Nper** is the total number of periods, that is, 36
- **PV** is the loan amount taken which is ₹1,00,000
- *FV* is the future value and is left blank
- **Type** is taken as 0.

It can be seen in Figure 14.7 that the interest amount that is to be paid at the end of the 5th month is ₹753. This function has made the work much simpler and easier.

Check Your Understanding

Mr X now also wants to find out the interest amount he will have to pay in his 25th instalment.

Ans. ₹88.36

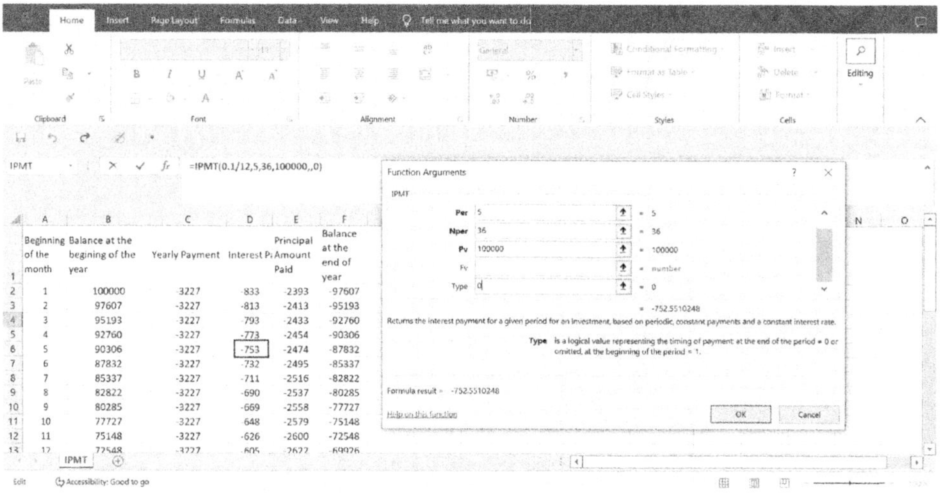

FIGURE 14.7 IPMT Function in Excel

14.7 Effective Annual Interest Rate

Arun is facing a situation of whether to take a loan of ₹1,000 for one year at an interest rate of 10 per cent per annum compounded annually or at an interest rate of 10 per cent compounded quarterly. Which option should he opt for? To find out a solution for Arun, let us first consider Option 1. By the usual formula of compound interest rate, we can find out how much he will have to repay at the end of one year.

$$FV \text{ of this loan} = P + Pr,$$

equivalently $\quad P(1+r)^n$

That is, $1,000(1 + .10)^1$

$= ₹1,100$

(1)

Let us look at Option 2 now. Notice carefully that the interest rate is 10 per cent per annum, but compounding is done quarterly, meaning it is compounded four times a year. Adjusting the r and n, the formula becomes as follows:

$$FV = 1000\left(1 + \frac{10}{4}\right)^4$$

$= ₹1,103.813$

In Option 2, Arun has to pay ₹1,103.813 compared to ₹1,100 in Option 1. The amount in Option 2 is more as the amount is compounded four times in a year as compared to Option 1 where the compounding is only once in the year.

But instead of working through this formula which does not take compounding effect into account, we can directly find out the effective interest rate by converting the stated interest rate. The effective interest rate formula can be derived as follows:

From Equation 2, $₹1,103.813 = \mathbf{1,000}\left(\mathbf{1} + \dfrac{\mathbf{10}}{\mathbf{4}}\right)^4$

$$\dfrac{1,103.813}{1,000} = \left(1 + \dfrac{10}{4}\right)^4$$

$$\dfrac{1,000 + 103.813}{1,000} = \left(1 + \dfrac{10}{4}\right)^4$$

[1,000 + 103.813 => principal amount plus interest amount]

It is equivalent to: $1 + 0.1038 = \left(1 + \dfrac{10}{4}\right)^4$

$$0.1038 = \left(1 + \dfrac{10}{4}\right)^4 - 1$$

So, 0.1038 or 0.1038 * 100, which is equal to 10.38 is the effective interest rate. The previous formula for the effective annual rate (EAR) can be generalized as follows:

$$\mathbf{EAR} = \left(\mathbf{1} + \dfrac{\mathbf{r}}{\mathbf{n}}\right)^{\mathbf{n}} - \mathbf{1}$$

Thus, by comparing the EAR, we can conclude that Option 1 is better for Arun as the interest rate of 10 per cent is less than 10.38 per cent in Option 2. It is worth emphasizing that in the case of any investment or loan, we must look at the interest rate and the frequency with which it is being compounded.

This exercise can also be simply performed using the **EFFECT** function in Excel. To use this function, we click on f_x function and choose **EFFECT** from the dialogue box. The two arguments required to solve it are **Nominal_rate** which is the nominal interest rate, that is, 10 per cent in our case. The second one is **Npery** which is the number of times the compounding takes place, that is, 4. The answer turns out to be the same at 10.38 per cent as shown in Figure 14.8.

To sum up, this chapter has provided the nitty-gritty of loans and introduced us to the functions that can help reduce the burden of extensive manual calculations. The application of the concepts of loans discussed is widely used in our day-to-day life. Therefore, it is imperative to study such concepts diligently and thoroughly.

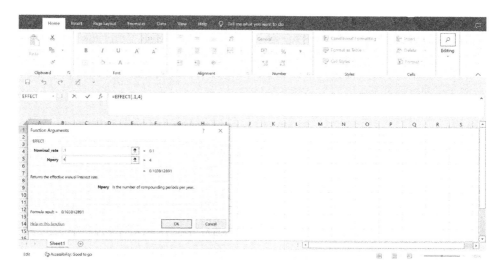

FIGURE 14.8 Effective Annual Rate Function

PRACTICE QUESTIONS

1. Ram borrows ₹3,000 to be paid back at the compound rate of 5 per cent per annum by the end of three years in three equal yearly instalments. How much will each instalment be? (rounded to the nearest whole rupee)

2. Mr X borrows ₹50,000 at 8 per cent compound interest. How much must he pay equally at the end of each year to settle his loan in five years? (round off decimals)

3. Ten years from now, Mr A will start receiving a pension of ₹3000 a year. The payment will continue for 16 years. How much is the pension worth now, if the interest rate is 10 per cent?

4. Ramesh is purchasing his first car. The car costs ₹10,00,000. They need to pay 20 per cent down payment and refinance the rest of the amount. He is considering a fixed rate 30-year mortgage at a 5.25 per cent APR with monthly payments. How much will his first monthly payment be?

5. You have been living in the house you bought ten years ago for ₹300,000. At that time, you took out a loan for 80 per cent of the house at a fixed rate of a 15-year loan at an annual stated rate of 9 per cent. You have just paid off the 120th monthly payment. The interest rate has meanwhile dropped steadily at 6 per cent per year, and you think it is time to refinance the remaining balance. However, the fee to refinance the loan is ₹4,000. Should you refinance the remaining balance? How much would you save/lose if you decided to refinance?

6. Two years ago, Ram purchased the mobile at ₹10,000, he paid ₹2000 down and borrowed the rest. He took a fixed rate 60-month instalment at a rate of 8 per cent per year. The interest rate has fallen during the last two years. He has the option of refinancing the balance amount at a new fixed rate of 6 per cent per year for three years. Should the amount be refinanced? How much amount will be saved per month for the next three years in case of refinance?

7. Which of the following represents the lowest cost of credit on an effective annual rate of interest rate basis?
   A: 10 per cent APR, interest compounded semi-annually
   B: 9.5 per cent APR, interest compounded quarterly
   C: 9.25 per cent APR, interest compounded monthly
8. If a mortgage requiring monthly payments is advertised of having a 6 per cent APR, what is the effective annual rate on this mortgage?
9. Suppose your credit card states that interest on unpaid balances is 22 per cent APR, with interest compounded monthly. What is the effective annual rate of interest on unpaid balances?
10. Complete the following table for a loan of ₹80,000 that is repaid with five annual payments of ₹21,104.

Period	Beginning Balance	Payment	Interest	Principal Repayment	Ending Balance
Today	–	–	–	–	₹80,000
1	₹80,000	₹21,104			
2		₹21,104			
3		₹21,104			
4		₹21,104			
5		₹21,104			

Note

1 Display of ₹2 instead of 0 is on account of rounding off errors.

WEB REFERENCES

Retrieved from https://finance.yahoo.com/quote/INR%3DX/history? period1=1563608203&period2=1595230603&interval =1mo&filter=history frequency=1mo

Retrieved from www.moneycontrol.com/financialstatebankindia/balance-sheetVI/sbi

Department of Commerce, Ministry of Commerce and Industry, Government of India. *Annual Report 2018–19*. Retrieved from https://commerce.gov.in/writereaddata/uploaded file/MOC_637036322182074251_Annual%20Report%202018–19%20English.pdf.

BSE. Retrieved from www.bseindia.com/

NSE. Retrieved from https://www1.nseindia.com/index_nse.htm

Database in Indian Economy-RBIs Data Warehouse. Retrieved from https://dbie.rbi.org.in/DBIE/dbie.rbi?site=home

Ministry of Statistics and Programme Implementation. Retrieved from www.mospi.gov.in/web/mospi/home

Census of India, Government of India. Retrieved from https://censusindia.gov.in/census.website/

Directorate of Economics and Statistics, Department of Agriculture and Farmer welfare, Ministry of Agriculture and Farmer welfare, Government of India. Retrieved from https://eands.dacnet.nic.in/Default.htm

The World Bank. Retrieved from https://data.worldbank.org

UNdata-A world of Information. Retrieved from https://data.un.org/

UNDP Human Development Reports. 2018. *Statistical Update: Human Development Indices and Indicators*. Retrieved from http://hdr.undp.org/en/content/human-development-indices-indicators-2018.

ANSWER KEY

Chapter 2. Basic Arithmetic Operations in Excel

1.

Roll No	Name	Physics		
		Theory	Practical	Total
		(out of 70)	(out of 30)	(out of 100)
1	Neetu	65	27	**92**
2	Harshit	53	25	**78**
3	Kashish	45	29	**84**
4	Riya	55	26	**81**
5	Tannu	48	28	**76**
6	Khushi	55	25	**80**
7	Vaibhav	60	29	**89**
8	Archit	**54**	27	81
9	Sonia	43	**47**	90
10	Shruti	**50**	28	78
11	Mannu	**35**	22	57
12	Aastha	**58**	27	85
13	Shubham	57	**22**	79
14	Amit	68	27	**41**
15	Atul	55	22	**33**

2.

Roll No	Name	Physics		
		Theory	Practical	Total
		(out of 210)	(out of 90)	(out of 300)
1	Neetu	195	81	276
2	Harshit	159	75	234
3	Kashish	135	87	252
4	Riya	165	78	243
5	Tannu	144	84	228
6	Khushi	165	75	240
7	Vaibhav	180	87	267
8	Archit	162	81	243
9	Sonia	129	141	270
10	Shruti	150	84	234
11	Mannu	105	66	171
12	Aastha	174	81	255
13	Shubham	171	66	237
14	Amit	204	81	123
15	Atul	165	66	99

3. Theory: 801; Practical: 411; Aggregate: 1124
4. 53.4 and 27.4
5. 602
6. 7
7. Neetu and Atul

Chapter 4. Visualization of Data Using Charts in Excel

1. Histogram
2. Line graph
3. Pie Chart
4. Scatter Graph
5. Column Graph

Chapter 5. Measures of Central Tendency

1. Mean = 3,36,850; Median = 3,75,500
2. Median = 32; Mode = 32
3. 62,669.18
4. 17.71531
5. Shipra = 89.2; Shraiya = 73

Chapter 6. Measures of Dispersion

1. 9 degrees Celsius
2. a) ₹2,652; b) ₹2,915; c) Firm A; d) Firm B
3. $19,511
4. Standard deviation = ₹97,709.98, variance = 9,547,240,000
5. We cannot compare the standard deviation for both datasets as they are in different units. Hence, we calculate the coefficient of variation to determine the variability as it is a measure of relative variability.

    Coefficient of variation of height = 6.184404545; Coefficient of variation of weight = 13.26249927

    The weight data has more variation in relation to its mean than height.
6. S_k = 0.033, comparatively symmetrical
7. Skewness = 0.9318, asymmetrical distribution, highly skewed to the right (positively skewed). Kurtosis = 0.3719, Leptokurtic distribution, Heavy tails or larger outliers than a normal distribution
8.

Mean	54,546.66667
Standard Error	7,626.892429
Median	44450
Mode	28400
Standard Deviation	41,774.21027
Sample Variance	1745084644
Kurtosis	10.48164561
Skewness	2.707047832
Range	2,19,300
Minimum	11,700
Maximum	2,31,000
Sum	16,36,400
Count	30

Chapter 7. Correlation Coefficient

2. Covariance for population = **2,609,286,231.88**, Positive or direct relationship

    Covariance for sample = **2,899,206,924.31;**

    The correlation is 0.9416, a very strong positive relation

3. Pearson's correlation coefficient = −0.8294, strong negative correlation
4. Spearman correlation coefficient = −0.2478, low negative correlation, that is, the student scoring high in the economics exam is less likely to score high in the statistics exam.
5. Pearson's correlation coefficient = + 0.5954; Spearman correlation coefficient = + .63474; Based on correlation coefficients, it can be concluded that an increase in 10 marks in one subject will lead to an increase in 5.9 and 6.3 marks respectively in other subject, according to Pearson and Spearman estimations.

Chapter 8. Regression Analysis

1. β_0 (constant) = 558.9582717 and β_1 (slope) = 27.9934892: The regression equation can be written as: Electricity consumption = 558.9582717 + 27.9934892 * working hours. This can be interpreted as the working hours' increase; the electricity consumption in the factory also tends to increase. The value of β_1 as 27.9934 demonstrates that increasing the working hours by an hour (a unit of the independent variable) will increase the electricity consumption by 27.9934 megawatts (dependent variable).

2. β_0 (constant) = 557.4474 and β_1 (slope) = −12.8294260; The regression equation can be written as: Demand for loans = 557.4474 − 12.8294 * interest rate on loan; R^2 (coefficient of determination) is equal to 0.863318, which indicates a good fit model. It tells that the interest rate on a loan (X) explains 86.3318 per cent of the variation in the demand for loans (Y).

3. β_0 (constant) = 3,465.17985 and β_1 (slope) = 5.9151203; the regression equation is Rent = 3,465.17985 + 5.9151203 * area of the flat; the value of rent (predicted) when the area of the flat is 7,500 sq. ft is 3,465.17985 + 5.9151203 * 7,500 = ₹47,828.58.

4.

Observation	Predicted Share Prices	Residuals
1	7,931.314789	−131.315
2	7,394.566344	−1,394.57
3	7,126.192122	−326.192
4	6,052.695232	747.3048
5	5,247.572564	652.4274
6	4,710.824119	989.1759
7	4,308.262785	1,191.737
8	4,308.262785	191.7372
9	3,637.327229	662.6728
10	3,503.140117	−703.14
11	2,832.204561	−332.205
12	2,832.204561	−232.205
13	2,563.830339	−463.83
14	2,161.269005	−1,161.27
15	1,490.333449	309.6666

Interpretation: In (the 1st year, 2nd year, 3rd year, 10th year, 11th year, 12th year, 13th year and 14th year) – the negative residual implies that the regression model overpredicts the share prices. Similarly, in (the 4th year, 5th year, 6th year, 7th year, 8th year, 9th year, and 15th year) – the positive residual implies that the regression model is underpredicting the share prices.

5.   Summary Output

Regression Statistics	
Multiple R	0.952024899
R Square	0.906351408
Adjusted R Square	0.89914767
Standard Error	3,251.083536
Observations	15

Multiple R is the correlation coefficient that measures the strength of a linear relationship between two variables. The correlation coefficient of 0.95 indicates a strong correlation between the dependent and independent variables.

R-square of 0.90635 indicates that 90.635 per cent of the variation in the orders placed (dependent variable) can be explained by the price of jewellery (independent variable).

The adjusted R square of 0.899 is the R^2 adjusted for the number of independent variables in the model. It is helpful to compare the models in case an additional independent variable is added to the model.

Analysis of Variance ANOVA

	df	SS	MS	F	Significance F
Regression	1	132,98,26457	1.33E + 09	125.8168221	4.67505E − 08
Residual	13	137,404,074	10569544		
Total	14	1,467,230,531			

SS (Regression): Explained variation = 1,329,826,457
SS (Residual): Sum of Squares of errors or Unexplained variation = 137,404,074
SS (Total): Total variation = 1,467,230,531

	Coefficients
Intercept	94,509.14895
Price	−16.32876797

Intercept (β_0) is equal to 94,509.14895, indicating the units of orders placed when the jewellery price is ₹0. As stated, we ignore the interpretation of β_0 as it will be irrational in practice to find the price of jewellery as ₹0.

The negative sign of the slope coefficient (β_1) means that as the price increases, the number of orders placed tends to decrease. The value of $\beta_1 = -16.329$ (rounded off) demonstrates that by increasing the price by one rupee (a unit of the independent variable), the number of orders will decrease by 16 units (dependent variable).

Chapter 9. Hypothesis Testing in Regression Analysis

1. H_0: $\beta_1 = 0$; H_1: $\beta_1 \neq 0$; t-statistics = 9.403576788, residual df = 18 and critical value = 2.101; Since the value of the t-statistics falls to the right of the positive cut-off value, *we reject the null hypothesis* and conclude that there is a significant relationship between the area of the house and the electricity bill.

2. H_0: $\beta_1 = 0$; H_1: $\beta_1 \neq 0$; t-statistics = 22.95098679, p-value = 0.0000. The p-value of 0.00 is less than the significance level of 0.05, that is, $p < \alpha$. Therefore, *we reject the null hypothesis* and conclude that there is a significant relationship between the taxes paid (dependent variable) and the average annual income earned by the individual (independent variable).

3. H_0: $\beta_1 = 0$; H_1: $\beta_1 \neq 0$; t-statistics = 1.617637; p-value = 0.1231; $\alpha = 5\%$. The p-value of 0.1231 is more than the significance level of 0.05, $p > \alpha$. Therefore, we *do not reject the null hypothesis* and conclude there is no significant relationship between the likes (dependent variable) and the views (independent variable) on a video. The belief of Abhinav that the number of views has a significant impact on the number of likes on the videos is incorrect.

4. H_0: $\beta_1 = 0$; H_1: $\beta_1 \neq 0$

Regression output: 95% confidence intervals

	Coefficients	Standard Error	t-Stat	p-Value	Lower 95%	Upper 95%
Intercept	74.99175186	3.703232912	20.2503471	7.76988E−14	67.21154821	82.7719555
Literacy Level	−0.751277881	0.050736835	−14.80734613	1.59998E−11	−0.857872016	−0.64468375

The lower and upper limits for the 95 per cent confidence interval specified in the regression output are (−0.8578) and (−0.6446), respectively. Since our hypothesized value $\beta_1 = 0$ does not fall within the confidence intervals, *we reject the null hypothesis*, which implies a significant relationship between the people below the poverty line (dependent variable) and literacy rate (independent variable). Regression output: 99 per cent confidence intervals

	Coefficients	Standard Error	t-Stat	p-Value	Lower 95%	Upper 95%
Intercept	74.99175186	3.703232912	20.2503471	7.76988E−14	64.33221637	85.65128735
Literacy Level	−0.751277881	0.050736835	−14.80734613	1.59998E−11	−0.897320841	−0.605234921

The lower and upper limits for the 99 per cent confidence interval specified in the regression output are (−0.8973) and (−0.6052), respectively. Since our hypothesized value $\beta_1 = 0$ does not fall within the confidence intervals, *we reject the null hypothesis*, which implies a significant relationship between the people below the poverty line (dependent variable) and literacy rate (independent variable).

5.   SUMMARY OUTPUT

Regression Statistics	
R Square	0.868283369
Adjusted R Square	0.858151321
Standard Error	3325.932545
Observations	15

	Coefficients	Standard Error	t-Stat	p-value	Lower 95%	Upper 95%
Intercept	79592.30045	2704.490341	29.4296856	2.77836E-13	73749.60429	85434.99662
Rainfall	1240.792659	134.0346561	9.257252531	4.37177E-07	951.2283893	1530.356929

Rainfall (X variable) coefficient: β_1 = 1,240.7926 indicates that if the rainfall increases by one inch (a unit of the independent variable) the rice production increases by 1,240.7926 thousand million tonnes (dependent variable).

H_0: β_1 = 0

H_1: $\beta_1 \neq 0$

t-statistics = 9.2572 and cut-off value = 2.160; p-value = 0.1231; α = 5%

a.   Since the value of the t-statistics falls to the right of the positive cut-off value, *we reject the null hypothesis* and conclude that there is a significant relationship between rice production (dependent variable) and rainfall (independent variable).

b.   The p-value of 0.00 is less than the significance level of 0.05, that is, $p < \alpha$. Therefore, we *reject the null hypothesis* and conclude that there is a significant relationship between rice production (dependent variable) and rainfall (independent variable).

c.   Since our null value β_1 = 0 does not fall within the confidence intervals, *we reject the null hypothesis*, which implies a significant relationship between rice production (dependent variable) and rainfall (independent variable).

The claim made by the agriculture officer is that if rainfall increases by 1 inch, rice production increase by 1,400 thousand million tonnes. The hypothesis can be stated as H_0: β_1 = 1,400; H_1: $\beta_1 \neq 1,400$. Using the 95% confidence interval approach, we observe that the hypothesized value = 1,400 falls within the lower and upper limit of the interval, that is, 951.2283893 and 1,530.356929. Hence, we do not reject the Null Hypothesis. It is possible that the true value of the increase in production can be 1,400 thousand million tonnes. The claim of the officer may be true.

Chapter 10. Understanding Growth Rates

1. Growth rate = 425 per cent
2. Growth rate = 17.638 per cent
3. 6.15 percent
4. 9.6 percent
5. 20.97 percent

Chapter 11. Growth Rate Using Regression Analysis

a) β_0 = 7.08026
   β_1 = 0.14698
   Instantaneous growth rate = 14.69%
   CAGR = Antilog of 0.14698 − 1
   = 1.15833 − 1
   = 0.15833 or 15.833%
b) Simple growth using LINEST = ₹458.396 crores
c) CAGR using LOGEST = 15.833%

Chapter 12. Compounding: Future Value of Money

1. 109
2. ₹17,417.76
3. Ananya: ₹1,935
4. Option 2: ₹1,816
5. ₹4,53,412
6. ₹22,705

Chapter 13. Investment Decision Criteria: NPV and IRR

1. ₹976.13
2. ₹13,838
3. Investment A is more preferred because it is more profitable at ₹1,171 than ₹810.55 in investment B
4. Investment B
5. ₹5,000, and 11.59 per cent
6. Project B

Chapter 14. Loan Amortization

1. ₹1,102
2. ₹12,523
3. ₹9, 954
4. ₹4,418
5. A gain of ₹4,647
6. Yes, ₹4.73

7. C, 9.65 per cent
8. 6.16 per cent
9. 24.36 per cent

Period	Beginning Balance	Payment	Interest	Principal Repayment	Ending Balance
Today	–	–	–	–	₹80,000
1	₹80,000	₹21,104	₹2,110	₹18,994	₹61,006
2	₹61,006	₹21,104	₹6,100	₹15,004	₹46,002
3	₹46,002	₹21,104	₹4,600	₹16,504	₹29,498
4	₹29,498	₹21,104	₹2,950	₹18,154	₹2,950
5	₹2,950	₹21,104	₹295	₹20,809	0

APPENDIX 1

Present Value and Future Value Tables

TABLE A-1 Future Value Interest Factors for One Rupee Compounded at r Percent for n Periods: $FVIF_{r,n} = (1 + r)^n$

Period	1%	2%	3%	4%	5%	6%	7%	8%	9%	10%	11%	12%	13%	14%	15%	16%	20%	24%	25%	30%
1	1.0100	1.0200	1.0300	1.0400	1.0500	1.0600	1.0700	1.0800	1.0900	1.1000	1.1100	1.1200	1.1300	1.1400	1.1500	1.1600	1.2000	1.2400	1.2500	1.3000
2	1.0201	1.0404	1.0609	1.0816	1.1025	1.1236	1.1449	1.1664	1.1881	1.2100	1.2321	1.2544	1.2769	1.2996	1.3225	1.3456	1.4400	1.5376	1.5625	1.6900
3	1.0303	1.0612	1.0927	1.1249	1.1576	1.1910	1.2250	1.2597	1.2950	1.3310	1.3676	1.4049	1.4429	1.4815	1.5209	1.5609	1.7280	1.9066	1.9531	2.1970
4	1.0406	1.0824	1.1255	1.1699	1.2155	1.2625	1.3108	1.3605	1.4116	1.4641	1.5181	1.5735	1.6305	1.6890	1.7490	1.8106	2.0736	2.3642	2.4414	2.8561
5	1.0510	1.1041	1.1593	1.2167	1.2763	1.3382	1.4026	1.4693	1.5386	1.6105	1.6851	1.7623	1.8424	1.9254	2.0114	2.1003	2.4883	2.9316	3.0518	3.7129
6	1.0615	1.1262	1.1941	1.2653	1.3401	1.4185	1.5007	1.5869	1.6771	1.7716	1.8704	1.9738	2.0820	2.1950	2.3131	2.4364	2.9860	3.6352	3.8147	4.8268
7	1.0721	1.1487	1.2299	1.3159	1.4071	1.5036	1.6058	1.7138	1.8280	1.9487	2.0762	2.2107	2.3526	2.5023	2.6600	2.8262	3.5832	4.5077	4.7684	6.2749
8	1.0829	1.1717	1.2668	1.3686	1.4775	1.5938	1.7182	1.8509	1.9926	2.1436	2.3045	2.4760	2.6584	2.8526	3.0590	3.2784	4.2998	5.5895	5.9605	8.1573
9	1.0937	1.1951	1.3048	1.4233	1.5513	1.6895	1.8385	1.9990	2.1719	2.3579	2.5580	2.7731	3.0040	3.2519	3.5179	3.8030	5.1598	6.9310	7.4506	10.604
10	1.1046	1.2190	1.3439	1.4802	1.6289	1.7908	1.9672	2.1589	2.3674	2.5937	2.8394	3.1058	3.3946	3.7072	4.0456	4.4114	6.1917	8.5944	9.3132	13.786
11	1.1157	1.2434	1.3842	1.5395	1.7103	1.8983	2.1049	2.3316	2.5804	2.8531	3.1518	3.4785	3.8359	4.2262	4.6524	5.1173	7.4301	10.657	11.642	17.922
12	1.1268	1.2682	1.4258	1.6010	1.7959	2.0122	2.2522	2.5182	2.8127	3.1384	3.4985	3.8960	4.3345	4.8179	5.3503	5.9360	8.9161	13.215	14.552	23.298
13	1.1381	1.2936	1.4685	1.6651	1.8856	2.1329	2.4098	2.7196	3.0658	3.4523	3.8833	4.3635	4.8980	5.4924	6.1528	6.8858	10.699	16.386	18.190	30.288
14	1.1495	1.3195	1.5126	1.7317	1.9799	2.2609	2.5785	2.9372	3.3417	3.7975	4.3104	4.8871	5.5348	6.2613	7.0757	7.9875	12.839	20.319	22.737	39.374
15	1.1610	1.3459	1.5580	1.8009	2.0789	2.3966	2.7590	3.1722	3.6425	4.1772	4.7846	5.4736	6.2543	7.1379	8.1371	9.2655	15.407	25.196	28.422	51.186
16	1.1726	1.3728	1.6047	1.8730	2.1829	2.5404	2.9522	3.4259	3.9703	4.5950	5.3109	6.1304	7.0673	8.1372	9.3576	10.748	18.488	31.243	35.527	66.542
17	1.1843	1.4002	1.6528	1.9479	2.2920	2.6928	3.1588	3.7000	4.3276	5.0545	5.8951	6.8660	7.9861	9.2765	10.761	12.468	22.186	38.741	44.409	86.504
18	1.1961	1.4282	1.7024	2.0258	2.4066	2.8543	3.3799	3.9960	4.7171	5.5599	6.5436	7.6900	9.0243	10.575	12.375	14.463	26.623	48.039	55.511	112.455
19	1.2081	1.4568	1.7535	2.1068	2.5270	3.0256	3.6165	4.3157	5.1417	6.1159	7.2633	8.6128	10.197	12.056	14.232	16.777	31.948	59.568	69.389	146.192
20	1.2202	1.4859	1.8061	2.1911	2.6533	3.2071	3.8697	4.6610	5.6044	6.7275	8.0623	9.6463	11.523	13.743	16.367	19.461	38.338	73.864	86.736	190.050
21	1.2324	1.5157	1.8603	2.2788	2.7860	3.3996	4.1406	5.0338	6.1088	7.4002	8.9492	10.804	13.021	15.668	18.822	22.574	46.005	91.592	108.420	247.065
22	1.2447	1.5460	1.9161	2.3699	2.9253	3.6035	4.4304	5.4365	6.6586	8.1403	9.9336	12.100	14.714	17.861	21.645	26.186	55.206	113.574	135.525	321.184
23	1.2572	1.5769	1.9736	2.4647	3.0715	3.8197	4.7405	5.8715	7.2579	8.9543	11.026	13.552	16.627	20.362	24.891	30.376	66.247	140.831	169.407	417.539
24	1.2697	1.6084	2.0328	2.5633	3.2251	4.0489	5.0724	6.3412	7.9111	9.8497	12.239	15.179	18.788	23.212	28.625	35.236	79.497	174.631	211.758	542.801
25	1.2824	1.6406	2.0938	2.6658	3.3864	4.2919	5.4274	6.8485	8.6231	10.835	13.585	17.000	21.231	26.462	32.919	40.874	95.396	216.542	264.698	705.641
30	1.3478	1.8114	2.4273	3.2434	4.3219	5.7435	7.6123	10.063	13.268	17.449	22.892	29.960	39.116	50.950	66.212	85.850	237.376	634.820	807.794	*
35	1.4166	1.9999	2.8139	3.9461	5.5160	7.6861	10.677	14.785	20.414	28.102	38.575	52.800	72.069	98.100	133.176	180.314	590.668	*	*	*
36	1.4308	2.0399	2.8983	4.1039	5.7918	8.1473	11.424	15.968	22.251	30.913	42.818	59.136	81.437	111.834	153.152	209.164	708.802	*	*	*
40	1.4889	2.2080	3.2620	4.8010	7.0400	10.286	14.974	21.725	31.409	45.259	65.001	93.051	132.782	188.884	267.864	378.721	*	*	*	*
50	1.6446	2.6916	4.3839	7.1067	11.467	18.420	29.457	46.902	74.358	117.391	184.565	289.002	450.736	700.233	*	*	*	*	*	*

TABLE A-2 Future Value Interest Factors for a One-Rupee Annuity Compounded at r Percent for n Periods: $FVIFA_{r,n} = \dfrac{(1 + r)^n - 1}{r}$

Period	1%	2%	3%	4%	5%	6%	7%	8%	9%	10%	11%	12%	13%	14%	15%	16%	20%	24%	25%	30%
1	1.0000	1.0200	1.0300	1.0400	1.0500	1.0600	1.0700	1.0800	1.0900	1.1000	1.1100	1.1200	1.1300	1.1400	1.1500	1.1600	1.2000	1.2400	1.2500	1.3000
2	2.0100	2.0200	2.0300	2.0400	2.0500	2.0600	2.0700	2.0800	2.0900	2.1000	2.1100	2.1200	2.1300	2.1400	2.1500	2.1600	2.2000	2.2400	2.2500	2.3000
3	3.0301	3.0604	3.0909	3.1216	3.1525	3.1836	3.2149	3.2464	3.2781	3.3100	3.3421	3.3744	3.4069	3.4396	3.4725	3.5056	3.6400	3.7776	3.8125	3.9900
4	4.0604	4.1216	4.1836	4.2465	4.3101	4.3746	4.4399	4.5061	4.5731	4.6410	4.7097	4.7793	4.8498	4.9211	4.9934	5.0665	5.3680	5.6842	5.7656	6.1870
5	5.1010	5.2040	5.3091	5.4163	5.5256	5.6371	5.7507	5.8666	5.9847	6.1051	6.2278	6.3528	6.4803	6.6101	6.7424	6.8771	7.4416	8.0484	8.2070	9.0431
6	6.1520	6.3081	6.4684	6.6330	6.8019	6.9753	7.1533	7.3359	7.5233	7.7156	7.9129	8.1152	8.3227	8.5355	8.7537	8.9775	9.9299	10.980	11.259	12.756
7	7.2135	7.4343	7.6625	7.8983	8.1420	8.3938	8.6540	8.9228	9.2004	9.4872	9.7833	10.089	10.405	10.730	11.067	11.414	12.916	14.615	15.073	17.583
8	8.2857	8.5830	8.8923	9.2142	9.5491	9.8975	10.260	10.637	11.028	11.436	11.859	12.300	12.757	13.233	13.727	14.240	16.499	19.123	19.842	23.858
9	9.3685	9.7546	10.159	10.583	11.027	11.491	11.978	12.488	13.021	13.579	14.164	14.776	15.416	16.085	16.786	17.519	20.799	24.712	25.802	32.015
10	10.462	10.950	11.464	12.006	12.578	13.181	13.816	14.487	15.193	15.937	16.722	17.549	18.420	19.337	20.304	21.321	25.959	31.643	33.253	42.619
11	11.567	12.169	12.808	13.486	14.207	14.972	15.784	16.645	17.560	18.531	19.561	20.655	21.814	23.045	24.349	25.733	32.150	40.238	42.566	56.405
12	12.683	13.412	14.192	15.026	15.917	16.870	17.888	18.977	20.141	21.384	22.713	24.133	25.650	27.271	29.002	30.850	39.581	50.895	54.208	74.327
13	13.809	14.680	15.618	16.627	17.713	18.882	20.141	21.495	22.953	24.523	26.212	28.029	29.985	32.089	34.352	36.786	48.497	64.110	68.760	97.625
14	14.947	15.974	17.086	18.292	19.599	21.015	22.550	24.215	26.019	27.975	30.095	32.393	34.883	37.581	40.505	43.672	59.196	80.496	86.949	127.913
15	16.097	17.293	18.599	20.024	21.579	23.276	25.129	27.152	29.361	31.772	34.405	37.280	40.417	43.842	47.580	51.660	72.035	100.815	109.687	167.286
16	17.258	18.639	20.157	21.825	23.657	25.673	27.888	30.324	33.003	35.950	39.190	42.753	46.672	50.980	55.717	60.925	87.442	126.011	138.109	218.472
17	18.430	20.012	21.762	23.698	25.840	28.213	30.840	33.750	36.974	40.545	44.501	48.884	53.739	59.118	65.075	71.673	105.931	157.253	173.636	285.014
18	19.615	21.412	23.414	25.645	28.132	30.906	33.999	37.450	41.301	45.599	50.396	55.750	61.725	68.394	75.836	84.141	128.117	195.994	218.045	371.518
19	20.811	22.841	25.117	27.671	30.539	33.760	37.379	41.446	46.018	51.159	56.939	63.440	70.749	78.969	88.212	98.603	154.740	244.033	273.556	483.973
20	22.019	24.297	26.870	29.778	33.066	36.786	40.995	45.762	51.160	57.275	64.203	72.052	80.947	91.025	102.444	115.380	186.688	303.601	342.945	630.165
21	23.239	25.783	28.676	31.969	35.719	39.993	44.865	50.423	56.765	64.002	72.265	81.699	92.470	104.768	118.810	134.841	225.026	377.465	429.681	820.215
22	24.472	27.299	30.537	34.248	38.505	43.392	49.006	55.457	62.873	71.403	81.214	92.503	105.491	120.436	137.632	157.415	271.031	469.056	538.101	*
23	25.716	28.845	32.453	36.618	41.430	46.996	53.436	60.893	69.532	79.543	91.148	104.603	120.205	138.297	159.276	183.601	326.237	582.630	673.626	*
24	26.973	30.422	34.426	39.083	44.502	50.816	58.177	66.765	76.790	88.497	102.174	118.155	136.831	158.659	184.168	213.978	392.484	723.461	843.033	*
25	28.243	32.030	36.459	41.646	47.727	54.865	63.249	73.106	84.701	98.347	114.413	133.334	155.620	181.871	212.793	249.214	471.981	898.092	*	*
30	34.785	40.568	47.575	56.085	66.439	79.058	94.461	113.283	136.308	164.494	199.021	241.333	293.199	356.787	434.745	530.312	*	*	*	*
35	41.660	49.994	60.462	73.652	90.320	111.435	138.237	172.317	215.711	271.024	341.590	431.663	546.681	693.573	881.170	*	*	*	*	*
36	43.077	51.994	63.276	77.598	95.836	119.121	148.913	187.102	236.125	299.127	380.164	484.463	618.749	791.673	*	*	*	*	*	*
40	48.886	60.402	75.401	95.026	120.800	154.762	199.635	259.057	337.882	442.593	581.826	767.091	*	*	*	*	*	*	*	*
50	64.463	84.579	112.797	152.667	209.348	290.336	406.529	573.770	815.084	*	*	*	*	*	*	*	*	*	*	*

TABLE A-3 Present Value Interest Factors for One Rupee Discounted at r Percent for n Periods: $\text{PVIF}_{r,n} = 1/(1 + r)^n$

Period	1%	2%	3%	4%	5%	6%	7%	8%	9%	10%	11%	12%	13%	14%	15%	16%	20%	24%	25%	30%
1	0.9901	0.9804	0.9709	0.9615	0.9524	0.9434	0.9346	0.9259	0.9174	0.9091	0.9009	0.8929	0.8850	0.8772	0.8696	0.8621	0.8333	0.8065	0.8000	0.7692
2	0.9803	0.9612	0.9426	0.9246	0.9070	0.8900	0.8734	0.8573	0.8417	0.8264	0.8116	0.7972	0.7831	0.7695	0.7561	0.7432	0.6944	0.6504	0.6400	0.5917
3	0.9706	0.9423	0.9151	0.8890	0.8638	0.8396	0.8163	0.7938	0.7722	0.7513	0.7312	0.7118	0.6931	0.6750	0.6575	0.6407	0.5787	0.5245	0.5120	0.4552
4	0.9610	0.9238	0.8885	0.8548	0.8227	0.7921	0.7629	0.7350	0.7084	0.6830	0.6587	0.6355	0.6133	0.5921	0.5718	0.5523	0.4823	0.4230	0.4096	0.3501
5	0.9515	0.9057	0.8626	0.8219	0.7835	0.7473	0.7130	0.6806	0.6499	0.6209	0.5935	0.5674	0.5428	0.5194	0.4972	0.4761	0.4019	0.3411	0.3277	0.2693
6	0.9420	0.8880	0.8375	0.7903	0.7462	0.7050	0.6663	0.6302	0.5963	0.5645	0.5346	0.5066	0.4803	0.4556	0.4323	0.4104	0.3349	0.2751	0.2621	0.2072
7	0.9327	0.8706	0.8131	0.7599	0.7107	0.6651	0.6227	0.5835	0.5470	0.5132	0.4817	0.4523	0.4251	0.3996	0.3759	0.3538	0.2791	0.2218	0.2097	0.1594
8	0.9235	0.8535	0.7894	0.7307	0.6768	0.6274	0.5820	0.5403	0.5019	0.4665	0.4339	0.4039	0.3762	0.3506	0.3269	0.3050	0.2326	0.1789	0.1678	0.1226
9	0.9143	0.8368	0.7664	0.7026	0.6446	0.5919	0.5439	0.5002	0.4604	0.4241	0.3909	0.3606	0.3329	0.3075	0.2843	0.2630	0.1938	0.1443	0.1342	0.0943
10	0.9053	0.8203	0.7441	0.6756	0.6139	0.5584	0.5083	0.4632	0.4224	0.3855	0.3522	0.3220	0.2946	0.2697	0.2472	0.2267	0.1615	0.1164	0.1074	0.0725
11	0.8963	0.8043	0.7224	0.6496	0.5847	0.5268	0.4751	0.4289	0.3875	0.3505	0.3173	0.2875	0.2607	0.2366	0.2149	0.1954	0.1346	0.0938	0.0859	0.0558
12	0.8874	0.7885	0.7014	0.6246	0.5568	0.4970	0.4440	0.3971	0.3555	0.3186	0.2858	0.2567	0.2307	0.2076	0.1869	0.1685	0.1122	0.0757	0.0687	0.0429
13	0.8787	0.7730	0.6810	0.6006	0.5303	0.4688	0.4150	0.3677	0.3262	0.2897	0.2575	0.2292	0.2042	0.1821	0.1625	0.1452	0.0935	0.0610	0.0550	0.0330
14	0.8700	0.7579	0.6611	0.5775	0.5051	0.4423	0.3878	0.3405	0.2992	0.2633	0.2320	0.2046	0.1807	0.1597	0.1413	0.1252	0.0779	0.0492	0.0440	0.0254
15	0.8613	0.7430	0.6419	0.5553	0.4810	0.4173	0.3624	0.3152	0.2745	0.2394	0.2090	0.1827	0.1599	0.1401	0.1229	0.1079	0.0649	0.0397	0.0352	0.0195
16	0.8528	0.7284	0.6232	0.5339	0.4581	0.3936	0.3387	0.2919	0.2519	0.2176	0.1883	0.1631	0.1415	0.1229	0.1069	0.0930	0.0541	0.0320	0.0281	0.0150
17	0.8444	0.7142	0.6050	0.5134	0.4363	0.3714	0.3166	0.2703	0.2311	0.1978	0.1696	0.1456	0.1252	0.1078	0.0929	0.0802	0.0451	0.0258	0.0225	0.0116
18	0.8360	0.7002	0.5874	0.4936	0.4155	0.3503	0.2959	0.2502	0.2120	0.1799	0.1528	0.1300	0.1108	0.0946	0.0808	0.0691	0.0376	0.0208	0.0180	0.0089
19	0.8277	0.6864	0.5703	0.4746	0.3957	0.3305	0.2765	0.2317	0.1945	0.1635	0.1377	0.1161	0.0981	0.0829	0.0703	0.0596	0.0313	0.0168	0.0144	0.0068
20	0.8195	0.6730	0.5537	0.4564	0.3769	0.3118	0.2584	0.2145	0.1784	0.1486	0.1240	0.1037	0.0868	0.0728	0.0611	0.0514	0.0261	0.0135	0.0115	0.0053
21	0.8114	0.6598	0.5375	0.4388	0.3589	0.2942	0.2415	0.1987	0.1637	0.1351	0.1117	0.0926	0.0768	0.0638	0.0531	0.0443	0.0217	0.0109	0.0092	0.0040
22	0.8034	0.6468	0.5219	0.4220	0.3418	0.2775	0.2257	0.1839	0.1502	0.1228	0.1007	0.0826	0.0680	0.0560	0.0462	0.0382	0.0181	0.0088	0.0074	0.0031
23	0.7954	0.6342	0.5067	0.4057	0.3256	0.2618	0.2109	0.1703	0.1378	0.1117	0.0907	0.0738	0.0601	0.0491	0.0402	0.0329	0.0151	0.0071	0.0059	0.0024
24	0.7876	0.6217	0.4919	0.3901	0.3101	0.2470	0.1971	0.1577	0.1264	0.1015	0.0817	0.0659	0.0532	0.0431	0.0349	0.0284	0.0126	0.0057	0.0047	0.0018
25	0.7798	0.6095	0.4776	0.3751	0.2953	0.2330	0.1842	0.1460	0.1160	0.0923	0.0736	0.0588	0.0471	0.0378	0.0304	0.0245	0.0105	0.0046	0.0038	0.0014
30	0.7419	0.5521	0.4120	0.3083	0.2314	0.1741	0.1314	0.0994	0.0754	0.0573	0.0437	0.0334	0.0256	0.0196	0.0151	0.0116	0.0042	0.0016	0.0012	*
35	0.7059	0.5000	0.3554	0.2534	0.1813	0.1301	0.0937	0.0676	0.0490	0.0356	0.0259	0.0189	0.0139	0.0102	0.0075	0.0055	0.0017	0.0005	*	*
36	0.6989	0.4902	0.3450	0.2437	0.1727	0.1227	0.0875	0.0626	0.0449	0.0323	0.0234	0.0169	0.0123	0.0089	0.0065	0.0048	0.0014	*	*	*
40	0.6717	0.4529	0.3066	0.2083	0.1420	0.0972	0.0668	0.0460	0.0318	0.0221	0.0154	0.0107	0.0075	0.0053	0.0037	0.0026	0.0007	*	*	*
50	0.6080	0.3715	0.2281	0.1407	0.0872	0.0543	0.0339	0.0213	0.0134	0.0085	0.0054	0.0035	0.0022	0.0014	0.0009	0.0006	*	*	*	*

TABLE A-4 Present Value Interest Factors for a One-Rupee Annuity Discounted at r Percent for n Periods: $\text{PVIFA} = [1 - 1/(1 + r)^n] / r$

Period	1%	2%	3%	4%	5%	6%	7%	8%	9%	10%	11%	12%	13%	14%	15%	16%	20%	24%	25%	30%
1	0.9901	0.9804	0.9709	0.9615	0.9524	0.9434	0.9346	0.9259	0.9174	0.9091	0.9009	0.8929	0.8850	0.8772	0.8696	0.8621	0.8333	0.8065	0.8000	0.7692
2	1.9704	1.9416	1.9135	1.8861	1.8594	1.8334	1.8080	1.7833	1.7591	1.7355	1.7125	1.6901	1.6681	1.6467	1.6257	1.6052	1.5278	1.4568	1.4400	1.3609
3	2.9410	2.8839	2.8286	2.7751	2.7232	2.6730	2.6243	2.5771	2.5313	2.4869	2.4437	2.4018	2.3612	2.3216	2.2832	2.2459	2.1065	1.9813	1.9520	1.8161
4	3.9020	3.8077	3.7171	3.6299	3.5460	3.4651	3.3872	3.3121	3.2397	3.1699	3.1024	3.0373	2.9745	2.9137	2.8550	2.7982	2.5887	2.4043	2.3616	2.1662
5	4.8534	4.7135	4.5797	4.4518	4.3295	4.2124	4.1002	3.9927	3.8897	3.7908	3.6959	3.6048	3.5172	3.4331	3.3522	3.2743	2.9906	2.7454	2.6893	2.4356
6	5.7955	5.6014	5.4172	5.2421	5.0757	4.9173	4.7665	4.6229	4.4859	4.3553	4.2305	4.1114	3.9975	3.8887	3.7845	3.6847	3.3255	3.0205	2.9514	2.6427
7	6.7282	6.4720	6.2303	6.0021	5.7864	5.5824	5.3893	5.2064	5.0330	4.8684	4.7122	4.5638	4.4226	4.2883	4.1604	4.0386	3.6046	3.2423	3.1611	2.8021
8	7.6517	7.3255	7.0197	6.7327	6.4632	6.2098	5.9713	5.7466	5.5348	5.3349	5.1461	4.9676	4.7988	4.6389	4.4873	4.3436	3.8372	3.4212	3.3289	2.9247
9	8.5660	8.1622	7.7861	7.4353	7.1078	6.8017	6.5152	6.2469	5.9952	5.7590	5.5370	5.3282	5.1317	4.9464	4.7716	4.6065	4.0310	3.5655	3.4631	3.0190
10	9.4713	8.9826	8.5302	8.1109	7.7217	7.3601	7.0236	6.7101	6.4177	6.1446	5.8892	5.6502	5.4262	5.2161	5.0188	4.8332	4.1925	3.6819	3.5705	3.0915
11	10.368	9.7868	9.2526	8.7605	8.3064	7.8869	7.4987	7.1390	6.8052	6.4951	6.2065	5.9377	5.6869	5.4527	5.2337	5.0286	4.3271	3.7757	3.6564	3.1473
12	11.255	10.575	9.9540	9.3851	8.8633	8.3838	7.9427	7.5361	7.1607	6.8137	6.4924	6.1944	5.9176	5.6603	5.4206	5.1971	4.4392	3.8514	3.7251	3.1903
13	12.134	11.348	10.635	9.9856	9.3936	8.8527	8.3577	7.9038	7.4869	7.1034	6.7499	6.4235	6.1218	5.8424	5.5831	5.3423	4.5327	3.9124	3.7801	3.2233
14	13.004	12.106	11.296	10.563	9.8986	9.2950	8.7455	8.2442	7.7862	7.3667	6.9819	6.6282	6.3025	6.0021	5.7245	5.4675	4.6106	3.9616	3.8241	3.2487
15	13.865	12.849	11.938	11.118	10.380	9.7122	9.1079	8.5595	8.0607	7.6061	7.1909	6.8109	6.4624	6.1422	5.8474	5.5755	4.6755	4.0013	3.8593	3.2682
16	14.718	13.578	12.561	11.652	10.838	10.106	9.4466	8.8514	8.3126	7.8237	7.3792	6.9740	6.6039	6.2651	5.9542	5.6685	4.7296	4.0333	3.8874	3.2832
17	15.562	14.292	13.166	12.166	11.274	10.477	9.7632	9.1216	8.5436	8.0216	7.5488	7.1196	6.7291	6.3729	6.0472	5.7487	4.7746	4.0591	3.9099	3.2948
18	16.398	14.992	13.754	12.659	11.690	10.828	10.059	9.3719	8.7556	8.2014	7.7016	7.2497	6.8399	6.4674	6.1280	5.8178	4.8122	4.0799	3.9279	3.3037
19	17.226	15.678	14.324	13.134	12.085	11.158	10.336	9.6036	8.9501	8.3649	7.8393	7.3658	6.9380	6.5504	6.1982	5.8775	4.8435	4.0967	3.9424	3.3105
20	18.046	16.351	14.877	13.590	12.462	11.470	10.594	9.8181	9.1285	8.5136	7.9633	7.4694	7.0248	6.6231	6.2593	5.9288	4.8696	4.1103	3.9539	3.3158
21	18.857	17.011	15.415	14.029	12.821	11.764	10.836	10.017	9.2922	8.6487	8.0751	7.5620	7.1016	6.6870	6.3125	5.9731	4.8913	4.1212	3.9631	3.3198
22	19.660	17.658	15.937	14.451	13.163	12.042	11.061	10.201	9.4424	8.7715	8.1757	7.6446	7.1695	6.7429	6.3587	6.0113	4.9094	4.1300	3.9705	3.3230
23	20.456	18.292	16.444	14.857	13.489	12.303	11.272	10.371	9.5802	8.8832	8.2664	7.7184	7.2297	6.7921	6.3988	6.0442	4.9245	4.1371	3.9764	3.3254
24	21.243	18.914	16.936	15.247	13.799	12.550	11.469	10.529	9.7066	8.9847	8.3481	7.7843	7.2829	6.8351	6.4338	6.0726	4.9371	4.1428	3.9811	3.3272
25	22.023	19.523	17.413	15.622	14.094	12.783	11.654	10.675	9.8226	9.0770	8.4217	7.8431	7.3300	6.8729	6.4641	6.0971	4.9476	4.1474	3.9849	3.3286
30	25.808	22.396	19.600	17.292	15.372	13.765	12.409	11.258	10.274	9.4269	8.6938	8.0552	7.4957	7.0027	6.5660	6.1772	4.9789	4.1601	3.9950	3.3321
35	29.409	24.999	21.487	18.665	16.374	14.498	12.948	11.655	10.567	9.6442	8.8552	8.1755	7.5856	7.0700	6.6166	6.2153	4.9915	4.1644	3.9984	3.3330
36	30.108	25.489	21.832	18.908	16.547	14.621	13.035	11.717	10.612	9.6765	8.8786	8.1924	7.5979	7.0790	6.6231	6.2201	4.9929	4.1649	3.9987	3.3331
40	32.835	27.355	23.115	19.793	17.159	15.046	13.332	11.925	10.757	9.7791	8.9511	8.2438	7.6344	7.1050	6.6418	6.2335	4.9966	4.1659	3.9995	3.3332
50	39.196	31.424	25.730	21.482	18.256	15.762	13.801	12.233	10.962	9.9148	9.0417	8.3045	7.6752	7.1327	6.6605	6.2463	4.9995	4.1666	3.9999	3.3333

APPENDIX 2

t-Distribution: Critical Values of t

Significance level

Degrees of	Two-Tailed Test:	10%	5%	2%	1%	0.2%	0.1%
Freedom	One-Tailed Test:	5%	2.5%	1%	0.5%	0.1%	0.05%
1		6.314	12.706	31.821	63.657	318.309	636.619
2		2.920	4.303	6.965	9.925	22.327	31.599
3		2.353	3.182	4.541	5.841	10.215	12.924
4		2.132	2.776	3.747	4.604	7.173	8.610
5		2.015	2.571	3.365	4.032	5.893	6.869
6		1.943	2.447	3.143	3.707	5.208	5.959
7		1.894	2.365	2.998	3.499	4.785	5.408
8		1.860	2.306	2.896	3.355	4.501	5.041
9		1.833	2.262	2.821	3.250	4.297	4.781
10		1.812	2.228	2.764	3.169	4.144	4.587
11		1.796	2.201	2.718	3.106	4.025	4.437
12		1.782	2.179	2.681	3.055	3.930	4.318
13		1.771	2.160	2.650	3.012	3.852	4.221
14		1.761	2.145	2.624	2.977	3.787	4.140
15		1.753	2.131	2.602	2.947	3.733	4.073
16		1.746	2.120	2.583	2.921	3.686	4.015
17		1.740	2.110	2.567	2.898	3.646	3.965
18		1.734	2.101	2.552	2.878	3.610	3.922
19		1.729	2.093	2.539	2.861	3.579	3.883
20		1.725	2.086	2.528	2.845	3.552	3.850
21		1.721	2.080	2.518	2.831	3.527	3.819
22		1.717	2.074	2.508	2.819	3.505	3.792
23		1.714	2.069	2.500	2.807	3.485	3.768
24		1.711	2.064	2.492	2.797	3.467	3.745
25		1.708	2.060	2.485	2.787	3.450	3.725
26		1.706	2.056	2.479	2.779	3.435	3.707
27		1.703	2.052	2.473	2.771	3.421	3.690

28	1.701	2.048	2.467	2.763	3.408	3.674
29	1.699	2.045	2.462	2.756	3.396	3.659
30	1.697	2.042	2.457	2.750	3.385	3.646
32	1.694	2.037	2.449	2.738	3.365	3.622
34	1.691	2.032	2.441	2.728	3.348	3.601
36	1.688	2.028	2.434	2.719	3.333	3.582
38	1.686	2.024	2.429	2.712	3.319	3.566
40	1.684	2.021	2.423	2.704	3.307	3.551
42	1.682	2.018	2.418	2.698	3.296	3.538
44	1.680	2.015	2.414	2.692	3.286	3.526
46	1.679	2.013	2.410	2.687	3.277	3.515
48	1.677	2.011	2.407	2.682	3.269	3.505
50	1.676	2.009	2.403	2.678	3.261	3.496
60	1.671	2.000	2.390	2.660	3.232	3.460
70	1.667	1.994	2.381	2.648	3.211	3.435
80	1.664	1.990	2.374	2.639	3.195	3.416
90	1.662	1.987	2.368	2.632	3.183	3.402
100	1.660	1.984	2.364	2.626	3.174	3.390
120	1.658	1.980	2.358	2.617	3.160	3.373
150	1.655	1.976	2.351	2.609	3.145	3.357
200	1.653	1.972	2.345	2.601	3.131	3.340
300	1.650	1.968	2.339	2.592	3.118	3.323
400	1.649	1.966	2.336	2.588	3.111	3.315
500	1.648	1.965	2.334	2.586	3.107	3.310
600	1.647	1.964	2.333	2.584	3.104	3.307
∞	1.645	1.960	2.326	2.576	3.090	3.291

INDEX

addition 15–16
advanced filter tools 10
Agricultural Statistics at a Glance 49
All India Crop Situation 49
alternative hypothesis 178
Annual Survey of Industries 47
ANOVA 180
arithmetic calculations 1
arithmetic mean 76–80; demerits 79–80; illustration 77–78; merits 78
asymmetrical distribution 115
autofill option 34
auto prompt 34
AutoSum function 21–22
average annual growth rate 193–197, 204

basic arithmetic operations, in Excel 15–32; addition 15–16; AutoSum function 21–22; COUNT and COUNTIF functions 24–25; division 20; MAX and MIN functions 23–24; multiplication 18–19; overview 15; power function 25; relative and absolute references 21; subtraction 16–18; SUMIF function 22–23
bins 66
Bombay Stock Exchange (BSE) 39, 52–53
Bretton Woods Agreement 53
BSE see Bombay Stock Exchange (BSE)

CAGR see compound annual growth rate (CAGR)
cash flows 231
categorical data 66
Census digital library 42
Census of India 40–44
charts and data visualization 60–73; column 63–65; histogram 66–69; line graph 60–63;
overview 60; pie chart 69–71; pivot tables 25–31; scatter plot 71–73
chi-squared test 180
chi-square statistics 180
class intervals see bins
coefficient of variation 101, 113–114; calculating using Excel 114
column chart 63–65
comma-separated values (CSV) 36, 42
compound annual growth rate (CAGR) 197–202, 204; Logest function and 213–217
compounding 219
compound interest 220–224
confidence interval approach 184–187
Consumer Confidence Survey 40
Consumer Price Index 46
copy and paste option 34
corporate sector 39
correlation 134–136; negative 135, 136; perfect negative 136; perfect positive 135; positive 134, 136; zero 135
correlation coefficient 130–151; correlation 134–136; covariance 130–134; Karl Pearson's Coefficient of Correlation 136–143; Spearman's Coefficient of Correlation 143–151
COUNT and COUNTIF functions 24–25
covariance 130–134; illustration 131–133; interpretation of results 133; negative 131; positive 130–131; zero 131
CSV see comma-separated values (CSV)

data 33–59; datasets available in public domain 37–59; entry 34–36; importing 36–37; management 1; overview 33; primary and secondary 34; qualitative and quantitative 33
data analysis 2; using Excel 122–125; visual 1

Database for Indian Economy (DBIE) 37–40
datamarts 57
DBIE *see* Database for Indian Economy (DBIE)
Department of Economic and Social Affairs 56
Department of Programme Implementation 44
Department of Statistics 44
Department of Statistics and Information
    Management 37
Deposit Insurance and Credit Guarantee and
    Corporation 39
descriptive statistics 75, 122; arithmetic mean
    76–80; geometric mean 92–94; harmonic
    mean 94–97; median 80–84; mode 84–88;
    relationship between arithmetic, geometric,
    and harmonic mean 97–98; weighted
    arithmetic mean 89–92
Development Data Group 53
Directorate of Economics and Statistics 48–49
discounting 219
discount rate 231
division 20

Economic Censuses 47
economic growth 191
EMI *see* equated monthly instalment (EMI)
empirical relationship 116
endowment plans 240
EPWRF India Times Series 58
equated monthly instalment (EMI) 247, 248
excess kurtosis 120
EXIM Bank 39
explained variation 167, 168, 170
extended internal rate of return (XIRR) 242
external sector 39

financial market 39
financial sector 39
fixed interest *vs.* reducing balance method:
    arithmetic derivation of payment/EMI
    249–250; calculating payment/EMI using
    present value interest factor of annuity
    (PVIFA) 250
Forex market 39
formatting axes 63
F-statistics 180
future value interest factor (FVIF) 222, 226
FVIF *see* future value interest factor (FVIF)

GDP *see* gross domestic product (GDP)
GDP per capita 57
geometric mean 92–94; calculating using Excel
    93–94; illustration 92–93
Government of India 40, 48
graphs *see* charts and data visualization
gross domestic product (GDP) 55, 60, 63, 64,
    191, 193

growth rate 191–202; average annual 193–197;
    compound annual growth rate (CAGR)
    197–202; measuring 191–192; simple 192–193
growth rate using regression analysis 204–217;
    Linest function 210–213; and logarithms
    204–205; Logest function 213–217; OLS
    method 205–210

harmonic mean 94–97
histogram 66–69
hypothesis testing, in regression analysis 177–187;
    alternative hypothesis 178; confidence interval
    approach 184–187; null hypothesis 178, 183,
    185–187; *p*-value 182–184; *t*-statistics 178–182;
    two-tail test 183, 187

Index of Industrial Production (IIP) 38
Industrial Financial Corporation of India 39
Inflation Expectations Survey of Household 40
interest amount paid 251
interest payment 247
internal rate of return (IRR) 235–245;
    applications 239–241; *vs.* extended internal
    rate of return (XIRR) 242; illustration
    236–239; merits and limitations 242–245
International Bank for Reconstruction and
    Development *see* World Bank
investment decision criteria 230–245; internal
    rate of return (IRR) 235–245; net present
    value (NPV) 231–235
IPMT function 257

Karl Pearson coefficient of skewness 116–117
Karl Pearson's coefficient of correlation 136–143,
    151; illustration 137–141; interpretation of
    results 141–143
kurtosis 101, 118–122, 129n1; illustration
    120–122; leptokurtic distribution 119;
    mesokurtic distribution 119; platykurtic
    distribution 119–120

labelling chart 61–63
Large-Scale All-India Sample Surveys 47
least-square criterion 167
leptokurtic distribution 119
linear regression model 155–157
linear relationship 150, 151
line of best fit *see* regression line
Linest function and growth rate 210–213
loan amortization 247–260; cumulative principal
    and interest amount 254–258; effective
    annual interest rate 258–260; fixed interest
    vs. reducing balance method 247–250; loan
    amount after *n* periods 251–253; payment/
    EMI using Excel 253–254; with table 250–251
Logest function and growth rate 213–217

MAX and MIN functions 23–24
measures of central tendency 75–98; arithmetic
  mean 76–80; descriptive statistics 75;
  geometric mean 92–94; harmonic mean
  94–97; median 80–84; mode 84–88;
  relationship between arithmetic, geometric,
  and harmonic mean 97–98; weighted
  arithmetic mean 89–92
measures of dispersion/variability 101–125;
  coefficient of variation 113–114; data
  analysis using Excel 122–125; kurtosis
  118–122; range 103–105; skewness
  114–118; standard deviation 105–109;
  variance 109–113
median 80–84; demerits 84; formula 81;
  illustration 81–83; merits 83
mesokurtic distribution 119
Microdata Library 56
Microsoft Excel 1–14; basic data manipulation 3;
  display of 2–3; filtering data 8–11;
  finding number of rows and columns
  in data 3; formatting decimal places 3, 5–6;
  freezing panes 11–12, 14; sorting data 6–7;
  unhiding and hiding rows and columns 8;
  see also individual entries
Ministry of Agriculture and Farmers Welfare 48
Ministry of Home Affairs 40
Ministry of Statistics and Programme
  Implementation (MoSPI) 44–48
MIRR *see* modified internal rate of
  return (MIRR)
mode 84–88; demerits 88; illustration 84–86;
  merits 88; using if data is given in discrete
  series 86–88
modified internal rate of return (MIRR) 245
moneyback policies 240–241
Monthly Estimates Of Index Of Industrial
  Production 46
MoSPI *see* Ministry of Statistics and Programme
  Implementation (MoSPI)
multiplication 18–19

National Accounts Statistics 45
National Bank for Agriculture and Rural
  Development 39
National Housing Bank 39
national income 38
National Statistical Office (NSO) 44–45
National Stock Exchange (NSE) 39, 50–52
negative correlation 135, 136
negative covariance 131
negatively skewed distribution 115
net present value (NPV) 231–235; accept/
  reject criteria 231; calculating 231–232; cash
  flows 231; demerits 235; discount rate 231;
  illustration 232–234; merits 234

Nifty 131
non-linear relationship 150, 151
normal distribution 114
NPV *see* net present value (NPV)
NSE *see* National Stock Exchange (NSE)
NSO *see* National Statistical Office (NSO)
null hypothesis 178, 183, 185–187

Office of the Registrar General and Census
  Commissioner of India 40, 41
OLS *see* ordinary least squares (OLS) method
one-tailed test 178, 180, 190
ordinary least squares (OLS) method 166–167,
  173, 205–210

Pearson product-moment correlation coefficient
  136, 138
perfect negative correlation 136
perfect positive correlation 135
PI *see* Programme Implementation (PI)
pie chart 69–71
pivot tables 25–31
platykurtic distribution 119–120
Pocket Book of Agricultural Statistics 49
positive correlation 134, 136
positive covariance 130–131
positively skewed distribution 115
positive residuals 167
power function 25
PPMT function 256–257
present value interest factor of annuity (PVIFA)
  250, 251
primary data 34
principal amount repaid 251
principal payment 247
Programme Implementation (PI) 45
public finance 39
p-value 182–184, 187
PVIFA *see* present value interest factor of
  annuity (PVIFA)

qualitative data 33
quantitative data 33, 66
quick access toolbar 35, 36

range 101, 103–105; demerits 105; illustration
  103–104; merits 104
raw data 60
real sector 38
regression analysis 154–173; coefficient
  of determination 167–173; coefficients
  estimation 157–162; definition 155; estimated
  coefficients interpretation 162–163; forecasting
  values of dependent variable 163–166; linear
  regression model 155–157; residuals/errors
  and OLS method 166–167

regression line 167
relative and absolute references 21
Reserve Bank of India (RBI) 37, 40
residual sum of squares *see* unexplained variation
rule of thumb 105–107

scatter plot 71–73
secondary data 34
Sensex 131
SI *see* simple interest (SI)
simple growth rate 192–193
simple interest (SI) 219
simple pension plan 241
skewness 101, 114–118; asymmetrical
    distribution 115; illustration 116–117;
    normal distribution 114; symmetrical
    distribution 114
Small Industrial Development Bank of India 39
socio-economic indicators 39
Spearman's coefficient of correlation 143–151
SSE *see* sum of squared errors (SSE)
standard deviation 101, 105–109; demerits
    109; illustration 107–109; merits 109; rule of
    thumb 105–107
Statistics as a Public Good 56
Statistics Division 56
subtraction 16–18
SUMIF function 22–23
sum of squared errors (SSE) 167, 173, 210
symmetrical distribution 114

time-series publications 40
time value of money 218–228; compound interest
    220–224; concept 218–219; future value of
    annuity 224–228; simple interest (SI) 219
total variation 167, 168, 170
trendline 72–73
t-statistics 178–183, 186
t-test 180, 181
two-tail test 178, 179, 183, 187, 190

UNdata 56–59
unexplained variation 167, 168, 170
United Nations 57
unit level data 40
UN Secretariat 56

variance 101, 109–113; demerits 113; illustration
    110–112; merits 113

weighted arithmetic mean 89–92
weighting factor 89
World Bank 53–56

XIRR *see* extended internal rate of return (XIRR)
XY plot *see* scatter plot

zero correlation 135
zero covariance 131
z statistics 180
z-test 180

Printed in Great Britain
by Amazon

39774565R00170